P9-CPZ-457

❀ *Garden Way's*
Joy of Gardening

Harry,
Happy Birthday
June 6, 1983

Garden Way's
Joy of Gardening

by Dick Raymond

GARDEN WAY PUBLISHING CHARLOTTE, VERMONT 05445

Garden Way's
JOY OF GARDENING

Editor: George Thabault
Art Director: Ann Aspell
Designer: Charles Cook
Cover Design: Evans Kerrigan
Production Manager: Bruce Williamson
Production Consultant: Irv Garfield
Production Assistants: Dennis Versweyveld, Bonnie Woodford-Potter, Jennifer Adsit,
  Andrea Gray, Leslie Fry
Research Assistants: David Moats, Mark Hebert
Photo Files & Typing: Joan Hebert
Photography: Paul Boisvert, George Robinson, Charles Cook, Erik Borg, Mark Hebert,
  George Thabault, and the W. Atlee Burpee Seed Company (pages 226 and 242).
Illustrations: Elayne Sears
Illustrations (pages 213, 219, 232, 278, 297, 305): Kurt Musfeldt

Garden Way Incorporated   Garden Way Publishing
Dean Leith, Jr., President   M. John Storey, Publisher

Separations by Graphic Process, Inc., Nashville, Tennessee
Printed in the U.S. by W. A. Krueger Company, New Berlin, Wisconsin

Copyright © 1982 by Garden Way Inc.

All rights reserved. No part of this book may be
reproduced without permission in writing from
the publisher, except by a reviewer who may
quote brief passages or reproduce illustrations in
a review with appropriate credit; nor may any part
of this book be reproduced, stored in a retrieval
system or transmitted in any form or by any
means—electronic, photocopying, recording, or
other—without permission in writing from the publisher.

Printing (last digit): *10 9 8 7 6 5 4 3 2*

Library of Congress Cataloguing in Publication Data

Raymond, Dick.
  Garden Way's joy of gardening.

  Includes index.
  1. Vegetable gardening. I. Sears, Elayne.
II. Boisvert, Paul. III. Garden Way Publishing.
IV. Title. V. Title: Joy of gardening.
SB321.R337 1983   635   82-12075
ISBN 0-88266-319-4

Contents

Preface   vii
Introduction   xiv

MY WIDE ROW GARDENING SYSTEM   1

What do I mean by a wide row?   2
Wide rows provide a continual harvest   8
Save hours of weeding and watering   10
My three big harvest garden plans   14
The Salad Garden (6′ × 8′)   16
The Summer Garden (30′ × 40′)   24
The Eat 'N Store Garden (60′ × 80′)   30
Seed varieties   38
Planting a wide row   42
Thinning, weeding, and harvesting   54
Multicrop rows   60
Block planting   66
Double and triple rows   70

GETTING THE SOIL READY   72

An early start cuts weeding   78
Soils, pH and fertilizers   80
Raised bed technique   92
Terrace garden   100
Garden in a strip of lawn   102

STARTING PLANTS   104

Count backwards for starting dates   106
Soil, pots and light   107
Cold frames and hotbeds   118
Stressless transplanting   120
Tunnel growing   126
Meet my friend the radish   131

STOP WEEDS COLD   132

Stop annual weeds early   134
Introducing the In-Row Weeder   136
My favorite hoes   138
How to fight perennials and win   142
The buckwheat story   144

GARDEN CARE   148

My favorite mulch   151
Watering, only two rules   152
Side-dressing guarantees top nutrition   156
Quick recipe for home compost   162
Harvesting for best yields   166
Succession crops keep garden green   168
My fall garden   172

GREEN MANURES   176

Peas feed soil   185
Beans are soil's summer nourishment   187
Buckwheat easy to turn under   188
Annual ryegrass blankets garden   190
Planting a green manure crop   192
Eternal Yield gardens   194

THE ROOT CELLAR   198

System to maintain cool temperatures   199
Root Cellar know-how   202

A VEGETABLE TREASURY   204

The Bean Family   206
The Cabbage Family   214
Corn   226
Eggplant   234
The Greens Family   236
Okra   247
The Onion Family   248
Peanuts   256
Peppers   261
Potatoes   264
Potatoes, sweet   270
The Root Crop Family   272
Sunflowers   282
Tomatoes   284
The Vine Crop Family   298
Garden Perennials   318

Garden pests   330
Insects and diseases   336

HANDY GARDEN CHARTS   346

Index   362

FARM WORK *built the foundation for Dick Raymond's knowledge of the soil. "I just wheel-harrowed my garden," said Dick of this June, 1955 snapshot at age 24. "That garden and roadside stand paid for my first home." He told me: "I always loved to drive a tractor. You could do so much work, with so little effort!" His worksaving gardening techniques seemed to be based on just that idea.*

I met Dick Raymond,

naturally enough, on his knees in a garden, his hands in the soil, and mumbling to himself. He was convinced there was a way to grow sweet potatoes up north, even though it was supposed to be crazy just to try.

"They're real long-growing, actually tropical vegetables," Dick said. "They love the heat. Well, I tell you, fellow, when it comes to gardening, I love a challenge!"

That was back in 1966, when Dick joined up with Garden Way. And sure enough, within a few years, Dick Raymond had not only grown a bountiful, fully ripened crop of sweet potatoes in northern Vermont, but developed a whole new technique of "raised beds."

Dick will often explain to gardeners, eager for his advice, that raised beds "keep those tender, finicky vegetables from getting their feet wet." He says elevating plants solves a host of problems all at once: helping slow-drying spring soil to drain excess moisture faster . . . keeping plant roots 5 to 10 degrees warmer than beds on the level, which tomatoes, melons and peppers really appreciate . . . creating an extra half-foot or so of finely textured topsoil so that root crops have all the "shoulder room" they need to grow big and healthy.

"Plants are like people," I've often heard Dick say, in one of his classes, or to visitors to his beautiful test gardens. "They catch cold. They windburn and sunburn. I often lick some tricky garden problems just by putting myself in *their* place."

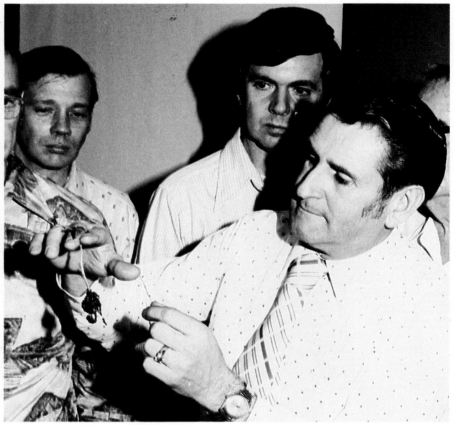

IN THE EARLY 70's the U.S.I.A. (the United States Information Agency) made a film called "FOOD: Will There Be Enough?", to bring the best of American know-how to developing countries. "They sought out individuals who were helping themselves," said Dick. "I was real flattered to be asked to demonstrate my methods in the film."

HERE'S DICK IN 1974 during a break in one of his gardening classes. He's explaining one of his favorite techniques—how to transplant a tomato seedling so as to bury most all the stem, in order to encourage the strongest possible network of roots.

"Take carrots, for example. They need sandy, loose soil. Or at least soil that's spongy with lots of organic matter. Well, most gardeners have heavy, compacted *clay* to start with! I've found carrots really thrive to a juiciness you wouldn't believe in my adaptation of raised beds."

And this is just *one* of the many exciting, new techniques Dick has developed.

How is it that this man, a former dairy farmer and cattle dealer, has come to know as much about growing spectacular vegetables as anyone you could ever hope to meet?

He has *not* been an "overnight sensation," that's for sure. It's taken Dick Raymond 40-plus years of hands-in-earth "trial and error," and a pure love of gardening. His practical bent of mind dates back to his early life in rural Vermont during the Depression days. "Every family gardened to keep food on the table, simple as that," Dick says of his growing up, "and I always had my share of work in the garden." As the youngest of nine children, Dick worked side by side with older folks, and pestered them for information. "I've spent a fair amount of time with farmers, too,"

viii

Dick told me. "Farmers are very smart people. They have to make do with what they've got. I don't care how much money they have, farmers must be practical. I didn't get much of what I've learned from the library. I got it from shrewd individuals."

For years before I met him, Dick and his wife Jan grew all the food for their young family, and made some extra cash from a one-acre market garden. This is when he devised methods for raising the earliest, sweetest corn, the plumpest, juiciest tomatoes, *up to four weeks ahead* of other growers in the area.

"I've never been satisfied with ordinary results, or shrugging at apples full of worms, or always doing battle with cabbage moths. I figure there's got to be an easier way, and a perfectly safe way too, if we just use our heads."

I can vouch for Dick's being an incurable tinkerer. He's constantly trying to stretch the gardening season, or honing his fishing and hunting skills (which are already razor-sharp), or getting his chores done a little faster and more effectively.

The truth is, Dick Raymond was hired as a caretaker and handyman back in 1966 by Lyman Wood, one of Garden Way's founders. In those days Lyman was running our only tiller test gardens, at his place in Charlotte, Vermont. Needless to say, it didn't take long for him to realize that Dick was a "dirt genius" when it came to farm tools and novel garden ideas.

At the time, I was just starting out as sales manager for Garden Way's Troy-Bilt tiller factory in Troy, New York. So I visited our Vermont gardens regularly. "What do you think of our tillers?" was my first question to Dick.

THIS ONE'S OF DICK helping a class of fifth graders to start a successful school garden—in the autumn. *He has always claimed that leaves are "a goldmine" of plant nutrients, and act as free fertilizer when broken down the following spring.*

WHEN IT COMES to garden tools, Dick Raymond has an opinion about every angle, curve, measurement, you name it. He's been invaluable from a practical, gardening point of view in many improvements in the Troy-Bilt Roto Tiller-Power Composter.

MY WIFE LIZ AND I CALL the Raymonds a real gardening partnership. Jan Raymond has authored many booklets and advice columns on great recipes for the gardener. Take my word—their root cellar of gleaming jars and beautiful winter-storage crops is a sight to behold.

He had quite an answer for me. "It's a beauty of a machine, but those short, stubby 'chopper tines' just aren't doing the trick. If you'd try 'bolo' tines, they'll slice and chop crop residues and organic material with much less tangling. The folks who buy your Troy-Bilt tillers to do power composting must be darn disappointed the way it is now. Switch to bolo tines and your tillers will get more work done a lot more easily, and you'll have a much better machine."

Dick grabbed a stick and drew a sketch right there in the soil—a longer, more curved shape for our rear-end tines. A few days later, Dick gave demonstrations on standing cornstalks, the toughest of all vegetation to chop and turn under. The following week our engineer went to work on *his* drawing boards. At that point, our Troy-Bilt rotary tiller also became a real power-composter.

George Done, our Chief Engineer and the man who has designed every machine that's been built in the tiller factory, was quick to recognize Dick's "farm-trained" equipment savvy. Over the years, Dick continued to give George his thoughts, good, bad, and otherwise. The result has been what most folks consider the best tiller in the business.

I'm forever hearing Dick Raymond call himself a "lazy" gardener. "Why plant extra rows of potatoes when you can reach under and 'rob' lots of the new ones? The plants don't mind. They just keep producing dozens of replacements!"

It was this sort of experimenting that led Dick to develop his breakthrough system of "wide-row" growing—easily doubling the yield (and for some crops, growing 5 and 6 times as much) *in the very same space.* Broadcast-planted bands, Dick discovered . . . shade the ground, retain moisture in dry spells, actually form a "living mulch," choke out weeds, cut way down on otherwise wasted walkways or aisles, and greatly simplify harvesting.

As many home gardeners know by this point, Dick Raymond was encouraged seven years ago to get all this down on paper, so

DICK IS DISCUSSING with me the marvels of high vitamin kale, "the winter wonder crop," which he harvests under snow. "I recommend planting a wide row like this," he said. "A family will have all the leafy green vegetable they need."

more people could share in his short-cuts to success. He wrote *Down-to-Earth Vegetable Gardening Know-How*, brought out by Garden Way Publishing, in 1975. It has been, in the gardening world, a real bestseller.

Also to his credit have been *Improving Garden Soil With Green Manures*, 1974, *Wide-Row Planting*, 1976, and *Cover Crop Gardening*, 1976. Most recently, Garden Way co-sponsored with Gardens for All, the non-profit National Association for Gardening, the publishing of Dick's *Your Independence Garden for the 80's*, 1980, and *Home Gardening Wisdom*, 1982. He has developed the most popular lecture series ever at our Garden Way Living Centers. I hesitate to use the word "lecture," because when Dick Raymond "talks gardening," he really makes the subject come to life. (Dick's comment on handling onion sets: "You can't kill an onion with a hammer!") When he appears on a radio or television phone-in show, which he does around the country, calls are often backed up for thirty minutes!

It got to the point that all of us at Garden Way realized that there should be one, easy-to-read-and-follow volume that pulled the whole treasury of this man's wisdom together. In recent years, Dick has travelled widely, listening to other experienced gardeners, giving classes, picking up even *more* wonderful tips, on everything from soil improvement to fool-proof bug control.

And then, in 1981, Dick Raymond was launched as the host of the most exciting, colorful, and instructive new television series for Garden Way, called JOY OF GARDENING. This new nationally syndicated video show is now bringing thousands of gardeners right into Dick's backyard every week. He is a plain "natural" as a friendly, helpful gardening coach. So, of course, more people than ever have been asking for more of Dick Raymond's practical know-how.

IT'S HARD TO FIND time for small groups these days, but Dick has always managed to lend friends and strangers a helping hand. In the case of this photo, Dick is offering hints for successful transplanting of broccoli and cauliflower.

DICK CONSTANTLY PREACHES TO ALL OF US: "The soil is the soul of your garden." Here he's reminding me that "if you feed your garden (in this case, old mulch), it'll gladly feed you!"

WE AT GARDEN WAY HAVE always urged our owners of Troy-Bilt tillers to follow Dick's advice. He was instrumental in pioneering the use of "green manure cover crops," such as this one of winter rye, for rapid home soil building and weed control.

GARDEN WAY'S "JOY OF GARDEN-ING" which features Dick, is a half-hour TV series. It was produced in Dick's own backyard—frosty spring mornings right through to mouth-watering harvest. We're tremendously proud of Dick Raymond, and the enthusiastic response to this show, now going into its second season.

This big, new book, which has taken several years of researching, writing, and illustrating, is a companion to the television series of the same title. It is needed now, more than ever, as so many of us get a bit more thoughtful and realistic about home vegetable raising. We don't want to spend decades to master the craft. Probably the single-best thing about this book is that it shows us that it's not necessary to have a full-blown country spread to reap the benefits of homegrown food. Nor do we need to devote every spare hour in order to have a beautiful, trouble-free garden. Dick shows us how to grow 65 onions in an 8-inch pot right on the windowsill! Step-by-step, he makes gardening truly fun and productive, from a postage-stamp summer salad garden to a real money-saving, fresh-eating "cut and store" garden.

I believe the generous use of gorgeous and inspiring color photographs of Dick's garden makes this book like no other. We can see in vivid close-ups just how to profit from Dick's proven advice.

But the real excitement, to my mind, is the experience in store for every reader of making the acquaintance of this most remarkable man and gardening friend—Dick Raymond.

Here's wishing you the most successful *and enjoyable* garden ever, with Dick's new book as your guide.

Sincerely,

Dean Leith, Jr.

Dean Leith, Jr.
President Garden Way, Inc.

Introduction

For a long time I've been perfecting some unbelievably easy ways to plant vegetables, to harvest, to get rid of weeds and to improve soil.

Wide row growing methods are at the heart of this new system. I grow over 30 different crops in wide rows. Wide row growing means planting seeds and many transplants in wide bands, instead of one behind the other in conventional single rows. A wide row puts much more of your garden to work producing food.

I realize there are probably as many ways to garden as there are to bake a cake, and my way is one of them. So I won't ask you to change all your gardening habits. But if you give some of my methods a try, even in just a tiny section of your garden, I promise you'll have a better garden.

Your soil and climate conditions might be different from mine, but my gardening methods will work for you, too. All you have to do is adjust planting dates to fit your area and choose your own favorite vegetable varieties.

I grew up on a farm during the Depression years, so I guess I started out with an advantage in developing my gardening system. We were always trying to outsmart Mother Nature to harvest as much food as possible from each growing season.

When my wife, Jan, and I started raising a family of our own, I grew a one-acre market garden for extra cash and to keep our own food costs down. It was strictly a spare-time operation. I had my hands full with a job, three children, and a home to keep up. By switching from the traditional single rows to wide rows I saved a lot of time, weeded less, and used less water; plus, I doubled the yields of many crops without making the garden an inch bigger.

We don't run the roadside stand anymore, but gardening is still a challenge. I try to have the earliest and latest harvest in the neighborhood, and as much as possible in between. To me, that's what home gardening is all about—enjoying the longest possible harvest of fresh produce each year. The day I sow my first seeds in the spring I harvest some scallions and parsnips which have wintered over. And in late November, when our ground is freezing, I pick the last broccoli and brussels sprouts from my fall garden.

To me, there are always newer, easier and better ways to grow a good garden, and I've spent a lifetime trying to find them. That's why I've written this book. I have a lot to share with you about my wide row growing, keeping the garden covered with plants, harvesting and cutting way down on weeding, and there are plenty of new tips for growing the most popular vegetables, as well as new information about raised planting beds, watering, and dealing safely with pests and diseases.

In my travels, I've met many gardeners with helpful knowledge and experience. But few are as fortunate as I am to have the support and encouragement of friends and of Garden Way to put a book like this together. I am grateful and honored.

Just one more thing—if you have a question about any of the techniques shown in this book, or want to share with me how they work in your garden, please write to me. I'd appreciate hearing from you, and I'll do my best to answer any questions you have. My address is Box 97, Ferry Road, Charlotte, VT 05445.

Dick Raymond

MY WIDE ROW GARDENING SYSTEM

I promise you more production in less space with less work! Up to three times the harvest from your same garden. And my wide row gardening system works with more than 30 vegetables, in all soils, and in all climates, too!

During the past 30 years I have tested almost every gardening technique. I've spent most of my gardening life trying to perfect the easiest and most rewarding techniques for growing a satisfying home garden.

The way I grow my garden now—using my wide row method whenever I can—is tops by far. I get more food and enjoy longer harvests than with any other system. And I spend only about one-third the time planting, thinning, weeding and caring for my garden.

Each year, gardening with the wide row method simply gets easier, more enjoyable, and more productive.

1

What do I mean by a wide row?

Single row—skimpy harvest! Wide row—double, even triple the harvest

Look at the *wide row* of carrots on the right. On the left, planted in the traditional way, is a *single* straight-line row. It's easy to notice the main features of *wide row* growing—thick wide rows, more plants in the row, and much more garden soil being used to grow food. The result is more food for you and your family.

Plant 144 onions in 1 square foot

I love scallions and I pull well over 100 from each square foot of my onion wide rows, leaving a dozen or so to grow into keeping-size bulbs. When thinning *single* rows of onions, however, I get only a handful of scallions. By planting onion sets 1 inch apart and harvesting most of them for scallions I can easily get 10 times the harvest of a single row of the same length.

I doubled my chard harvest

I planted these chard rows on the same day. Both rows were 10 feet long. The *single* row (left) yielded 17 pounds, 8 ounces through the season. The 15-inch *wide* row (right) produced 34 pounds, 4 ounces. It takes the same amount of time to get the soil ready and sow the seeds, so why not try the wide row?

In my wide row system I broadcast the seeds in wide bands

The easy way to plant a wide row is by "broadcasting" seeds . . . scattering them evenly the entire length and width of the row. The plants come up quite close together, but with my thinning and harvesting techniques they never get too close.

Here's why I love wide rows

In this 30-foot by 40-foot garden I planted 8 of 13 rows wide!

I grew this backyard vegetable garden as an experiment. I used wide rows whenever possible. There were 13 rows of crops and 8 of them were planted "wide." Only the pole beans, tomatoes (two rows), broccoli, and summer squash were in straight-line narrow rows.

Even cabbage and cauliflower are great in wide rows

I fit many more cauliflower, cabbage and head lettuce plants into my garden by using the wide row method, and I harvest much more over *a longer period of time*. There are other benefits, too—see how the leaves of these plants shade the ground. The sun can hardly hit the soil in this row. The soil stays cool and moist, and weeds are rarely a problem.

so much!

The best way to grow head lettuce

Better than supermarket lettuce, that's for sure! Most people can grow two wide row crops of firmhead *Iceberg* lettuce—one in the spring and one in the fall. Head lettuce does not do well in hot weather, but growing in wide rows keeps the soil cool so the plants will head up well even if you get some unexpected warm weather. The leaves grow out, touch those of neighboring plants, and together they protect the ground from the sun.

A 3-foot-long wide row of leaf lettuce yields all a family can eat

It's simply amazing how much fresh leaf lettuce you can harvest from a short wide row. I get basket after basket by cutting the plants in a short swath right down to an inch above the ground. This encourages them to bounce back with tender new leaves while I harvest the rest of the row.

"Block" planting—just plant and pick!

Jan and I are looking over a large block of peas in our experimental garden. This is quite a pea patch—it's 12 x 24 feet. To plant it, I sprinkle the seeds over the entire area and run my roto-tiller over them, mixing them into the top of the soil. Some seeds wind up too shallow, others are too deep to germinate, but most are at the right depth for sprouting well. By using a little extra seed I insure a good stand of plants. I never have to weed in a square like this—it's a plant and pick crop.

We used 3 or 4 pounds of seeds and we picked 150 pounds of fresh peas. It's easy to harvest a square of peas like this—we take stools right into the patch, sit down and pick plenty, then move to another spot.

A wide row 3 feet across!

Wide rows can be planted to whatever width suits you best. This wide row of kale is 3 feet across. I've grown crops in wide rows from 10 inches across, all the way up to 25 feet wide. A 3-foot width is very manageable. I can reach any plant from one side or the other, so I never have to step in the row and compact the soil.

From the very same row I harvest five different vegetables

The most interesting and colorful wide rows in the garden are my new "multicrop" rows. Here I grow up to five different vegetables in the same row. They are all planted on the same day, but the harvest from the row extends for weeks. (More about multicrops on page 60.)

Planting a wide row is as easy as scattering grass seed

With all the plants I have in my wide rows you might think I spend a lot of time planting. Well, I don't.

Planting a wide row takes only a few seconds because I broadcast seeds, scattering them fairly close together the entire width and length of the row. I never bend over to space seeds exactly. With my way of seeding, I probably spend more time opening the seed packet than sowing the seeds. There's very little bending and kneeling on the ground for me. Whenever I plant, I try to do it standing up.

Wide rows provide a continual

Now harvest earlier and longer than ever

Perhaps what I like most about my method is the *continual harvest* possible from wide rows.

With more plants in the row there's obviously going to be a bigger harvest. But the nice thing about wide rows is that this larger harvest comes over a much longer period of time than conventional single rows. With many crops, the harvest can easily be stretched out 5 or 6 weeks longer than usual.

In a wide row there's a natural competitiveness among plants growing near each other. They are all trying to get as much sun, water, and food as possible. But, just as in uncultivated woods or meadows, not every plant can win.

The strongest plants get an edge over the others and dominate for a short period of time. That's okay. These plants are the first ones to get to the eating stage, so I pick them first.

In a row of carrots, beets, lettuce, cabbages, or whatever, I always start the harvest with the largest. Because there are so many plants in the row I don't have to wait like other gardeners for the crop to get big—I can enjoy plenty of vegetables when they are tender and small.

I can start harvesting *earlier,* take the best of the row, and still look forward to much more to come. With each early harvest, I end some of the competition between plants, and more plants receive their full dose of sun and food.

With this harvesting style I multiply the days when I can go out into the garden and bring back some produce for a meal. As a backyard gardener, this is the ultimate—a steady, extra-long harvest.

harvest!

MY BONUS SYSTEM OF HARVESTING GREENS

1st Cutting

When the plants are 4 or 5 inches tall they are in prime shape for a first cut. I slice them only 1 inch above the soil. They are so tasty at this stage.

2nd Cutting

A few weeks later the plants have produced a new set of tender leaves ready to cut again. While waiting for these leaves to grow I've made first cuttings on other sections of the row.

3rd Cutting

After another 3 or 4 weeks the chard leaves have reached eating size again. Chard can be cut like this all season long, but I usually get only three cuttings of leaf lettuce before the quality peters out.

Wide rows save hours of weeding and watering

The "living mulch" formed by close-growing plants stops weeds

The most amazing aspect of my wide row growing method is how little weeding has to be done. The secret is in growing plants close together. As long as the vegetable seeds sprout and grow *ahead* of the weeds (and the planting and thinning techniques I'll show you later will guarantee this), their leaves will work to block out the sun. And weeds cannot last long or grow far without sun.

I like to seed my rows thickly so that this living mulch over the soil is created early, when plants are small. Then in succeeding weeks I thin out the crowded row so that the plants get room to grow. But I always keep enough plants in the row to maintain the important shade mulch over small weeds struggling to grow.

Saves water three ways

First, the leaf canopy over the row keeps the sun from hitting the soil and drying it out. In effect, the plants in the row create a mulch to slow down water loss due to evaporation.

Second, the plants on the edges of the row act as *windbreaks* for the others in the micro-climate of the row. When a plant is sitting all by itself it is terribly vulnerable to drying winds. The winds may cause the plant to release water into the air faster than it can take water up through the roots.

In a wide row, however, most of the plants are *inside* the boundaries of the row. They do not take the full brunt of the winds; in fact, they're pretty well protected and lose moisture at a much slower rate. In my test gardens I can spot this important difference easily on a hot windy day.

Third, the leaf canopy of wide rows can trap the dew which forms on the soil under the row and on the undersides of the plant leaves. In a single row, this valuable moisture is quickly lost to morning evaporation because there's nothing there to hold it back. But in a wide row, the canopy of leaves slows this evaporation, allowing some of the moisture to be absorbed into the soil to help the plants.

I stumbled onto the benefits of wide row growing by accident 30 years ago.

It was the spring after Jan and I were married and we were starting our garden together.

We decided to grow some extra fresh peas to sell at the market because the price was good—$8 or $9 a bushel. I bought 10 pounds of pea seed.

On planting day I prepared the area that I had set aside in my plan for peas. I planted the seeds in straight-line rows, one after another, with lots of walkspace between them just as my father and I had always done. When I finished seeding the rows, I had about 3 pounds of seed left over.

To use them up I sprinkled the seeds by the handful over another patch of ground in the corner of the garden and mixed them into the soil with a spading fork.

This was my first wide row—a 10-foot by 20-foot section of garden that was solid peas with no walkways.

Watching the peas grow, I was amazed. They grew so close together that they actually held themselves up. I didn't have to fiddle with any brush or fencing to stake them up as I had to do with my other rows.

The plants grew close enough together to shade the soil underneath them. I noticed that the soil was always moist and cool under that canopy of shade—and peas like that environment.

To my delight, the plants also blocked the sun from reaching any tiny weeds. So, I didn't do any weeding.

The harvest was a big surprise. The wide row pea patch was much more abundant than we expected. Though it was thick, Jan and I had no problem picking all the peas. Actually it was fun because we discovered we could just take stools into the pea patch, sit down and pick a peck of peas before having to move.

Many years of experimenting

That was 30 years ago, and ever since I've planted peas in wide rows. I've planted them in rows from 10 inches wide, all the way up to big blocks 25 feet on each side.

After my first success with wide rows, I experi-mented with other crops to see if they could be as easy and productive to grow as the wide row peas.

How would beets, onions, and carrots grow in wide rows? How much seed should I use? How wide could I make the rows? How could I weed easily in a row with plants growing so closely to-gether? Before long I found the answers, and I was able to double the profits from our little market garden (which grew after a few years to 1 acre in size) just by switching most crops to wide rows. I found that wide rows took a lot less time for weed-ing and watering. Even though I was growing more food, harvesting took less time. I appreciated this because I had a full-time job and had to make my time in the garden really count.

My wide row method works in all kinds of soil and climates. I know—from experience!

When I travel around the country and give slide shows on gardening, I always hear this question: "Sure *looks* good, Dick. But will your wide row method work here where we live?"

This is a question that I've been answering "Yes" to for a long time, both in the lecture hall and out in the garden.

I began experimenting with wide row growing at my home market garden in Vermont. Later, as more and more people became interested in my techniques and as I started to do consulting for garden-related companies, I was able to plant and supervise wide row demonstrations in other parts of the country.

I saw for myself in Georgia, in Florida and on the West Coast, that my wide row method not only produced more food in less space but had special benefits for hot-climate gardens. The water, mulch and time-saving aspects of wide rows are es-pecially helpful to southern gardeners.

I've also had the chance to visit many different states—Pennsylvania, Tennessee, Iowa, New York, California, and others for a few days at a time—to help individuals and groups plant successful dem-onstration gardens featuring wide rows.

I also hear by mail from gardeners all over the country who report they are growing vegetables in wide rows and liking it. These are folks who may have heard a lecture or a radio talk or read about wide rows in my earlier books.

11

Just how much *more productive* are wide rows?

Here are typical results from my test plots

Single Row 10 ft. long	Average Harvest	Wide Row 10 ft. long
Onions		16 inches wide
12 lb. 3 oz.		28 lb. 1 oz.
Carrots		16 inches wide
19 lb. 8 oz.		30 lb.
Lettuce		16 inches wide
13 lb. 8 oz.		32 lb. 12 oz.
Cabbage		20 inches wide
35 lb. 12 oz.		110 lb.

Gardeners from across the country say they love my wide row gardening techniques

Here are some of the letters I've received:

"A few years ago I tried some wide rows in my garden. The results stopped neighbors in their tracks. They couldn't believe how nice those rows looked.

"I started with beans, carrots, and beets, but now I do most of my planting in wide rows. I use half a row where I used to use a whole row.

"I had more produce in ¼ acre with wide rows than I had in ½ acre the other years. It's the most practical way to garden."
> Henry Carty
> Elkton, MI 48731

"We studied your wide row planting chart during the winter and changed our whole garden. Last year, thanks to the wide row method, we grew all our own food. We didn't buy any vegetables at all.

"The wide row method is super. I wouldn't garden any other way. I do the rake thinning bit—I drag it across the row just like you say. It works well, but I was afraid to use it at first. It's casual for me now."
> Richard Kirchner
> New Fairfield, CT 06810

"I tried your wide row method with lettuce, carrots and radishes. I am very well pleased with the results. I have told people of this better system, but if they don't listen it's their hard luck."
> Leland Klukkent
> Prineville, OR 97544

"Wide row gardening as inspired by Dick Raymond is the greatest! My fall garden is started and I am looking forward to fresh vegetables all winter, including kale, cabbage, broccoli, cauliflower, green peas, onions, Swiss chard, spinach, turnips, beets, carrots and lettuce."
> Frederick H. Myers Jr.
> Augusta, GA 30906

"I'm experimenting this year with your wide row idea. I'm planting peas, carrots, beets and lettuce in 15-inch wide rows. I like the results very much so far."
> Walter Hinkley, Sr.
> Sabbattus, ME 12601

"Let me express my thanks for introducing me to wide row planting—it's the only way to fly! I've got most of my friends doing it also and the results have been superb."
> Don Hollis
> Rapid City, SD 57701

"I have read a great deal about your wide row planting method in several publications and have used it to a limited extent with great success. This year I plan to use it for cabbage, cauliflower, and broccoli, in addition to beans, peas, beets, carrots, etc."
> Robert J. Dolansky
> Poughkeepsie, NY 04280

Popular crops I now plant using my wide row method

Beans	Chinese cabbage	Leeks	Peppers
Beets	Collards	Lettuce	Radishes
Cabbage	Endive	Mustard	Rutabagas
Carrots	English peas	Onions	Southern peas
Cauliflower	Garlic	Parsley	Spinach
Celery	Kale	Parsnips	Turnips
Chard	Kohlrabi		

My Three Big-Harvest Wide Row Garden Plans

Wide rows of vegetables fit in any garden plan. To help you come up with your own wide row garden I've included three of the simple, but amazingly productive wide row gardens I've designed for the backyard garden. I've grown each of these gardens, the Salad Garden (6 by 8 feet), the Summer Garden (30 by 40 feet) and the Eat 'N Store Garden (60 by 80 feet). They feature wide rows of vegetables wherever possible, and cut down on the open, unproductive walkspace.

   All the plans allow for succession crops in rows where early planted vegetables will be finished before the season is over. The cabbage and greens family crops are excellent for succession planting because they perform very well in the cool weather of fall. I've included plenty of them in my plans. Growing succession crops is a great way to get more production from a garden without making it bigger.

Salad Garden

Beautiful variety-packed design for a small garden. For a beginning gardener or perhaps a busy person with only a few spare minutes a day. There's a host of salad items here, and the easy way I grow them assures a long harvest.

Summer Garden

Designed to get high production from a wide variety of vegetables—over 25 of them. Plenty of succession crops included so you can stretch summer's good eating into the fall months.

Eat 'N Store Garden

This garden is big. But it emphasizes best-to-store crops such as potatoes, carrots, winter squash, and onions, along with easy-to-freeze broccoli, beans and peas. The way to make a garden pay off is to store or preserve some of the harvest. With an Eat 'N Store Garden like this, you can chop hundreds of dollars from your food bill.

MY SALAD GARDEN

A lush Salad Garden to last all season long!

All the mixings for salads are included in this compact Salad Garden—lettuce, cucumbers, onions, tomatoes, peppers, and more. Choose a sunny spot for this garden, one that's not too far from the kitchen. With its wide row design, this Salad Garden is made to order for regular harvesting, especially the multicrop row (Row 1 in plan). Steady harvesting will keep the greens young and tender, the carrots and onions properly thinned, and the cucumbers, tomatoes and peppers blossoming and producing new fruit.

You won't see any "miniature" varieties of lettuce, spinach or other vegetables in my garden plan. Seed catalogs sometimes advertise them as "space savers," but I find they don't yield anywhere near enough produce for the space they take up.

18

Salad Garden Plan

This is a super-productive small space garden—and it's easy to plant and care for. My vegetable selections for this garden are further explained on the next pages, but don't limit yourself to them. If you don't like the chives and parsley in Row 1, for example, fill in with something different. Be sure to plant in wide rows—that's what makes this garden so good.

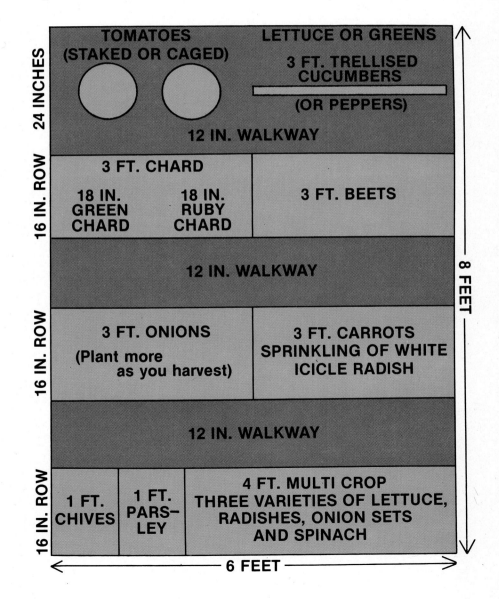

TOMATOES (STAKED OR CAGED)

LETTUCE OR GREENS

3 FT. TRELLISED CUCUMBERS

(OR PEPPERS)

24 INCHES

12 IN. WALKWAY

16 IN. ROW

3 FT. CHARD

18 IN. GREEN CHARD

18 IN. RUBY CHARD

3 FT. BEETS

12 IN. WALKWAY

16 IN. ROW

3 FT. ONIONS

(Plant more as you harvest)

3 FT. CARROTS SPRINKLING OF WHITE ICICLE RADISH

12 IN. WALKWAY

16 IN. ROW

1 FT. CHIVES

1 FT. PARS-LEY

4 FT. MULTI CROP THREE VARIETIES OF LETTUCE, RADISHES, ONION SETS AND SPINACH

8 FEET

6 FEET

Row 1

2 ft. chives and parsley

4 ft. multicrop sections using three varieties of lettuce with radishes, onion sets, and spinach

Follow up: sprinkle lettuce seeds or plant late onion sets after spinach is harvested.

Lettuce and three other vegetables in one row!

What a wonderful variety of food you can grow in a small space! Along with spinach and lettuce leaves, I have crisp radishes and scallions in the row. It's perfectly okay to mix and match your favorite greens in a multirow. However, it's a good idea to include radishes, onions and perhaps a few carrots in every section.

Row 2

3 ft. carrots, Nantes or Danvers (include sprinkling of White Icicle radishes)

3 ft. onion sets for scallions

Follow up: plant more sets as you harvest. Carrots will last all season.

Plant onions and carrots thick and harvest early

The onion sets here are planted very closely together—no more than 1 or 2 inches apart. I plan to harvest at least two out of every three onions when they are at the young, delicious scallion stage.

It's important to go after the carrots early, too. Start pulling them when they get as long and as thick as your little finger.

Row 3

3 ft. chard (two varieties, Swiss and Ruby)

3 ft. beets, Detroit Dark Red or Lutz Green Leaf (include sprinkling of radishes)

Beet greens and chard for tasty salads

I start crew-cutting my chard when it's only a few inches high. Like tiny spinach leaves, at this small stage chard tastes great and mixes well in a fresh salad with lettuce. I'm a big chard fan; you might want to plant another green more to your liking, such as mustard or spinach.

Row 4

3 ft. trellised cucumbers, variety such as Spacemaster or Bush Champion

3 ft. of staked or caged tomatoes (3 or 4 plants)

Big climbing cukes and tomatoes

I try to set out two early tomato plants, such as *Pixie* or *Early Girl*, and two of a later variety such as *Better Boy*. I stake or cage them so they'll grow up instead of out.

To save even more space I use a trellis to grow my cukes in this garden. Once I install the trellis it's not much work to maintain. I train the cucumbers up the wire and tie the vines to the mesh.

In just 3 feet of row you can have plenty of peppers, if you want to substitute for cucumbers. Plant your peppers in a staggered wide row.

You can grow a Salad Garden

anywhere

I know you can grow a Salad Garden with your favorite vegetables just about anywhere . . . even in a driveway.

I planted a little "driveway garden" (top) after a friend heard me say that people could garden just about anywhere—even in a driveway. He challenged me to prove it, so I did. I used a roto-tiller to slowly loosen the hard-packed gravel and soil, mixed in a cartful of compost, and planted. Left: Tomatoes and onions can be prolific in small containers or tubs set out on the back patio. They need sun and a steady supply of water.

MY SUMMER GARDEN

My most popular garden—I designed it for The National Association for Gardening

I planned this high-yield garden a few years ago at the request of The National Association for Gardening. Each year I've been amazed at how much top-quality food comes out of it.

This Summer Garden can keep a family in fresh produce all season long, plus provide some extra for entertaining or to store or preserve. With my wide rows I get extra beets, carrots, potatoes, and onions for the root cellar, and ample broccoli, beans, and peas for freezing.

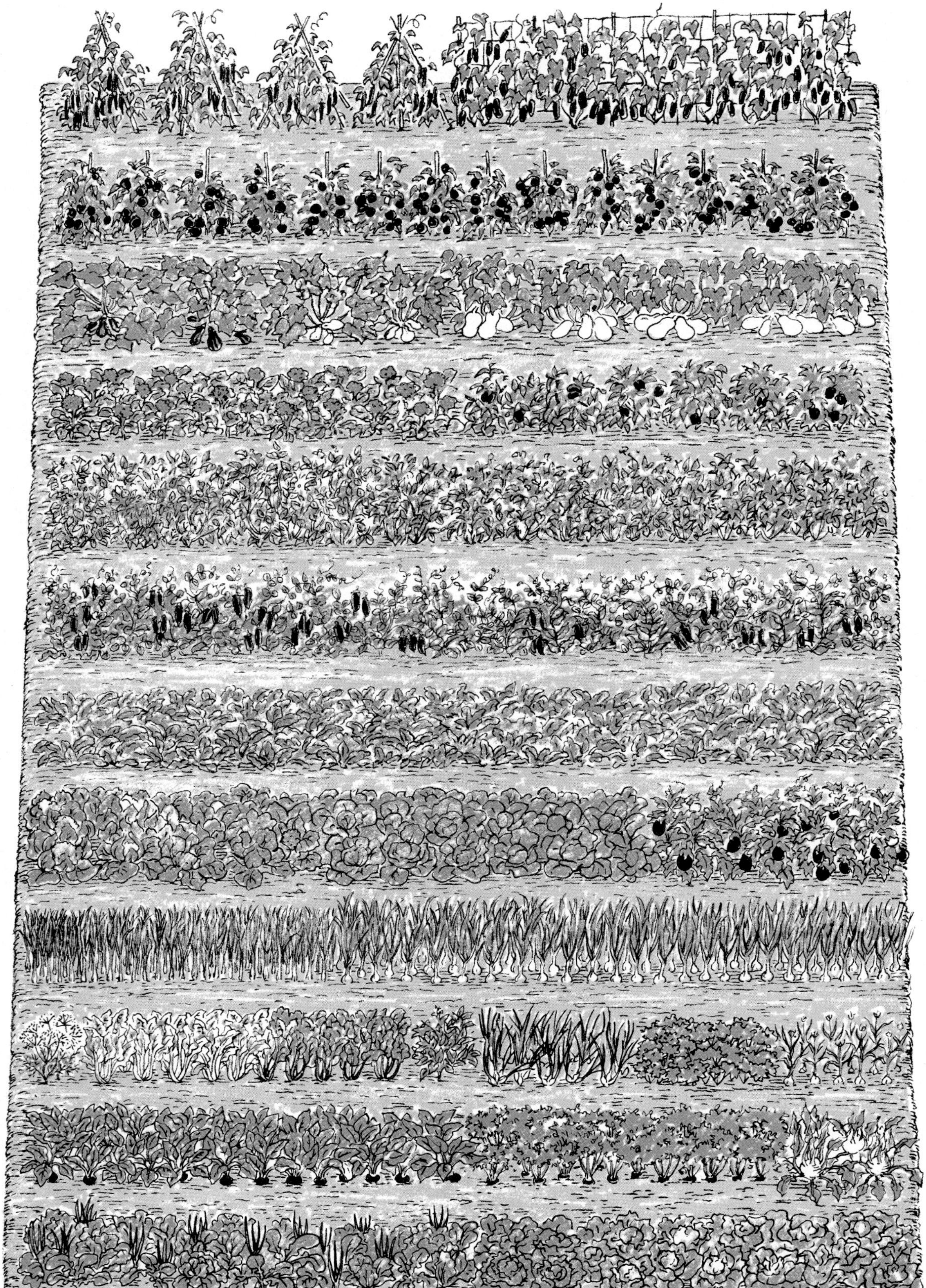

Summer Garden Plan

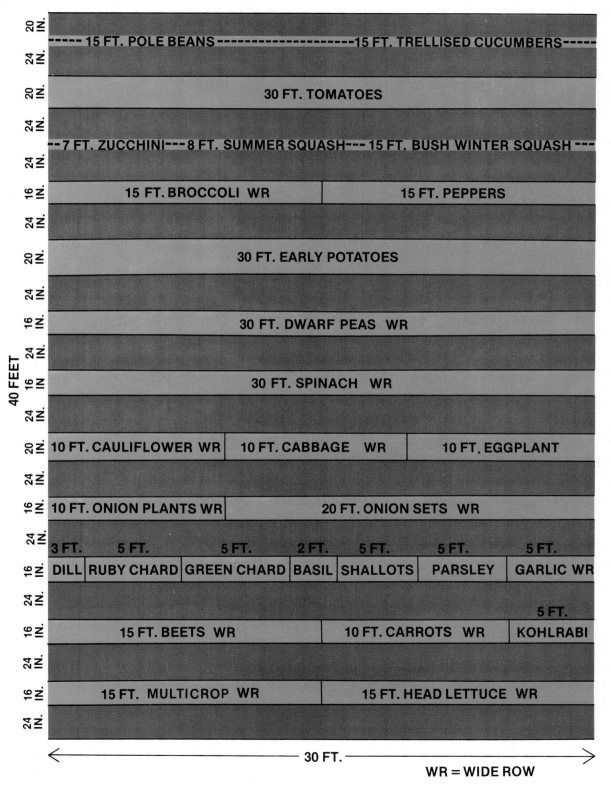

40 FEET

20 IN.
----- 15 FT. POLE BEANS ----------------------15 FT. TRELLISED CUCUMBERS-----

24 IN.

20 IN.
30 FT. TOMATOES

24 IN.

---7 FT. ZUCCHINI--- 8 FT. SUMMER SQUASH--- 15 FT. BUSH WINTER SQUASH ---

24 IN.

16 IN.
| 15 FT. BROCCOLI WR | 15 FT. PEPPERS |

24 IN.

20 IN.
30 FT. EARLY POTATOES

24 IN.

16 IN.
30 FT. DWARF PEAS WR

24 IN.

16 IN.
30 FT. SPINACH WR

24 IN.

20 IN.
| 10 FT. CAULIFLOWER WR | 10 FT. CABBAGE WR | 10 FT. EGGPLANT |

24 IN.

16 IN.
| 10 FT. ONION PLANTS WR | 20 FT. ONION SETS WR |

24 IN.

3 FT.	5 FT.	5 FT.	2 FT.	5 FT.	5 FT.	5 FT.
DILL	RUBY CHARD	GREEN CHARD	BASIL	SHALLOTS	PARSLEY	GARLIC WR

16 IN.

24 IN.

5 FT.

16 IN.
| 15 FT. BEETS WR | 10 FT. CARROTS WR | KOHLRABI |

24 IN.

16 IN.
| 15 FT. MULTICROP WR | 15 FT. HEAD LETTUCE WR |

24 IN.

←———————————————— 30 FT. ——————————————————→

WR = WIDE ROW

27

Row 1

15 ft. multicrop: 1 pkt. lettuce for each 3-ft. section; ½ pkt. spinach; ½ pkt. carrots; ½ pkt. beets; ½ pkt. radishes. 15 ft. head lettuce: 60 plants (fall turnips and rutabagas: 1¼ oz. each)

Start cutting some heads of lettuce early—well before they make firm heads. With 60 plants in the row there's plenty to eat, so don't wait.

Row 2

15 ft. beets: ½ oz.; 10 ft. carrots: ½ oz.; 5 ft. kohlrabi: 1 pkt.

Pull some early beets for greens. If there's a little beet on the bottom, toss it into the pot with the greens—delicious. Many gardeners will have enough time to make a second sowing of kohlrabi.

Row 3

3 ft. dill: 1 pkt.; 5 ft. Ruby chard: 1 pkt.; 5 ft. Swiss chard: 1 pkt.; 2 ft. basil: 1 pkt.; 5 ft. shallots: 2½ lb. of sets; 5 ft. parsley: 1 pkt.; 5 ft. garlic: 8 bulbs (separate into cloves before planting)

Plant dill very early so that if you want to pickle some of your own cucumbers you can use your own fresh dill. Keep soil lightly moist until parsley seeds come up.

Summer Garden planning tips

Row 7

30 ft. peas: ½ lb. (followed with 15 ft. green beans: ¼ lb.; and 15 ft. yellow beans: ¼ lb.)

When you seed a wide row of either peas or beans the seeds should land 2 or 3 inches apart. Peas are easiest to roto-till or dig into the soil after the harvest when they are still quite green. Pea vines decompose fast so it's okay to plant beans right away.

Row 8

30 ft. potatoes: 30 sets or 5 lb. seed potatoes; (15 ft. fall head lettuce: 60 plants; 15 ft. turnips or mustard: 1¼ oz.)

Choose an early variety of potatoes, such as Red Norland, and plant early. This will leave you ample time to grow good fall succession crops. Start harvesting potatoes early by reaching into the hills for small "new" potatoes.

Row 9

15 ft. broccoli: 16 plants; (15 ft. fall kale: 2 pkts.); 15 ft. peppers: 25-30 plants (fewer if you plant high number of bell peppers).

Set out broccoli plants about 2 weeks before the expected last spring frost and peppers 1 week after the frost date. Keep broccoli going as long as possible by picking all side shoots which grow after you cut the main head.

Row 4

10 ft. onion plants: 180 plants; 20 ft. onion sets: 9 lb.

Put your onion sets 2 inches apart— planted to their full depth—so you can pull every other one as they reach a nice scallion size—8 to 12 inches tall and as thick as your finger.

Row 5

10 ft. cauliflower: 30 plants; (fall spinach: ¼ oz.); 10 ft. cabbage: 30 plants; 10 ft. eggplant: 20 plants

Plant cabbage and cauliflower 2 or 3 weeks before the average last frost date, but set out eggplants when cold weather has passed. Cut biggest heads of cabbage and cauliflower first for a continual harvest.

Row 6

30 ft. spinach: ¾ oz.; fall 15 ft. kale: 2 pkts.; 7 ft. collards: 2 pkts.; 8 ft. broccoli: 10 plants; or 8 ft. Chinese cabbage: 1 pkt.

Plant spinach as early as you can and you may get two productive cuttings before it goes to seed. Be sure to thin fall kale and collards to 6 or 8 inches between plants by the time they reach a foot in height.

Row-by-row ideas on how much to plant, succession crops, saving space, and harvesting

Row 10

7 ft. zucchini: 1 pkt.; 8 ft. summer squash: 1 pkt.; 15 ft. bush winter squash: 1 pkt.

Plant squash seeds 6 inches apart but then thin all plants in this row to a foot or two apart after 3 weeks of growth. The small zucchini and squash (under 6-8 inches long) are best. Use winter squash any time after they've reached full size.

Row 11

30 ft. tomatoes: 18 plants

To get more plants in the row I cage or stake tomatoes in the Summer Garden. Of 18 plants, try to get at least three or four varieties. You'll have a longer harvest, different tastes, and less chance of disease hurting your harvest.

Row 12

15 ft. pole beans: 3 oz.; 15 ft. cucumbers: 1 pkt. slicing variety, 1 pkt. pickling

Tepees are the best supports for pole beans. They are sturdy and easy to erect. With more time on your hands you can try a string trellis system. You can grow more plants and the picking is easy.

MY EAT 'N STORE GARDEN

Three varieties of sweet corn plus 12 months of home-grown produce

This 60- by 80-foot Eat 'N Store Garden has plenty of long wide rows of peas, cabbage family crops, beets, carrots, onions and more! These vegetables are easy to freeze or store in the root cellar. The great advantage of putting storage crops in wide rows is that there is always plenty to eat during the season as well. In fact, you have to harvest beets, carrots and onions along the way in order to have some good-sized keepers in the fall.

With the Eat 'N Store plan, there's room for lots of cucumbers, potatoes, and a dozen 30-foot rows of sweet corn. I've got three varieties of sweet corn planned for the longest possible harvest: early, mid-season and late. If you're using up valuable garden space for sweet corn, there's no sense in having too much all at once. The later varieties are usually the best for freezing.

A garden this size may seem like a lot of work, but by planting in wide rows and using the other special planting and weeding techniques shown in this book, you can save loads of time caring for the garden. You'll spend most of your garden time harvesting!

My Eat 'N Store

---- SUNFLOWER ----
---- CORN ----
30 In. Walkway
---- CORN ----
30 In. Walkway
---- CORN ----
30 In. Walkway
---- CORN ----
30 In. Walkway
---- CORN ----
30 In. Walkway
---- CORN ----
30 In. Walkway
---- CORN ----
30 In. Walkway
---- CORN ----
30 In. Walkway
---- CORN ----
30 In. Walkway
---- CORN ----
30 In. Walkway
---- TOMATOES ----
36 In. Walkway
---- SUMMER SQUASH ----
6 Ft. Walkway
---- MELONS ----
6 Ft. Walkway
---- CUKES ----
6 Ft. Walkway
---- POTATOES ----
36 In. Walkway
---- POTATOES ----
36 In. Walkway
30 FT. PEAS
30 In. Walkway
20 FT. PEPPERS/10 FT. EGGPLANT
30 In. Walkway
30 FT. CAULIFLOWER
30 In. Walkway
30 FT. ONIONS
30 In. Walkway
25 FT. CARROTS/5 FT. KOHLRABI
30 In. Walkway
15 FT. HEAD LETTUCE/15 FT. MULTICROP

4 FT. WALKWAY

← 30 FEET →

Garden Plan

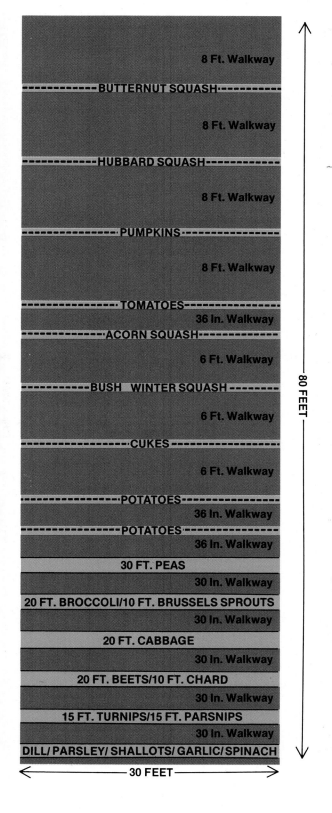

8 Ft. Walkway	
--------------**BUTTERNUT SQUASH**-------------	
8 Ft. Walkway	
--------------**HUBBARD SQUASH**--------------	
8 Ft. Walkway	
-----------------**PUMPKINS**-----------------	
8 Ft. Walkway	
-----------------**TOMATOES**-----------------	
36 In. Walkway	
----------------**ACORN SQUASH**---------------	
6 Ft. Walkway	
-----------**BUSH WINTER SQUASH**-----------	
6 Ft. Walkway	
-------------------**CUKES**-------------------	
6 Ft. Walkway	
----------------**POTATOES**-----------------	
36 In. Walkway	
----------------**POTATOES**-----------------	
36 In. Walkway	
30 FT. PEAS	
30 In. Walkway	
20 FT. BROCCOLI/10 FT. BRUSSELS SPROUTS	
30 In. Walkway	
20 FT. CABBAGE	
30 In. Walkway	
20 FT. BEETS/10 FT. CHARD	
30 In. Walkway	
15 FT. TURNIPS/15 FT. PARSNIPS	
30 In. Walkway	
DILL/ PARSLEY/ SHALLOTS/ GARLIC/ SPINACH	

80 FEET

← 30 FEET →

Potatoes

I feel good digging storage potatoes in early fall. I take four or five bushels into the root cellar each year . . . hefty *Kennebec* potatoes like these. They are a fine all-purpose potato, good for baking, boiling, and making french fries.

Sweet Corn

The flavor of just-picked sweet corn is indescribable. In this garden I grow three varieties—*Sugar 'N Gold, Butter 'N Sugar,* and *Silver Queen.* They mature at different times so I stretch out the harvest. We gobble up the early *Sugar 'N Gold* and freeze a portion of the later varieties—they're sweeter.

Space for the space-loving

Crowder Peas

This plan allows lots of room for regional favorites. For example, if you live in the South, make room for crowder peas (actually members of the bean family.) Blackeye peas are the best-known crowder. I've grown them in the North and in the South. Harvest them when they're fully formed but still soft, or let them dry in the pods.

Pumpkins

A big garden without pumpkins is a crime. At least the family and neighborhood children think so. Those you don't use for Halloween can be stored for several months in a cool, dry space. I grow two varieties—one for big jack-o'-lanterns and a smaller "pie-size" variety with plenty of meat for cooking.

Winter Squash

Winter squash will keep for 5 or 6 months with no processing, so I grow three rows of it in the Eat 'N Store Garden. We store it in the root cellar but it keeps very well in any dry, cool room such as a spare closet. The Blue Hubbard is my favorite, but most any winter squash variety is delicious and nutritious.

Dry Beans

Dry beans are easy to grow, easy to extract from their pods, and easy to store. They are a terrific source of protein. I grow 4-foot-wide swaths of them between my winter squash rows. We fill some big jars with *Soldier* beans and *Red Kidney* beans for the winter.

vegetables

Cucumbers

Keep your cucumber crop healthy and you'll have plenty of pickles. I choose *Wisconsin SMR 18,* a pickling variety that is well-suited to my climate and resistant to several troublesome diseases. It sounds highly specialized, but it's available in most garden stores and seed catalogs. A few feet of dill in a wide row gives us all we need for many quarts of dill pickles.

Melons

Melons love sun, heat, and room to run. Because I have a short summer season, I start a few plants early indoors and also sow some seeds out in the garden earlier than recommended. I cover them with plastic tunnels to capture heat. I prefer hybrid varieties of melons. They're earlier and more reliable in my neck of the woods.

Snapshots from my garden

Quick Reference
Wide Row Planning Chart

PLANTS	RECOMMENDED SIZE OF WIDE ROW	LENGTH OF ROW TO PLANT PER PERSON	AMOUNT TO PLANT PER PERSON
Beets, carrots, rutabagas turnips, radishes, kohlrabi	Rake width (15-16 inches wide)	2-3 feet	½ packet
Onion sets, plants, shallot sets, garlic cloves, leeks	Rake width (15-16 inches wide)	3-6 feet	1 lb. onion sets, ½ lb. shallot sets, 2 bulbs garlic (break into cloves before planting), 10-12 onion or leek plants
Leaf lettuce, spinach, endive, chard, mustard, kale	Rake width (15-16 inches wide)	2-3 feet	¼-½ packet
Cauliflower, cabbage, head lettuce	20 inches wide	3 feet	6-8 plants, ¼ packet
Broccoli, brussels sprouts, peppers	10-12 inches staggered row	3 feet	4-6 plants, ¼ packet
English and southern peas, snap beans, lima beans, dry and shell beans	Rake width (15-16 inches wide)	7-10 feet	¼ lb., (½ lb. lima beans)
Herbs: dill, chives, basil, parsley, etc.	Rake width (15-16 inches wide)	1 foot	¼ packet

Yes, wide rows take more seed, but buying extra seed is like getting a hired hand

Planting in wide rows means you need a little bit more seed. This is only to be expected since more of your garden space will be planted.

I seed my rows rather thickly, knowing that what I get from each individual seed is usually lower than it would be in a single row. But the overall harvest is *much greater* because there are so many extra plants in a wide row. The extra seeds and extra plants actually go to work in the garden, like a hired hand. They help get a solid stand, help keep weeds down, and help save water.

Exactly how much extra seed you need depends on the crops you plant, how long and wide your rows will be, and how skillful you become in sprinkling the seeds evenly over the seedbed. Some people who have switched to wide rows say their total seed costs go up 20 percent or so. To me, that's not very much when you consider that growing in wide rows can increase your harvest by 50 to 100 percent in the same sized garden.

Many gardeners, however, believe they didn't purchase a whole lot more seed when they switched to wide rows because they made better use of their seeds. They had fewer half-used packets, and no overcrowded straight-line rows where seeds had been dumped.

If you go in for wide rows in a big way, get your seeds from a garden store or mail order company with good bulk-purchase prices.

Seed varieties:
here are my "old reliables"

It's fun to experiment and compare by growing a few new varieties, but I never forget my "old reliables." The tried-and-true varieties are first with me. Because they've excelled year after year I pick them again every spring. After all, I want an abundant supply of good-tasting vegetables. If you're trying to save money, feed a family, and have the most productive garden possible, stick with varieties you've tried, liked, and know to be good.

Some crops are more climate-conscious than others. I find that gardeners everywhere grow pretty much the same varieties of carrots, beets, and lettuce. But it's a different story with sweet corn, beans, tomatoes, and onions. Varieties of these crops have often been developed for very specific regions, so I think it pays to know these "best bets" of the garden. The varieties I've listed below may not be the very best ones for you. Check with experienced gardeners nearby to find the trustiest varieties in your area. You'll probably hear the same names over and over.

The local County Extension office should have a list of varieties recommended for your area. Staple a copy of it in this book.

A seed company located in your region may offer more seeds adapted to your area. They're also more likely to carry the latest varieties introduced by state universities in your region where new plants are developed.

MY OLD RELIABLES

BEANS (dry): Soldier, Red Kidney, Yellow Eye
BEANS (green): Tendercrop, Contender
BEANS (Lima): Fordhook 242, Henderson Bush
BEANS (pole): Blue Lake, Kentucky Wonder
BEANS (yellow): Golden Wax, Eastern Butterwax
BEETS: Detroit Dark Red
BROCCOLI: De Cicco (spring) Green Comet (fall)
CABBAGE: Stonehead, Penn State Ballhead, Ruby Ball
CARROTS: Nantes types, Danvers types
CAULIFLOWER: Early Snowball
CHARD: Ruby, Fordhook Giant
CHINESE CABBAGE: Michili
COLLARDS: Vates
CUCUMBERS: Wisconsin SMR 18 (picklers), Marketmore 76 (slicer), Spacemaster (bush)
DILL: Bouquet
DWARF PEAS: Little Marvel, Progress No. 9, Wando
EGGPLANT: Black Beauty
GARLIC, SHALLOTS: whatever is available
HEAD LETTUCE: Ithaca, Great Lakes
KALE: Blue Curled Scotch
KOHLRABI: Early White Vienna

LEAF LETTUCE: Black Seeded Simpson, Salad Bowl, Ruby Prizehead, Oak Leaf
MUSTARD: Tendergreen
OKRA: Clemson Spineless
ONION SEEDS OR PLANTS: Yellow Bermuda, Red Hamburger, White Sweet Spanish
ONION SETS: Stuttgarter
PARSLEY: Curled Dwarf
PEPPERS: California Wonder or New Ace Hybrid (bell), Sweet Banana, Cayenne (hot)
POTATOES: Red Norland (early), Kennebec (storage)
RADISHES: Cherry Belle (red), White Icicle (white)
RUTABAGAS: American Purple Top
SPINACH: Bloomsdale varieties
SUMMER SQUASH: Early Prolific Straightneck
SWEET CORN: Sugar 'N Gold, Butter 'N Sugar, Platinum Lady, Silver Queen
TOMATOES: Pixie, Early Girl, Supersonic, Better Boy, Jet Star
TURNIPS: Purple-Top White Globe
WINTER SQUASH: Gold Nugget (bush), Blue Hubbard, Waltham Butternut, Table Queen Acorn
ZUCCHINI: Aristocrat

WHAT TO LOOK FOR IN A NEW VARIETY

Here are some things I think about when picking out a new variety to try:

Good taste: I like vegetables with a lot of flavor, so I pay attention when a seed company uses words like "unsurpassed sweetness" or "most flavorful variety yet" or "most delicious." If I'm not already growing it, I'll try it to see if the praise is deserved.

Heavy yielder: New varieties may often be labeled "heavy yielder" or "prolific producer." I'm interested in these—except if the vegetable is zucchini squash because they're prolific enough already. A lot goes into growing a heavy yielder—good soil, adequate rain, good weather, and good care.

Disease resistant: I check to see if a new variety is resistant to such diseases as wilts, blights, and mosaics. The ones that are resistant will say so. The resistance qualities are usually right after the name of the variety. The *Better Boy VFN* tomato indicates the variety is resistant to disease. "V" stands for resistance against verticillium wilt; "F" for fusarium wilt, and "N" for nematodes. If any of these letters appear after the name of a variety, that variety is resistant to the disease. For example, *Roma VF* is a tomato that is resistant to verticillium and fusarium wilts.

The more letters you see, the better chance you have to get a good harvest.

Days to harvest: I like to plant varieties of beans, sweet corn and peas that mature at different times so I can spread out the harvest. I always check how long a new variety will take to mature.

For example, I may plant all these early and mid-season varieties of sweet corn at the same time:

Spancross	62 days to harvest
Sugar 'N Gold	67 days to harvest
Butter 'N Sugar	73 days to harvest
Platinum Lady	80 days to harvest

If they all ripen on schedule we'll enjoy fresh corn for several weeks.

Space savers: People often leave watermelons and winter squash out of the garden plan because they take so much room. But I've tried some of the new compact bush varieties of winter squash, melons, cucumbers, and pumpkins and found them excellent. One of my favorites is *Gold Nugget,* a delicious winter squash that yields tremendously but doesn't spread much. Although pole beans need staking, they need less garden space than bush beans. The opposite is true of peas; you get more out of bush varieties like *Progress No. 9* and *Little Marvel,* which grow without support.

Hybrids: Hybrid varieties are the results of special breeding techniques. Hybrid seeds cost a little more, but the advantages of stronger plants, earlier harvest, more flavor, better keeping qualities or improved disease resistance are worth the extra cost. I especially like hybrid varieties of peppers, tomatoes, melons, and corn.

Check the date on seed packets

A seed, though it's dormant, is a living thing. If it's to sprout and grow in your garden, it must be kept under dormant conditions—in a cool, dry place—until planting time.

If you go into a store and the seed packets are placed in direct sun or near a heater, don't buy them. High heat causes changes inside the seeds and they may not germinate well.

Buy seeds from stores or seed companies that have a good track record. I always plant seeds from packets that have the current year's date printed on them. There is nothing more discouraging than planting old seeds which fail to germinate. You can lose as much as 2 weeks of the gardening season this way, and it's just not worth it.

Treated or untreated seeds

The biggest threats to seedlings growing indoors and outdoors are fungus diseases known as *damping-off* and *seed rot* which thrive in cool, wet soil in early spring.

In order to protect seeds against these diseases some seed companies treat their seeds with a fungicide. This protectant colors the seeds pink, yellow, or white. You will see it most often on seeds of peas and beans, sweet corn, and vine crops. You can purchase seed protectant and treat any of your seeds.

Follow these directions for treating a small quantity of seeds:

1. Tear off the corner of the seed packet.

2. Dip the small blade of a penknife into the fungicide.

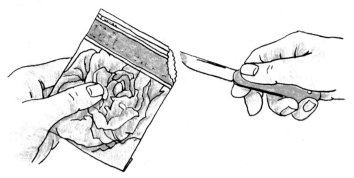

3. Lift out as much as will go on the tip of the blade.

4. Insert the fungicide through the hole in the packet.

5. Fold down the corner of the packet.

6. Shake the seeds thoroughly.

The directions on the package will tell you how much fungicide to use for treating a large quantity of seed. Place it and the seeds in a closed container. Shake the container 1 to 2 minutes.

Do not eat treated seed or feed it to livestock. It's poisonous. Using seed protectant is most important when you're planting early in the year. That's when soils are moist and cool, just what the damping-off and seed rot organisms prefer. I always use seed protectant on peas, beans, corn, and vine crops and often on seeds of lettuce, spinach, chard, beets and carrots.

Test old seeds in a towel

There's an easy way to determine before planting if old seed is good. Stack two or three paper towels and wet them with a mister.

Place 10 seeds on the top towel from the batch you want to test.

Roll up the towels with the seeds inside,

and wrap the roll in a damp terry cloth towel.

Enclose the whole bundle in a plastic bag and put it in a warm place such as the top of the refrigerator.

After four or five days unwrap the towels and count the number of seeds that have germinated. If 8 of the 10 seeds have sprouted, you have an 80 percent germination rate, which is good for old seed.

If you discover low germination rates, plant more seeds, or better yet, buy fresh packets.

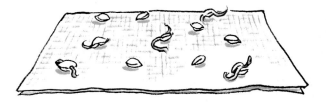

1 First and most important, prepare a deep, loose seed-bed. (And don't walk on it!)

Wide row growing is an intensive way to raise food. Plants are closer together in the row, and their roots compete for food and water. These roots must be able to grow down into the soil easily. So the first goal of working the soil before planting is to create a loose seedbed about 6 to 8 inches deep. I use my roto-tiller to work up most of my seedbeds because it's easy and fast. Excellent seedbeds can be readied with hand tools also.

Planting a wide row

2 Use a string to establish the edge of the row

Once the planting area is tilled, I run a string along what's going to be the edge of my first wide row. That tells me where my first walkway will be so I always stay right there in the *walkway* to plant. I only work from *one* side of the row. As you'll see, the soil in the other walkway across the row must be loose. All your gardening chores can be done from the walkway. There's no reason to set foot in the planting area all season long.

A loose seedbed is important for your plants, so don't ever step where you'll be planting seeds. When the soil is loose and "footprint-free," the roots can travel down much more easily.

I want to show you the easy practical steps of planting and caring for a wide row

3 I use a rake to mark the exact width of rows

I grow most vegetables in wide rows that are about as wide as my rake—15 or 16 inches. I drag my rake down the row, keeping the edge of the rake close to the string. This marks off a 16-inch wide row. I don't need to set another string along the outer edge of the planting area.

Don't bother to rake the entire garden; rake only the areas within the rows where you're going to broadcast seeds.

You can make your rows a little wider or narrower, of course, but I've found 15 or 16 inches to be a practical width for most crops.

4 Sprinkle fertilizer over the row

Once I've marked off the rows, I usually sprinkle some fertilizer in the area where the seeds will grow. This is in *addition* to the general broadcast fertilizing I do over the entire garden, explained a bit later. The extra fertilizer is optional, but it helps me get the best possible harvest.

I use commercial fertilizer such as 5-10-10, or a natural fertilizer such as dehydrated manure. To fertilize a wide row seedbed 10 feet long requires about 2 cups of commercial fertilizer or 4 cups of dehydrated manure.

For my root crops and onions, I use some high phosphorus fertilizer, such as bone meal, because phosphorus helps plants grow strong roots.

I spread the fertilizer and mix it into the soil, with my garden rake.

5 Smooth the soil with the back of the rake

When the rows are staked out and the fertilizer is mixed in, there's one more important chore before planting—smoothing out the seedbed.

I flop my rake over and move soil gently until my seedbed is as smooth and level as possible. In smoothing the row, I remove large stones, clumps of soil, and large pieces of organic matter.

Believe me, a smooth seedbed is important for getting seeds in a wide row off to a good start. If the seedbed is smooth, it means you'll be able to broadcast seeds, firm them, and cover each and every one with the *correct amount of soil.* This is so important! If your seedbed is bumpy, some seeds will be covered with too much soil and others with too little. As a result some plants come up at different times, making early weeding harder; some seeds may not come up at all, producing a spotty row with a lot of "skips."

6 Broadcasting seeds: daredevil at first, but second nature with a little practice

For the most even distribution over the entire row here's the way I pass my hand up and down the row.

The easiest way to sow seeds in a wide row is by sprinkling or broadcasting them over the bed like grass seed. The broadcasting method is simple—I don't have to make any furrows or little holes for seeds. I can sow a wide row 100 feet long in just a couple of minutes. But for some people, switching from the old system of putting each seed down one by one to the new "daredevil" scatter method probably will take a little practice.

The idea is to land the seeds over the full width of the row without clumping a bunch together or leaving a bare patch.

46

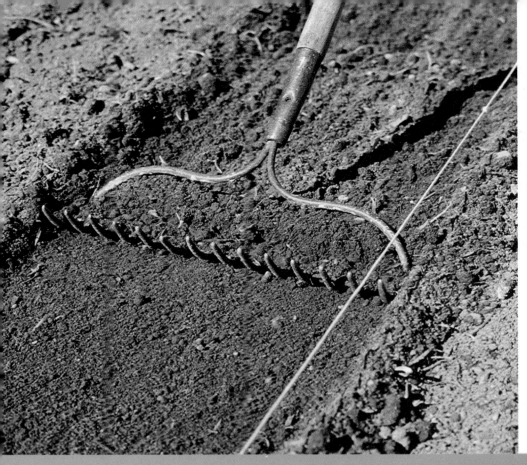

The rake is my measuring tool for wide rows.

When seeds are planted on a level seedbed and each covered with the same depth of soil, they will emerge at about the same time. This makes thinning easy.

The easiest way to plant small seeds is to use empty herb jars with different-sized holes in the tops. I shake the seeds onto the soil like shaking pepper on scrambled eggs.

Thickness to sow seed

I never have any trouble broadcasting bigger seeds such as chard, beets and spinach. They're so much easier to control—you can let them roll off the end of your fingers one or two at a time. You can space them evenly because it's easy to see where they land.

Peas and beans are also a cinch. They are the only crops I won't thin with my rake when they come up, so I sprinkle them 3 or 4 inches apart.

To plant my onion sets in a wide row is a little different. I push them into the ground one by one and then tamp them all in with the back of my hoe. I usually plant them about 1 or 2 inches apart and pull quite a few scallions to give the remaining ones more room to bulb out. Onion plants also go in my wide rows one by one.

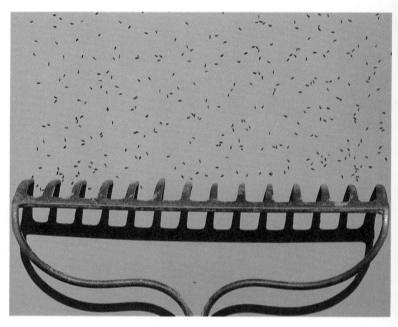

LETTUCE

7 Sprinkle in a few radish seeds

With just about all my wide rows, I sprinkle some radish seeds—not many—right in with the main crop of seeds. Radishes are my favorite companion plants and they are very important to my gardening method. They serve as "row markers" because they sprout up ahead of other vegetables. They also loosen and aerate the soil like any cultivator when I pull them out of the row.

8 Firm in the seeds for good germination

Once the seeds are sprinkled over the soil, I firm them down gently with the back of a regular hoe. To germinate well, a seed should come in good contact with warm, moist soil on all of its sides. Tamping down gives them this necessary contact.

PEAS BEANS

9 Cover them with soil my way

Now comes an important step—covering the seeds with just the right amount of soil.

Small seeds like lettuce and carrots usually need about ¼ to ½ inch of covering. Larger seeds such as peas and beans need about 1 inch of soil. The rule of thumb for all seeds is to cover them with enough moist soil to equal *four times their own diameter*.

The easy way to cover seeds is to use a rake and pull soil from 1 or 2 feet beyond the row up onto the seedbed. This may sound tricky, but it isn't.

Going down one side of the row, I rake up and lift soil up onto the middle of the seedbed. If the soil I'm moving is loose, the job is easy.

I don't worry about getting each seed covered by the proper amount of soil at this point. I simply pile soil in the center of the seedbed. The important thing is to lift the soil up onto the bed and not to rake *into* the seedbed.

10 Level the soil over the seeds

Once I have little mounds of soil sitting on the entire seedbed I smooth them out.

I use the back of the rake to push the soil around until it spreads evenly over all the seeds. Each seed should be covered by the same amount of soil. Since they've already been tamped down, the seeds won't move as I push and pull soil above them. After a little experience, this leveling action will be almost second nature. You'll get the knack of just how much soil to pull up to cover small or large seeds.

11 Tamp down the seedbed again

Once the seeds are covered evenly, tamp the whole seedbed down gently with a hoe. This packs soil and moisture around each seed and protects it from air which could dry out the seed as it's germinating.

12 Keep the seedbed moist

If the soil is dry on planting day and there's no rain in the forecast, you can use a sprinkler on your rows *after* you've planted. It's important to keep the soil slightly moist until the seedlings come up. Once the seeds begin germination, you can't let them dry out.

Early in the spring, most garden soils have quite a bit of moisture, and watering is usually unnecessary. But later in the season when the days are longer, sunnier, and hotter, the soil surface will dry out faster. Keeping the seedbed moist will be more of a job.

To save on my hot-weather watering, I put ½ inch or so of light mulch over the row after it's planted to hold in moisture and to keep the sun from baking a hard crust on the surface. I use hay, peat moss, or straw, and the plants will grow right up through it.

Once I put mulch on a seedbed I don't want to pick it up again.

After a rain or watering, clay soil may occasionally develop a hard, crusty surface as it dries. Sometimes the soil gets so hard that young seedlings don't have the strength to burst through and are deprived of needed oxygen.

Here's how to beat crusty soils: 4 or 5 days after planting, drag a garden rake or an In-Row Weeder (a new tool I've designed) over the seedbed with just enough force to break up the crust—the tines should penetrate the soil only about ¼ inch. You may have to water hard-packed seedbeds before loosening your soil ¼ inch down. This will allow plants to emerge and continue their growth.

I set many transplants in wide rows too!

When I made the switch to wide row growing, I concentrated only on vegetables seeded in the garden. But I soon began experimenting with crops started indoors and set out later, such as head lettuce, cauliflower, and cabbage, and learned some very interesting things. For example, I discovered wide rows yielded more usable produce and gave a longer harvest than single rows.

How far apart do you plant cabbages in your garden? Most gardening books advise 18 to 24 inches between plants, but I get terrific results spacing them only 10 inches apart. When cabbages are planted this close, I can harvest some heads while they're small and "table-size." These 2- or 3-pound early cabbages are just right for a family meal. After all, big cabbages can be a bother. Too often we cut a big one, use part of it, and hide the rest in the fridge for a week. I'd rather cut a smaller cabbage when we need one, and eat the whole thing.

I start my spring crop of cabbages in flats. When the time is right and my plants are hardened off, I plant the first two cabbages on opposite edges of a *20-inch wide row*. Then I set the third one between the first two, which leaves 10 inches between plants. I move 10 inches down the row and this time plant two cabbages, each one 5 inches in from the edge of the row. I continue alternating three plants, then two, until the row is complete.

This is the planting scheme for what I call my "3-2 staggered row." I put three plants side by side, then move down the row and plant two more. They're pretty close together, but close planting has many advantages.

I harvest cabbage, head lettuce, and cauliflower early

Early picking from my 20-inch wide rows of crops planted in the 3-2 pattern is very important. I start harvesting as soon as there's something big enough to eat, always taking the largest of the row. This frees up space, water, and plant food for some of the slower-growing plants nearby.

Crops don't all mature at the same time in one of my 3-2 rows. Picking early stretches out the harvest. My wide rows have plenty of plants, and even though I pick quite a few early, there are still many growing to full size.

Cabbage

Small heads of cabbage are all you need for a meal. There's little left over to spoil in the fridge. There are plenty of smaller heads to choose from in this row. The plants here are just 10 inches apart. I prefer to grow early varieties which produce round heads, such as *Stonehead Hybrid*. The varieties with pointed heads, such as *Early Jersey Wakefield*, seem to go past the prime eating stage too quickly. If you want to get plenty of early cabbage, try to set out your plants 2 or 3 weeks before your last spring frost date.

Cauliflower

I love early cauliflower that's tender and creamy white. It pays to cut some early heads—you never know when warm weather will hit and cause the quality to drop a little.

Head Lettuce

My first harvest comes before the plants have started to make firm heads. They're delicious at this stage, and the dark green leaves are loaded with vitamins.

Thinning my wide rows once with an ordinary garden rake accomplishes three of the most important steps in my gardening system

Rake-thinning gives plants growing room

All my wide row crops planted from seed (except peas and beans) must be thinned out when they're quite small—about ¼ to ½ inch high. This is true for most methods of planting, but I consider it *essential* with wide rows because the plants are so numerous.

To most people, thinning means work—but not to me. I never did like the idea of spending hours bent over a row in the hot sun pulling out tiny plants one by one. Years ago I discovered that I could thin out any crop properly using an ordinary garden rake. Since then I've been doing my thinning standing up—and spending only a couple of minutes on each row.

Here's how I do it

When the plants are ¼- to ½-inch high, I drag the rake *across the width of the row* so that the teeth dig into the soil only about ¼ to ½ inch. The teeth in an iron garden rake catch just enough seedlings, and pull them from the row.

One thing I have to admit—thinning this way seems drastic—maybe even cruel. I tell beginners, "Don't look down when you thin with a rake. Just trust me. It works. After a few days the row will look fine again. I know, I've been thinning this way for many years."

4 days after thinning

2 weeks later

Rake-thinning gets rid of weeds

Thinning with a rake is actually my first weeding. Most weed seeds are so small that they must be close to the surface in order to sprout. Most annual weed seeds do not have much of a taproot anchoring them in the soil when they sprout. So the rake kicks many of them out of the soil just as they germinate but before they anchor themselves in. Soon the vegetable plants start shading the soil, preventing many weeds from getting anywhere.

Rake-thinning allows oxygen and water to flow freely into the soil

After a rake-thinning, the soil around the vegetables is left loose, so it can take in oxygen and water easily.

Soil life and plants need this supply all season if they are going to grow properly. When folks thin a row by hand they just pluck the plants out. This doesn't loosen up the soil much.

Loose soil around the plants is important if you have clay soil because clay soil tends to bake hard. When you grow crops in wide rows, the plants shade the soil very early on, and this protects the soil from crusting and insures that air and water can get into the soil.

An early pass over the row with a rake gets rid of tiny weeds just starting to grow.

Crops I thin with a rake

In case you're wondering about thinning with a rake, I've listed the wide row crops that get a rake-thinning in my garden. With all these crops, I thin them as soon as the plants are ¼ to ½ inch high.

Endives	**Leaf lettuce**
Parsley	**Kohlrabi**
Chard	**Spinach**
Collards	**Turnips**
Kale	**Rutabagas**
Chinese cabbage	**Parsnips**
Radishes	**Mustard**
Herbs	**Beets**
Onions planted from seeds	**Carrots**

Notes:
Do not thin peas or beans with a rake. Their stems are tender and break off too easily.
I find most crops are thinned correctly with one pass of the rake, but if the crop is a bit thick, another pass is required. I sometimes draw the rake across from a different direction on the second pass.

My In-Row Weeder nips small weeds early, with no harm at all to the spinach plants.

Weeds are no problem in wide rows

My In-Row Weeder eliminates weeds before you can see them

About 5 or 6 days after thinning with a rake, I use my In-Row Weeder for the next 2 weeks to prevent weeds from getting a start in my wide rows. This new tool is indispensable in my strategy to get weeds *before* they become a problem. (All my weeding ideas are spelled out in more detail on pages 132–147.)

The flexible tines of the In-Row Weeder stir up the top ¼ inch of soil as I drag it over the plants down the row. This action disrupts many tiny weed seeds that are germinating. However, *the In-Row Weeder does not harm my small vegetable plants.* Vegetable plants may be tiny, but they are firmly rooted—much more so than weed seedlings. So the tines of the In-Row Weeder do not pull out vegetables—they pass around them. This is the secret of the In-Row Weeder.

How often do I use the In-Row Weeder on a wide row? Well, that depends a little on the weather and on how fast things are growing. But on the average I go over my wide rows once every 4 or 5 days until the crops are too big to pass through the tines without harm or until they shade the seedbed completely.

A few weeds may escape the In-Row Weeder and put on some size. These lonely weeds are easy to pull.

(Dick Raymond's In-Row Weeder and other tools pictured in this book are available by writing to Dick Raymond, Box 97, Ferry Road, Charlotte, VT 05445.)

Weeding in a nutshell

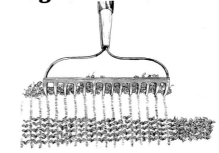

1. Drag a rake across the row when plants are ¼-½ inch high.

2. After a few days, start passing over the plants with an In-Row Weeder and repeat every 4 to 5 days.

3. Pull any remaining weeds by hand.

Harvesting a wide row

FIRST CUT

I harvested this tender chard for the first time by cutting off the entire plant.

SECOND CUT

After making several more harvests down the row I came back to make a second cut from the area where I first harvested.

THIRD CUT

I can harvest chard three or more times from the same spot. The tall chard in the picture is where I haven't harvested at all yet.

Don't pick at lettuce and greens! Get three or four better harvests with my "cut and grow again" method

The way I harvest my wide row greens—spinach, lettuce, chard, and others—actually encourages more production. I take a long knife and cut the plants all across the row 1 inch above the ground. It doesn't take much row space or time to fill up a large picking basket.

The best thing is that each trimmed plant will grow back with fresh, tender growth. That's because these plants want to fulfill their life cycle—they want to produce seed. When you frustrate them by cutting them back, the plants simply renew their drive to put out seed pods. They spurt back with some incredibly tender leaves.

Many years I get three harvests from a row of lettuce. Chard can be cut many times, from early summer until fall. I only cut part of a row at a time. When I've reached the end of the row, it's time to start in on the second harvest from the sections I cut earlier.

To help my greens come back quickly, I often sprinkle a little natural fertilizer or compost over the area I've just harvested.

Wide rows give you an abundant early harvest of small, tender beets, carrots, onions, greens, and more

As soon as something in my wide rows gets big enough to eat, I'm after it. Because there are so many plants, you can harvest lots of food quite early and still have plenty left for later. In a single row, you simply can't afford to harvest early; there wouldn't be enough plants left for later eating. In my garden I can pull carrots all season long from a 20-foot row and still have plenty left in the fall to store in the root cellar. Small carrots are the tastiest anyway—and the best ones for freezing.

A hidden benefit from harvesting small root crops

Years ago I noticed an important benefit from pulling small root crops from the row regularly. Removing a carrot or beet is an easy method of thinning and loosening the soil around plants to let in air and moisture.

As long as I harvest regularly I know that the soil in the row is being loosened from time to time. The holes left by pulling out some early root crops provide needed shoulder room for other plants and are wonderful traps for water and air.

With carrots in a wide row (left), you can afford to pick many at the tasty "fingerling" size. Pulling young beets (right) thins the row and loosens soil around other beets.

HERE ARE THE CROPS I HARVEST EARLY:		
Cabbage	Beets	Turnips
Kale	Carrots	Lettuce
Kohlrabi	Chard	Collards
Onion family	Mustard	Radishes

MULTICROPPING

I grow five crops together

Do you want to grow practically a whole salad in one wide row? I grow five different vegetables together in a wide row 15 or 16 inches across. It's almost like growing a chef's salad in one row. It's fun, easy, and surprisingly productive. I combine radishes, onions, lettuce, carrots, or beets, and spinach, and add a splash of color by planting several different colored lettuce varieties. There are lots of other combinations which work, too.

Here's spinach, onions, and Ruby lettuce in a multi-crop row. Sharp eyes will spot some carrots, too. I've already harvested radishes from this row.

61

Here's how I plant a multicrop

3 I tamp down the seeds and rake up some soil onto the row to cover them.

4 I smooth the soil over the seeds to cover them with about ¼ inch of soil.

1 First I prepare a good, deep seedbed, just as in planting a regular wide row.

2 Then I sprinkle the seeds of lettuce, carrots, spinach, and radishes over the entire seedbed. Naturally, I use less of each seed than in a regular wide row. When I'm done, the seeds are spaced about ½ inch apart.

5 Now it's time to plant the onions! I push in onion sets or onion plants so that they are 3 or 4 inches apart in all directions. (Don't plant onion seeds—they won't make it because the other plants will shade them out. But you can try garlic bulbs or leek plants.)

6 Then I tamp the whole row down with the back of my hoe to bring everything—seeds and sets—into good contact with the soil.

Harvesting a multicrop is like stepping up

In my multicrop there's a little of everything. My radishes are ready to pick and eat first. Pulling them cultivates within the row, leaving loose pockets for the other crops to grow toward.

Spinach, onions, and lettuce are ready to pick or pull next. I usually pull up a few lettuce and spinach plants from the row each time I harvest to make room for other crops to grow. Soon my beets or carrots start to come on, so I keep pulling more onions and any remaining radishes to give the others more room and sunshine. Once the carrots and beets reach "eating size," I start picking them. They will usually yield until the very end of the season.

You also can plant a few garlic sets with your onions and leave them in until the end of the season to get as big as possible.

I let some of the onion plants grow until their tops fall down so I can get a few large, sweet, slicing onions.

To me, a multicrop of vegetables is as pretty as any flower garden. And I've only scratched the surface as far as colorful, mouth-watering combinations go.

to a salad bar!

From left, Dick harvests the multicrop; marigolds, carrots, and beets are neighbors in a multicrop row; colorful **Ruby** lettuce planted in front of a multicrop area; a basketful of veggies! Below: plenty of tasty **Oak Leaf** lettuce in this multicrop row.

"BLOCK" PLANTING

Big squares of solid vegetables to harvest

I plant many vegetables in superwide rows that are anywhere from 3 to 25 feet wide. It's a fantastically easy way to put every inch of soil to work and to reap a tremendous harvest. I grow crops such as kale, collards, onions, peas, and beans in wide rows that are actually *blocks,* measuring perhaps 3 feet by 3 feet, or 4 feet by 4 feet. There are no walkways through the blocks—they are solid vegetables. Blocks this size can provide all a family can eat and store.

In my larger blocks, up to 25 feet by 25 feet, I grow thick crops of peas, beans, and lima beans. The way I plant them, there's absolutely no weeding to do, and the harvest is overwhelming.

Large blocks nourish the soil, too. Peas, beans, and soybeans are "legumes"; they belong to a group of crops that captures nitrogen from the air and adds it to the soil. And nitrogen is one of the three most important plant foods.

After the harvest, I roto-till all the plants back into the soil to give my earthworms and other soil life plenty of organic matter to feed on. That's important. Without a steady diet of fresh organic matter, soil will become lifeless.

Why I'm sold on block planting

- puts all available space to work growing food
- very easy to plant by broadcasting seeds
- inexpensive way to get large harvest, especially if you buy seeds at bulk prices
- produces large amount of organic matter for tilling in after harvest
- very little or no weeding in small blocks
- no thinning or hoeing necessary for big blocks

Here are Jan and I harvesting peas from a 12x24-foot block. There's no thinning, hoeing, or staking needed at all for peas with my block planting method.

My special techniques for planting blocks

A 4x4-foot block is easy to plant by hand. Here's how I do it. First, I work up the soil in about a 6x6-foot area, getting the soil loose and crumbly to a depth of 6 inches. Mixing in a few cups of 5-10-10 fertilizer or some compost will help.

Then I stake out the square, 4 feet on each side, and smooth out the soil. As with rake-width wide rows, I never step on the seedbed. I try to stay on one side of the bed since I'll need some of the loose soil on the far side of the 4x4-foot area. I don't want to pack it down with footsteps.

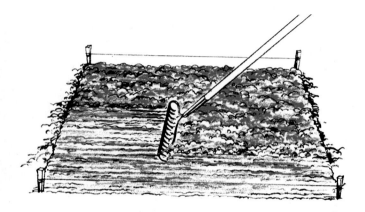

I broadcast seeds over *one-half* of the bed. Then I tamp them down to bring them in good contact with the soil for germination.

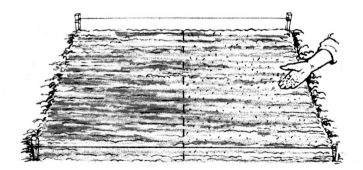

To cover the seeds, I rake up soil *from the other half of the bed* and smooth it evenly over the seeds—most will need ¼ to ½ inch of soil over them— and tamp down again. Now, half the square is planted.

In the area where I pulled soil to cover the first half of the row, I smooth out the soil. Then I sow more seeds and tamp them down. To cover them with soil, I reach to the loose soil *outside the bed*, lift some up onto the square and smooth it over the seeds. Then I tamp down again to finish the job.

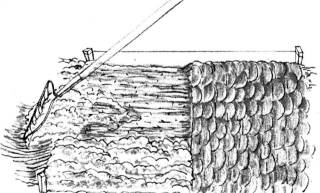

Small squares of lettuce, chard, and any other crop except peas and beans can use a rake-thinning—easy to do if you work one-half of the bed at a time. Thinning these squares is important. Without thinning, the center of the bed will be unproductive.

68

I planted almost an entire garden in 4 × 4-foot blocks—and it took only minutes!

Let me tell you about one of the easiest gardens I ever planted. It was a long row of 4x4-foot blocks. I used a roto-tiller to work all the seeds into the soil at once.

I first tilled the area deeply, and then broadcast and mixed in some fertilizer. Then I marked off a long 4-foot wide row and smoothed it out. Going down the row I planted a different crop every four feet, scattering the seed a little more thickly than usual. (I'll tell you why in a second.)

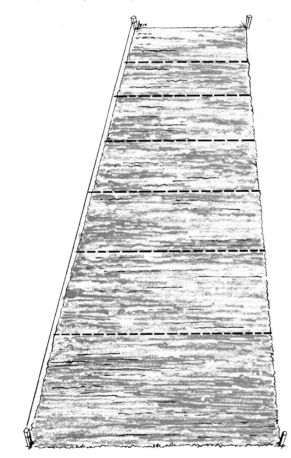

I sowed mustard, two kinds of lettuce, and three kinds of chard, as well as beets, turnips, kale, beans, and so on. Using my roto-tiller, I covered them with soil. By making a shallow 2- or 3-inch deep pass over the seedbed with my tiller, I worked some seeds into the soil a little too deep. They didn't come up. This is why I needed a little extra seed in the row. But most were at the right depth to sprout quickly, so I didn't have to tamp seeds down or bring soil onto the row.

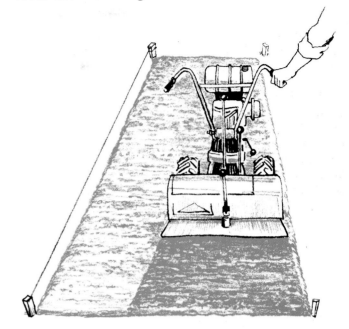

The seeds germinated perfectly after tilling them in. I could have taken a lot of time to plant each one and cover it separately, but I don't like to waste time. The way I see it, seeds don't really care how they are planted. They just want to grow.

After a rake-thinning and a little maintenance with my In-Row Weeder, I was harvesting. This block garden was so successful that I still plant part of my garden this way.

BEST CROPS FOR BLOCK PLANTING

Chard	Onions
Kale	Collards
Head lettuce	Cabbage
Cauliflower	Peas*
Mustard	Beans* (such as snap beans, limas, dry beans, southern pea varieties)
Turnips	

(Only crops I plant in large blocks.)

Planting a double or triple row

To plant double and triple rows I sow two or three single lanes of seed close together. I plant beans and lima beans this way, because they appreciate the extra growing room. But you can plant almost any crop in double or triple rows.

I've found that double or triple rows take more time to plant and require more weeding than a normal wide row. But once the plants are high enough to create a shade mulch over the soil, they are just like wide rows; they'll need little weeding and watering. If you're nervous about giving up the single-row style of planting, these double and triple rows are a good stepping-stone to a regular broadcast wide row.

Double and triple rows are the next best thing to wide rows.

1. Prepare a loose, smooth seedbed—6 to 8 inches deep and a foot or more wide. Toss out large rocks and break up any big clods of soil. Mix fertilizer into the soil with a rake.

2. Line up your double or triple rows with a string tied to stakes at both ends of the row. Individual rows should be 3 to 5 inches apart for greens and root crops. For beans and peas, 4 to 8 inches is good. This distance can vary to fit different crops or the weeding tools you use.

3. Drag the corner of your hoe or the handle end along the string to make shallow furrows for the seeds.

4. Drop the seeds in the furrow. Space larger seeds such as peas and beans so you won't have to thin—about 3 to 4 inches apart. (Small-seeded crops will usually need thinning with a rake when they come up.)

5. Gently firm the seeds into the soil with a hoe.

6. Cover the seeds by running a hoe alongside each row to spill soil into the furrow. Small seeds will need ¼ to ½ inch of covering; larger seeds such as peas or beans 1 to 1½ inches.

7. Tamp down over the furrow so soil is in good contact with the seeds.

8. Water the row gently if soil is dry. Keep seedbed moist until plants come up.

9. Thin the plants out when they are ¼ to ½ inch high. Use a rake and the job will only take a minute.

Points to Remember for Successful Wide Rows

Follow these basic steps and you'll grow more food with less work and far less weeding

---

Prepare a seedbed that is 6 to 8 inches deep and quite loose.

Never step on the seedbed or compact it in any way.

Try a 15- or 16-inch width for your wide rows, about the width of an ordinary garden rake.

Don't be stingy with seeds. Sowing thickly is much better than sowing thinly.

Sow a few radishes in every wide row.

Pull soil with a rake from beyond your rows to cover seeds. Then smooth the soil with the rake upside down so all the seeds are covered with the same amount of soil.

Use a garden rake to thin plants as soon as they grow ½ inch. Drag the rake across the row with the teeth going in the soil just ¼ inch.

Use an In-Row Weeder to keep weeds from getting anchored in the row.

Start harvesting as soon as something is big enough to eat. Keep "pickin' 'n thinnin' " as the crop grows.

GETTING THE SOIL READY

When I first till at my place the geese are flying north

The bluejays are perched near the tool shed, I hear cardinals in the woods, the air is sharp and clean—and sometimes I can even see the last patches of melting snow under the trees. It feels great!

I'm a firm believer in working the soil as early in the season as possible. When I say "early" I mean early—weeks ahead of Valentine's Day, St. Patrick's Day, Good Friday, Memorial Day, or whatever the traditional planting date is in your area.

In Vermont, tradition says you can plant a garden on Memorial Day, but some advice years ago from an experienced market gardener got me rototilling the garden at the end of March and planting a few days later, almost 8 weeks before our last spring frost.

Ralph Spade, a neighbor up the road, had a good vegetable growing business. He's retired now, but when I was starting out and trying to sell my own vegetables for income, I asked him how early I should plant. He answered, "Dick, if you don't *lose* some of your *first* planting or some of your *last* planting, you just aren't planting early enough or late enough." I took that message to heart and began planting a little bit earlier each year. After a while, I learned that as soon as I can work the soil, I can plant some of my early crops.

A big advantage of working the soil early is that I can also mix plenty of organic matter into the soil—such as old leaves or a green manure soil improvement crop that has died over the winter—and give it time to decompose before planting.

Organic matter is food for my garden soil. It keeps the earthworms and other soil life in my garden working. And since my soil is on the sandy side, organic matter plays a big role in holding moisture for my crops. Without organic matter, a sandy soil loses water rapidly.

Fall is considered the best time for adding or-

73

ganic matter, but I like to mix some into the soil in spring as well. The important thing is to give organic matter time to start decomposing. The many kinds of soil life that attack organic matter and break it down need energy to work. They get it from nutrients in the soil. If the soil is low in nutrients, the soil life can "tie up" all available nutrients. Crops will sprout, but then stop growing because there's little in the soil for them to use.

Give organic matter at least *2 weeks* or so in the spring to start decomposing. I put my spring organic matter where I'll be planting a late crop, such as corn or melons. I don't put it where my earliest crops are going.

Working wet soil early

Some people say the ground is dry enough to work when you can pick up a clump of soil and knock it apart with a light tap. I think a better test is stepping on the soil. If your footprint is shiny, the soil is still too wet to work.

Occasionally, I'm too impatient to wait until the soil's 100 percent ready. On soil that is a little too wet, I till or rake *just the top crust.* Once the crust is broken, air gets in and dries the soil out in a hurry. After a few days, it is ready for a deeper tilling.

In my old market garden I had a large muddy area that stayed wet for weeks in the spring. I dried it out by going over the soil with a roto-tiller in high gear. I couldn't go down deep, so I just broke up the surface. I never could have planted that section without opening up the ground to dry first.

Depending on your soil type, you might be able to loosen the surface crust of your garden with a rake or tiller and get some crops planted up to 2 weeks earlier than usual.

If you have heavy, clay soil, be careful. Working it too early can cause it to cake up and bake hard like pottery.

Preparing garden soil

Choosing the right tool to prepare the garden will lighten the chore and help you finish the job sooner. The best tool for working the soil is a round-pointed shovel. It's easy to drive into the soil and chop clumps of earth, and it's usually lighter than other digging tools. My shovel has a long handle so I don't have to bend much to dig up and turn the sod.

The spading shovel is a good tool for cutting and digging a straight border around your garden because it has a sharp flat edge. That's about all it's good for. You'll do a lot of bending if you dig a whole garden with it, unless you can find one with a long handle.

The spading fork has four strong tines. It's good for preparing soil in an established garden. It will break up clumps of soil easily. The spading fork is also good for loosening any layers of hard-packed soil or hardpan below your topsoil.

You don't need all three, of course. The long-handled round-pointed shovel will do most jobs very well.

I turn over *new* sections of the garden *in the fall* to expose weed seeds and to give roots and grass sod a chance to decompose over the winter.

If you can't work the soil in the fall, don't fret. You can turn over new ground in the spring and still plant a garden. There will probably be more weeds to contend with during the first season, though.

with a shovel

1. *Stake out the dimensions of your new garden.*

2. *Starting at the outside edge (with your back to the garden site), turn up a chunk of sod and earth. Continue digging across the width of the garden.*

3. *Place all soil from this first row in a garden cart. When you finish you'll have an open furrow down one edge of your garden.*

4. *To start the next row, face the open furrow with your back to the garden site and again dig into the sod. Turn this chunk upside down into the open furrow.*
By flipping every chunk into the open furrow ahead, you make sure that all the roots and pieces of sod end up below the soil where they will decompose.

5. *Dig up the rest of the garden, always turning the sod upside down into the open furrow in front of you.*

6. *After you've dug the soil out of the last furrow, take the garden cart with the sod chunks to the last row and turn the sod pieces upside down into the open furrow.*

7. *After a couple of days, chop up the clumps as well as you can with a strong hoe. It pays to do this several times.*
Some gardeners handle sod in a new garden differently. They dig up the sod pieces, shake out the soil over the garden and toss the grass and roots into the compost pile. The green matter increases the nitrogen content of the pile, and the soil clinging to the grass roots helps activate the heap.
If you remove sod from the garden site, you'll find the soil a little easier to dig and smooth out for planting and you'll probably have fewer weeds, too.

8. *In subsequent years it's a good policy to spade the garden at least twice before planting. The first time, dig in 6 or 8 inches, turn the soil over into the holes, and break up any big clumps of soil.*
After a week or so, spade the area again, but only to half the depth of your first spading. This makes for easier spading, but also gets rid of many weeds in the top 2 or 3 inches of soil and helps keep it loose and aerated for planting day.
If you have enough time to do this half-depth spading two or three times before planting day, go ahead. It will pay off in reduced weeding and it will keep the soil loose and crumbly.

A good roto-tiller makes soil preparation easy and fast

I have a large garden and I use a Troy-Bilt Roto-Tiller to work the soil in the spring and to do many other chores throughout the season. A good roto-tiller like the Troy-Bilt makes spring tilling easy and fast. Even if I have only a few minutes at the end of the day I can get a lot done.

Years ago, I plowed and harrowed my market garden with a tractor. When I started to use a roto-tiller in the garden, it changed my whole way of gardening. I was able to work the soil earlier because the tiller is much lighter and doesn't get stuck in moist soil like heavy equipment does. I was able to plant many small areas, work in tighter quarters, grow more succession crops, till more organic matter into the soil, and do spot tilling, weeding and planting.

My Troy-Bilt is about the most important tool in my garden. Without it I couldn't garden so intensively or quickly, or build up my soil the way I do. For example, when a crop is finished in the garden, I can quickly till it under while it's still great food for the soil.

One important feature of a Troy-Bilt tiller is that its tines are in the rear of the machine. The tines chop up any imprint the wheels make, which means the soil is left loose provided that I walk

76

alongside and don't step where it has tilled. With the engine in front and the tines in the rear, the machine has a nice balance. And it's no problem to operate when tilling in crop leftovers.

The Troy-Bilt is tops by me, but I guess I'm a little biased. You see, I've been involved with the people at the Troy-Bilt factory as a gardening consultant, and even had a hand in improving several features of their machines to make them better products for home gardeners. There are other good tillers on the market, of course; it's just that after so many years of gardening, farming, and testing all kinds of equipment, I think the Troy-Bilt is the best all-around gardening machine.

What a good roto-tiller should do for you

Basically, a roto-tiller should "do it all." Without a lot of fuss and strain, a good tiller should help you with many chores, all season, not just spring plowing, such as:
• Turning over tough sod or garden soil. A machine should be able to till down to a depth of 6 inches or more.

• Mixing organic matter, lime, or fertilizer into the soil quickly.
• Preparing deep, loose, level seedbeds. A good tiller lets you walk alongside it so you don't have to walk in the newly prepared seedbed.
• Cultivating quickly with control of tine depth so you can weed at a shallow depth between rows without harming plant roots.
• Tilling under all crop residues right after the harvest—even tall cornstalks—to add important organic matter to the soil.
• Chopping and turning into the soil large amounts of organic matter such as mulches, compost, manures, and leaves.
• Preparing areas to seed green manure crops and later turning them under to improve soil fertility.
• Making straight, deep furrows for planting potatoes and many other crops.
• Hilling soil around potatoes, corn and other crops to kill weeds, anchor plants and provide better growing conditions for plants.

A good roto-tiller should be easy to maneuver in the garden and easy to maintain, too. Buying a roto-tiller is an important investment and if you take care of it, it should last a lifetime.

Here are some things I've learned about tilling

An early start can cut later weeding in half

I till the soil three or four times before planting. This cuts my weeding time during the growing season in half.

Scattered throughout the soil are thousands of tiny, almost invisible, weed seeds. Weed seeds located deep in the soil don't have the strength to push up through a lot of soil. But each time the soil is worked, hundreds of these weed seeds are brought up close to the surface of the soil where it's warm, moist, and a short step to the sun. It's here in their "germination zone" where they will sprout.

When I work the soil again 3 or 4 days later, I eliminate those weeds that have sprouted, by spilling them up into the sunshine or by burying them deep in the soil. This gets rid of a lot of weeds, but a few more are brought close to the surface in the process. If I continue to turn the soil every few days, I'll get rid of hundreds of them just as they start to sprout. By planting day a large number of potentially troublesome weeds will be gone.

When it is time to plant, I work the soil once again, often just a few minutes before getting my seeds in the ground. This last tilling eliminates any weeds sprouting in the germination zone. I don't want a single weed to get a head start on my plants. I may bring up a few new weed seeds to the germination zone, but that's okay. My vegetable seeds will sprout and grow ahead of them. Their seed coats are softer than those of weeds. They take in moisture faster and sprout more quickly.

Tilling clay soil can be a little tricky. Before you get the tiller out, take the footprint test to see if it's dry enough to work. Remember, if you walk on clay soil and it shows a shiny footprint, it's too wet. Tilling would only clump the soil together.

I managed several farms with clay soils and learned that it's best to work the soil and plant it within a day or two. If you till the soil when it's too wet, you may come back in a few days to plant and find the soil all caked up. That's not good; it's hard to plant seeds and get them to come up when the soil is full of large clods.

Clay can be very hard even when it's dry enough to work, so it may take a few passes before you can till 6 to 8 inches deep.

"I CAN'T SAY THIS TOO OFTEN: ALWAYS TILL OR TURN THE SOIL ONE LAST TIME RIGHT BEFORE PLANTING."

All garden soils are loaded with weed seeds. They will only germinate close to the surface.

Deep tilling or spading brings many seeds to their germination zone where they sprout. But tilling a few days later kills them.

Each time you work the soil before planting there will be fewer and fewer weed seeds to bother you later. Make your last tilling or spading the very day you plant.

Several passes for organic matter

The soil in my garden is rich in organic matter. It's a *joy* to till, but it didn't start out in top condition. Over the years I've mixed plenty of organic matter such as crop residues and green manure crops into it.

Adding organic matter to the soil is an important part of my gardening technique. I put it this way, "The more you add, the easier the soil is to work."

When turning over crop leftovers or a green manure crop, I till the area two or three times to chop and mix the organic matter thoroughly into the soil.

Don't curse rocks

People curse them, but rocks are not all that bad in a garden because they deposit many minerals in the soil. In fact, they are usually a sign of a fertile garden.

When I till rocky soil, many rocks will come to the surface. I don't worry about any that are tennis ball size or smaller. Bigger ones I toss aside.

Try new ground in fall

In ground that has never been gardened before it's best to prepare the soil in the fall. Tall, tough weeds should be cut or mowed down and removed before tilling. Don't go too deep on the first pass of the tiller; on the return pass overlap the tiller area by half the tiller's width. Continue across the garden taking on a small strip of sod each time. Go over the area two or three times, first one way, then crossways, going deeper each time.

Turn the soil a few times to dig in organic matter (top). Rocks often indicate very fertile soils.

79

Now a little common sense talk about soils, pH and fertilizers

Sandy soils are easy to work

If your soil reminds you of a children's sandbox, you've got sandy soil. I'm pretty familiar with sandy soil because that's basically what I work with in my garden.

You can plant in sandy soil early in the season because it dries out and warms up quickly. You can also work sandy soil very soon after a rain.

Sandy soil was a blessing when I had a market garden. I could get an early start at planting time, and it paid off with the earliest scallions, lettuce, peas, beans, cukes, and most importantly, tomatoes and corn.

Sandy soil drains well. If you pick up a handful of sand at the beach and let it run out of your hand, you can get an idea why this is so. The soil particles do not stick together very much. If you look at them through a microscope you'll see it's because they are rough-edged. They don't fit together well so they allow water to seep through quickly. I sometimes have to water the garden when we have a short dry spell.

To improve my sandy soil, I constantly add organic matter to it—mainly green manure crops, vegetable plant residues after the harvest, and leaves. Organic matter acts like a spongy glue in sandy soil. It helps to hold the soil particles together, and it also soaks up water and nutrients, keeping these near plant roots.

Clay soils are like a deck of cards

Clay soils are usually fertile, but they're heavy, often prevent good drainage, and can't be worked as early as sandy soils. The soil particles in a clay soil are flat. They remind me of a deck of cards. When it is wet, clay soil acts a lot like a deck of cards thrown on the floor. If you step on the cards, you'll slip—and it's like that with clay soils. The soil particles compress and become slick; they shut off the flow of air and water to the roots of plants.

The best way to improve clay soil is by adding organic matter such as leaves, old mulches, and green manure crops. As the organic matter breaks down, it acts like millions of little wedges, keeping soil particles from sticking together. The wedges create openings for air, water, and roots to penetrate. This allows plant roots to take in oxygen and water.

Some people try to improve clay soil by adding a few truckloads of sand to it. Well, that doesn't work. You need a mountain of sand to make a difference and that's not worth the expense.

One way to make gardening in clay soil a lot easier is to prepare some raised beds. They help overcome drainage problems and allow the soil to dry out and warm up earlier. (More on raised beds later.)

"If you've got loam, you've got it made"

Loam is almost a catchword with gardeners—if you've got loam soil you've "got it made." Loam soils are usually rich in organic matter and fertile.

They're easy to work, too. Loam soils have good drainage but still hold enough moisture for plants to thrive. They're the best soils for gardens.

No matter what kind of soil you have, adding organic matter will make it better

All soils need organic matter and all soils benefit from it. You'll hear me talk many times in this book about organic matter. It's very important in my gardening system, and should be in yours, too.

What it is

Organic matter is something that is alive or once was. For example, after harvesting my peas I till all the green living matter from above ground back into the soil. That's a lot of organic matter. The extensive roots of the pea plants are another source of organic matter.

Most people don't realize how much organic matter is in the roots of their crops. Believe me, there is plenty—scientists say the root system can often amount to half the weight of the crop parts above ground. That's why I like to grow wide rows whenever I can. A wide row has lots of plants, so there will be many roots to decompose in the soil.

Some common sources of organic matter for the garden are a green manure crop of buckwheat, a pile of leaves, some old hay, manure, pine needles, weeds, wood ashes, and straw.

Food for the earthworms and other creatures

When soils are moist and the temperature is warm, organic matter in the soil will decompose. Many kinds of soil organisms—bacteria, fungi, earthworms, mites, and others—attack organic matter. Earthworms are probably the most familiar. They are good workers in the garden but they need a steady supply of food to stay on the job. People write to me, "Dick, how do I get earthworms into the garden?" The answer is organic matter. Put it in the garden, keep things loose so the soil can breathe, and earthworms will come.

Earthworms digest organic matter, subject it to

their own particular enzymes, and deposit casts that are high in nitrogen, phosphorus, potassium, and magnesium. Wherever earthworms work on organic matter, you'll have extra nutrients available for growing plants.

As organic matter is worked on by earthworms and other soil life, nutrients contained in it are released into the soil. Nitrogen is one of the prime elements released in this process.

Keeps soil open, retains water

When it is still fresh and starting to decompose, organic matter may be chunky. Its bulkiness helps to break up clods in the soil and keep the soil open and porous so air and water can enter the soil easily.

When organic matter is broken down as far as it can go, what remains is called "humus." Both decomposing organic matter and humus can hold water very well. Many kinds of organic matter will hold 100 percent more moisture than soil particles nearby. I was amazed when a soil scientist once told me that in some sandy soils, 80 to 90 percent of the moisture and minerals in the soil may be held by the *organic matter alone.* You can see why sandy soils with little organic matter are a problem for gardeners.

Makes soil easier to work

As organic matter in clay soils breaks down and becomes more like humus, its value increases. The tiny bits of organic matter wedge between the flat clay particles and keep them apart. The result: air and water can circulate; drainage is improved; and the soil is easier to work.

In all soils, including loam soils, a steady supply of organic matter is the only way to keep earthworms and other beneficial soil creatures busy. A soil teeming with active microorganisms and earthworms is a fertile soil and a darned good place to garden.

Your soil is alive! So keep feeding it regular helpings of organic matter and it will feed you in return.

Soil tests can help

Some gardeners postpone testing their soil as long as their crops are healthy. But everyone should test the soil every 3 or 4 years, and new gardens should be tested before planting. A soil test tells you the strengths and weaknesses of your soil; it keeps your soil improvement and fertilizing efforts on track, and it can pinpoint a soil problem before it hurts you.

The first thing to look for in a soil test is pH—the acidity or alkalinity—of the soil. Soil pH is expressed in numbers on a scale. The scales goes from 0 to 14; 7 is considered neutral. A pH above 7 is alkaline or sweet; below 7 is acid or sour.

Most vegetables require a pH between 6.0 (slightly acidic) to 6.8 (almost neutral). Fertilizers work best when the soil pH is in this range.

New gardens in most parts of the nation have soils that are slightly acidic, (pH 6.8 or lower). Lime is the best material to add to raise the pH to the proper range. In several western states the soil test might indicate a pH of above 7.0. The ingredient used to lower the pH is sulfur.

Since most gardeners need to add lime, here's my formula to keep my soil pH about right. I spread a 10-quart bucket of lime on every 1,000 square feet of garden space. If you do this once every 3 to 4 years on sandy soil, and every 4 to 5 years on clay soil, your soil will stay pretty much within the 6.0 or 7.0 range.

Wood ashes are a good substitute for lime, but they should be used sparingly. Spread no more than one or two 10-quart pails of ashes over each 1,000 square feet of garden per year. Coal ashes should not be used.

To bring the pH down, mix some form of sulfur into the soil. To bring a slightly alkaline soil into a good pH range (a drop of about 1 point), takes about ½-1 pound of sulfur per 100 square feet of garden space.

Since I have a large garden, I do soil tests in several areas. But if you have a small garden you can take a single soil sample for the whole area. Here's how:

TAKING A SOIL TEST

1

Dig a 6-inch hole with a garden trowel, then cut a thin slice of the soil down the side the full depth of the hole, and place it in a clean bucket. It's important to get a full 6 inches of soil—a sample from only the top inch will not be accurate.

2

From several other locations in the garden take samples the same way until you have five or six. Combine all samples in the bucket and mix them together thoroughly. Don't touch the soil with your hands.

3

Scoop out a trowelful from the bucket. Empty it into a clean plastic bag and seal it. Now you have a sample ready to send to a soil testing lab or to use in a home gardener's test kit.

SOIL TEST REPORT

Name: _DICK RAYMOND_   **Lab. No.:** _1408_

County: _ADDISON_

Date tested: _NOV. 18_   **Location:** _SUMMER GARDEN_

Texture (Clay, Sand, or Loam): _SAND_

pH: _6.1_   **Lime Requirement:** _1089 lbs./Acre_
(25 lbs./1,000 sq. ft.)

Available phosphate: _41 (HIGH)_ **Reserve phosphate:** _519 (HIGH)_

Available potash: _430 (VERY HIGH)_ **Available magnesium:** _186 (HIGH)_

The pH of this plot is slightly low; 25 lbs. of lime per 1,000 square feet is recommended. This will bring the pH closer to 6.8, which is ideal for most vegetables.

The phosphorus and potash (or potassium) nutrients in this plot are in good supply.

The nitrogen in the soil has not been analyzed because it's hard to do accurately. I always add some nitrogen fertilizer to the soil at planting time.

Some laboratories will analyze "organic matter content"; the higher the percentage of organic matter in the soil, the more nitrogen is likely to be released during the season. Good soils will contain perhaps 4 or 5 percent organic matter; where the weather is quite warm, this percentage will be lower.

pH SCALE

```
0
1   Hydrochloric acid
    Phosphoric acid
2   Lemons
    Vinegar
3   Grapefruit
    Apples
4   Superphosphate
    Tomatoes
5   Very strongly acid      Grass silage
    Strongly acid           Boric acid
6   Medium acid             Distilled water
    Slightly acid           Fresh corn
7   Very slightly acid
    Very slightly alkaline  NEUTRAL
8   Slightly alkaline       Manure
    Medium alkaline         Sea water
9   Strongly alkaline       Bicarbonate of
    Very strongly alkaline  soda
10  Milk of magnesia
11  Ammonia
    Washing soda
12  Trisodium
    phosphate
13  Lye
14
```

OPTIMUM pH RANGE FOR VEGETABLE CROPS

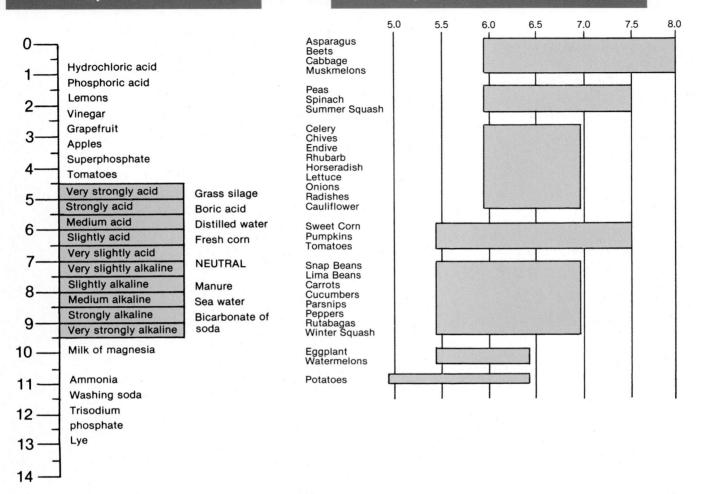

Asparagus, Beets, Cabbage, Muskmelons — Peas, Spinach, Summer Squash — Celery, Chives, Endive, Rhubarb, Horseradish, Lettuce, Onions, Radishes, Cauliflower — Sweet Corn, Pumpkins, Tomatoes — Snap Beans, Lima Beans, Carrots, Cucumbers, Parsnips, Peppers, Rutabagas, Winter Squash — Eggplant, Watermelons — Potatoes

TO RAISE SOIL ONE UNIT OF pH

	Hydrated Lime	Dolomite	Ground Limestone
Light Soil 100 sq. ft.	1½ pounds	2 pounds	2½ pounds
Heavy Soil 100 sq. ft.	3½ pounds	5½ pounds	6 pounds

Note: The amount of lime you use doesn't have to be as precisely measured as this chart suggests.

TO LOWER SOIL ONE UNIT OF pH

	Sulfur	Aluminum Sulphate	Iron Sulphate
Light Soil 100 sq. ft.	½ pound	2½ pounds	3 pounds
Heavy Soil 100 sq. ft.	2 pounds	6½ pounds	7½ pounds

Keeping the soil stocked up with plant food

Vegetables use 16 *different* foods. Luckily for us, most of these 16 nutrients are taken from the soil in very small quantities—and they're already present in most soils.

Only three of the 16 elements are taken up by plants in hefty doses—nitrogen, phosphorus, and potassium. It's important for every garden soil to have an adequate supply of these three "major nutrients," or plants simply won't do well.

NITROGEN

key to quick start and tender greens

Nitrogen (N) is essential to almost all the complex chemical activities in every plant. Greens such as spinach, lettuce, and chard especially like it because it gives the plants lots of healthy, tender, dark green leaves. Sweet corn, onions, and potatoes also need plenty of nitrogen.

Where does nitrogen come from? A steady, slow-release supply of it comes from decomposing organic matter in your garden soil. But I like some commercial nitrogen fertilizer to supplement this natural source, particularly in early spring when the soil is still cool. You see, the bacteria that help break down organic matter and release nitrogen don't become active until the soil warms up. By providing a little nitrogen boost at planting time, I help plants get off to a fast start.

Most crops use more nitrogen than any other plant food. The leaves of these plants will let you know when your soil is low in nitrogen—they will turn pale and start to yellow. It's important to add some form of nitrogen fertilizer to your garden every year. But you must be careful about putting on too much. When you add nitrogen to the soil, plants naturally spurt up quickly. When a plant grows too fast it concentrates on producing leaves, leaves, and more leaves. You may not get enough blossoms and fruit on some crops. Other crops might actually be late in giving a harvest.

Onions are one of the crops needing plenty of nitrogen.

A gardening friend in the next town once called me up at the end of summer and said he couldn't understand why his tomato plants had formed so few tomatoes. When I got to his house and saw a row of 8-foot, leafy, dark green plants, I knew why—he had used too much nitrogen fertilizer.

Heavy applications of nitrogen can burn seeds and transplants if it's put too close to them.

PHOSPHORUS
my root crops love it

A good supply of phosphorus (P) in the soil helps me grow terrific potatoes, sweet potatoes, and root crops such as carrots, beets, and turnips. Phosphorus is important for the early growth of young plants because it stimulates root growth. It's also important to any vegetable that forms underground, such as carrots and potatoes.

Although a soil test is the best way to find out if you need phosphorus, many plants will produce telltale signs of a deficiency. Lower plant leaves may turn purple or an unusually deep green; if you dig up such a plant you may find stunted roots.

Spreading commercial phosphorus fertilizer, marked 0-20-0 on a bag, will correct a deficiency. This fertilizer is often called "superphosphate" and is rock phosphate treated with an acid to help it spread through the soil.

Rock phosphate is a good natural source of phosphorus which you can find at some garden centers. Spreading 6 to 8 pounds of rock phosphate per 100 square feet of garden will also take care of this deficiency.

Sometimes I mix a little bone meal, which is high in phosphorus, into the seedbed where I'm planting root crops. This provides handy phosphorus for the roots. Bone meal won't burn seeds so I can sprinkle it right over them.

POTASSIUM
for healthy, heavy-fruiting plants

Scientists are still trying to pinpoint all the ways potassium (K) or "potash" helps vegetable crops stay vigorous, fight off disease, and yield tasty produce. One thing is sure—all gardens need it.

If your soil test shows a lack of potassium, spring is a good time to mix it in the soil. Wood ashes are a good source of potassium—but even if you have a big pile of ashes, go easy because wood ashes raise the soil pH. I mix in no more than one or two 10-quart pails for each 1,000 square feet of garden.

Potassium is also available in a natural product called "greensand," which I've seen recently in some garden centers, though at a high price. Greensand comes from the ocean floor and has small quantities of many nutrients in addition to potassium. Apply 5-6 pounds for every 100 square feet a week or so before planting.

In some stores you may spot a bag of fertilizer labeled "muriate of potash." This is also a fine source of potassium.

A small potassium deficiency is hard to detect because it shows up as a general reduction in growth. A serious deficiency is indicated when the leaves turn yellow on the tips and edges. In corn, the tips of the yellow area get broader and the leaf edges turn brown. The stalks will be weak and short with small, poorly filled ears. Tomatoes will rarely set fruit, and beets will be shaped more like carrots than the plump bulbs they ought to be.

Purple leaves may mean a phosphorus deficiency in the soil.

More vital nutrients

Besides the three major nutrients, there are three elements known as *secondary plant nutrients*—calcium, magnesium, and sulfur. Calcium and magnesium are usually supplied in lime. Sulfur is supplied in some chemical fertilizers, but it comes from the air and from decomposing organic matter as well.

Less crucial are the six elements known as *trace minerals*. They are iron, chlorine, zinc, manganese, copper, and boron. These six nutrients are every bit as vital to plant growth as any of the others, but are only needed in very small quantities.

New gardens will seldom lack any of these trace minerals, but if you garden a long time using only commercial fertilizers, you may eventually have a deficiency in one or more of the minor nutrients.

Leaves furnish a safe and easy source of trace minerals. Deep tree roots bring them up from deep in the subsoil where they are in good supply. If you feed your soil with leaves every year, there's little chance of a shortage of minor nutrients in your garden.

A helping hand from fertilizers

A balanced or "complete" fertilizer is one that contains all three of the major nutrients—nitrogen, phosphorus, and potassium (NPK). I use some in my garden each season to guarantee that these three important nutrients will be in my soil. Of course, I also fertilize the soil with compost, dehydrated manures, and green manure crops.

There's a wide range of fertilizers available. You'll find many at good garden stores. On the bags there will be numbers, perhaps 10-10-10 or 5-10-10 or 8-16-16. What do these numbers mean?

Let's say you have a 100-pound bag of 5-10-10. The first number indicates the percentage of nitrogen in the bag by weight. In this case it's 5 percent, or 5 pounds. The second number is the percentage of phosphorus—10 percent or 10 pounds. The last number is the percentage of potassium, again 10 percent or 10 pounds. Incidentally, the numbers will always be in this order—nitrogen, phosphorus, and potassium.

So there are actually only 25 pounds of fertilizer in the 100-pound bag. The remaining 75 pounds is a chemical carrier because nitrogen, phosphorus and potassium cannot be handled in pure form. Some fillers may contain a little magnesium or sulfur or other minor plant food, but these bonus nutrients won't be mentioned on the bag.

OTHER PLANT FOOD SOURCES

Nitrogen	percent
Ammonium nitrate	33.5% N
Ammonium sulfate	21% N
Urea	45% N
Phosphate	
Rock phosphate	about 30%
Superphosphate	17-20% P
Triple superphosphate	45-54% P
Potassium	
Muriate of potash	60% K
Potassium sulfate	50% K
Potassium nitrate	44% K
Wood ashes	5% K
Sulfur	
Ammonium sulfate	24% S
Superphosphorus	12% S
Epsom salts	14% S
Gypsum	17% S
Magnesium	
Dolomitic limestone	variable
Epsom salts	9.6 Mg
Calcium	
Calcitic limestone	32% CA
Gypsum	29% CA
Phosphorus rock	32-43% CA
Superphosphate	20% CA
Hydrated lime	46% CA

5-10-10—one of the handiest fertilizers

I find that a 5-10-10 fertilizer is one of the handiest balanced fertilizers. It has the right amount of nitrogen for all of my fertilizing jobs. I use it without worrying that I'm feeding my vegetables too much nitrogen. I mix it into the top few inches of soil at planting time or a day or two be-fore. If you work it into the soil too early, some of it may leach too far down into the soil to help get your crops off to a good start.

About 3 or 4 pounds of 5-10-10 per 100 square feet of garden is all you need. That's about a 10-quart pail for 1,000 square feet of garden.

I also use 5-10-10 to spoon-feed my home-grown transplants when I set them out and to fertilize them later in the season.

I've noticed that 5-10-10 fertilizer is not available in all parts of the country. The most common balanced fertilizer in some parts of the South, for example, is 6-8-8, in other regions it's 8-16-16. Go right ahead and use them at the same rates I recommend for 5-10-10.

There's a good chance you'll spot some 10-10-10 fertilizer on the store shelves. This balanced mixture has twice as much nitrogen as 5-10-10. I reserve it for crops that need and can handle a good dose of nitrogen—corn, asparagus, and onions. But there's hardly any risk in broadcasting 10-10-10 over a wide area before planting, and mixing it into the soil a few inches down.

The prices for fertilizers at the stores and garden centers are going up. *It pays to get the most helpful fertilizer, to buy only as much fertilizer as you need, and to use it at the right time.*

Manures may cause a big weeding headache

I learned a lesson years ago in my market garden about mixing manure into the garden soil in the spring. Back then, I could get all the cow manure I wanted from a farm down the road. One season before spring planting, I spread 2 or 3 inches of manure over my one-acre garden and worked it into the soil. I didn't realize how many weed seeds were in that manure—or that 99 percent of them would sprout! I had the biggest weed problem ever.

Now I never spread manures in the garden unless they are dehydrated or thoroughly composted to kill the weed seeds. Leaving a pile of manure behind the shed for it to age won't kill the weed seeds; the seeds will stay, and the nutrients will leach into the ground.

Don't get me wrong—there is a place for barnyard manure in the garden. Manure usually has good amounts of nitrogen and other plant foods. It's a wonderful source of organic matter to help improve the soil. If you mix fresh or uncomposted manure into the soil it will certainly do some good—but you'll have to expect a much bigger crop of weeds.

If you can get some manure close by at a reasonable price, have the manure delivered in the summer or early fall—and immediately start working it into your compost pile. If you get a lot of manure, build another compost pile. The pile must heat up to about 160°F. to destroy the weed seeds. (There's more information later on how to make sure that happens.)

The next spring mix the compost into the soil, use it in the cold frame, or keep it to fertilize vine crops, tomatoes, and other hungry plants through the season.

Alfalfa meal—a wonderful natural fertilizer

When I worked on dairy farms, we used alfalfa meal as a feed supplement for our cows. Alfalfa meal is the alfalfa plant dried and ground up into a fine powder. Like fresh-cut alfalfa from the hay field, it has a high protein content. Cows love it. If someone spills a little alfalfa meal on the barn floor a cow always stops and licks it right up like candy.

Plants love alfalfa meal, too. I glimpsed the potential of alfalfa meal in the garden in an unusual way. I was putting my market garden to bed late in the fall. When mulching my strawberries I ran out of clean straw for the bed before I could finish. I grabbed a few bales of alfalfa hay from the barn to finish the job.

The next spring, the berry plants seemed healthier, greener, and taller where I had put the alfalfa mulch. That made me curious about how they would produce. It didn't take long to find out. By early summer the plants produced bigger berries and *more* of them than the plants I had mulched with straw. I knew there was something in the alfalfa helping my berries grow.

The following year I decided to try alfalfa meal directly in the garden as a fertilizer. I spread a pail of alfalfa meal over a swath straight across the garden. I sprinkled it over the ground instead of ordinary fertilizer and mixed it into the soil. I

scattered it a little on the thin side to be careful. I didn't know what it would do to seeds and plants.

After the garden grew a little, there was no doubt that the alfalfa meal helped. Along the swath where I sprinkled it, the plants were unmistakably taller!

Alfalfa meal as a natural fertilizer for garden crops makes sense. After all, the roots of alfalfa plants out in the hay field go deeper than all the others. This extensive root system must be bringing back plenty of lost nutrients from deep in the soil. And there's also the important fact that alfalfa is a legume; it's one of those miracle crops that can take nitrogen from the air and fix it onto its roots.

I spent years experimenting with alfalfa meal in the garden, using it on almost every crop at one time or another. During this time, I kept an eye out for articles by other growers or scientists about alfalfa meal. I wanted to know the scientific reason why it did such a great job in my garden. But I couldn't find any.

Finally, in the mid 1970s, scientists at Michigan State University isolated a primary growth stimulant in alfalfa called triacontanol. The discovery launched experiments all over the world. Researchers are now creating this key stimulant in the laboratory. Someday it may be reproduced easily and made available to growers and gardeners everywhere at low cost.

Where to find alfalfa meal

Alfalfa meal is still inexpensive if you can find it at a farm feed store. Where I live, it's available only in 50-pound bags, which cost around $12 each. One 50-pound bag is enough to use on two or three average-size gardens.

If you can't find it at a feed or garden store, look for alfalfa meal in the *supermarket!* Check the aisle with pet food and pet supplies. If you find the kitty litter product called "Litter Green" you've got a source for alfalfa meal. Litter Green is 100 percent *alfalfa pellets.* It is an excellent substitute for alfalfa meal, and you can use it in the garden or on your compost pile just like the powdery alfalfa meal. Since it's concentrated in pellets, you don't have to use as much as the powdery form. It's a little more expensive this way, but still worth a try. (Be sure to use Litter Green straight out of the bag, and not after it's been in a kitty box.)

Three good ways to use alfalfa meal

1. Sprinkle it over the garden soil before planting. Rate: one 10-quart bucket of alfalfa meal for each 1,000 square feet of garden. Mix it into the top 2 or 3 inches of soil.

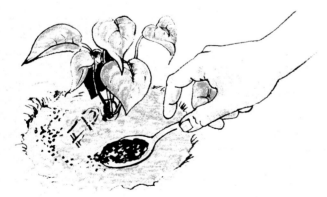

2. Spoon-feed it to crops as they start producing to give them an extra boost of plant food. When cucumbers, tomatoes, peppers, pole beans, squash, and melons blossom, give each plant one tablespoon of alfalfa meal. Sprinkle it around the plants and mix it gently into the soil so the wind doesn't blow it away.

3. Sprinkle a fine layer on your compost pile

every time you add organic matter. Alfalfa meal is high in protein, and it helps activate a compost pile.

Shopping tips for natural fertilizers

There are many excellent natural fertilizers—all kinds of dehydrated manures, mineral products, and helpful soil additives. Most natural fertilizers work over an extended period and include trace elements not found in standard commercial fertilizers.

But, just because someone recommends dried blood meal or dehydrated sheep manure for the garden, it doesn't mean you should automatically spend an arm and a leg to get some. A high price for a natural fertilizer usually means a lot of people are handling the package before it gets to you or that it's been shipped quite a distance.

I prefer to use natural fertilizers and organic matter that I can find in my neighborhood or town. It's a good way to recycle local resources, and keep the cost of gardening down. Seaweed is a great plant food but since I live 300 miles from the ocean, it's hardly a practical fertilizer for my garden.

Instead, I use leaves or dehydrated manure or alfalfa meal—all available free or at low cost in my county.

Check around your community. You might be overlooking wonderful low-cost sources of organic matter and plant foods.

KNOW YOUR PLANT FOOD ELEMENTS

PRIMARY PLANT FOOD ELEMENTS

Element	Symbol	Function in Plant	Deficiency Symptoms	Excess Symptoms	Sources
Nitrogen	N	Gives dark green color to plant. Increases growth of leaf and stem. Influences crispness and quality of leaf crops. Stimulates rapid early growth.	Light green to yellow leaves. Stunted growth.	Dark green. Excessive growth. Retarded maturity. Loss of buds or fruit.	Urea Ammonia Nitrates
Phosphorus	P	Stimulates early formation and growth of roots. Gives plants a rapid and vigorous start. Is important in formation of seed. Gives hardiness to fall-seeded grasses and grains.	Red or purple leaves. Cell division retardation.	Possible tie up of other essential elements.	Superphosphate Rock Phosphate
Potash	K	Increases vigor of plants and resistance to disease. Stimulates production of strong, stiff stalks. Promotes production of sugar, starches, oils. Increases plumpness of grains and seed. Improves quality of crop yield.	Reduced vigor. Susceptibility to diseases. Thin skin and small fruit.	Coarse, poor colored fruit. Reduced absorption of Mg and Ca.	Muriate or Sulphate of Potash

SECONDARY PLANT FOOD ELEMENTS

Element	Symbol	Function in Plant	Deficiency Symptoms	Excess Symptoms	Sources
Calcium	Ca	Part of cell walls. Part of enzymes.	Stops growing point of plants.	Reduces the intake of K and Mg.	Lime Basic Slag Gypsum
Magnesium	Mg	Aids photosynthesis. Key element in chlorophyl.	Loss of yield. Chlorosis of old leaves.	Reduced absorption of Ca and K.	Magnesium Sulphate (Epsom Salts) Dolomite is ⅓ Mg.
Sulfur	S	Helps to build proteins.	Looks like nitrogen deficiency.	Sulfur burn from too low pH.	Sulfur Superphosphate

MINOR (OR) MICRO ELEMENTS

Element	Symbol	Function in Plant	Deficiency Symptoms	Excess Symptoms	Sources
Boron	B	Affects absorption of other elements. Affects germination of pollen tube.	Small leaves. Heart rot and corkiness. Multiple buds.	Leaves turn yellowish red.	Borax
Copper	Cu	Enzyme activator.	Multiple budding. Gum pockets.	Prevents the uptake of iron. Causes stunting of roots.	Copper Sulphate Neutral Copper
Iron	Fe	A catalyst. In the enzyme system. Hemoglobin in legumes.	Yellowing of leaves, the veins remaining green.	None known.	Iron Sulphate (Copperas) Chelated Iron
Manganese	Mn	In enzyme system.	Mottled chlorosis of the leaves. Stunted growth.	Small dead areas in the leaves with yellow borders around them.	Manganese Sulphate (Tecmangam)
Molybdenum	Mo	Helps in the utilization of N.	Symptoms in plants vary greatly.	Poisonous to livestock.	Sodium Molybdate
Zinc	Zn	Aids in cell division. In enzymes and auxins.	Small, thin, yellow leaves. Low yields.	None known.	Zinc Sulphate

ELEMENTS FROM AIR AND WATER

Element	Symbol	Function in Plant	Deficiency Symptoms	Excess Symptoms	Sources
Carbon	C	Keystone of all organic substances.	None known.	None known.	Air (Carbon Dioxide)
Oxygen	O	Respiration.	White areas at leaf veins. High nitrates.	None known.	Air and Water
Hydrogen	H	Necessary in all plant functions.	Wilting.	Drowning.	Water

RAISED BEDS

My simple, problem-solving raised bed technique

Most people don't realize how many benefits come from two or three raised beds in the garden. A raised bed can help *every* gardener, and for some it will mean a whole new way to grow food.

I used to think that making raised planting rows or beds was something strictly for gardeners who had heavy soil which stayed wet too long.

But in the last few years I have grown terrific crops on raised beds in different soil conditions and in different climates. I believe that all gardeners, no matter what their soil or climate, could profit from at least one or two raised beds.

Raising a few beds is not hard work. And with my wide row method, you can grow enough food to make it worthwhile. What may be hard is seeing how this technique can help you.

When to make raised beds?

There's no one set time of the year to make them. It depends on your soil, length of season, weather, and gardening schedule.

Here are three possible times:

Fall—Fall is the most popular time for creating one or two beds because they enable you to plant on time in the spring, even when there's too much rain. Heavy soil such as clay can take many weeks to dry out in the spring. But soil raised up in beds the previous fall can be easily worked and planted early come springtime.

Spring—If your soil can be worked in early spring, raising beds lets you plant earlier and provides insurance against flash rains, lengthy unexpected wet spells, and other bad weather.

It also allows crops to be irrigated during the summer. Late-planted storage crops of carrots, parsnips, beets, and onions will love the loose, elevated soil of a raised bed.

Late summer—Planting on raised beds in late summer helps fall crops get through any long rainy spells. If you live where winters are mild but often wet, you can keep crops such as kale, collards, spinach, lettuce, and cabbage growing on these beds long after the first frost.

Raised beds solve a host of problems

Plant on schedule even after a spell of wet weather

I remember introducing raised beds at a demonstration garden near Atlanta, Georgia, where a rainy spring can set planting back for weeks. We made several long raised beds in the fall and they kept their shape well through the winter.

When it was time to start planting the next February, some extended heavy rains hit the area and kept most gardens too soggy to plant.

But in our demonstration garden, the top of the raised beds did not collect any water—the rains simply ran off into the walkways. A day or two after the last rain the beds were dry enough to plant, even though the walkways were still soaked with water and the rest of the garden could not be worked at all. We put on rubber boots, went out, raked the beds smooth, and planted our early crops of English peas, spinach, cabbage, collards, onions, chard, and radishes.

Turn wet, low-lying areas into productive gardens

When you make raised beds, drainage improves immediately. In a low-lying wet area, raise some beds 4 or 6 inches above ground level. Rainwater won't sit on the soil and pack it down. Instead, the water will drain off the beds into the walkways where slow drainage won't hurt as much. On top of the seedbed you'll have loose soil that dries out faster, and easily allows air to enter.

Seeds won't wash out in a hard rain

Ever get a lot of rain in a hurry? If you've just planted some seeds you know what can happen—part of a row washes out.

A few summers ago we had a very hard, fast rain—1.2 inches fell in 20 minutes. I had just planted some lettuce, carrots, and radishes on raised beds the day before. After the rain let up, I checked the area. The walkways between the raised beds were choked with water, but there were no puddles on the seedbeds and nothing had washed out. A few days later the seedlings came up—everything was in place!

Gardening in clay soil is easier

Many problems connected with clay soil gardening disappear when using raised beds. The soil dries out earlier in the spring. Seedbeds don't bake down because water doesn't settle on top of the beds; it drains off. Carrots and other root crops have an easier time growing in clay soil when it's raised up and kept loose.

Raised beds help these onions and peas (far left) to prosper in wet conditions. A hard rain won't wash out this newly-planted seedbed (center). Root crops, such as **White Icicle** *radishes, can grow deeper on raised beds.*

Helps northern gardeners grow better warm-weather crops

I've found that the soil on top of a raised bed can be as much as 10 degrees warmer than soil at ground level. That's because a raised-bed planting area is more exposed to sunlight. And the soil is usually drier on a raised bed; drier soils are warmer than moist soils. This makes a raised bed a wonderful place to put your tomatoes, melons, cucumbers, and lima beans.

Easy to irrigate

Some gardeners in the South and West get practically a whole season's rainfall during a few spring days. Then it will be dry for weeks. Raised beds help protect the seedlings if the rains are heavy, and they also allow you to mulch and irrigate with ease later if you don't get the rain you need.

When plants are small their roots have not reached too far into the bed. Using a sprinkler or a soaker hose directly on the bed are the two best ways to irrigate. Later, when the plants are bigger and their roots have grown deep into the bed, you can water right into the walkways between beds; the moisture will seep sideways into the root zone of the plants.

Longer, straighter root crops

There's more topsoil to work with on a raised bed because in making beds you scoop out soil from the walkways and place it directly on the planting row. If you happen to have a shallow layer of topsoil, this extra 3 or 4 inches of soil is a godsend. You'll be able to grow longer and straighter carrots, and your beets, turnips, white radishes, and parsnips will expand more easily.

I've noticed that when root crops grow on beds, people don't step near them and compact the soil. The worst thing for a carrot or beet is a footprint next to it, because in packed soil the carrot or beet must struggle to expand.

Small benefits add up

• Raised beds are easier to weed and harvest because they are 6 to 10 inches above the walkway. There's a lot less bending and stooping—which makes gardening more enjoyable.

• They help control traffic through the garden. Kids stay in the deep walkways and don't walk accidentally over a seeded row or into a group of small plants. Pets stroll straight down the walkways in raised-bed gardens—it's almost as if they had gone to an expensive obedience school!

• A well-tended raised-bed garden is darned pretty to look at, too.

Once your soil is nice and loose you can quickly make raised beds with hand tools. I also use my roto-tiller and special attachments to form and maintain the beds. That's shown on the following two pages.

1 Work the soil by hand or with a tiller down at least 6 or 8 inches until it is quite loose.

My easy way to build a raised bed

4 Stay in the walkway and continue bringing up soil the length of the row. Then repeat the process from the other side to complete the bed.

5 Add some compost or fertilizer and mix it into the top few inches of the bed if you haven't already fertilized the area.

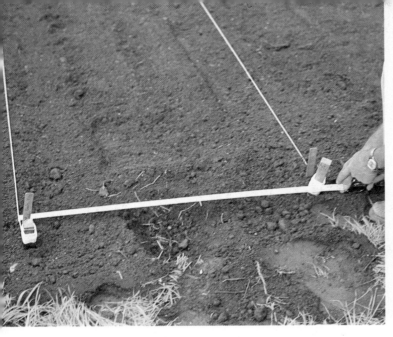

2 Use stakes and string to mark the dimensions of each bed. I like beds with a planting surface 15 or 16 inches wide—about the width of a rake. I keep my walkways 18 to 20 inches wide.

3 Stand at the head of a walkway and pull up soil from the next walkway and build up your bed. I like to use a rake—it moves a lot of soil quickly. Try to rake up 4 to 6 inches of soil.

6 Smooth out the top of the bed with your rake until it is level. It's easy if you flop the rake over and keep the tines up.

7 Once the seedbed is smoothed out, you're ready to plant. To make the most of my raised beds, I grow many crops in wide rows.

Here's how I make raised beds in minutes with my tiller

1. Till twice and till deep

A deep tilling helps you make well-shaped, long-lasting raised beds. Till the area at least twice, going 6 to 8 inches deep into the soil.

The last pass with your tiller should be at right angles to the direction of the beds. In other words, if your beds will run east-west, you should work the soil on the last pass going north-south. This will make it much easier to create straight walkways and beds.

Broadcast fertilizer over the area after you are finished tilling the soil. Then when you form the beds, the fertilizer is automatically mixed into the soil and covered.

2. Stake out the walkways

Decide how wide your raised planting beds will be on the top. I recommend 16 inches, which is perfect for wide rows of lettuce, peas, carrots, and onions and for larger crops such as peppers, caged tomatoes, and broccoli.

To make beds 16 inches wide on the top with my tiller, I set stakes 46 inches apart at both ends of the garden. When I take the tiller from stake to stake, I'm actually moving down the middle of what will be the walkway.

3. Use a hilling attachment

I slip my furrowing and hilling attachment onto the tiller and set the hilling wings to the highest position so they'll push a lot of soil upward.

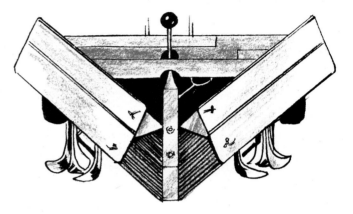

4. Hill up the beds

I line up the center of the tiller with the first stake at the end of the garden. I point the machine directly towards the stake at the other end of the garden. Keeping my eye on this stake, I guide the machine straight at it. This helps make straight beds.

When I get to the end, I turn the tiller around and line it up with the next stake. I head back across the garden with my eye on the far stake. This pass raises the rest of the soil to complete the first bed and forms one side of the second bed.

5. Rake tops

After the soil has been hilled up, I smooth the tops of the beds with a rake. This is important for planting seeds properly or for setting in transplants.

If I did not broadcast fertilizer over the area earlier, I add some and rake it in.

Now, I'm ready to plant.

Watering, weeding, and replanting a raised bed

Watering: Some people look at a raised bed garden and say, "Gee, with those high beds you must have to water a lot."

Most raised beds need very little watering. The loose soil of a raised bed makes it easy for roots to grow deeply in a hurry. If you have to water, it's easy.

For instance, if you are planting on raised beds when the weather is warm and dry, you may have to water to keep the seedbeds moist until the plants come up. If you have only one or two beds to water, use a hose with a water breaker nozzle. It's fast and won't wash out any seeds.

If you are watering a large raised bed area, a sprinkler works fine. I set mine on a sawhorse to get a little additional reach. If you're trying to use as little water as possible, you can bypass the sprinkler and water each bed with a canvas soaker hose. Lay it on top of the bed, and the water will ooze out slowly right where you want it. It should soak slowly into the soil and not spill into the walkways.

If your beds are close together, say 12 to 18 inches apart, fill the walkways with water. This is a quick way to water, and is more efficient than using a sprinkler. The water seeps down, of course, but much of the water seeps across to nourish the plant roots in the bed. There is more of this sideways movement of water in clay soil than in sandy soil.

Mulching: Mulch is important in raised bed gardens in the South. It's not needed early in the season when the ground is very wet and rains are frequent. But in the summer when the weather gets hot and the rains disappear, the beds can get hot and parched. So, pack the sides of the beds and the pathway with a thick layer of mulch to hold in moisture.

Weeding: I use my tiller with hilling attachment to weed and loosen soil between raised beds. It takes me only a few minutes. The tines loosen the soil in the bottom of the walkway to keep the channels open for air and water. The hilling blades push loose soil against the sides of the beds and scrape away any small weeds.

To weed with a hoe, loosen up the walkway by working your hoe through the soil only an inch or so deep. Then if the beds need a little extra soil on the sides, lift some of the loose soil up onto the sides.

Knocking down a bed and replanting: After my early crops are harvested, I till right on top of the bed to plow under crop residues. With small crops the bed usually stays intact through this job, so I only have to rake the top of the bed before planting another crop.

With taller crops, such as corn or broccoli, I wind up knocking the bed down in the process of working the crop residues into the soil. It's easy to reshape the bed because the soil is left in such a loose condition by the tiller. I set up a string as a guideline, and rake up the loose soil to form another straight, wide bed. Then I mix in a little fertilizer and plant another crop.

My terrace garden solves the problem of sloping ground

An easy way to turn hilly sections of your yard into productive growing areas is to create a series of level steps, or terraces, built into your hillside.

I've developed two such terraces on a steep bank at my place for vegetables, flowers, and herbs. They are about 30 feet long, but terraces as short as 5 or 6 feet will provide a great harvest.

The important thing is to prepare a *wide* terrace so you can use wide row growing methods to make the most of your space.

Good terraces also help control water and soil runoff and will enhance the beauty of your property. Notice the strip of grass sod between my two terraces; this keeps soil of the top terrace from washing out.

I did the work on my terraces with a roto-tiller, starting with the inside edge of the top terrace. It's easy to do this work with hand tools; in fact, if you have a slope that pitches 10 degrees or more, it's probably safer to do so. You have to be careful with power equipment on hills.

Terraces which are 3 feet wide or less usually allow you enough room to plant some wide rows and to work the area easily with hand tools.

No garden space?
Plant a strip-garden
in the lawn!

If you need good growing space, how about taking a look at your lawn? It's probably a perfect spot for a productive strip of food crops. Why? Well, a good lawn has just what most vegetables need: a lot of sun, soil that has good drainage but enough organic matter in it to retain water during dry spells, and a soil pH in a range that fits most vegetables.

I've been growing a small lawn garden in front of my house just to show people how easy it is and how nice it looks. I plant short sections of rake-width wide rows so that there's not a bare spot in the whole strip. It looks beautiful, especially when I plant combinations of vegetables in a multi-row.

One good benefit about planting in thick wide rows is that you don't need much lawn to get a big harvest. Also quick-growing vegetables can shade out the weeds that might try to come up during the first season.

The best time to start a lawn garden strip is in the fall because you can work the soil and expose many grass roots and weeds to the elements all winter to kill them off. I started my lawn strip in the spring, however, and things turned out fine. To keep down the number of grass roots that would come back as weeds, I tilled the strip several times before planting. If you're working by hand, do the same thing—chop up the roots on several occasions and expose them to the sun and wind before planting. If you till several strips, be sure to leave room to get between them with your lawn mower.

You can make your lawn strip look terrific after the season. Work the plants into the soil or pull them up and put them in your compost pile. Then smooth out the lawn strip with your rake and broadcast annual ryegrass seed over it, just as you would regular grass seed. Annual ryegrass is just that—annual. It will stay green through the fall and into the early winter (some folks might not even *notice* that you had a food strip in your lawn) and then it will die down. Through the winter it will protect the soil from washing out. Annual ryegrass won't come back in the spring. You can chop and dig it into the lawn garden and plant your garden as early as you want in the spring.

After discussing it with my wife, Jan, I roto-tilled a strip of lawn in front of our house in the spring . . .

. . . and kept a wide bed of vegetables growing all season. Though I have a big garden out back, I wanted visitors and friends to see how productive a little lawn space could be.

Starting Plants Indoors

I start many crops indoors while there is still plenty of snow on the ground. That's the way to get the earliest harvests possible—especially the first tomatoes in the neighborhood.

If you've never grown vegetable plants indoors, try a few. You'll get earlier harvests of many crops and give your long-season crops more time to produce. In northern parts of the country, if you want tomatoes, peppers, eggplant or big onions, you need indoor-started plants, and you'll be amazed at all the vegetables and varieties to choose from. The greenhouse in our town usually has four or five kinds of tomato plants on sale in the spring, perhaps *Jet Star, Better Boy, Moreton,* and a couple of others. But in one or two seed catalogs I can find 30 or more tomato varieties—all the way from the tiny *Patio* to the giant *Beefsteak.*

Years ago I planted ordinary yellow and white onion sets every season. But when I started to plant onion seeds indoors, I found dozens of varieties to pick from—new extra-long keepers, hamburger slicers, and the big *Sweet Spanish* and *Bermuda* onions.

You'll find quite a selection in most mail order seed catalogs. Even if you don't start your plants indoors, it's a good idea to check out the catalogs—they have plenty of solid gardening information.

Buying plants from a nursery is convenient, of course, and I always get some as insurance to go along with those I grow myself. I sometimes wonder about them. How have they been cared for? Have they been properly fed? Are they free from insects and diseases?

I have peace of mind when I grow my own plants. I can pick out the varieties I want, use the soil mix I think best, and fertilize them the way I want to. The nicest thing is I'm free to experiment.

I count backwards for starting dates

I keep the average date of our last spring frost in mind when I make up a schedule for starting different crops. If you don't know the average last frost date in your area, see the map on page 355. It's an important date.

Here's a quick look at when I start my most important vegetables. This schedule is good for most gardeners—you might delay a week or two if you have heavy clay soil.

WHEN TO SOW SEEDS

Crop	Weeks before last frost date
Onions, leeks	10-12
Early tomatoes	10-12
Celery	8-10
Mid-season and late tomatoes	6-8
Early peppers	6-8
Eggplant	6-8
All other peppers	4-6
Cabbage	4-6
Cauliflower	4-6
Broccoli	4-6
Head lettuce	3-4
Melons and cucumbers	3-4

Note: Onions, leeks and tomatoes need plenty of time to develop a strong root system. That's why I start them so early. Cabbages, head lettuce, cauliflower, and broccoli develop quickly, and I can set them outside a week or two before the last spring frost. That's the reason for their later start. My melons get only a short head start inside because I like to transplant them small. There's less risk in disturbing their sensitive root system.

Why I like to start these crops indoors

Tomatoes, peppers, and eggplant—Seed for seed, tomatoes yield more food than any other vegetable in the garden. With a little luck, one tiny seed can yield a bushel of tomatoes.

I like a lot of tomatoes, and I like them early. That's why I push the season. I start *Pixie* and other early varieties almost in the dead of winter.

To get a good harvest where I live, peppers and eggplants must be started inside and set out when they're 6 or 8 weeks old. And unless I start them myself I won't be able to grow many of the unusual hot peppers which Jan likes in her relishes. Some of our favorite varieties are not available at local greenhouses.

Onion family—Leeks and sweet onions, such as the sweet Spanish and Bermudas, need a very long growing season to reach maturity, so I have to start them 10 to 12 weeks before setting them out.

Cabbage family—Cabbage, broccoli, and cauliflower germinate easily in just a few days at 70°—75°F. and grow quickly.

You can start these cool-weather crops directly in the garden in early spring, too, but sometimes early hot weather slows them just as they're getting ready. So I get the best chance for a big, tasty harvest if I start my crops indoors and set plants in the garden early.

106

Head lettuce—Lettuce germinates and grows so quickly that I start some every couple of weeks in late winter and early spring. I start more *Iceberg* or firm-headed lettuce than other kinds because it needs more growing time in cool weather to make a firm head.

Lettuce seeds are tiny and paper thin, so I sometimes seed them too thickly. To thin, I pinch some off at soil level, or transplant them to other flats. Lettuce seeds are sometimes available in pellet form. Spacing them is definitely easier, but the seeds are more expensive.

Melons and cucumbers—I start a few melons and cukes indoors to see if my house-started plants can produce cukes and melons ahead of those plants I start directly from seed in the garden. If you have a short summer, try growing a few inside—it's easy. There's just one important rule to remember: once they start growing you must not jar their roots.

Squash also can be started indoors, but I prefer to seed mine directly into the garden.

Crops started outdoors

I usually sow the following seeds directly in the garden:

Beans	Okra	Potatoes (seed
Beets	Onions (sets	pieces)
Carrots	and seed for	Radish
Chard	scallions)	Rutabagas
Corn	Parsnips	Spinach
Kale	Peanuts	Turnips
Leaf lettuce	Peas	

I rarely start seedlings in real soil

I start almost all my seedlings in a sterile, soil-less mix. Each spring I pick up several bags of seed-starting mix at the garden store. I prefer Pro Mix but other mixes are good, providing they are "soil-less."

A soil-less mix is easy to use and safe for plants. There's practically no chance of damping-off or seed rot diseases spoiling your efforts. These disease organisms are not present in sterile mixes, but are a problem with garden soil. Another good thing about mixes is that they are at the right pH for good growth. Some mixes also come with a little fertilizer mixed in.

Regular potting soil isn't as good for starting vegetable seedlings. It's heavy, packs down too much in my seed trays, and doesn't stick well to the roots of my seedlings when I transplant them. If potting soil is all you have, add 50 percent peat moss to it, a quart of peat moss for every 2 quarts of potting soil to improve it. It's best to save potting soil for houseplants.

You can also make up a soil-less mix. Homemade soil-less mixes are usually a little less expensive than commercial blends. Here's a simple formula: mix 4 quarts of vermiculite, 4 quarts of peat moss, and a couple of tablespoons of lime. Don't add fertilizer at this time. Once the plants are up, you can give them a little plant food in their water.

Be sure to moisten any mix before putting it in your pots.

Backyard sod pots

My dad showed me how to make natural pots that don't cost a penny. I get them right out of the backyard in late fall or early spring, or even during our January thaw.

Using an old butcher knife, I cut several strips of sod about 2 inches thick and about a foot square. I bring the sod strips inside, turn them bottom-side-up, grassy-side-down, and cut them into pieces about 2 inches square. In each square I plant a seed or two, using treated seeds because the soil may contain disease organisms.

After the seed has germinated and the plant has grown 3 or 4 inches, I put the plant, sod and all, directly into the garden without ever disturbing its tender roots. The soil in the sod is usually quite rich, and as the grass decomposes, more nutrients for the plants are released. I use sod pots to start vine crops, such as cucumbers and melons.

INDOOR SUNSHINE

Indoor seedlings need lots of light. I like to grow them under fluorescent lights because we have short days and lots of cloudy weather. Many plants get leggy growing near the window by natural light alone.

If you have room, lay a half-sheet of ½-inch plywood (4 by 4 feet) across a couple of sawhorses. You'll need six 4-foot fluorescent lights (three units) above this grow table if you fill the area with plants.

I've found that cool-white fluorescent bulbs work fine for vegetable seedlings. The more expensive grow lights are best for flowering houseplants, not vegetables.

FOR SEEDLINGS

It's also easy to build a set of free-standing "bookshelves" for your indoor vegetable plants. Four shelves, 2 feet deep, 4 feet long, and 18 inches apart, can hold 16 large seed flats. The shelves, each with a two-bulb light unit, occupy only 8 square feet of floor space.

Ready-made light stands are perfect for starting seeds or raising houseplants. I'll give you a shopper's tip: look for a unit on which you can raise or lower the lights easily. *I keep fluorescent lights just 1 or 2 inches away from small plants. As the plants grow, I raise the lights to stay ahead of them.* If the light units don't move easily, put the flats on blocks. As the plants grow, remove the blocks.

How long should a plant sleep ?

I give indoor vegetable plants 12 to 16 hours of direct light every day. Plants have to "sleep" at least 8 hours. I have a timer on my fluorescent lights which turns them on and off at the right time if I'm not there to do it.

Since there's less light generated at the ends of fluorescent bulbs, I move the end flats to the middle and the middle ones to the end every week to make sure all the plants get an equal share. As the plants get older, I increase the distance between light and seedlings to 5 or 6 inches.

Handy extra supplies

If you're going to set flats or pots on a windowsill or on wood furniture, you'll need waterproof saucers or trays to protect the finish. Plastic trays from the supermarket or disposable aluminum pie plates work well.

I use a houseplant mister or an old Windex or hairspray bottle to water my seedlings when they're small. A watering can with a thin spout is also good for small plants. When I water the cold frame outside, I use a mist nozzle on the garden hose.

Clear plastic bags from the dry cleaner or grocery store are good to wrap around seed trays until the plants sprout.

I use plant stakes and a weatherproof marking pen such as the "Sharpie" pen to keep my flats and varieties in order. What I write with the Sharpie pen lasts through all kinds of water and weather.

Soil, you may have to bake it

One way to save money is to use soil from the garden. What you save in money, however, you may spend in time and energy, since garden soil should be sterilized to kill the damping-off organisms and bacteria that might hurt seedlings.

The traditional way to sterilize soil is to bake it, but I stopped doing that a long time ago. My wife, Jan, told me, "If you're going to bake something, try some food!" Besides, we found that the baking soil gave off an unpleasant order. Still, if you live alone and want to try it, here's how: preheat the oven to 350°F. Place moist soil in a 2-inch deep baking pan, and set it in the oven for 30 to 90 minutes. The soil temperature should reach 180°F. The deeper the soil layer, the more time it takes to achieve this temperature.

A money-saving tip

You can save some money by using unsterilized garden soil on the bottom of your container, with a thinner layer of sterile starting mix on top. Plant your seeds in the top layer and cover with more mix. By the time the roots reach the soil below, the seedlings will usually be out of danger.

The soil in my garden is rich, sandy loam, so I can use it as is for the bottom of my flats. However, if you have heavy soil, you should add vermiculite, peat moss, or compost to lighten it before planting your seeds.

One thing I've learned over the years is that adding fertilizer to my starting soil *before planting* seeds can be harmful to tender sprouts.

I remember visiting a fellow's small greenhouse where nearly 60 tomato seedlings died practically overnight. He was baffled because he thought he had followed the same steps as in previous years. But together we discovered he had done something different. Hoping to save some time later, he had tossed some potent dried chicken manure in with his starting mix. Those few handfuls of fertilizer were too much for his tomatoes.

PICK A POT

Be wary of seed-starting pots that absorb too much of the seedlings' water supply — like cardboard egg cartons. They could come apart.

Containers needed for broadcasting seeds

trays and flats	milk cartons
wooden flats	plastic flats
fruit cartons	dish pans

These are good for broadcasting seeds and growing many plants in a group. I use them to start onions and leeks. They're also good for plants such as tomatoes and cabbages which will be lifted out and repotted after they grow a few inches.

For individual seeds or seedlings

milk cartons	plastic trays
peat pots	"sod pots"
(round or square)	clay or plastic pots
tin cans	Styrofoam cups
pyramid planter trays	

Melons, squash, and cukes must be started and grown in individual pots until transplanted into the garden. Individual pots are also good for tomatoes, eggplants, and other crops—especially if you want large, healthy plants that are easy to transplant.

100% success with my favorite planter tray

I want to tell you about some exciting seed trays that take all the worry out of growing and transplanting. Plants from these trays won't wilt or need a lot of water when put in the garden—even in 90°F. weather on a sunny day!

They're called *pyramid planters*. I use them for lettuce, cabbage, tomatoes, melons—just about all my started plants. The pyramid planters are made of Styrofoam or plastic. They don't weigh much and last for years. These trays have many individual compartments which are shaped like upside-down pyramids.

At the bottom of each individual compartment is a very important small hole. When the roots of each seedling poke through this hole they are "air pruned." The tray must be raised off the table an inch or so to create an airflow before this can happen. The pruning encourages side or "feeder" roots to grow. Before long there's a tight network of sturdy roots all through the compartment.

At transplanting time this network has bound soil and roots together. You can actually lift a plant out without dropping a speck of soil or budging any of the roots. The plants don't feel much stress; consequently, I don't have to water them very much or worry about them when I put them in the garden. I don't think I've lost a single plant since I started using these pyramid trays.

The trays come with various-sized compartments up to 4 inches square. I seed head lettuce in the 1-inch square compartments; my melons and vine crops go in the 2-inch units. The 3-inch and 4-inch compartments are reserved for tomatoes, peppers, and eggplants which I transplant from a smaller flat.

1-inch square pyramid compartment	2-inch square	3-inch square	4-inch square
lettuce	melons	cabbage	tomato*
	cukes	broccoli	pepper*
	squash	tomato*	eggplant*
	cabbage	pepper*	
		eggplant*	

I put in tiny seedlings rather than seeds

The only drawback I've found is that these trays dry out faster than most flats because of the airflow above and below them. They must be watered nearly every day.

Starting Plants in Trays

**Follow these easy steps
if you want quick germination of seeds and smooth,
healthy growth of your vegetable transplants.**

2.

After each flat is filled to the top with moist starting mix, use a wood shingle or a small thin board to smooth out the soil surface.

1.

Moisten the starting mix *before* putting it into flats or pots. If you water a dry mix from the top after planting, you'll have a mess on your hands. The seeds and mix will spill out.

3.

Broadcast seeds in the flat, spreading them evenly over the soil surface. Once in a while I'll put vegetable seeds in rows, using the edge of the shingle to make shallow furrows.

4.

After sowing the seeds, firm them down with the flat side of the shingle or board.

6.

Smooth out the covering of soil and firm the soil down again. Seed must be in good contact with moist soil to germinate well.

5.

Cover the seeds with more moist starting mix. All seeds, no matter where they're planted, should be covered with firm, moist soil to a depth three to four times their own diameter. For melons and cucumbers that's no problem, but it can be trickier with lettuce, cabbage, tomatoes, peppers, and herb seeds which are no bigger than a grain of fine salt. For those fine seeds, ¼ inch of moist soil is sufficient.

7.

Before setting flats aside to germinate, make sure the soil is moist but not soggy. To keep it moist, cover every flat or pot with plastic wrap and seal it. This way you don't have to do any more watering until the seedlings come up.

Let's take the mystery out of cold frames and hotbeds

Cold frames and hotbeds have earned the nickname "Poor Man's Greenhouses." Both are simple, inexpensive structures to house hardy transplants once they've started to grow—or even radishes, onions, lettuce, and spinach sown directly in soil.

A cold frame is heated by the sun, and a hotbed is heated by the sun and by sources underneath it—perhaps fresh horse manure, which gives off heat as it decomposes, or electric cables which heat the soil.

The easiest cold frame I ever built required only six bales of hay and an old storm window. I set the bales in a rectangle over some tilled soil, set the storm window on top, and I was in business.

Keep cool—prop the top

During the day, a cold frame or hotbed can become an oven. It may be sunny and 50°F. outside, but it can easily get 100°F. or more in the cold frame. That's too hot for plants. Keep a thermometer inside the box. If the temperature rises above 80°F., prop up the top, or remove it, to allow the cooler outside air to enter.

Some preconstructed cold frames have automatic vents which open and close at specific temperatures. These can be a lifesaver when you're away from home all day.

A cold frame traps heat inside during the day, but as soon as the sun goes down the heat escapes rapidly. That's why you should keep it covered on cold nights to protect tender seedlings. Use an old blanket, a piece of canvas, or straw.

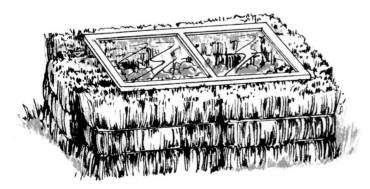

You can also make a simple cold frame or a hotbed by nailing the ends of four fairly wide boards together to fit glass, an old window sash, or clear plastic. If you have a slope that slants a few degrees to the south, put the frame there to catch more of the sun's rays.

TIPS FOR GENTLE TRANSPLANTING

Indoors you've been babying your plants for weeks, giving them lots of time and attention. They're precious. If you get them into the soil without much "transplant shock," they'll grow quickly and give you an early harvest.

Mistakes, such as rushing the plants into the ground before they are properly hardened off, or roughing up their roots while handling them, or leaving them on the ground almost bare-rooted while you look for a tool, can set the crop back. Plants should get four-star transplanting service—a quick and gentle ride from pot to garden.

The best time to transplant well-hardened plants is on a cool, cloudy, windless afternoon or evening. Be over protective; don't let hot sun or fierce winds intensify the shock of transplanting.

1.

I always give my flats or pots a good soaking before taking out any plants. The wetter the soil, the fewer roots will be exposed to the air when I lift them from their containers. I stop short of washing away any soil, though.

While the water is soaking into the flats, dig the furrows or holes where plants are headed.

2.

A teaspoon of 5-10-10 fertilizer or a handful of compost mixed in with soil in the bottom of the hole helps. I always fertilize on the light side—too much could shock the roots and set the plant back.

It's important to cover fertilizer with a couple of inches of soil, or mix it well with the soil at the bottom of the hole. That way fertilizer won't come in direct contact with plant roots.

3.

It's important to cup the roots of each seedling when you lift it from the flat or individual compartment. That way, shock to the roots will be reduced. Keep as much soil around the roots as possible.

4.

I pinch off lower leaves of lettuce, cabbage family and tomato transplants. Trimming the bottom foliage only relieves the often shocked root system from supporting too much top growth. With less to support on top, the root system recovers faster. Do not snip the center growth of lettuce or cabbage family plants; if you do, the plants will not produce. On tomatoes, be sure to leave the top cluster of leaves, as I've done in the photo above. The tomato on the left with bare stem is ready to be put in the ground. The one on the right will have more leaves removed.

Do not pinch leaves off eggplant, peppers or any vine crop family transplants.

5.

Be sure to protect young plants against cutworms before setting the plants in the ground. Cut newspaper into pieces measuring about 3 inches square. Wrap a piece around the stem of each plant so that half the paper is above the soil. This prevents the cutworms from attacking the stems until the plants are able to withstand them on their own.

Cutworms are usually gray or black, about an inch long and about ½ inch in diameter; they winter over in established gardens. Often they are more abundant in a freshly turned garden, one that has been recently lawn or pasture.

6.

Cup each plant by its roots and set it in the prepared furrow or hole about an inch deeper than it was in its container.

7.

I plant my tomatoes lengthwise in a trench about 2 or 3 inches deep. A shallow, horizontal planting allows them to quickly develop more roots along the buried stem. Plus, the plant is close to the surface; it gets warm faster than if I set it in a deep hole. That's important because tomatoes like heat.

8.

Quickly cover the roots with soil and firm them in well. With tomatoes, pack soil all the way up the stem, leaving just the top cluster of leaves exposed. Don't worry about propping up this top cluster; Mother Nature will send the plant growing in the right direction.

9.

Water generously. Don't be afraid of overwatering at this stage; in fact, you should almost drown your plants for a couple of days.

You can also water with a "starter solution" after transplanting. A starter solution is usually just a phosphorus fertilizer (for example, 0-15-0) which helps roots develop quickly.

Most transplants take a few days or a week to recover from transplanting. If your plants look a bit peaked initially, don't worry. Just keep them watered and they'll perk up like these pepper plants.

TRANSPLANT WARMUPS

I gamble every year and put some transplants out in the garden before it's totally safe. I give these early tomatoes, peppers, and eggplants plenty of protection against tough spring winds and cool nights.

I surround the plants with a protective cylinder made from a roll of plastic-sheeted chicken wire. I cut the wire into 2- or 3-foot strips about 18 inches wide. Then I stand the strip up in a circle around each plant and dig it into the soil a little so it doesn't blow over.

The plastic cylinder blocks the wind from striking the plants, and also catches a lot of heat during the day, which tomatoes, peppers, and eggplants like. If the weatherman announces a frost warning or a cold Vermont night, I use a standard hot cap, or I push a piece of newspaper into the cylinder. Then frost can't get the plants.

Since the cylinders are quite large I can leave them in place for a couple weeks. The heat they gather brings me an earlier harvest.

A few years ago I started using strips of black

Three ways to protect and warm up your transplants.

felt roofing paper to circle plants. First I set a small wire cage around a transplant, then I wrap the roofing paper on the outside of the frame and staple it together.

This works beautifully to stop wind and collect heat during the day.

When it's windy or cold, put something around your transplants. Cardboard boxes, paper bags, even a little shroud of cloth will work.

If a frost is predicted, you also can protect transplants by covering them with newspapers or old sheets. Take an armful of old newspapers out to the garden at dusk when it is still light enough to see. Spread one layer of newspaper over your wide rows of beans, for example, and drop a sheet over each tomato, eggplant, or pepper plant. Usually dew will hold the paper on the plant. There's no wind when a frost hits, so the newspaper will stay put. Leave the papers in place until just after the sun comes up the next morning. Then collect them, because if the wind should come up, your neighbors won't be very happy.

When there is a spring frost warning I cover my early bean rows overnight with newspaper sheets. Milk and cider jugs (right) can trap heat for transplants or seeded crops such as cucumbers. Don't use caps during the day.

Tunnel growing

I recently began experimenting with "tunnel growing" to find out just how much *earlier* and *later* in the year I could grow crops and get away with it.

By fashioning 18-inch-wide pieces of plastic into tunnels over my rows, I've been able to plant watermelons and cantaloupes 4 or 5 weeks *before* the average last frost date. The plastic traps heat and moisture, and this early start guarantees that I'll have ripe, juicy melons here in my short frost-free growing season. In the old days we spent a month watching our watermelons and cantaloupes, hoping they would ripen before the first frost. Now we spend that month eating melons.

I've been pushing up the planting dates for my cucumbers and summer squash, too. This past year, for example, I planted cukes and squash on April 23 under heat tunnels. We had our last spring frost May 18. (The frost did not harm any of my tunnel crops.) These plantings gave me excellent summer squash and cucumbers about 2 weeks earlier than I've ever harvested them. If I were running my old market garden, how plastic tunnels would bring in more early profits!

I've used two kinds of plastic material with excellent results: "Instant Greenhouse" which comes in 3-foot by 25-foot rolls, and "Keylite" which comes in 3-foot by 25-foot, 3-foot by 100-foot, and 6-foot by 100-foot rolls. Both materials are reinforced with light wire mesh which makes them hold the shape I give them over the row.

Small openings at tunnel ends are important for air circulation; they can be closed when night temperatures are expected to be quite low.

A bigger opening at each end becomes important with plantings in later spring. Keep a good flow of air going through the tunnels on sunny days. One idea is to use only small sections, or to keep each 25-foot section separate, and not hook up two or three pieces to make a long tunnel. I started some early okra in high-peak tunnels but restricted the tunnels to 10-foot sections. Excess heat found a way out of the tunnel but enough was captured and retained to help the plants until they got too tall for the tunnel. The okra under tunnels produced earlier and grew taller than the rows I grew conventionally.

Tunnels are now a must in my fall garden

There's extra satisfaction in harvesting vegetables when no one else is, so I've started to use my tunnels to extend the season into late fall.

A couple of years ago I hitched together two 3-foot sections of Instant Greenhouse and made an extra-large tunnel over a late wide row of beans. I harvested fresh green beans 3 weeks past the first hard frost. At that point the leaves were pressing against the inside of the plastic. When the next frost hit, the cold passed right through the plastic and killed many leaves and plants. For the best frost protection, a layer of air between the tops of the plants and the tunnels is important.

I cut the 3-foot by 25-foot rolls in half with tin snips or heavy-duty scissors, giving me 50 feet of 18-inch-wide material. The 18-inch-wide sections are easy to roll up and store for use in the fall or next spring.

After I plant the seeds I shape the plastic into a low tunnel over the row. I bend each edge up a little so I can easily anchor it down with soil. My tunnels have stood up to the hardest spring winds.

I close in the ends of each tunnel, leaving a small opening for air circulation. That's important on sunny days because even if it's cold outside, a bright sun will create plenty of heat inside the tunnel. One year I neglected to bend the tunnel ends in and a hungry (or cold) skunk worked his way right through the tunnel. He dug up and pawed over every single plant.

MY BEST TUNNEL CROPS

Spring	Fall
Cucumber	Lettuce
Zucchini	Beans
Summer squash	Spinach
Melons	Chinese cabbage

Lettuce does very well under a tunnel late in the year. I put head lettuce seedlings about 8 or 9 inches apart in a wide row and use a 36-inch tunnel to cover them. They grow fast in the hot tunnel but don't bolt or taste bitter. At night, the tunnel protects them from frost. I'm still getting crisp heads of lettuce from the tunnels when everybody else is back buying expensive heads in the supermarket.

1

Before planting seeds, rake out any bumps or valleys to get a smooth seedbed, and then drag the corner of your hoe alongside the string to make a furrow 4 to 6 inches deep.

Easy Single Row Planting

How I plant corn,

3

Cover the fertilizer with 2 or 3 inches of soil to prevent the seeds from coming in contact with it because nitrogen can burn seeds. To do this job, walk along one side of the furrow and hoe a hefty amount of soil into it from the other side. I angle the hoe like a snowplow.

4

Drop the seeds in the open furrow at the correct spacing. I usually sow a little more thickly than is recommended on seed packets. I want to get a good stand of plants—I can always thin later.

2

Along the bottom of the furrow, place a thin band of 5-10-10 fertilizer at the rate of about 2 or 3 pounds every 100 feet. Don't spill the fertilizer into the furrow—lay it carefully on the bottom, not along the sides of the furrow.

cucumbers, melons, squash, pumpkins, and other single row crops

5

Cover the seeds with the right amount of soil. Small seeds need about ½ inch of soil; larger ones such as squash or bean seeds need 1 to 1½ inches.

Firm the soil one more time with the back of your hoe. That's all there is to it.

Vegetables that need a lot of room to grow are planted in single rows, or in "hills." A hill is *not* a raised area of soil. In gardening, hill refers to planting a group of seeds in a circle on flat ground. To sow a hill of corn, for example, I put four or five seeds 6 inches apart in a circle. I put the hills 18 to 24 inches apart.

Hills of summer squash, cantaloupes, and cucumbers are usually 4 to 6 feet apart; pumpkins, winter squash, and watermelons need 6 to 10 feet between hills.

I prefer planting in rows for two reasons: first, it's a lot easier to cultivate between rows with my tiller, or with hand tools. Second, if insects attack a hill there are not many plants to go around. If all of them are damaged, there are no plants nearby to fill in and keep the area covered with plants. In a row, however, plants easily take up room left by plants lost to insects.

SPACING SEEDS IN A SINGLE ROW

Crop	Distance between seeds before thinning
corn	6-10
cucumbers	6-8
melons	6-8
summer squash	6-10
winter squash	6-10
pumpkins	6-10

Companion planting with single row crops

While I think red radishes are the best all-around companion crop for vegetables, there is great interest in other companion schemes wherever I go. Companion planting is an unproven science, but it can be fun trying to confuse insects and animals with colors, smells and unusual neighboring plants.

Vegetable	May benefit by planting it next to:
Corn	Potatoes, peas, beans, cucumbers, pumpkin and squash
Cucumbers	Beans, peas, radishes, sunflowers, and corn
Melons	Corn, sunflowers, morning glory
Okra	Peppers and eggplant
Potatoes	Beans, corn, cabbage, horseradish, and marigolds
Pumpkin	Jimson weed (in vicinity), and corn
Squash	Icicle radishes, nasturtium
Tomatoes	Chives, onions, parsley, marigolds, nasturtium and garlic

Source: adapted from Carrots Love Tomatoes, *Secrets of Companion Planting for Successful Gardening, by Louise Riotte, Garden Way Publishing, Charlotte, VT.*

Meet my friend, the radish!

Most of my rows — wide and single — work better when I include some radishes. I plant them with carrots, melons, onions, lettuce, parsnips, well, with practically everything except corn, peas, and beans. To me, radishes are the best companion plants of all.

I use about 5 percent radish seeds in just about every row I plant. I sprinkle them in with the main crop before I tamp down the seeds.

Here's how they help:

Radishes come up quickly. Because they sprout in 3 to 7 days they act as row markers. I can see where to weed between the rows even before the main crop has come up.

Radishes act as natural cultivators. Think of a wide row of beets, turnips, lettuce, or carrots that has a smattering of radishes in it. These radishes mature quickly and when I pull them, they loosen the soil in the row and also leave holes in the ground. These cavities catch water and provide breathing space so the neighboring plants can expand easily.

Radishes help me grow better root crops in clay soil. I plant the long, *White Icicle* radishes which grow deep, even in the heaviest soil, loosening the earth as they do. I let them grow large so that when I pull them, they will leave lots of room for other root crops to muscle into.

Radishes distract bugs. Bugs seem to wait around early in spring until there's something to munch on, and then usually pounce on the first shoots that appear. Many times those are radishes. I suspect that since the early food for some bugs consists of radishes, they wind up developing a taste for it. Meanwhile, other plants may have time to grow with very little damage. The same may be true of the insects and other pests which attack underground. Perhaps because radish roots grow quickly, pests seem to be attracted to them first, leaving the main crop alone.

I lose some radishes to insect damage each year, but since I plant them all over the garden I get plenty of perfect ones to eat. In fact, if you don't watch it, you'll have radishes coming up all over. I got a letter from a woman a few years ago who said, "Thanks a lot, Dick, for your idea on putting radishes in my rows. I now have a zillion of them in my garden!"

STOP WEEDS COLD!

We all know weeds can be the biggest headache and time drain in the garden. But they don't have to be. If you know what makes a weed tick and understand the hidden ways weeds can enter and spread in your garden, you can learn how to stop them cold.

You *can* have a garden that's practically weed-free, without spending a lot of time hoeing or pulling weeds by hand.

I've said it before, and I'll say it again: "I'm a lazy gardener." I'd rather sit on the porch and drink iced tea on a hot summer day than be in the garden pulling weeds. That's why I've spent years figuring out the easiest ways to prevent most weeds from getting started in my garden, and to take care of those that do come up—and almost always without bending down.

One of the first steps to a weed-free garden is understanding the difference between *annual* and *perennial weeds*. It's important because there are different techniques for controlling each kind.

Annual weeds grow only one season. Their goal is to produce seeds before cold weather kills the plant. If you let annual weeds grow they will create hundreds, even thousands, of seeds. These seeds then tumble down to the ground or get blown all over the garden.

Many of these will germinate the following year, and then it's their turn to make a new batch of seeds.

Perennial weeds spread by means of underground stems and root parts, but they will go to seed also. A single hoeing or tilling doesn't do much to them because pieces of their roots left in the soil have enough energy to send up new shoots right away.

The new green growth captures energy from the sun and begins to replenish the root system. As long as the roots have energy they will be able to send up new growth.

If you understand a few basic principles, it won't take much work to keep a garden this neat and clean.

Annuals

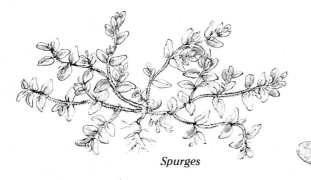

Spurges

Purslane

Lamb's-quarters

Green Amaranth

Chickweed

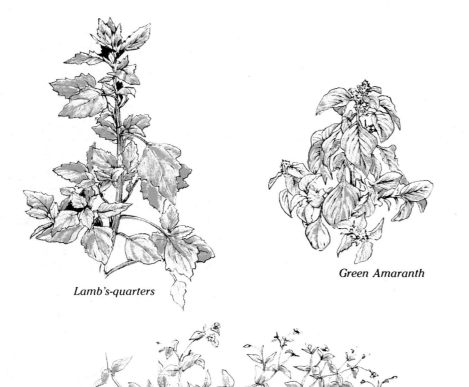

I get rid of annual weeds before I see them!

The seeds of annual weeds are so small that they can germinate only in the top ¼ inch of soil. If the seeds are deeper, they don't have enough strength to push up through the soil.

When weed seeds begin to sprout below the surface, you can't see them, of course, but this is the time they are easiest to get rid of.

I saw this clearly years ago when I planted alfalfa in a large experimental glass grow box to see its root system. I covered the glass most of the time so the roots would grow toward it and not shy away from the light.

I peeked behind the cover occasionally to see the extensive alfalfa roots expand throughout the box. One day I noticed that a few weeds had sprouted. Looking more closely at the area just under the soil surface, I saw that more small weed seeds were germinating right below the soil surface. What fascinated me was that these seeds did *not* send down a deep taproot before poking through the soil as many vegetables do. Scuffing the soil lightly knocked them loose and killed them.

Annual weed seeds sprout the same way out in the garden. The soil is full of them, but because they're so small they only sprout when they wind up very close to the surface, to what I call their "germination zone."

134

Work the soil just before planting

When you work the soil deeply in the spring, you bring up thousands of these tiny seeds to this germination zone. If you let the soil sit for 2 or 3 days and then plant your seeds, many of the tiny weeds in the zone would germinate and overwhelm your vegetables. That's getting your garden off on the wrong foot!

I *never* work the soil one day and plant it the next. I always roto-till it *immediately* before setting up my stakes and string and planting. If you don't have a tiller, stir up the soil in the seedbed with a rake or hoe.

This last-minute stirring of the soil turns up hundreds of weed seedlings. They are so tender at this point that the slightest disturbance kills them.

With most of the germinating weeds out of the picture, my seeds have a darned good chance to germinate and sprout ahead of any more weed seeds near the surface.

Remember, thinning with a rake is one of the best weeding steps of all

Thinning my wide rows with a *rake* is one of the most important weed-fighting steps of all. As soon as my wide-row vegetables get ¼ to ½ inch high, I drag an iron garden rake *across* the row with the tines going in about ¼ inch. This thins out some of the closely planted vegetables, but more importantly, the rake tines shake up hundreds of sprouting weed seeds. (Remember, peas, beans, and onion sets and plants do not get this rake-thinning.)

Tiny weed plants are not anchored into the soil, so they spill out easily and die. In most cases, *one* pass across the row will do the job, but if my plants appear too thick after the first pass, I drag the rake over the row a second time.

Even when my plants are slow to come up, I still use the rake. I know that if I *don't* stir up the soil in the seedbed within 10 days after planting I will have a weed problem, and the only way to get them will be by hand-pulling. Raking across the seedbed may pull out some plants just starting to push through the soil. That's okay. All my wide rows need thinning anyway. I'm thinning a little early but getting a whole mess of weeds on time.

Two good things happen with shallow cultivation

The best time to get rid of annual weeds in the germination zone is shortly after a rain or watering. A rain brings moisture to hundreds of weed seeds and they start sprouting.

When the surface of the soil gets dry, I stir up the top inch or 2 of soil between my rows and near the plants. This stirring or "cultivation" wipes out hundreds of weeds before they come to the surface.

Two good things happen when I cultivate at a shallow depth. First, I don't bring any new weed seeds into the germination zone from deeper layers of soil; and second, I avoid cutting any roots of my vegetables which grow out under the walkways.

So if you're using a hoe, a roto-tiller, or a push-cultivator to weed your garden, don't go down more than an inch or so.

After four or five shallow cultivations, most of the annual weed seeds in the top layer of soil have germinated. You won't have to do much weeding after that.

Another good thing about regular shallow cultivation is that it helps the soil absorb and hold water. Packed soil doesn't hold much moisture. Loosening the soil lets water seep down.

Here are a few more cultivating tips

Let plants dry off before you weed. If the leaves are wet, it's possible to spread a disease by brushing your legs against them as you move down a row.

Do any hand weeding around the plants *before* tilling or hoeing the walkways. Leave the walkways with as few footprints as possible. That lets water drain into the soil easily, and keeps weeds from sprouting because they need firmed soil for that.

Work weeds into the soil or throw them on the compost pile. As long as they haven't produced seeds, they're good organic matter which you should try to get into your soil.

Weed after the harvest, too! Annual weeds will keep trying to produce seeds no matter how late in the season. Keep after them.

INTRODUCING THE IN-ROW WEEDER

I drag my In-Row Weeder across this row of onions every 4 or 5 days to uproot weeds just as they are sprouting.

My new weeding tool passes harmlessly around vegetables to uproot small weeds

Four or five days after rake-thinning, I use my In-Row Weeder, a tool with long, flexible prongs that lightly stirs the soil surface as I drag it over the plants in each row. I don't want to use the garden rake again because I've already thinned out enough plants with it.

Walking quickly alongside each row, I drag the In-Row Weeder lightly over the plants. The tines stir up only the top ¼ inch of soil and kill annual weed seedlings that are starting to grow there. The vegetables are rarely hurt, because their roots are much deeper and sturdier and have a taproot anchor. The light flexible prongs of the In-Row Weeder merely flex and pass around the vegetables, and only weeds are uprooted.

Once in a while the weeder may pull up a vegetable plant or two along with the weeds, but usually that happens when the plants are too thick to begin with.

I use the In-Row Weeder every 4 or 5 days during their first 3 weeks of growth. After that, most plants are too big for the In-Row Weeder, but there are few weed seeds left near the surface ready to spring to life.

Sometimes a weed will get anchored and the In-Row Weeder won't pull it up, so I let it grow 3 or 4 inches. Then it's big enough to pull out easily.

The In-Row Weeder is not only for wide rows. I can drag it over small transplants, such as head lettuce, cabbage and peppers, my onion plants and sets, and my corn rows.

The In-Row Weeder will not stop perennial weeds. Their roots are anchored well below the surface. You have to either pull them or adopt a strategy that will get rid of perennial weeds in your garden for good.

"I thought of the In-Row Weeder design lying flat on my back in the hospital . . ."

In the winter of 1973 I broke my back in an accident. The doctors told me I had to stay in the hospital and recuperate for at least two months. It would be a lot longer, they said, before I knew if I'd be able to bend, stoop and carry things.

While recuperating and staring at the hospital wall, I thought a lot about what the doctors had told me. Since spring wasn't too far off, I wondered if I'd be able to take care of my garden. I didn't want to cut down the size of the garden—it was too important to the family. I knew my wife and daughters could plant the garden. But I wanted to do my share later. I was always proud of having a neat garden, so I had to come up with a way to keep the garden free of weeds without having to bend over and pull them by hand.

One day I thought of the In-Row Weeder design. There I was, lying flat on my back, when I remembered a weeding tool I had used when I was 12 years old.

I remember dad called me to the barn one day and brought out what he called "The Weeder." It was a wide heavy attachment with about 35 springy tines, each a foot long. He said, "Hitch this up to the horse and drag it cross-ways through the cornfield." The corn was only about 3 inches tall at the time so I said, "Dad, won't this thing pull up the corn?" My dad looked at me sternly and said, "Don't worry, son. It'll dig out the weeds, but not the corn." I knew it didn't pay to argue.

Remembering this old "Weeder" helped me design my new tool.

I hitched "The Weeder" to the horse and went across the corn rows just as dad told me. I still thought that we were going to ruin all the corn plants, so I was amazed to see that the tines of the weeder just bumped into a plant here and there and passed around it. All the corn stayed rooted, but those tines passing over them kicked the soil up and kept plenty of weeds from getting started. About 10 days later I used The Weeder again on the cornfield. After that, the corn plants got too tall for it.

Perfecting my idea

This corn weeder from my younger days gave me the idea for a tool, a *new* weeder that could pass over small vegetable plants without pulling them out of the ground. In the hospital I refined the design in my mind, and as soon as I got out I started to build one. I had to get the right number of tines with the right spacing between them and with the right kind of metal so they would be flexible. Also the weeder had to have enough weight to lightly penetrate the soil. It couldn't be too heavy or it would yank out vegetables by their taproots.

After a few prototypes I had a real good product. Later when I tried it out, I thought of the name "In-Row" Weeder because the tool was so good at keeping weeds from getting started *right in the row* close to the vegetables where it's hardest to weed.

Peas and beans were the only crops I didn't weed with this tool; the tines caught too many of their tender stems.

Using my In-Row Weeder just a few minutes each week, I discovered the joy of having practically a weed-free garden without having to bend over and pull weeds by hand. I could weed my rows just as fast as I could walk by them.

Just a couple of years ago I spotted an old "Weeder" like the one my dad and I used. It was in the back of a barn at the home of a retired farmer. After a little dickering, I swapped one of my new In-Row Weeders for it. Now at my place I've got both weeders—the old and the new.

MY FAVORITE HOES AND

COMMON GARDEN HOE

A common garden hoe for weeding should be light with a narrow head. To weed with it, lightly draw the hoe underneath the soil with the blade going in 1 to 1½ inches. This will loosen the soil and dislodge most weeds. Don't chop around plants with your hoe. That brings up more weed seeds to where they can germinate; and it also can damage the roots of your plants.

I like an ordinary hoe with a broad head for my planting and hilling chores. I can move a lot of soil easily and tamp down seeds quickly.

A wide garden hoe is best for hilling, planting and other chores.

ONION HOE

This light, maneuverable hoe is one of the best for weeding. Its head is about 2 inches deep and 4 or 5 inches wide. Because the head is thin you can sneak between plants that are close together. It's perfect for double and triple rows. I don't really know why it's called an onion hoe; my father called it that because we used it sideways to weed between onion plants without disturbing any onion roots.

The slim blade of the onion hoe can work near closely-spaced plants.

138

HOW TO USE THEM

FINGER HOE

I haven't found a more versatile weeding tool in the world than the finger hoe. I always grab it before going in the garden because there's bound to be some way for me to weed with it—by its point, by the blade edge, or even by yanking a weed out with the hoe's curved, looping neck.

The best thing about the finger hoe is that I can pull weeds very close to plants without bending down and without disturbing any plant roots. Why? Well, you'll notice that the blade edge is fashioned completely on one side of the head. It's not like a regular hoe with the blade extending to each side. So with the blade to one side I can get the hoe very close to a plant—and actually bump the stem if I want to. When I pull the blade through the soil, it's impossible for me to accidentally slice into a plant.

Besides having a thin blade which gets into very tight spots, the finger hoe's curved neck allows you to lift weeds and their roots from the soil.

Is your hoe sharpened on the right side?

I'll bet 99 percent of garden hoes are sharpened on the wrong side. At least that's what I find when I look in hardware stores.

Hoes should be sharpened only on the inside edge—that's the side facing up when you're pulling it toward you through the soil. You'll find it pulls into the ground more easily; you won't have to force it.

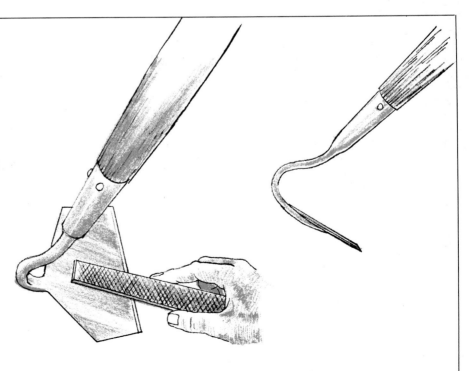

139

It's been years since I've pulled a weed by hand around my corn and potatoes

Instead of hand-weeding around my potatoes and corn, I hill the plants to get rid of weeds. Hilling means piling up soil around the base of each plant. This smothers small weeds and avoids disturbing the roots of vegetables.

Hilling with my roto-tiller and hilling attachment takes only a few minutes. It takes a bit longer to hill with a hoe, but even that is quicker and easier than weeding around each plant.

If I'm in the mood for a little exercise, hilling potatoes or corn with a hoe is just the thing.

I plant my corn and potatoes to make hilling easy. I put the corn rows exactly 30 inches apart, and the potatoes 36 inches apart. I hill the corn for the first time when it's just a few inches tall. I run my tiller with hilling attachment between the rows. The tiller tines loosen up soil in the patch,

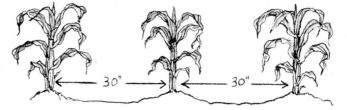

For easy hilling, my corn rows are planted 30 inches apart.

and the hilling wings spill it from the middle of the row out to the base of the corn plants. I hill the corn again when it's about a foot tall. The extra soil around each stalk helps the plant stand up to strong winds. If you've ever had corn blow over in your garden, try hilling it up once or twice for protection.

The hilling attachment of my tiller scrapes away weeds and pushes soil against potato plants at the same time.

My potato rows are 36 inches apart because they need more room to grow and more soil for the hilling operation. I hill most of my potatoes three times. Again using my roto-tiller and hilling wings, I till down a little deeper so I can push a lot of soil up around the plants. Potatoes need lots of soil mounded around them to produce the best potatoes. Here is when I usually hill potatoes: first when most of the plants have grown 2 or 3 inches above ground; (this hilling may completely cover many of the plants with soil, but that's okay, the plants will grow through it quickly); second time when the plants are about 8 to 10 inches tall; third time about 2 weeks after the second hilling.

After three hillings there really aren't any weeds in the rows. Toward the end of the season some weeds do grow, but these weeds are usually tilled in right after the potato harvest before they've had a chance to produce any seed. I think of them as bonus organic matter.

Hilling also keeps weeds down near okra, tomatoes, peppers, eggplant, and broccoli. If I hill these crops, I use a hoe. I'm very careful around pepper plants, though; they don't like too much soil around their stems, especially when they are still quite young. About an inch or 2 of soil is the most I bring up around them.

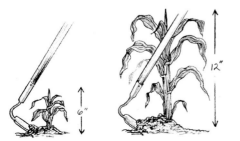

Hill corn first when only a few inches tall; hill later when plants are 1 foot or so tall.

Tomatoes need lots of soil mounded around them.

141

Perennials

How to fight them and win!

If you're having trouble with grass and other perennial weeds, an all-out attack on them is in order. You can't control them the way you do annual weeds.

Some perennial weeds are much more of a problem than others. Quack grass, Bermuda grass, and nut grass are the worst because they have extensive root systems. Their stored energy lets them send up new shoots when others are cut down. After a tilling, you may think your soil is rid of them, but in a few days they've started up again thicker than ever. It's important to realize that each time they rebound with new growth, they have used up some of their reserve. They draw on these reserves until there's enough top growth to start capturing the sun's energy and replenishing the root reserves. Usually this starts when the plants are ½ inch or so high.

But if you *prevent* perennials from putting on this ½ inch of growth, you'll starve out their root reserves and they'll die. It is not an overnight process. One way to do this is to till the soil and then quickly cover it with black plastic sheeting or a very heavy mulch for a whole season. Another way to starve the roots is by continuous tilling at a shallow depth to kill the small blades coming up without chopping up a lot of the root system. If you till for a *whole season* whenever the grass first appears—probably every 4 to 7 days—you can force the roots to use all their energy. When they're out of energy, you win.

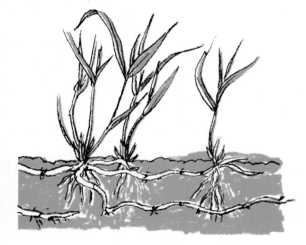

The toughest perennial weeds spread by underground root systems as well as by scattering seeds. Perhaps the best way to get rid of these troublesome weeds is to completely starve out the root system. This is done by preventing the plants from developing any top growth. You can cover the ground with black plastic or rototill the soil regularly at a shallow level.

142

Some of the toughest perennials

BERMUDA GRASS. You might think of Bermuda grass as the South's version of quack grass. As a lawn or pasture grass in the South, it's fine—but in a garden it's big trouble. It spreads by both seed and creeping roots.

If the ground in your area freezes during the winter, kill Bermuda grass by a thorough tilling in late fall to expose the roots to the cold. This won't work in areas with mild winters, but smother crops will. Starting in the fall, plant a smother crop such as rye, and follow it the next year with two or three thick crops of buckwheat. Their dense shade should destroy most of the grass.

QUACK GRASS. One of the worst perennial weeds for gardeners in the North. It will grow through most mulches and can produce abundant seed.

Quack grass competes with vegetables for light, water, space, and nutrients. It may take a full season to weaken and kill a heavy infestation. During this time it's important to prevent new shoots from getting much more than 1 inch high.

Quack grass likes cool weather so it is most aggressive during the spring and fall months.

NUT GRASS. There's a northern and southern version of nut grass. The northern variety, sometimes called "yellow nut grass," prefers poorly drained soils. Both species can be identified by their shiny, erect blades and the hard little tubers or "nuts" that form on the roots.

Even when the roots are chopped and tilled thoroughly, the little nuts survive to send up new plants. When pulling nut grass by hand, pull very carefully so that the tubers don't break off and remain in the soil.

BINDWEED. Bindweed must hold some kind of record among pesky weeds. Its extensive root system can penetrate as deep as 16 feet. It's most abundant and troublesome in the West.

This viney perennial is a member of the morning glory family, and can reproduce both by seed and by creeping roots. Don't even try to plant a garden where bindweed is a bad problem. To get rid of it, till the plot every 2 or 3 weeks to drain root reserves. After a while, plant successive smother crops of buckwheat and till them in. The next year you'll be able to plant a garden without much trouble.

Bermuda grass

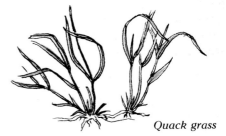

Quack grass

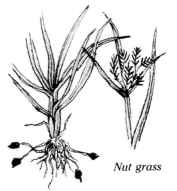

Nut grass

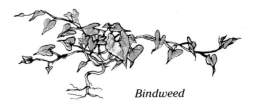

Bindweed

THE BUCKWHEAT STORY

How I smothered perennial weeds so they never came back, and improved my soil in the process

When Jan and I bought the land where we now live, our garden spot was an old, abandoned pasture, completely overgrown with thick perennial grasses like quack grass and nut grass. Those roots were so dense that I could hardly dig my shovel into the soil. I knew I'd never enjoy my garden until I got rid of those perennial weeds.

The first year, I decided to grow only a small salad garden near the house and to plant a crop of buckwheat throughout our main garden. I didn't grow buckwheat for flour, but because it is the best crop to smother perennial grasses. I hired a tractor to turn over and harrow the garden—about an acre in size. Then I *immediately* sowed the buckwheat seed at a rate of 3 to 4 pounds for each 1,000 square feet.

Buckwheat sprouts very quickly in warm weather, and in just a few days it was up. Because I seeded it thickly, the leaves of each plant started to touch their neighbors' within 2 weeks. As buckwheat leaves come together they create a thick shady canopy over the ground. It's like putting a giant tarp over the garden. The sun is blocked off; it can't penetrate the canopy and nourish the perennial grasses coming back after plowing.

When the buckwheat started to blossom, I tilled it back into the soil because I didn't want it to go to seed. It's all right to let honeybees work the blossoms for a few days, but buckwheat should be turned under before any dark seeds appear.

Tilling the buckwheat back into the soil added huge amounts of organic matter to the soil. It also chopped and buried the perennial grasses which had used much of their root reserves trying to overcome the buckwheat canopy. Many of the perennials were low on root reserves, but I knew they still had enough punch to grow again if I let them.

I tilled and reseeded the garden the very next day with a second crop of buckwheat. I didn't want to let the weeds grow, capture sunlight, and start building up their root reserves again.

The second crop of buckwheat was up and shading out the weeds within days. When this second crop hit the blossom stage, I turned it all back into the soil again. This was just about the finishing blow for the perennials.

After a few days I tilled again, and because it was getting toward the end of the growing season, I sowed a final crop of *annual ryegrass*. Like buckwheat, annual ryegrass is fast-sprouting and provides a thick cover. It continued the work of blocking out the weeds until early winter when the hard freezes killed it.

The annual ryegrass protected the soil over the winter and was almost totally decomposed by spring. It was easy to work into the soil before I fertilized and planted my first big garden at my new home.

Did the buckwheat and annual ryegrass eliminate the perennials? You bet they did! Weeds which might have taken me 3 or 4 years to clean out took only one season. Here and there during my first full gardening season I found a few perennials making a last-ditch effort to come back, but a little hoeing kept them from getting any sunlight and they pooped out.

Buckwheat is the best of the smother crops

Soybeans, field peas, garden peas, and beans will grow quickly and shade out weeds, but I like buckwheat better if I'm working a big area. It grows faster, and the seeds are cheaper. In a small area, peas and beans are perfect because not only do you shut out the weeds, you get a large harvest, too.

Turning a buckwheat smother crop into the soil is easy with a roto-tiller, but you'd be amazed at how little effort is needed to dig the crop in by hand. Buckwheat stems are hollow and very tender at the blossom stage, so they're easy to chop. Because the crop grows so thickly and shades out the sun, the soil is quite loose and moist underneath, giving you perfect conditions for mixing the crop into the soil.

Buckwheat is the best choice for a smother crop or super soil-building crop. Plant it when the soil has warmed up, around the average last spring frost date. Buckwheat grows well in all types of soil and in all climates of the country. It is especially good for clay soil, because its roots break up clay and help keep it loose. The seed is reasonably priced, too.

Where to find buckwheat seed

Look for buckwheat seed at your local feed and grain store or a garden supply center. Your local Extension horticultural agent can help you find a local source.

Two mail-order seed companies offering buckwheat are Wyatt-Quarles Seed Co., Box 2131, Raleigh, NC 27602, and Johnny's Selected Seeds, Albion, ME 04919.

My 12-point system for fewer and fewer

1

Till or work your soil minutes before planting. Don't give hidden sprouting weed seeds a head start on your vegetables.

2

"Weed and thin" with a garden rake when your plants are ¼ to ½ inch high or within 10 days after planting. You must stir the soil in your seedbed early. (Don't do this with peas, beans and onion sets.)

3

Lightly drag the In-Row Weeder over your crops three or four times before they are 2 or 3 weeks old. Use the In-Row Weeder on corn and around transplants, too.

4

Plant two or more crops of buckwheat to smother perennial weeds.

5

Devote a small section of your garden to a series of thick pea and bean crops which shade out weeds. In the same spot next season plant in wide rows those crops that can't handle weed competition—carrots, onions, and lettuce. There will be fewer weeds to bother them.

6

Avoid using horse, cow, or sheep manures in your garden unless they are dehydrated or thoroughly composted. Manures and bedding materials are full of weed seeds.

weeds each year

10

Cultivate at a shallow depth—no deeper than 1 or 1½ inches. The best time to cultivate or pull weeds is when plants and soil dry out after a rain or watering.

11

Keep stirring the top ¼ inch of soil because this is where weed seeds sprout. Don't wait until the weeds come up. In spring and early summer, work this germination zone every 4 or 5 days.

12

Clean the garden at the end of the season when weeds are making their last big push to produce seeds before cold weather. Till in crop residues and plant end-of-season green manure crops such as annual ryegrass.

7

Don't use mulches that are loaded with weed seeds such as hay or straw. It's better to mulch with pine needles, grass clippings, and other materials with few weed seeds.

8

Don't let weeds go to seed in or near your garden. Weeds never give up trying to make seeds, so take a few minutes each week to clip or mow near the garden.

9

Till deeply around the edge of your garden occasionally to keep perennial lawn grasses from creeping into the garden.

GARDEN CARE

In the following pages I want to explain the easy steps and labor-saving tips which can make caring for the garden as enjoyable and satisfying as planting or harvesting it.

My approach to many garden chores is to picture them from the plant's point of view—what does this crop need for best health at this point in its growth? Then I can figure out the easiest way to do what's best for the crop.

This tactic works especially well when mulching, watering, or giving a crop a side-dressing of fertilizer.

I've also outlined here some basic steps for increasing garden production into the fall months. Every garden I've seen recently—including my own—could have more fall vegetables growing. That's why succession planting and careful planning for fall crops should be on everyone's garden checklist.

MULCHES

Every garden needs a little mulch. Mulch is a thick blanket of material laid on the ground near plants or in the walkways. It blocks sunlight, keeps weeds from growing, holds moisture in the soil, and keeps the soil temperature steady and cool. Mulch is a must for many dry-country gardeners who are trying to cut down on their watering, and for folks who haven't got the time to stir up the soil every week to stop weeds from getting started.

People use all kinds of organic matter and material for mulch—grass clippings, bark chips, peat moss, pine needles, leaves, sawdust, black plastic, and so on.

If you have a little extra space you can even grow some mulch. I've had good luck with planting winter wheat or winter rye in the fall and letting it grow 3 or 4 feet tall the next spring. Then I scythe the crop before it produces seed and use the plants as mulch around tomatoes, peppers, and other crops. They help feed the soil when I work everything back into the soil after the season.

My favorite mulch is a living mulch of wide row vegetables. I grow most of my vegetables close together so that as they grow their leaves form a canopy over the soil. This canopy blocks out the sun from tiny weeds trying to grow, and conserves water.

Mulches you can eat

An edible mulch keeps weeds down, shades the soil to hold water in, and also provides a harvest of food.

Take my rows of broccoli, for example. The plants are small when I set them out in spring. As they get bigger I put in lettuce plants or some other green throughout the row to grow as an edible mulch. The lettuce grows quickly and helps cover the soil to keep it cool—and broccoli loves cool soil. Because lettuce is a shallow-rooted vegetable, it doesn't compete with the broccoli for food.

A living mulch of lettuce under broccoli plants.

My favorite mulch is a living mulch

Lettuce also works well under my pole bean te-pees and near eggplants as an edible mulch.

Spinach and chard are good edible mulches be-cause they can take a little shade and have shallow root systems.

Hay for mulch—take care

Many mulches have weed seeds tucked into them and hay is probably the worst. If you mulch with hay, chances are good you'll add many more weeds to your garden. Most hay is a mix of differ-ent grasses such as timothy, orchard grass, June grass and others. By the time the first cutting of hay takes place each year, many of the grasses have gone to seed. These seeds are cut down and baled with the hay. I used some bales of early hay for mulch 10 years ago in the back section of my garden. After all these years, more weeds try to come up there than in any other part of the garden!

Avoid a first cut of hay for mulch. It's better to scout around later in the season, when farmers are putting up bales of second cut or third cut hay. These will have fewer weed seeds because meadow grasses usually produce seeds early.

The ideal hay mulch is a late cutting from an al-falfa field. Alfalfa is one of the most common hay crops and it's very high in protein. When you turn alfalfa hay into the soil at the end of the season, you're giving your soil life a good meal.

Once you find later cuts of hay, it's usually too late in the season to use them in your garden. I buy broken bales of late cut hay out in the fields at a low price, haul them home, and keep them under cover until I need them the next season.

Some people think straw mulch is free of seeds, but it isn't. Straw is what's left of grain plants like oats or wheat after the seed is taken off. But in re-moving the seeds, some get mixed with the leftover straw. Oat straw always has many seeds which are as much trouble as any weed.

I've mulched these peppers with straw which has few weed seeds.

Where I used a mulch of seedy hay 10 years ago I get more weeds sprouting than anywhere else in the garden.

151

Watering

Only two rules for thirsty plants

Water from this "impact" sprinkler hits a deflector, causing the head to rotate continuously. In most cases, sprinklers should run until soil is moist to a depth of 4 or 5 inches.

There are only two rules for watering the garden correctly: *water at the proper time* and *water deeply*.

Too many gardeners, especially beginners, feel they must water a garden. But you should water your plants only when they really need it. How do you tell? Look at your plants in the morning. If they are wilted, it's a sure sign that the soil has very little moisture left to provide for plants. *It's time to water!*

Plants often look fine in the morning but start to droop in the afternoon when it gets hot. Drooping plants means they are losing more water than they are absorbing. Don't rush to the water hose if you see this. Hold off for a while. Plants usually recover in the evening and overnight when the sun goes down and moisture moves up in the soil. But if your plants are wilted in the morning, get busy and water them.

Water morning or evening

I water in the morning because that's when I can see plants need it. After a morning watering they'll have enough moisture to get through a hot day and perhaps two or three more before the next rain or watering.

If you water in midday, some of the water will evaporate before the plants get to use it. If water is scarce or the price high, avoid midday sprinkling. It's okay to water in the evening if you can't do it in the morning, even though some people say that it increases the chances of disease. Sure, plant leaves often stay wet overnight from an evening watering. But that's exactly what happens during many summer nights when dew coats the leaves—or when it rains.

Think deep when you water

It takes a lot of water to give the garden a decent dose. Gardens need 1 inch of rain or irrigation water each week to grow well. Do you know how much water an inch is? Well, it takes 62 gallons to put an inch of water on a 10-by-10-foot garden. That's one 10-quart bucket of water for a single tomato plant!

The biggest watering mistake is *too little* water. Shallow watering discourages plant roots from diving deep. And since they get used to finding water near the surface, they grow only shallow roots. This becomes a serious problem when it's dry because without a deep root system the plants survive only if they are watered almost daily.

Deep waterings make the plant roots reach deep into the soil to find water. Then, should there be a dry spell they'll be able to live well between waterings.

If you don't water until the soil is moist 4 or 5 inches down, there's almost no point in watering. So soak the soil. Dig down after a while to make sure the soil is moist 4 to 5 inches deep.

Want to save water?

When soil is open and exposed to the beating hot sun, a heck of a lot of water is lost to evaporation, precious water that your garden *needs*.

Often people use heavy mulches to cover the soil. But there's a better and more productive way to keep the soil covered—grow more plants!

I once planted a test garden in Florida and stuck to this principle. As usual I planted most vegetables in wide rows or in blocks.

The man who owned the property next to our test garden sauntered over when we started to plant. It was late afternoon but still hot as the dickens.

"What are you going to have for a water system?" he asked. "We're not going to have one," I told him.

"Well then," he said, shaking his head slowly, "you won't be able to make a garden. You just got to have a water system down here."

"We'll see," I said. In the wide rows and blocks, the crops shaded the soil and kept it cool and moist. At night the leaves trapped an amazing amount of dew. We hardly had to water these crops. But across the fence, the man with the water system seemed to be sprinkling his single-row garden every other day. The plants in his narrow rows had exposed soil all around them. It didn't take long for his soil to get dry and dusty.

My favorite tools make watering easy!

Sprinkler—My sturdy oscillating sprinkler gets a lot of use in the bigger areas of my garden. It has a fine needle screwed into the end. With the needle I poke any holes that are clogged to get a smooth, even delivery of water.

I like to put sprinklers up on a sawhorse. Down at ground level the spray oftens hits nearby plants pretty hard. I also get a little farther reach with it mounted above the ground.

Breaker—Young plants like a soft shower and with a water breaker and extension wand I can give them a perfect one. The unit is very handy around my greenhouse and cold frames for plants and seed flats, but I use it in the garden as well. It delivers a good volume of water in a soft, gentle spray. It's perfect for spot-watering of seedbeds and transplants.

Soaker hose—I use a canvas soaker hose for any small area that needs water. Water oozes slowly out of it and drains into the root zone of my plants. The hose is so soft and flexible that I can snake it around the transplants in my wide rows. It's also excellent for single rows as well as wide rows where I can place it down the middle without harming plants.

Soaker hose delivers water close to plants.

Water-saving suggestions for drought years

1. Gamble and plant early

There's more moisture in the soil in early spring than any other time of the year. As soon as you can work the soil and prepare seedbeds, gamble some seeds and plant some early crops. Push ahead your plantings of corn and potatoes, too. These crops take lots of water, and the more growth they can put on before dry weather, the better it is for you.

2. Don't fertilize too much early in the year

You'd be amazed at how few roots will develop in over-fertilized soils. Plants can get all the food they need close to the surface with just a small root system. So they don't bother to go down deep. When a dry spell occurs, look out! They suffer quickly, you wind up watering them every day. It's better for your crops if they have to work for their food and water. Let them develop far-reaching root systems which penetrate deep in the soil *before* you give them big helpings of plant food.

3. Plant wide rows

Water escapes rapidly from the ground when the soil is bare. To hold water in, grow your vegetables in wide rows or blocks. They will trap plenty of moisture.

4. Use mulches— weed-free is best

Mulches hold in moisture by cutting evaporation. They also prevent weeds from stealing food and water.

The best time to apply a mulch is after a good rain. Use thick mulches so the sun can't possibly hit the ground.

Use mulches of lawn clippings, pine needles, or other material with few weed seeds.

5. Don't water weeds—more than once

The only reason to ever water a weed is to make it easier to pull. A deep watering leaves the soil loose and moist, and weeds come out of the ground like feathers. If some weeds survive rake-thinning and the In-Row Weeder, don't let them hang around. When they get big enough to pull, water and grab them.

6. Block the wind

Plants lose water when they're in the path of a breeze or stiff wind. Just think of your laundry. Doesn't a wet towel hanging on the line dry a lot faster on a windy day? The wind makes a tremendous difference! If you can stop the breezes from hitting your plants, they'll hold on to their water supply longer.

7. Skip thirsty crops

Some vegetables require more than their share of water. When water supplies are low, avoid growing corn, melons, and potatoes. But greens, beets, carrots, turnips, and onions are "moisture-efficient" because most of the plant can be eaten. Other plants that can grow on modest amounts of moisture include peas, beans, sweet potatoes, and eggplant.

8. Let your tomatoes sprawl

Staking and pruning tomatoes during a drought exposes too much of the plant to the drying effects of the sun and wind. Let your tomatoes sprawl if dry weather hits. Instead of being up in the wind like a flag, the tomato leaves will shade the ground and keep it cooler, thus slowing evaporation.

9. Catch the rain

Use a rain barrel, some plastic pails, an old tub or whatever you have to catch the rain. Plants love natural rainfall, and though you can't water the whole garden from a rain barrel, you'd be surprised at how many small transplants and seedlings you can keep moist with rain barrel water.

10. Keep walkways narrow . . . and few

You'll water less unproductive empty space when it gets hot. Plus, narrow walkways mean a better "canopy of food" over your garden soil.

11. Grow a garden in the fall

Look past the dry spells of summer to a fall garden and have your seeds and plants ready. Most areas of the country have good fall rains, so often it's much easier to grow a super garden in the fall than to battle the heat and dryness of summer. Fall is a perfect time for greens because they need a steady supply of water *and* cool weather to taste their best.

12. Use shade

Many plants will grow well with as little as 4 or 5 hours of direct sunlight a day. In the shade they will lose a lot less water than if they were out in the burning sun. Peas, collards, cabbage, broccoli, lettuce, chard, turnips, and parsley are shade-loving vegetables. If you don't have natural shade areas for them, grow some. Leave two rows empty in the middle of your corn patch and plant your crops there.

13. When you water, do it right

1. Make sure your plants need water. The best indication is when you spot wilted plants in the morning. A little drooping of plant leaves is natural on a hot afternoon. Plants should perk up later.

2. Water until the soil is moist to a depth of 4 to 5 inches. Plants like a deep soaking so their roots can stretch way down into the soil to get water. The deeper the roots of your plants, the easier it will be for them to get through a dry spell.

14. Cultivate around plants before watering

A gentle, shallow cultivation loosens the soil around your plants so that water can soak in easily. Without a cultivation, the soil may be so hard and crusty that it sends water *running off* instead of *soaking in.*

15. Above all, add organic matter

A soil that is rich in organic matter will hold plenty of moisture. This is the key to surviving a drought—gardening in soil packed with decomposing organic matter and humus. Soils aren't too fussy about what type of organic matter they get—composted manure, kitchen scraps, leaves, lawn clippings, green manure crops . . . all will help your soil retain more moisture.

SIDE-DRESSING
Guarantees top nutrition

Many vegetables don't like a big serving of fertilizer at planting time. They prefer to take their plant food from the soil a little at a time.

Giving crops an extra boost of fertilizer is often called "side-dressing" or "top-dressing." Good side-dressings help crops grow evenly and smoothly—and help deliver better harvests.

People often ask me, "Is side-dressing really *necessary*?" Well, that depends. If you've mixed plenty of organic matter into your soil over the years and grow green manure crops like peas, beans, and buckwheat, chances are your soil is pretty rich in nutrients. As long as you add a little fertilizer to the soil before planting, your crops probably will do very well without side-dressing. But it's a good idea to side-dress corn and onions, two crops with big appetites.

On the other hand, if you're just starting to improve your soil by adding organic matter, side-dressings are important. For example, in a sandy soil with little organic matter, plant foods drain down through the soil and away from the roots of your crops. To keep crops growing smoothly, you'll probably need to side-dress.

My soil is sandy and even though it's always getting plenty of new organic matter mixed into it, I like to side-dress most of my crops. I want to get as much high-quality produce from my garden as I can.

Not every crop needs side-dressing. My peas and beans, greens such as lettuce and spinach, and my root crops grow fine when fertilized only at planting time. My carrots, beets, and turnips get a little extra bone meal fertilizer at planting time. This assures a good supply of phosphorus, the plant food that helps my root crops develop the best roots.

Plants signal when it's time to side-dress.

Most crops signal when they'd like to get a little more plant food. To read this sign, think of a plant's life cycle as having two stages.

During the *first stage,* a plant builds its foundation or support system for producing seeds, which is what plants are trying to do. It develops a network of strong roots and puts out more and more leaves. Then the plant stops work on the foundation, before setting out on the *second stage* of its life cycle: making seeds.

When the plant starts to blossom, it needs extra food to develop buds and blossoms, to set fruit, and to grow seed pods.

When I see clusters of blossoms on tomato plants, for example, I know the foundation work is over. The plants now want to produce and ripen tomatoes; to help them I give each plant a small bit of fertilizer.

There's a danger in fertilizing *before* plants give their signal. With tomatoes, early side-dressing often encourages the plant to spend extra time on the foundation, adding more roots and lush top growth. Extra time here only delays the second stage of growth, and that means the harvest will be later.

Side-dressing and equivalents

If you have good natural fertilizers on hand and want to use them instead of the complete fertilizer 5-10-10, here's how to substitute in the list of vegetables given on pages 158–159.

1 tablespoon complete commercial fertilizer (such as 5-10-10) equals:

- 2 handfuls good compost or

- 2 handfuls dehydrated manure or

- 1 to 2 tablespoons alfalfa meal.

Three ways to apply side-dressing

BANDING

With the corner of a hoe open a furrow 1 or 2 inches deep in a straight line next to a row of plants. Keep the furrow about 5 or 6 inches from the line of plants. Then put the fertilizer in the furrow and cover it with soil. It's important to cover any commercial fertilizer so the rain doesn't splash it up onto plant leaves. The nitrogen can burn the leaves and set the plants back.

CIRCLE THE PLANTS

With tomatoes, peppers, broccoli, and other transplanted crops, dig a shallow circular furrow around each plant. Sprinkle the fertilizer in evenly and cover it. Put this circle of plant food about 5 or 6 inches away from the plant stem. But if the plant is quite large, put it right around the outer leaves or "drip line" of the plant. There are many shallow feeder roots there so the fertilizer will move down into the soil with the next rain and be taken up quickly.

TOP-DRESSING

Sprinkle natural fertilizers such as alfalfa meal, dehydrated manure, or compost over wide rows. With chard, for example, I cut all the plants 1 inch above the ground and fertilize right in the seedbed to encourage quick, new tender growth. I scratch the fertilizer in with my In-Row Weeder and then water.

SIDEDRESSING GUIDE

I measure fertilizer in teaspoons and tablespoons

I remember side-dressing a row of peppers with a pinch of complete fertilizer, and it helped me to get a great harvest of peppers. The next year I thought, "Well, this year I'll give the plants two pinches." It worked again, and I got a very fine harvest. The next season I said to myself, "Well, I got such good results from those two pinches of fertilizer, why not try even more?" Well, that's where I got my comeuppance! The extra fertilizer hurt the crop. I got plenty of green, but no peppers to eat. Since then I've always been cautious with side-dressing. It's much better to *under-fertilize* than to overdo it. I recommend side-dressing amounts in teaspoons and table-spoons. Keep a measuring spoon next to that bag of fertilizer.

BROCCOLI

Side-dress when the head begins to form. It may be only the size of a fifty-cent piece when you notice it, but go ahead and side-dress. Amount needed: 1 to 2 tablespoons complete fertilizer per plant.

BRUSSELS SPROUTS

I usually side-dress brussels sprouts when I harvest the first small marble-size sprouts. Amount: 1 table-spoon complete fertilizer per plant.

CABBAGE

The best time to side-dress cabbage is when it starts to form a head. In my wide rows of cabbage, that's when the leaves of the plants are about to completely shade the row. Amount needed: 1 tablespoon of complete fertilizer per plant.

CAULIFLOWER

Because cauliflower heads form so fast, side-dressing when you first see the head usually won't help. I side-dress when the plant's leaves seem to be as big as they're going to get, usually 5 or 6 weeks after transplanting. Amount: 1 to 2 tablespoons complete fertilizer per plant.

CHARD

To keep my wide rows of chard productive all season, I side-dress right after harvesting "crew cut" style. I cut the plants 1 inch above the ground and side-dress with a natural fertilizer such as dehydrated manure. Amount: 1 handful for each foot of wide row 16 inches wide.

CORN

Because corn takes more plant food than most other crops, I side-dress it twice. The first time it's about knee-high, the second time it starts to tassle and silk forms on the stalks. Fertilizer helps to make good ears. Amount: about 1 tablespoon complete fertilizer per plant or about 3 cups per 25 feet of row each side-dressing.

CUCUMBERS, MELONS, AND WINTER SQUASH

These vine crops should be fertilized before they start to spread out and run. At this point they stand up straight and tall. It's easy to get the fertilizer close to the plants where the main roots are. Amount: 1 tablespoon complete fertilizer per plant.

EGGPLANT

When blossoms or first small eggplants are visible, apply side-dressing. Amount: 1 tablespoon complete fertilizer per plant.

LEEKS

Leeks don't give a signal for side-dressing. Side-dress them when they're 8 to 12 inches tall. Pack several big handfuls of compost high around each stem. This provides a slow release of nutrients and shades or blanches the stalks somewhat so they will get white and tender. Amount: 2 to 3 handfuls compost mounded around each plant.

OKRA

Side-dress when the plant blossoms. If you have a long harvest of okra, you can side-dress again about a month after the first time. Amount per side-dressing: 1 tablespoon complete fertilizer per plant or 3 cups per 25 feet of row.

ONIONS

Don't try to follow the rule about side-dressing at blossom time with onions because they don't blossom until their second season. I side-dress them when they are to 6 to 8 inches tall and every couple of weeks after that until the bulbs start to expand. Onions can take quite a bit of fertilizer. I give them plenty because the size of the onion bulb is determined by how much green top the plant has. Bulbs are made with energy stored in the green leaves. The more green top I encourage, the bigger the bulbs I'll be able to harvest. Amount: 2 to 3 cups complete fertilizer per 10 feet of wide row 16 inches wide. Don't fertilize onions if their tops have started to fall.

PEPPERS

Peppers are very sensitive to fertilizer. They need it in small doses only at blossom time. Amount: no more than 1 tablespoon complete fertilizer per plant.

POLE BEANS

Beans usually don't need any side-dressing. But in long-season areas down South, side-dressing will keep plants in top shape. Side-dress within a week or so after your first picking and every 3 or 4 weeks after that. Amount: 1 teaspoon complete fertilizer per plant.

POTATOES

Side-dress potatoes about 6 or 7 weeks after planting. This is when some of the plants start to blossom and when it's time to hill the plants for the last time. Side-dress *before* hilling so you can cover the fertilizer with soil as you hill. Amount: 1 tablespoon complete fertilizer per plant or 3 cups per 25 feet of row.

SUMMER SQUASH AND ZUCCHINI

I side-dress when I see flower buds or blossoms. Amount: 1 to 2 tablespoons complete fertilizer per plant.

TOMATOES

I side-dress when I see the first blossoms. Sometimes I wait until I see the first small green tomatoes to be sure the extra fertilizer goes toward nourishing the fruits. Amount: 1 to 2 tablespoons complete fertilizer per plant.

Compost

The free wonder-working plant food

Composting is one of the most important things we gardeners can do. A good compost pile recycles vegetable scraps and other wastes from the garden and yard. We can "harvest" some *free* fertilizer for the garden, save money, and lessen our need for outside fertilizers. Composting also helps the community because it reduces the amount of garbage other people have to deal with. One of my dreams is to see every household in a town with a compost pile.

Good compost makes excellent fertilizer because in addition to some important nitrogen, phosphorus, and potassium, it often contains trace elements you don't ordinarily find in commercial fertilizer. With a wide variety of materials (coffee grounds, wastes from fruits and vegetables, wood ashes, etc.) in your compost pile, you're apt to get a good sampling of the secondary and minor nutrients needed for plant growth. You shouldn't have

any worries about deficiencies of trace minerals in your soil.

The best compost pile will heat up and start to decompose the material in it *quickly*. Research shows that the longer a compost pile sits, the less useful it will be for your garden. What happens is that the nutrients leach steadily through the pile into the ground. Later, when you put the compost in the garden, it hasn't got much fertilizer zing to it. If you compost the way I do, the pile will start to heat up in a day or two and you can start using the material in about 15 days. You won't lose much fertilizer through leaching.

In the decomposition process, a compost pile gets pretty hot. On a cool fall morning I can see the steam rising from the center of my compost pile. A pile that is decomposing well, or "cooking," will produce temperatures of 140-160°F. At these temperatures weed seeds and many plant disease organisms are killed. But high heat is not crucial; a good compost pile will break down material at much lower temperatures.

Compost piles rarely have a bad smell and shouldn't attract pests if you never put meat scraps or bones in the pile. Odors can occur when a pile is too big or packed too tightly and air can't circulate. Provide a good flow of air into and through the pile.

All compost piles need an activator— alfalfa meal is the best

To get a compost pile working, it's essential to have several layers of an activator throughout the pile. An activator is a source of both nitrogen and protein—ingredients that help all the various micro-organisms and bacteria break down compost material. Most old compost directions tell you to mix in horse or cow manure as the activator; today that's impractical for many people.

I've found *alfalfa meal* to be about the cheapest, quickest-acting activator. If you can't find any at your garden or feed store, look in the supermarket for "Litter Green," a kitty litter product that's 100 percent alfalfa meal.

Every time I add new material to the compost pile, I dust it thoroughly with alfalfa meal and moisten the pile a little. Alfalfa meal is an excellent source of nitrogen and protein. It is made from alfalfa hay and is usually 14 to 16 percent protein.

If you have had problems getting your compost pile to work, dust the pile with alfalfa meal as you add material. It not only improves the performance of a compost pile, but also cuts down any odor.

Alfalfa meal is the best way to break down a big pile of leaves quickly. Leaves stored in a big bin or stashed behind the garage may take *years* to break down. For this reason many people avoid putting them in their compost pile. Mix a thin layer of alfalfa meal between 4-inch layers of leaves, keep the pile moist, and you'll get a rich crumbly leaf compost in a hurry.

When you haven't got alfalfa meal . . .

Once I was invited to give a talk on composting and to start a model compost pile at a school about 2 hours from my home. When the day of the talk came, I loaded up my truck with everything I needed for the demonstration and drove to the school. As I was setting up my materials before the talk I realized I had forgotten my alfalfa meal compost activator. I rushed up to the teacher who had invited me. "Do you happen to have any alfalfa meal around here at the college?" I asked. "I've got to have it for the compost pile."

"What's alfalfa meal?" he asked.

"Never mind," I said. "I'm going to drive into town for a minute. I'll be back in a hurry."

I raced down into the village and dashed into the grocery store. There wasn't any alfalfa meal kitty litter anywhere on the shelves, so I got the next best thing, a big bag of high-protein dog food. Yes, dog food! It's a natural activator for a compost pile, too, because of all the protein in it.

Back at the school, it soon was time to talk about activators. So I told the students my story and explained why I was sprinkling dog food over the layers of compost material. A dog was standing at the edge of the students. I don't think he accepted my explanation too well. To him, I was just throwing good dog food away.

Besides alfalfa meal and dog food, good activators include barnyard manure, natural products such as bone meal, cottonseed meal, blood meal, and good, rich garden soil. If you can get some of these materials, keep them handy. Anytime you add to your compost pile, dust the works with a little activator.

1. Set up a wire collector

Choose a well-drained spot, preferably a shady one that's not too far from the house or garden. It's nice to be near a water source, too. Set up a wire collector for your pile. I use a strong turkey wire with a 2- or 4-inch mesh and a height of 3 feet. Cut off a 9-foot section of mesh and shape it into a circle, fastening the ends together. If you want, you can loosen the soil up a little where the collector sits. This will help drainage.

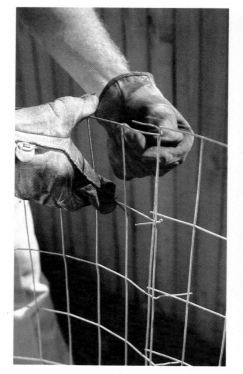 

HERE'S MY EASY RECIPE FOR

4. Do it again!

Repeat steps 2 and 3 by adding the same amounts of organic matter and meal as before.

5. Sprinkle with water

Moisten the pile thoroughly. Compost piles that don't work are usually too dry or too wet. The material should be moist but not soaked. In warm, dry weather you may have to water the pile every 3 or 4 days to keep it in good working condition.

6. Keep the center loose

Never compact the center of the pile—keep it loose. The composting process depends on the ability of the air, water, and alfalfa meal to contact all the material as completely as possible. Good circulation is a must. A good compost pile is a balance of thirds: one third air, one third material, and one third moisture.

7. Fill the collector

Whenever material becomes available, repeat steps 2 through 6 until the collector is full. Keep everything loose and never tightly packed down.

2. Make the first layer

Loosely place leaves, hay, straw, or other good compost materials in the bottom of the collector in a layer about 2 inches thick.

3. Add protein material

Sprinkle a large handful of alfalfa meal or other protein-rich meal over the first layer. Dust the entire surface. This material is often called an "activator."

QUICK HOME COMPOST

8. Turn the pile in a week

If the pile is made correctly, the temperature should reach 140 to 150° F. within 2 or 3 days. After a week or so of heating and decomposing, it's time to turn the pile.

Lift off the wire collector, set it up beside the pile, and then fork all the material back into it. Put the outside, drier material in the center of the new pile. If the material seems *too* dry, moisten it. The heating process will start up again. It should be ready to use—but still coarse—in 15 days.

Making precious compost count

I like to use compost before it is totally broken down. I'd much rather have a coarser compost with a lot of small, loose bits of organic matter than a fine compost, because a coarser compost still has the ability to hold plenty of moisture once it's worked into the soil. I like that.

I have three basic ways to use compost.

1. As an ingredient in my **seed-starting mixture** in early spring. I used to have a large shed where I kept a compost pile working for most of the winter. I found that a little compost worked into my commercial seed-starting mix really helped. The nutrients in compost are not concentrated, so tender seedlings and plants were never burned.

I don't have that shed anymore. Instead, I let some late fall compost work down to a much finer consistency than usual. Then I put 10 or 12 shovelfuls in a box or plastic bag and bring it into my cellar where I start plants under lights in late winter. The compost is well broken down, of course, and has no odor so it's no problem keeping it in the cellar. (I keep the bag open at the top, though, so it can breathe and stay odor-free.)

2. As a **starter fertilizer** for transplants. When I set out tomatoes, peppers, broccoli, head lettuce, and other transplants, I place a big handful of compost under each plant. The compost provides a light dose of fertilizer close to the roots, and it holds moisture well so the plants are less likely to go thirsty. When the last bits of organic matter in the compost break down, a little extra fertilizer is released.

3. As a **side-dressing** or top-dressing for plants through the season. I use compost on my onions, tomatoes, head lettuce, and pole beans, for example. I usually don't have enough compost for my big areas of sweet corn, potatoes, and winter squash.

Better composting ideas

- You may want to safeguard your compost collector against dogs, raccoons, or other animals, though usually it's not necessary. Put a liner of hardware cloth (¼-inch by ¼-inch wire screening) around the inside of the wire collector and create a lid for the top.

- You can start a compost at any time of year. I start a couple of new ones in early summer because there's a lot of food coming out of my garden then and that means there are carrot tops, potato peelings, and all sorts of goodies for composting.

- Commercial fertilizer, such as 5-10-10, will not help activate a compost pile. It has nitrogen, but the important protein is missing. Natural activators such as alfalfa meal have the best nitrogen-protein power to activate a pile.

- If you're in doubt about whether to add a certain material to the compost pile, ask yourself this question, "Will an earthworm eat it?" If yes, it's okay to use. If no, don't add it to your pile.

Sheet Composting

The no-fuss compost method

For large quantities of organic matter, such as leaves, grass clippings, and garden residues, don't go to the trouble of making a compost pile if you have a good roto-tiller.

Scatter the material to be composted over your garden area and till it into the soil. This is known as sheet composting.

It's the simplest way to compost organic matter. The leaves and plant wastes will rot quickly, since tilling chops them into fine pieces which are easy for soil life to work on.

Sheet composting has a big advantage over pile composting. Compost piles lose nutrients to leaching before they can be used in the garden. With sheet composting all the nutrients go into the soil.

There are a few things to watch out for when sheet composting. Be careful about using materials that could contain weed seeds, such as weedy mulches and manures. Don't overdo it when you add materials that decay very slowly, such as sawdust, pine needles, or bark. They may tie up the nitrogen in the soil for a long time.

Don't use any plant material that is severely diseased, and never use anything that an earthworm won't eat or that has been sprayed with herbicides.

Trench composting is ideal for kitchen garbage

Another way to compost is the trench method, which is excellent for disposing of kitchen wastes. Dig a trench across your garden, either by hand or with a tiller. Every time you have kitchen garbage, dump it in one section of the trench and rake dirt over it. (Don't dump meat scraps or bones because they attract animals.)

When the trench is filled, till or turn the row thoroughly to mix the composted garbage with the soil. Then start another trench.

You'll be surprised how quickly the garbage in the trenches will be decomposed and digested by soil organisms.

If it's close to planting time, I don't recommend planting a root crop immediately over the trench because a few parasites or undesirable bacteria might have been present in the garbage. It's safe to plant leafy and cole crops.

A few summers ago I taught a short course on gardening for the University of Vermont. The classes were held at my test gardens. During a discussion about root crops, Willie, one of the students, said, "Dick, I grow real nice carrots, but I don't like them too much. I can hardly eat them; they seem so woody."

"How big do you grow them?" I asked.

Willie smiled, "Oh, they get real good size. I've got nice loose soil for them."

I decided it was time for our morning walk through the gardens. I stopped the class near a wide row of carrots. "Willie, let's pick some to munch on, okay?" I said.

"Sure," he replied, "as long as they're not as woody as mine."

Together we bent over the row, found some of the darkest green tops, and reached down to pull some carrots. They were not much thicker or longer than my index finger. "They're so small," Willie said.

"Don't knock them 'till you try 'em," I told him.

He brushed off a few and started eating. "They're not woody," he exclaimed. "They're sweet and crisp! I never thought carrots this small could be worth much."

Small is beautiful, I told Willie and the class. To me, the whole point of gardening is to have the longest possible harvest of the best-tasting vegeta-bles. That's one reason why I plant as many crops as I can in wide rows, and why I start harvesting as soon as there's something big enough to eat in the row. Why let vegetables grow past their prime eating stage?

Small vegetables taste great; they are tender, and because they are young and growing fast, bugs, diseases, and animal pests have practically no time to bother them.

In my gardening method, early harvesting of small vegetables is important. With wide rows I must start pulling or picking vegetables in the row as soon as I can. By doing so, I thin the row. As plants develop in a wide row they need more growing space, extra food, and more water. Without regular thinning, too many plants would be deprived of these, and the harvest would be disappointing.

When I pull my first beet greens, for example, there are only thumb-sized beets on the bottom. The first cabbages from my wide rows weigh only a pound or two. From the *Iceberg* lettuce row, I cut heads that haven't begun to firm up. I pull many onions when they are just pickling size, no fatter than a quarter. I cut spinach when the biggest leaves are only 3 or 4 inches long.

When there's something big enough to eat, I go after it.

Zucchini tastes best when picked small . . .

. . . and the same is true for okra.

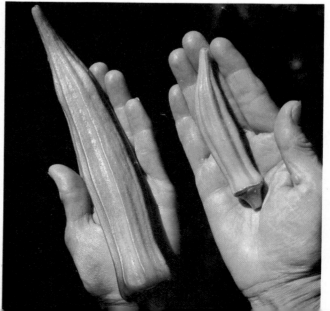

Pick, pick, pick

Plants have a purpose in life—to produce seeds. Before producing seeds, however, they produce their "fruit," and this is where the gardener steps in. With many vegetables, as long as you can keep a plant from making mature seeds, it will continue growing fruit to try and reproduce itself. This means the more vegetables you pick, the more some plants will produce. And, of course, this means a larger and longer harvest.

To prove it, try this experiment: plant two zucchini (or cucumber) seeds or plants near each other. When the zucchini or cucumbers appear, harvest from only *one plant*. Pick off every zucchini or cucumber when it gets 4 to 6 inches long. After 6 weeks of harvesting from that one plant, I bet you'll have harvested 25 or so little zucchini or cucumbers. After 6 weeks, stop harvesting and let the remaining fruit mature. Let the zucchini or cucumbers on the other plant mature also.

After all the fruits on both plants are mature, count them. The untouched plant will have 6 to 10 zucchini or cucumbers on it. The other plant—the one that's given you 25 already—will also have 6 to 10 on it.

Harvest all ready snap beans to keep plants productive.

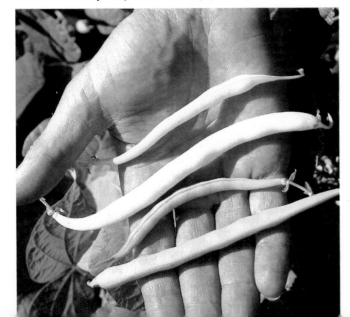

You can see how harvesting the vegetable when it's young lengthens the fruit-producing life of the plant. *Not* harvesting permits the plant to fulfill its normal life cycle, making and maturing seeds, and then closing down the shop.

Once you start picking beans, broccoli, peas, as well as zucchini and cucumbers, you shouldn't stop. Even if you can't eat it all, harvest anyway. It's the only way to keep the plants sensing they have *not* finished their life cycles. They'll keep trying, and producing.

If you have too much produce, sell it, give it away to friends and neighbors, or put it in your compost pile. The important thing is to keep the plant in the productive stage. You'll be glad you did later in the season when other folks' crops have petered out.

Remember to cut greens for a second and third harvest

I force many of my greens to give me a second and third harvest. I never pick only the outside leaves of my lettuce, spinach, chard, or mustard. They're the oldest and toughest on a plant. Instead, I give the row a clean cut, slicing the plants about 1 inch above the ground. This encourages the plants to send up new tender growth and to try again to develop seedpods. For the harvest, I have a pleasing combination of young, tender leaves from the center of the plant mixed with the older ones.

With some varieties of leaf lettuce, such as *Oak Leaf*, I can easily get three or four cuttings of young, tasty lettuce. Heck, if you have 4 or 5 feet of wide row lettuce and harvest it properly, a family of four can't keep up with it.

Can or freeze at prime time

A friend of mine once said, "Putting up second-rate vegetables means they'll be third-rate when you eat them." I agree. If you are canning or freezing, pick only the best vegetables, ones that are reaching the peak of tenderness and flavor. Process them immediately. One reason why home-preserved foods taste so much better than store-bought is the short time between harvesting and processing. Commercial processors just aren't as quick as we are.

We freeze a lot of corn at our house. We pick ears that are just shy of full ripeness because we don't want to freeze corn that has "started downhill." We pick our corn at about 4 in the afternoon when the ears have the highest sugar content and process them right away. Incidentally, the best-tasting corn varieties are the late ones.

For our many jars of pickles, Jan insists on young, small, unblemished cucumbers. We pick them early in the morning when they are still firm and crisp, before the sun and heat cause them to soften up slightly.

Morning is also the best time to harvest chard and beet greens for preserving. The leaves are crisp, the plants have a lot of moisture, and they are most tender.

We freeze our snap beans when they are pencil-size and very tender. They keep their flavor much better than older, fatter beans which seem very bland after being frozen.

Peas need quick processing. Because a big pea patch can take a while to harvest, it may be tempting to pick them one day and freeze them the next. Don't do it; the quality will go down. You can keep them in a plastic bag in a cool basement or in the refrigerator for a few hours, but you should try to take care of them right away.

A HARVESTING GOSPEL

- **When there is something big enough to eat, go after it.**
- **Small is beautiful, tasty, and tender, too.**
- **Cut greens so they'll come back—again and again.**
- **Keep picking! Don't let plants go to seed.**
- **For canning and freezing, harvest only the best—and at the right time of day.**

SUCCESSION CROPS

Bare soil in the garden during the growing season is lost opportunity and an eyesore. Whenever the sun's rays hit bare soil I lose the chance to capture some of that precious solar energy in food-producing or soil-improving plants.

In my gardening method, I keep things as green as possible all year long. When one of my early-planted crops such as peas, spinach, cauliflower, or head lettuce is finished, I work plant leftovers into the soil and sow a follow-up or "succession" crop.

Succession crops have a lot going for them

1. There's nothing more satisfying than getting a new crop of beans or broccoli when other gardeners are wishing they had some to pick. There's a very successful market gardener near me who plants corn as a succession crop and has all the end-of-season business to himself.

2. There's more organic matter for earthworms and soil life when this second (or third) crop is turned under.

3. The leaf canopy over the soil is restored, shading the soil, cutting down on evaporation, and blocking out weeds.

4. Succession crops of carrots, beets, turnips, and rutabagas usually mature late in the season when the root cellar is *cool,* and it's the best time to store them.

5. Pests and diseases may be avoided completely. For example, my first succession crops are planted in early summer when the weather and soils are warm. I know that the troublesome root maggots prefer cool soils so they are deep in the soil and won't be a problem. Diseases that thrive in cool soils, such as seed rot, are no problem either.

6. Succession crops get extra attention and "TLC." In early spring everybody is in a rush to get the soil tilled and crops in. But later, when it's time to plant succession crops, the pace is slower and more relaxed. I can take the time to pamper the new crop and get it off to a healthy start.

(Top) I've turned my early peas into the ground to plant a succession crop of wide row beans. (Bottom) There's plenty of summer remaining for these beans to grow and produce. Note how the soil is shaded even though the plants are still quite young.

Getting seeds and plants to grow in hot, dry weather

The only things I worry about with succession crops are getting seeds to germinate in hot, dry weather and keeping transplants watered so they'll root quickly with no moisture stress.

When it's hot and dry and the soil doesn't have much moisture, seeds can *start* to germinate only to *run out* of moisture. That kills them.

To avoid this, plant seeds a little bit deeper, an extra ¼ to ½ inch for small seeds, an extra ½ to ¾ inch for larger seeds. The very top of the soil may be dry, but you'd be amazed at how well seeds use the small amounts of moisture beneath the soil surface. Also, I time my succession crops so that they're sown just before or just after a rain. With clay soil it's wise to plant before a rain.

Another trick is to put a very light mulch over the row after planting. I use hay—as weed-free as I can get it—or a dusting of peat moss. The mulch should be light enough for the seedlings to grow through. Once you put mulch over the seedbed you don't want to take it off—that's a good way to pull up a lot of plants.

Transplant crops of head lettuce, broccoli, and cauliflower figure heavily in my succession plans. Since the weather is so good when I sow them, I grow them outside. I start some in a small section of the garden, but many others get their start in seed flats or pyramid planters which I park in a partially shady spot.

After harvesting, turn what's left of your crop into the ground

When you have finished harvesting a crop, work it into the ground right away—the greener it is the better it is for your soil. Leaving crop residues to wither away above ground is bad policy. They become a refuge for pests and disease organisms which could trouble you later. Green plants are the most beneficial for earthworms and other soil life, and are the easiest to digest and break down. Tough, old plants are the hardest to work into the soil.

If you have a good tiller, you can put crops back into the soil in just a few minutes. I make several passes over the area to chop up the residues and to mix them deep into the soil. This way they'll decompose faster.

Morning is the best time for tilling or spading crops. The plants have the most moisture in them early in the day and they cut a lot easier—even vining crops which are a problem for some gardeners to put under.

If you work with hand tools, use a long-handled, round-pointed shovel for spading. Chop up the plant remains a bit, turn them into the soil about 4 to 6 inches deep, and then drive the shovel down to chop them some more. Small pieces of green matter will break down best.

Wide row crops are easier to turn under than those in single rows because the soil is loose and moist in the row. No one ever tramps on it and the leaves provide a shade mulch to hold water in. To spade under a wide row of spinach or peas right after the harvest is hardly any work at all.

My tiller can handle all crop leftovers in the garden, including cornstalks. But if your machine can't, don't strain yourself trying to get the residues under. Sometimes you can pull heavy residues like cauliflower, broccoli, or early corn, or mow them down, or somehow chop them up before tackling them with your tiller.

Why soils need extra energy for succession crops

I usually plant my succession crop within 2 or 3 days of tilling under the old crop. Fertilizer at planting time is very important for succession crops in order for bacteria and other organisms in the soil to break down and decompose the old crop. They need nitrogen to do their thing. The more plant material turned into the soil, the more nitrogen they'll require. Sometimes, if their nitrogen needs are great, the soil organisms can claim or "tie up" much of the nitrogen in the top part of the soil. If you plant seeds at this time, they'll sprout but may stall for lack of nitrogen. Another reason you need more plant foods in the soil is weather. As your first crop grows, rains carry more and more of your early season fertilizer down into the ground, out of the root zone of plants.

I mix in 1 to 2 pounds of 5-10-10 or 3 to 4 pounds of dehydrated manure for every 50 square feet of succession planting area. This will satisfy the needs of soil organisms breaking down the old plant matter. And it will give the new crop important nourishment. Later, as the material in the soil decomposes further, extra plant food will be released.

If the crop will grow where I tilled in *peas* or *beans*, it's a little different. These two crops are special. They are legumes which add nitrogen to the soil by taking it from the air and fixing it onto little nodules attached to their roots. Because peas and beans collect some nitrogen and add it to the soil, follow-up crops don't need much extra fertilizer. About half the recommended fertilizer is sufficient in these areas.

PLANTING A MID-SEASON
SUCCESSION CROP

After digging in the old crop, be sure to add a little fertilizer to the planting area because soil organisms need nitrogen to break down the newly-added organic matter.

Rake the fertilizer into the top few inches of soil and then smooth out a seedbed before sowing seeds—the smoother the better.

Mark your row with a string, sprinkle the seed down and then tamp seeds firmly into soil—important for quick germination.

After tamping the seeds cover them with the proper amount of soil. In summer, seeds may require a little extra soil covering because the soil surface can dry out quickly.

MY FALL GARDEN

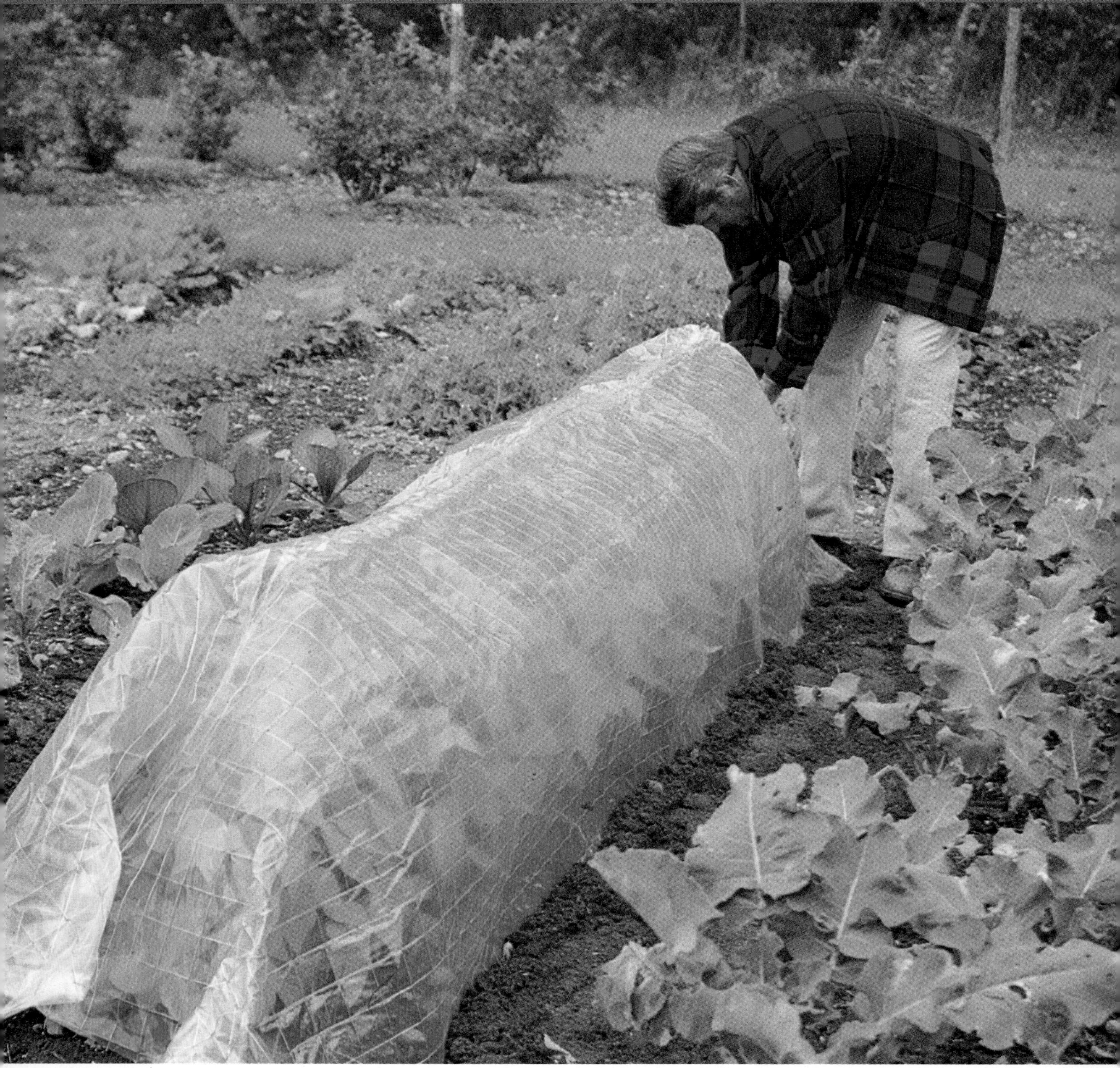

Fall. The weather cools off. Leaves start to drop from the trees. Rains become more frequent. Time for school, football, the World Series, raking leaves. Prices for fresh produce start to climb again in stores. Out in the garden the soil is moist and rich in organic matter, and there's no better time than fall to have a productive vegetable garden.

Most folks put their gardens to bed too early. I've been growing more and more crops later and later in the year, and I'm amazed at their productivity, flavor, and high quality.

Vegetables growing in the fall have everything they could ask for: soil with organic matter from summer crops spread throughout, plenty of moisture, a refreshing absence of insects, soil pests, and diseases; and cool temperatures which promote tender, tasty growth.

The fall garden has special satisfactions for me. It keeps me from having to go to the store for produce, especially lettuce and fresh greens. It gives me more time to tinker with my grow tunnels and cold frames, to try to extend the harvest of some crops further than ever. Now I pick broccoli, cauliflower, brussels sprouts, lettuce, kale, and radishes right up until the ground freezes hard. (Kale and brussels sprouts will last even *longer* than that!) It's kind of fun being known as the local gardener with the earliest and the latest vegetables.

A little planning will help

Timing is important in the fall garden. Most crops yield best if they attain most of their growth before it gets very cold. The "days to maturity" information on seed packets usually applies to spring-planted crops, most of which grow faster as the weather warms. In the fall, however, changes in day length, angle and intensity of the sun, and temperature add a week or more to the time most vegetables need to mature. This is important if you're growing broccoli, cauliflower, and cabbage, which need time to form decent-sized heads. It's less important with root crops, lettuce, and other greens which can be harvested when they are small and tasty.

FALL PLANTING DATES

Fall harvest	Weeks to plant before average first frost
Beans	7-10
Beets	8-12
Broccoli *	6-8
Brussels sprouts *	10-12
Cabbage *	6-8
Carrots	8-12
Cauliflower *	6-8
Chinese cabbage	6-8
Collards *	6-10
Head lettuce *	8-10
Kale	4-10
Lettuce	4-6
Mustard	6-10
Peas	6-10
Radishes	2-8
Spinach	4-6
Tomatoes	8-12

* Dates given indicate time to transplant seedlings. (These can be started earlier directly in the garden, or in flats or planters outside the garden.)

173

Fall garden know-how

Start transplants in the garden

Three or four weeks before the planting dates for cabbage, broccoli, head lettuce, and cauliflower, I sprinkle their seeds in short wide rows out in the garden. It's an easy (and cheap) way to grow a lot of transplants in a very small space.

For my fall garden, I choose the best-looking plants, dig them out of the short wide rows, and put them in another row with more room around them.

Seed wide rows as in spring

There's no adjustment to make in fall planting of seeds. Use the same broadcasting and thinning techniques I described earlier for wide rows. Include some radishes with your greens and root crops.

Try warm-season crops

Most people think only cool-weather vegetables will grow in the fall garden. Wrong. Even in Vermont, I harvest new crops of snap beans and *Pixie* tomatoes from the fall garden. Gardeners in more southern parts of the country look forward to growing their tomatoes, beans, and peppers in fall weather. Their summers are too hot, causing many blossoms to drop off these plants.

For the latest snap beans, use a "grow tunnel"

Where I live, nobody picks fresh snap beans in October—except at my place. Beans are so sensitive that I have to be good at protecting them from the cold. Once they start to blossom, I build a large heat tunnel over the row. It's important to keep some air space between the plants and the plastic; when the leaves press against the plastic, the cold is conducted through. The beans are slower to develop than in summer, of course, but they are still beautifully crisp and tender.

Pixie *suckers also can be potted for indoor growing (top). Water plants well and keep them out of direct sun for a few days.*

Grow *Pixies* from suckers

Late in the year tomatoes from a young *Pixie* plant taste a whole lot better than those from a tired ol' *Better Boy* that's been producing all summer.

To start plants, I cut 5- or 6-inch suckers from established *Pixie* plants in mid-summer and set them in water for an hour. Then I strip off the lower leaves and stick the suckers a foot apart in a row. I water the heck out of them for 3 or 4 days. They root quickly and by early fall many new clusters of tomatoes will be ripening. To make them last as long as possible, I cover them with light cloth when frost is possible, or I erect a tall plastic tunnel over them after planting and keep it there gathering heat as long as the plants are producing.

Broccoli, brussels sprouts, kale and onions were part of this last fall garden harvest Dec. 12 in Vermont.

Kale is the hardiest and perhaps the most nutritious fall garden crop

I like to plant a lot of kale. To harvest, I break off the outside leaves (the small ones are the most tender) and leave the center bud alone. The plants will grow taller and send out new leaves. Kale is noted for its high vitamin C and A content.

GREEN MANURES

How to turn heavy, hard clay and lifeless sandy soils into a garden like mine with green manure crops

My garden soil didn't start out the way it looks in pictures. It was poor and gravelly and didn't have much organic matter in it. Rain and fertilizer just washed down through it and seedbeds dried out very quickly. The soil needed lots and lots of organic matter. And I provided it by growing green manure crops and turning them under.

I've always believed that you can garden in any soil and I believe you can improve any soil, too. You can't do it overnight, of course, because nature doesn't work that way. Mixing one huge pile of organic matter into your soil might help a bit in the short run, but it won't last.

Organic matter is the key to creating a rich soil, but you must realize that it is always *temporary*. From the moment you mix organic matter in the soil, you start to lose it. Earthworms and countless other soil creatures start breaking it down into usable plant food and soil-improving humus. In warm weather they'll work through organic matter in no time, and if you don't have another helping ready for them, they'll die or leave your garden in search of food elsewhere. Once you've got a big crew of earthworms and bustling soil life working in your soil, don't lay them off. *Feed your soil and soil life with a series of green manure crops.*

Facing page: Organic matter feeds the soil. Part of my garden is always growing a patch of nutrient-rich green manure.

Top: I have a small test plot of clover. This is an excellent green manure crop, but because it's slow to establish itself and needs a full season or two for best results, I don't recommend it for most home gardens.

Bottom: Like clover, alfalfa takes a season or two to get established. A small, permanent area is good for growing some of your own mulch.

What is a green manure crop, and why is it so important to the garden?

If you've harvested peas and turned under the plants while they were still green and tender, you have put green manure in your soil. Any green plant spaded or tilled back into the soil can be called green manure. Some green manure crops are grown just to be plowed back into the soil while they are still green and rich in organic matter. Alfalfa, buckwheat, and annual ryegrass are a few examples. There are many others.

You might hear green manure crops being called "cover crops" or "catch crops." These names indicate two of the jobs of a green manure crop:

1. To *cover* bare soil at the end of the season. This protects it from erosion over the winter.

2. To *catch* fertilizer and moisture that have leached deep into the soil. Deep roots of a green manure crop retrieve nutrients that would otherwise be lost.

Nine Great Benefits

1.

Green manure is easier to use as a fertilizer and soil conditioner than barnyard manure. Heck, I'd rather stand knee-deep in green manure than ankle-deep in the "cow kind" any day.

A green manure crop might start out from as little as 5 or 10 pounds of buckwheat seed. Six weeks after planting you may have 2 or 3 tons of plant matter to work into the soil.

Animal manure as a fertilizer and soil conditioner is expensive if you don't have your own animals. It's usually full of weed seeds and hard on the back to lug around, spread, and till in. Besides, it takes a lot of animal manure to add a sizeable amount of fertilizer to the soil.

2.

Green manure crops are especially helpful to lifeless sandy soils. After a few crops, sandy soil will hold nutrients and water much better. Instead of washing right through the soil, the nutrients are trapped by the organic matter very close to the surface of the soil where plant roots can get to them. This trapping action saves on fertilizer—especially nitrogen—and on watering.

3.

Green manure crops provide a
tremendous amount of organic
matter for earthworms and bacteria in the soil. These soil creatures break down the organic
matter into elements to be used
by the next crop. Some acids
react with soil minerals to produce extra nutrients. A green
manure crop is a feast for your
soil.

4.

Roto-tilled into heavy, clay soils,
green manure crops improve and
condition the soil. The organic
matter wedges its way between
tight clay soil particles and that
allows air, water, and roots to
penetrate better. Buckwheat, one
of my favorite green manure
crops, is exceptionally good at
this. Clay soil with a lot of buckwheat decomposing in it won't
bake down and crust over as
much, which makes it easier to
till.

5.

When you cover the soil with a green manure crop, you control the loss of topsoil by water erosion and winds. If you have a large garden space, you may not want (or have the time) to plant it all to vegetables. Plant any unused sections to green manure crops and protect the soil there. It takes little time to plant a crop and till it in at the proper time.

I strongly recommend keeping as much vegetable-growing area as possible covered during the winter.

6.

Green manure crops can provide free fertilizer. Some of my favorite green manure crops, such as peas and beans, are legumes. Legumes are nitrogen factories. They take nitrogen from the air and fix it to their roots in little nodules. Tilling these crops into the soil replenishes much of the nitrogen that is removed by growing other vegetables. Legumes can provide two or three times more nitrogen than grasses and other green manure crops.

7.

Fast-growing green manure crops such as buckwheat smother weeds. Buckwheat can cover the soil like a tarp in just a few days after sprouting. The leaves are so close together that sunlight can't nourish any weeds. Two or three of these crops in succession will beat almost any weed problem, including the most persistent perennials.

8.

Green manure crops act as an insulating blanket over the soil. They keep the ground cooler in summer and warmer in winter. A green manure blanket covering the soil in fall and winter is especially important because earthworms are busiest and most numerous at this time. If you can keep them working close to the surface, they'll produce a rich store of nutrients for next year's crops located right where young plants can reach it. But if you leave the soil bare it will freeze early near the surface. This will force the earthworms down deep where it's still warm enough for them to work. The fertilizer produced down there will not be of much use to your early crops.

The best end-of-season blanket crop is annual ryegrass. It grows fast in the cool weather of fall, and won't be killed back until a hard freeze hits. Then it will lay like a thick mat through the winter.

9.

Green manure roots are "go-getters." They reach deep into the subsoil (where vegetable roots hardly ever reach) and recapture valuable nutrients. These plant foods pass through the roots, up into the plants, and wind up back in the topsoil when the crop is turned under.

What happens to the extensive deep roots when you till the plant in just 6 or 8 inches deep in the soil? The deeper roots will decay and contribute organic matter to the cause, and plenty of it. Another bonus: they leave paths for worms and vegetable roots to follow.

Peas

Beans

Buckwheat

Annual ryegrass

Why I like these four green manure crops best of all

Some green manure crops are easier to grow and work *better* than others. In my years of testing and improving backyard gardening methods, I've done a lot of work with green manure crops, both at my home in Vermont and at several test sites around the country.

In order to recommend to home gardeners which green manure crops are best, I've grown and studied just about all of them—clover, millet, Sudan grass, several types of vetch, oats, wheat, rye, alfalfa, bromegrass, lespedeza—and many others. After many years of trials and backyard-style experiments I realize that a good green manure crop for the home gardener must have these qualities:

- Seed should be inexpensive and easy to get.
- Seed should germinate quickly and get established fast.
- Plants should grow rapidly, even on "not so great" soils.
- If seeded at the proper rate, the plants should cover the ground quickly and shut off light from weeds.
- Plants should be easy to spade or till into the soil.

Four green manure crops meet these standards and fit best into my gardening system. They are: English peas, beans (green and yellow snap beans and sometimes soybeans), buckwheat, and annual ryegrass. Let me tell you why I like them so much.

Peas grown for green manure are doubly rewarding. We get plenty to harvest for eating and freezing, and then the soil receives a meal of fresh organic matter with a big helping of nitrogen fixed on pea roots.

Try to turn peas under as soon as possible after your last harvest.

PEAS

Fill your freezer as you feed your soil

Amount needed per 1,000 sq. ft. . . . 10 lbs.

Approximate cost/lb. . . . $1.40–$1.70

Varieties: Little Marvel, Wando, Progress No. 9

Best time to plant: early spring or early fall.

I like garden peas as a green manure crop because I can plant them very early and because they produce so much food for so little work. I call them an "edible" green manure crop because I don't till them in until after Jan and I harvest bushels of peas for freezing and eating, and to give to friends and neighbors.

I grow them every year in my Eternal Yield garden plots, starting almost as soon as I can work the soil. One year in an Eternal Yield plot 24 by 24 feet in size I planted 3 pounds of seed and got my normal close stand of plants. A neighbor remarked that it seemed to him a very expensive soil improvement crop, seeing as the seeds were priced at more than $1 per pound. "Oats are a lot cheaper," he said. I told him I would weigh all the peas from the patch and then we could judge.

We made two pickings from the pea patch. Jan and I took little stools in there and picked away while comfortably seated. We keep things orderly even though there are plants all around. We picked all the ready pods on one plant before moving to the next one.

We harvested 181 pounds of peas (weighed with pods) and then I roto-tilled all that luscious green matter back into the soil. I called my neighbor and gave him the final figures.

"You're kidding me!" he cried.

"No, I'm certainly not," I said. "We froze most of them but there were still plenty to give away. Let's see, if we charged 80 cents per pound as they are doing now at the market, I figure we made a pretty good profit."

"Yeah," he said quietly.

The best thing about growing peas this way is that I don't have to weed them. I plant them—and *that* takes only a minute or two—and then I return only for the harvest. The peas sprout quickly and since they're close to one another, they soon shade the soil. Struggling weeds are deprived of sun and most of them fall back. If a few weeds make it above the peas, I don't care. I'll just till them into the soil along with everything else after the harvest. The leaf canopy over the soil also keeps the soil cool and moist. We occasionally have dry spells in the spring, but I never have to water a green manure crop of peas.

I like to mix some inoculant into the pea seeds before planting. This guarantees a good supply of the bacteria necessary for the nitrogen-fixing process of legumes. The inoculant culture, which comes as a dark powder, can be purchased from most suppliers of legume seeds. Mix the inoculant with water according to the directions and evenly coat the seeds. After you till in a green manure crop of peas, there's still plenty of time to plant more vegetables there and reap the benefit of the nitrogen the peas provide.

Peas make a good fall green manure crop in many areas. I have planted them on occasion here in Vermont but the harvests aren't as rewarding as in spring. In the South a fall crop does much better.

When beans are sown thickly for a patch of green manure they require no weeding at all. The harvest is a terrific bonus, and I usually need help to keep up with the picking.

BEANS

Summary workers in your nitrogen factory

Amount per 1,000 sq. ft. . . . 10 lbs.

Approximate cost/lb. . . . $1–$2.

Varieties: your favorite green or yellow bush varieties, such as *Contender, Eastern Butterwax,* etc. Or shell beans such as *French Horticultural,* or lima beans (seeds are slightly more expensive). In South: plant favorite Southern peas.

Best time to plant: anytime after last spring frost and up to 8 weeks before expected first fall frost.

Beans are a wonderful green manure crop when warm weather arrives. All summer I fit in more beans whenever a spot opens up in the garden. Like peas, I grow them as an edible green manure crop. I harvest them before turning the tender green plant matter back into the soil.

In my Eternal Yield gardens, I plant beans after tilling in my early green manure crops of peas. Like peas, beans are a legume crop, so I continue the nitrogen fixing in that section of the plot throughout the summer. The next season I plant a variety of vegetables where the peas and beans grew in succession, and I won't add any extra fertilizer.

Beans sprout quickly in warm weather. The way I sow the seeds, bean plants come up about 3 or 4 inches away from their neighbors. Before long their leaves touch and the important

shading of the soil begins. Weeds don't grow in there, and the shaded soil retains water. Lima beans are the slowest of the group at shading the soil. That's because I sow the seeds less thickly than snap beans. But they still reach the point of shading the soil and blocking out weeds.

I've noticed an interesting trend among big-time commercial growers of beans. They are planting their rows and plants much closer together. Research is showing that yields go up and weed problems go down the quicker plants can reach out and shade the soil all around. This is exactly what happens with a well-planted green manure crop of beans.

A note on soybeans

I used to grow soybeans for green manure. At the time, I was

not interested in getting a harvest. Our season is a little short for most soybean varieties, and I don't particularly care for the taste of soybeans. What interested me was the quick, lush growth of the plants and that as a legume, soybeans produce plenty of nitrogen. The seeds are fairly cheap, too.

Since I have switched over to growing regular green and yellow bush snap beans as a green manure crop, I have not grown many soybeans. They still may be a good green manure crop for you. If you're not interested in picking and using lots of green and yellow beans, try soybeans. The seeds are available from feed and grain stores. You'll need 4 to 5 pounds per 1,000 square feet of garden space. Keep some on hand to "spot plant" if you have small sections of garden that become bare during the summer.

I plant big plots of buckwheat and roto-till them under just at blossom time. Small areas are easy to sow and spade under (above). Buckwheat grows fast and shades out weeds (left), even tough perennials.

Hollow, tender stems make buckwheat easy to turn back into the soil.

BUCKWHEAT

Even hip-high, a cinch to turn under with a shovel

Amount per 1,000 sq. ft. . . . 2-3 lb.

Approximate cost/lb. . . . $0.30-$0.40

Varieties: there are several, but "common" buck-wheat is the only one you'll see for sale. It's the one to get.

Best time to plant: from 1 to 2 weeks before last spring frost up to 4 to 6 weeks before first expected fall frost.

Every gardener should have a small bag of buckwheat seed on hand. Planting a little buckwheat is the easiest and cheapest way to produce lush green organic matter for your soil. It also attracts pollinating bees to your garden. I've planted it in spaces of 30 or 40 square feet, up to large blocks of 600 to 1,000 square feet. If it grows in warm weather it's usually ready to turn under in about 6 weeks.

The best time to till buckwheat into the soil is when it blossoms. I let the bees work the beautiful white blossoms for a few days and then roto-till the crop under. If it stays in blossom too long, some seeds will mature, and then you'll get buckwheat coming back as a weed. It's not a serious problem to have a few buck-wheat plants sprout among your next crops of vegetables because they are quite easy to hoe or pull. Still, it can be a nuisance.

Buckwheat is easy to chop and work into the soil by hand. The stems are tender and hollow and that makes it a breeze to dig the plants under. Also, the soil under a thick green manure crop of buckwheat is usually well-shaded. That keeps it moist, which is a help when you dig it under. If you have a small garden and you work it with hand tools, don't be afraid to plant some buckwheat to improve your soil.

Most experts say buckwheat should be planted only after the last frost and when the soil is warm. I always start some at least 2 weeks *before* the average last frost date and I have not been hurt by this practice yet. I figure that seed is cheap enough to gamble on an extra-early green manure crop.

189

At end of season, sow annual ryegrass between rows (top) and after turning under crop residues. Annual ryegrass is fast-growing and lush (bottom left) and dies down over the winter to form a protective blanket over soil (below). It can be turned under easily and does not delay early spring planting.

ANNUAL
RYEGRASS

A winter blanket for your garden

Amount per 1,000 sq. ft.... 2-3 lbs.

Approximate cost/lb.... $0.25-$0.35

Varieties: very important to buy only annual ryegrass. Don't be confused by similar crops or names.

Best time to plant: midsummer through early fall.

I plant annual ryegrass up to about 3 weeks before our first hard frost. It grows fast, but it needs time to put on some lush top growth before the cold weather hits. Like buckwheat, it can be planted in all regions and in all soils with good success.

Since it is an annual, the crop will not make it through our cold winters. By the time snow falls, it is pretty well killed off. The grass mats down as it dies and forms an insulating blanket over the soil. This blanket keeps the soil from freezing too deep, and allows earthworms and other soil life to work close to the surface. It also helps to stop water and wind erosion.

In the spring the annual ryegrass is partly decomposed and very easy to work into the soil. It does not delay planting of early vegetables. I can work the mat of dead grass into the soil and plant the same day. (I usually work the soil two or three times over the span of a week, however.)

Be very careful when shopping for annual ryegrass seed

Annual ryegrass is a widely available green manure crop, but some gardeners and seed store folks confuse it with "rye." *Ryegrass* is a grass which grows only a couple of feet tall. *Rye* is a grain crop from which we get rye flakes and rye flour. It grows 4 to 5 feet tall.

There are *two* kinds of ryegrass, and *two* kinds of rye.

Annual ryegrass

This is the kind of green manure seed to buy. Notice the word "annual." This crop will live only *one* season. I plant it toward the end of the growing season and by the following spring, all the plants have died and the grass is partly decomposed. It will not start any new growth. If winter kills it, it won't come back.

Perennial ryegrass

Perennial ryegrass is a real lawn grass and it looks just like annual ryegrass. Once you plant it, it will keep coming back each spring like a good lawn grass should.

Do *not* use perennial ryegrass as a green manure crop.

Winter rye

Winter rye is a grain crop, but many gardeners use it as a green manure crop. It is planted in the fall at least 2 or 3 weeks before the first fall frost. It grows right through fall until the cold weather stops it.

In the spring it resumes growth. Till it in when it is 10 or 12 inches high. If it gets much taller it is hard to till in. It also takes a while to decompose in the soil and can delay planting.

Spring rye

This grain crop is not grown much. The winters up North and in Canada are too harsh for a fall planting of winter rye to make it through in top shape. So folks plant spring rye in early spring and harvest it in late summer.

191

Planting a green manure crop

I roto-till harvested crops into the soil . . .

. . . then scatter seeds of a green manure crop evenly over the area . . .

1.

The first step is to prepare a deep, well-groomed seedbed. Many green manure seeds are small, so a fine, level seedbed will help produce an even stand of plants. Tilling down deep will help the crop's roots to dig in quickly. If you are working an old crop into the ground first, make an extra pass or two to get the plant residues chopped up small and mixed throughout the soil. If you have time, till the old crop and come back in a few days and till again. However you do it, till the area one last time *on planting day*. This helps your crop get ahead of any weeds.

Mix a little fertilizer into the soil before planting the seeds. Use just enough to get the green manure crop off to a good start. Spread about 2 pounds of a balanced fertilizer like 5-10-10 for each 100 square feet of crop area. Mix it into the soil 2 or 3 inches deep.

2.

It takes only a few minutes to broadcast green manure seeds over the seedbed. Carry the seeds in a bag. Get a handful of seed and with wide, "Ferris wheel" swings of your arm, scatter the seed evenly. Buckwheat and annual ryegrass seeds should land an inch or two apart (though some will wind up a little closer). Peas and beans should land about 2 to 4 inches apart.

With a tiller it takes only minutes

. . . and mix the seeds into the top inch or so of soil without stepping directly behind my tiller.

3.

There's a simple way to cover the seeds with my tiller. I zip across the seedbed in high gear with the tines going into the soil only an inch or two. I walk on the side of the tiller where I have not yet covered the seeds so there are no spots of heavy compaction when I get through.

The tines bury some seeds a little too deeply, and others are too close to the surface or even right on top. That's okay. The seeding rate takes this into account. There will be plenty of seeds at the right depth to germinate quickly and to give you a good stand of plants.

Planting a green manure crop with hand tools

1.

Prepare a good seedbed. If the area has plant residues, spade them into the soil or pull them and pile them on a compost pile. Some crops with heavy stalks and stems, such as corn, broccoli, and cauliflower, are best pulled out and worked into your compost pile. Some of the greens and vine crops are easier to dig in.

Loosen the soil to a depth of 6 to 8 inches. Give the area a final raking. As you do this, step backwards so that you can rake over your footprints.

2.

A little fertilizer will help the green manure crop get off to a quick start. About 2 pounds of a commercial fertilizer such as 5-10-10 or 10-10-10 per 100 square feet should suffice. Mix it into the soil with a rake. Do the work so you don't leave footprints.

3.

Broadcast the seed evenly over the area. You can walk around a small plot and scatter the seed without stepping on the soil.

4.

A light raking will mix most of the seed into the soil at the proper depth. A couple of friends who live on the other side of town have an unusual way to cover seed. They lay a long chain across the garden. They each take an end of the chain and walk along the edge of the seeded area. The chain tumbles through the soil and spills a little soil over the seeds. It works well and they don't put any footprints in the soil.

My never-fertilize Eternal Yield

I have not put an ounce of commercial fertilizer or manure on these test gardens in 10 years.

For the past 10 years I've been conducting a home garden experiment on eight 24 by 24-foot gardens. I started after a discussion with a soil scientist and agricultural researcher at our state university. Part of his job was to analyze trends in the food and dairy industries and to predict what was coming next. What he forecast scared me.

"Farmers aren't taking care of soil like they used to," he said. "Almost everywhere we are losing topsoil rapidly. We're wearing out and wasting in a few years what nature took hundreds of years to create. We want to get paid now, and have people in the next generation get the bill.

"People are depending on chemical fertilizers which quickly could become unavailable or too high-priced to buy. It's been cheap and easy for years, but it may not be for long," he noted.

"Also, there's the aspect of technology and specialized sciences. Dick, you wouldn't believe some of the things going on in laboratories right now. The simple act of growing food in a garden may someday be a lost art. Consider all the people we have to feed, and consider all the good land being taken for business and housing. You can understand why there's a frantic effort to come up with new sources of food.

"Someday, Dick, all your protein and vitamins—maybe your whole meal—could come in capsules."

My friend's thoughts are routinely voiced by experts these days, but 10 years ago they had a great impact on me.

I immediately began working on my 24 by 24-foot gardens, an ideal home-garden size for many people around the country, especially those in cities. I had a feeling then—and still do—that the small backyard garden is going to be important in the food picture as the years go by.

I did complete soil tests on each plot and limed them all to bring the soil pH close to 6.8, an ideal pH for most vegetables.

gardens

My goal was to plant different sequences of green manure crops to see if they *alone* could provide all the nutrients food crops need. My guidelines were simple: don't add any fertilizer, compost, or manures to the soil. As for organic matter, till under only the crops that grow on the plot. Do not bring in any outside material—no leaves, no mulch, nothing.

The number one crop rotation

In the test gardens I planted different green manure combinations and tested them by growing sweet corn in alternate years. Sweet corn is a heavy feeder. It takes a lot of nutrients, especially nitrogen, from the soil. So I included it in all my rotations to create a drain on soil nutrients.

Our best soil tests and best sweet corn have come from the plot which has recently had the following rotation schedule:

First year: Green manure crop of peas, followed by snap beans, followed by annual ryegrass.

Second year: One crop of sweet corn, followed by annual ryegrass.

Third year: Repeat first year rotation, and so on.

The local extension agent has often visited my "no fertilizer" test gardens and has handled the soil tests for them. Every time I get a report back on this "number one" plot, he says, "Dick, whatever you're doing is working. Your soil test looks great again." So far I've been able to keep this plot fertilized and replenished with organic matter grown right on the plot. My Eternal Yield garden experiments add weight to my belief that we home gardeners can provide for ourselves. I hope this method helps more people counteract the serious problems of soil, land, and fertilizer we're facing.

The Eternal Yield garden plan

I'm using my top green manure rotation scheme in another test plot to see if a typical garden can be nourished by green manure crops alone. So far I'm excited by the results. This may be the garden of the future. Here's what I do:

In half of the test plot (12 by 24 feet), I grow peas and follow them with snap beans and a final crop of annual ryegrass at the end of the season. We get 75 pounds of shelled peas and more than 125 pounds of beans from these crops before tilling them in.

In the other half of the plot I grow a mixture of vegetables. Greens, beets, carrots, onions, peppers, cabbage, squash, cucumbers, tomatoes, and corn. Four of the rows are thick wide rows. As in my other test plots, I don't use any fertilizer, manures, or anything else. I harvest these vegetables the way I harvest my other gardens, and when I'm done I till the residues into the soil.

The next season I switch crops, planting the vegetables where the peas and beans grew the previous year. They will use the nitrogen fixed by the plant roots and deposited in the soil, as well as the foods produced by soil life breaking down the plant material worked into the soil.

The peas, beans, and annual ryegrass are raised on the other side to replenish what was taken out of the soil by the vegetables.

So far, this "flip-flop" rotation is working well. The vegetables have been excellent. I've gotten some of the choicest beets and carrots ever from this garden, and a lot of them. I'm convinced that this plan will continue to work, giving me vegetables and providing lots of organic matter and soil nutrients year after year.

I can't guarantee that this Eternal Yield plan is the ideal combination for all climates and soils. Someday I'd like to test it in southern states because organic matter decomposes quickly in hot weather there. Different rotations might be required to keep the soil full of decomposing organic matter. Perhaps a little home compost would be needed in the vegetable area.

How it all started

Here's the history of *one* of my eight Eternal Yield test plots, year by year, to show you the type of rotation sequence I started out with, and how it has evolved.

Year 1   Complete soil tests, add lime to bring pH to 6.8. Crops: peas, soybeans, annual ryegrass

Year 2   Soybeans, replant soybeans, winter rye

Year 3   Sweet corn, annual ryegrass

Year 4   Peas, soybeans, annual ryegrass

Year 5   Sweet corn, annual ryegrass

Year 6   Peas, snap beans, annual ryegrass

Year 7   Sweet corn, annual ryegrass

Year 8   Peas, snap beans, annual ryegrass

Year 9   One-half of area mixed vegetables; one-half area peas followed by snap beans; annual ryegrass over whole plot at end of season

Year 10 Where vegetables were in year 9, peas followed by beans; in other half, mixed vegetables; annual ryegrass over whole plot at end of season

Future years 11, 12, etc. I will continue to alternate mixed vegetables with peas, snap beans, and annual ryegrass on this plot.

(Yearly soil tests for pH and nutrient levels are necessary to ensure we are "on track." Only lime is added.)

*Top: Peas and beans gather nitrogen from the air and "fix" it on root nodules like these. They **add** fertilizer to the soil. Center: Corn needs plenty of nutrients—it's a crop known as a "heavy feeder." Using my green manure rotation, I get excellent ears. Next year, I'll plant corn on the opposite side of this plot. Bottom: I always turn crops back into the soil right after the harvest. Note the annual ryegrass growing next to me on the left.*

Everyone wants the harvest to last as long as possible. In a good root cellar, many vegetables easily will keep 5 or 6 months. You don't have to process vegetables going into the root cellar. It's a true low-energy food preservation system. A steady cool temperature (35°-45° F.) is the main requirement.

If you have a basement, you may be able to partition off one corner and turn it into a root cellar for vegetables. The soil outside the house foundation remains at a fairly even temperature all year long—about 50°-55° F. degrees. It will provide some warmth on winter days when the air temperature is way below freezing. This even temperature of the soil is the reason why you don't have to insulate the root cellar floor or the two outside walls.

Because the northern part of the cellar is the coolest zone in the house, it's best to put your storage area there. The two inside partitions and the ceiling of your root cellar must be insulated. Regular 3½-inch building insulation is adequate. A solid door that seals tightly is also important. It is not a bad idea to insulate the inside of the door. A root cellar works by keeping warm air out.

In most cases, it is not necessary to have an outside window in the root cellar. If your basement is particularly damp, though, it may be a good idea either to build your partitions in a corner where there is a window for ventilation, or to add a vent. If you have a window, keep it blacked out. You don't want sunlight streaming into the root cellar. That will only heat things up and cause vegetables to spoil more quickly.

My system to maintain cool temperatures.

I've rigged up a ventilation and temperature control system to bring cold air in from outdoors if my root cellar gets too warm. It's been a lifesaver in early fall and in spring when the root cellar temperature ordinarily would vary quite a bit.

Here's how it works: I have a 6-inch duct running from the outside wall of the house into the root cellar. There's a low-energy fan positioned in the duct. The fan is controlled by two thermostats located on the outside wall of my root cellar. One thermostat has a capillary tube running into the root cellar; the other has a tube on the outside of the house.

Generally my root cellar temperature is between 35°-45° F. If the temperature inside the root cellar goes above 50° F., the thermostat signals the fan to bring in air. However, the outside thermostat (set at 50° F.) must also signal that the temperature out there is *below* 50° F. before the fan will kick on. Often, in the early fall, the fan will only run at night when it gets cool.

With this system I can rest assured that my root cellar will stay cool. In the middle of winter the fan hardly runs because the root cellar stays so cool. But in the first two months of storage in the fall, and the last two in the spring, it's very helpful.

I hang onions in the top "cool" zone because they need ventilation.

Store your crops in the proper temperature zone

Zone 3—cool

Zone 2—cold

Zone 1—coldest

The temperature in a root cellar is always a compromise. It's never equal in all parts of the cel-

lar. Most vegetables never get the perfect temperature.

· The temperature near the ceiling of many root cellars can sometimes be 10° F. or so higher than near the floor. This variance creates temperature zones in the root cellar. Your vegetables will keep better if you understand the temperature zones of your root cellar and store crops accordingly.

The temperature in a root cellar is always a compromise. It's never equal in all parts of the cellar. Most vegetables never get the perfect temperature.

There's another temperature zone around the halfway point of the root cellar's height. It is slightly warmer than at ground level but it is still cold. Here I put my pumpkins and winter squash, which don't like the very coldest storage.

Up top is the cool area. I hang my onions, shallots, and garlic there more for the air circulation than for the temperature.

VEGETABLES THAT STORE WELL IN THE ROOT CELLAR

Crop	Best zone to store	Average length of storage
Beets	1	3-4 months
Cabbage	2	1-2 months
Carrots	1	3-4 months
Garlic	3	6-8 months
Thick-skinned onions and shallots	3	6-8 months
Bermuda and sweet Spanish onions	3	1-2 months
Parsnips	1	2-4 months
Potatoes	1	4-7 months
Pumpkins	2	2-3 months
Rutabagas and turnips	1	3-4 months
Winter squash	2	4-6 months
Tomatoes, green	2	2-6 weeks

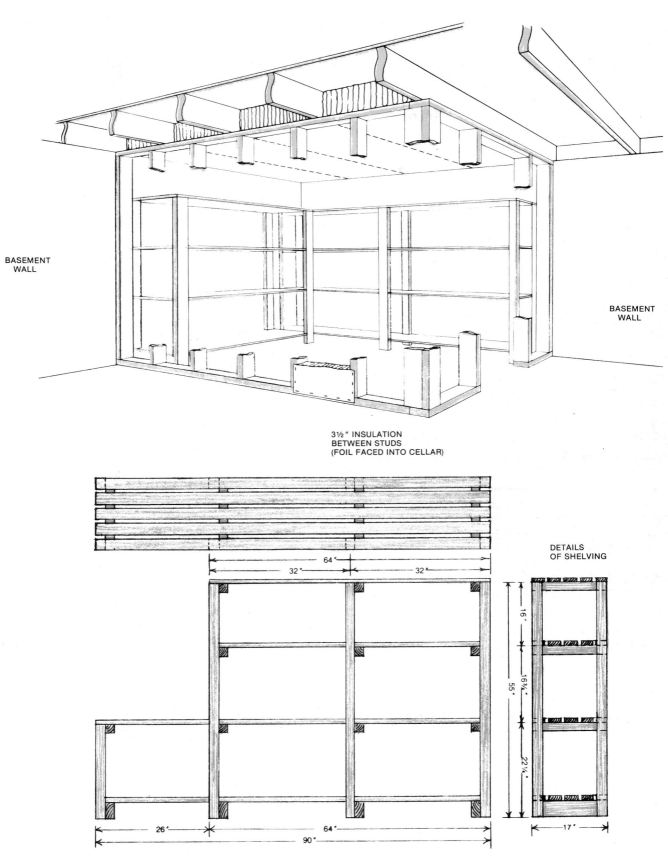

BASEMENT
WALL

BASEMENT
WALL

3½" INSULATION
BETWEEN STUDS
(FOIL FACED INTO CELLAR)

DETAILS
OF SHELVING

64"

32"   32"

16"

16¾"

55"

22¼"

26"   64"

90"

17"

201

Some specific root cellar know-how

BEETS

Keep ½ inch of tops on your beets, but do not cut the tails. Larger beets keep longer, so at harvest you may want to sort for size. Store in plastic bags, tied at top, with a few air holes punched in sides. Or pack in boxes of moist peat moss or sawdust.

CABBAGES

Bring into the root cellar at the latest possible time. Wrap each head in 10 or 12 sheets of newspaper and tie up with a rubber band. Use as quickly as possible. If cabbage goes by, it will send a strong odor throughout the house.

CARROTS

Cut tops off in garden. Don't wash carrots until you use them. Store in plastic bags with several holes punched in them, or pack in boxes of moist peat moss or sawdust.

GARLIC

Like onions, must be dried and cured before storing. Braid or hang in small mesh bags to increase air circulation.

THICK-SKINNED ONIONS OR SHALLOTS

Sort for size and hang onions in mesh bags in top zone of the root cellar. They need air circulation. Check onions and shallots regularly; if some soften or start to sprout, use them.

BERMUDA AND SWEET SPANISH ONIONS

To keep these as long as possible, don't crowd them. Put in small mesh bags or nylon stockings where they'll have air all around them. Use quickly.

PARSNIPS

Dig just before the ground freezes or after several hard frosts in fall. Trim the tops and store like carrots or beets. Good idea to leave some stored in ground over winter and to dig them in spring before growth resumes.

POTATOES

Best to have storage crop mature as late in the year as possible when the root cellar is cool. Total darkness and good air circulation around them is important. Don't pile too deeply or directly on floor.

PUMPKINS

Use the big pumpkins for jack o' lanterns and store the smaller pie pumpkins. Use them quickly. Cook and freeze them if you want longer storage.

RUTABAGAS AND TURNIPS

They keep best in plastic bags like carrots and beets, or in boxes of moist sawdust or peat moss.

WINTER SQUASH

Do not pile too deeply—squash have to breathe. If stems are broken off or squash show bruises, put them on top and use early—these will not keep as long as the others. They're easy to cook and freeze, too.

TOMATOES, GREEN

Put green tomatoes that are mature in size and have started to turn color on a rack or counter. Cover them all with a sheet or two of newspaper. If your root cellar is crowded, use an old dresser drawer and put it in cool place where you can check it often.

Getting the most out of a root cellar

No two home root cellars function the same. You'll have to learn about yours through trial and error. You'll know better than anyone else which crops will keep a long time in your root cellar and which ones won't.

Never put anything directly on the floor because vegetables need air circulation from all sides. If you set them on the floor, they will become moist underneath and start to rot much sooner. Set your boxes, barrels, and baskets on boards on the floor so air can circulate under them.

It is a mistake to store diseased or bruised fruits and vegetables. They certainly won't improve in storage. In fact, they will do you more good in the compost pile than in the root cellar. Keep them apart from the ones that you intend to store all winter, and use them first, because they won't last.

For crops to store well, the relative humidity should be above 60 percent. In a dry root cellar you can increase humidity with a small humidifier, or by spreading moist sawdust on the floor of the root cellar and wetting it down from time to time.

If the humidity is too high, you'll have to find a way to bring in dry air, or use a dehumidifier.

Don't expect every vegetable you put in the root cellar to keep forever. Check them periodically. If some start to deteriorate, eat the ones you can and throw the rest onto the compost pile. By the time some of your crops start to deteriorate—squash, for instance—your freezer will probably be partially empty. Cut away the rotting areas, cook the rest and freeze it. After all, the fuller your freezer, the less it costs to run it.

If you put canned vegetables in the root cellar, use them within 6 or 8 months. In a root cellar with high humidity, the metal caps and jar lids may rust. Keep an eye on them and use them promptly.

In the root cellar, your greatest enemies are rodents. In the country, mice do their best to come indoors when the weather starts turning cold. The basement is a convenient and safe place where humans rarely bother them. Secure your storage area from these hungry critters. When mice are hungry—and winter seems to whet their appetites—they'll eat anything, and that includes potatoes, cabbage, apples, root crops, squash, and pumpkins.

Keep your vegetable storage area clean. Once a year, remove your storage boxes and baskets for cleaning. Air them in the sun or spray with disinfectant.

Left: Metal caps may rust in humid root cellars if they're kept too long. Use canned produce promptly. With a selection like this, that's hardly a problem with us.
Right: Tomatoes ripen very well on a shelf under newspaper sheets. It's easy to check for ripeness.

MY
VEGETABLE
TREASURY

Vegetables
have families, too!

"When you learn how to grow *one* root crop, you have learned how to grow *every* root crop"

To give you as much information as I can on all the important vegetables, I've grouped many of them according to their "families."

Vegetables in the same family often need the same growing conditions, are planted at the same time, need the same plant food, and are bothered by the same insects and diseases. By telling the "family story" first, I won't have to repeat information for each family member. I'll use the space to pass on tips and tricks for planting, growing, and harvesting each family member.

There's a bonus in getting to know vegetables by family. Take the root crop family, for example. The information at the beginning of the section fits every root crop. When you learn how to grow *one* root crop, you have learned to grow them *all*. And if you identify an insect or disease causing trouble with one crop, you'll know to check all the other *family relatives* the same trouble may strike.

(Vegetables which do not belong to families are included in alphabetical order as they fall between the family names.)

Here's how I've grouped the vegetables:

The Bean Family
Snap beans
Shell beans
Dry beans
Soybeans

The Cabbage Family
Broccoli
Brussels sprouts
Cabbage
Cauliflower
Chinese cabbage
Kohlrabi

Corn

Eggplant

The Greens Family
Celery
Chard
Collards
Endive
Kale
Lettuce
Mustard
Spinach

Okra

The Onion Family
Garlic
Leeks
Onions
Shallots

Peanuts

Peas

Peppers

Potatoes

Potatoes, Sweet

The Root Crop Family
Beets
Carrots
Parsnips
Radishes
Rutabagas
Salsify
Turnips

Sunflowers

Tomatoes

The Vine Crop Family
Cucumbers
Gourds
Melons (Cantaloupes
and Watermelons)
Pumpkins
Summer squash
Winter squash

Perennials
Asparagus
Rhubarb
Horseradish
Strawberries

THE BEAN FAMILY

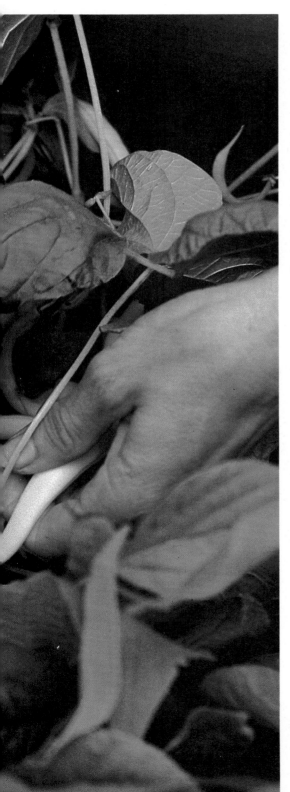

Beans have been *the most important* vegetable crop through the ages. They are the best vegetable source of life-giving protein, and today in many societies, beans are still the staple of life. Beans are also the one protein source you can keep for a long time without processing. And you can get a heavy harvest from a small amount of work.

Our family relied on dry beans when I was young. Every Saturday night (if not more often), the heart of our family meal, like the traditional New England Saturday supper, was baked beans.

Today, with so many bean varieties available, they certainly get the "most versatile" award for the home garden. No matter what kind of bean you grow, you're bound to be happy with the harvest.

I divide the bean family into four groups.

Green and yellow snap beans: These beans used to be called "string" beans because they had fibrous strings that ran the length of the pods. The string has been bred out of most varieties. Snap beans come in bush and pole varieties. They are harvested when the pods are young and tender, when they still "snap" into pieces easily.

Beans yield high rewards for little work. Planted in wide rows there is little or no weeding.

Shell beans: Lima beans, southern peas, and horticultural beans are the best examples of shell beans. To harvest, you have to open the pods or shells, and collect the soft beans inside.

Dry beans: Here's where all the protein is. Dry beans come from plants that have completed their growth and produced hard, dry seeds inside their pods. When mature, they are packed with protein. All you have to do is separate the beans from their hulls and store them.

There's quite a bit of overlap among these first three groups of beans. For example, *Red Kidney* beans (usually thought of as a dry bean) and *French Horticultural* beans (usually considered a shell variety) can be eaten first as a snap bean, later as a shell bean, and even as a dry bean at the end of the season.

Soybeans: Soybeans are in a class by themselves. These beans contain about three times more protein than other beans and are an important crop in many states. Most home gardeners don't grow them. I grow only a small patch of soybeans because I haven't found much flavor to them. It's hard for me to give space to soybeans when I could be growing tasty lima beans. Better-tasting varieties will be introduced before too long, I bet, and then we'll probably all be growing more protein-rich soybeans.

207

PLANTING

A good crop in any soil

Beans are warm weather vegetables. I plant almost all my beans when the danger of frost is *past* and the soil has warmed up. However, I always gamble and plant a few rows of snap beans early, 2 or 3 weeks before the average last frost date. Since even the lightest frost will kill them, I sometimes have to cover the small plants with newspapers to protect them on cold nights. It's easier work than it sounds— and worth it. Back in my market-gardening days I was usually first with early beans. I remember days when the cars lined up in front of the house and people waited for Jan and me to finish picking them.

Beans are not too choosy about where they'll sink their roots as long as it's sunny. They'll give you a good crop in soil that's loamy, sandy, rocky, rich, or poor. Beans don't like wet soil though, but if you grow them on raised beds, they'll probably do fine.

Beans don't need much fertilizer to produce abundantly. They are *legumes,* able to take nitrogen from the air and fix it on their roots. Since they can *make* some of their own fertilizer, I only add 2 pounds of 5-10-10 or other balanced fertilizer for each 100 square feet of beans.

Inoculate your beans just before planting to help them gather as much nitrogen from the air as they can. Bean-seed inoculant is available at most garden stores.

Beans belong in wide rows. It takes extra seed to plant beans in wide rows, but for a few extra seeds you can grow enough plants to shade out weeds and hold in lots of moisture.

A wide row, 16 or 18 inches, is easy to plant, care for, and harvest. I drop the seeds for snap beans about 3 or 4 inches apart. Lima beans need more room than snap beans so I plant them 4 or 6 inches apart.

Wide row beans require little weeding.

Beans do well in single and double rows too, but I've found they need more weeding. Put the seeds 3 or 4 inches apart in the row. Sow double rows 6 to 8 inches apart.

Try block plantings of beans if you have the room and want a big harvest. Block planting is good for growing dry beans because they are a "plant and pick" crop. You don't have to do much while they're growing, just harvest them when the seasons's over.

Have a healthy crop

Here is how to prevent disease problems in your bean patch:

*Anthracnose, bacterial blights, common bean mosaic, and rust are the most common bean diseases. Try to grow varieties resistant to these diseases. A good seed catalog will point these out.

*Before planting, use a seed protectant on your beans, especially those you plant early when the soil is a little cool.

*Stay out of the garden when plants are wet, because water is often the carrier of diseases.

*Rotate the bean crop each year to avoid soil-borne diseases.

*Well-drained soil is important for growing beans. If soil stays wet, raised beds are your best bet.

*Use mulch for walkways and wide-row growing to prevent raindrops from splashing soil and disease spores on the plants.

Bean insects

The Mexican bean beetle, a 16-spotted ladybug type, is one of the most common bean pests. The adult and the orange-to-yellow larvae feed on bean leaves, often working from underneath.

The bean leaf beetle, a yellowish bug with six spots, feeds on leaves, too, but it's not as common.

Many people find Japanese beetles on bean plants, but they can be brushed into a can and destroyed before doing much damage.

Bean plants can withstand a lot of damage before the yield is affected, so be careful about spraying them. Many times you can wait until the first big harvest is over.

SNAP BEANS
GREEN AND YELLOW

Snap beans are the first beans to give me a harvest, about 45 days after they come up. I plant them *early* and *often* to get a continuous supply of fresh, tender pods. From early summer to the first fall frost, snap beans are ready to pick in my garden. I plant them every 2 weeks until about 8 weeks before the average first fall frost date. Snap beans are a good succession crop because they are so easy to plant and they sprout quickly in warm soil. When my spinach starts to go to seed in early summer, I till it under and plant a wide row of beans on the same day. A couple of weeks later when some of my early peas are finished, I till them in and plant another row of snap beans.

I have three favorite green snap beans: *Bountiful, Tendercrop,* and *Tendergreen Improved.* I don't know how many bean varieties I've planted over the years, but *Bountiful* is still an old favorite. It produces early, and as long as I keep harvesting, I get more beans. *Tendergreen* is resistant to some major diseases, and *Tendercrop* is a heavy yielder for me. For yellow-podded snap beans or "wax beans," you can't beat *Eastern Butterwax* or *Pencil Pod.* They're delicious.

There are some purple-podded snap beans, too. A good one is *Royal Burgundy.* The pods are flavorful. As the name implies, they're purple. (They turn green when they're cooked.)

Southern gardeners sometimes grow a different type of bush snap bean, called "half-runners." They spread out more, but not enough to need staking. A reliable variety is the *White Half Runner* that matures in about 60 days.

I grow pole snap beans with tepees

There are a lot of nice things about pole beans. You can raise a bushel of them using just a few square feet of garden space; they have flavors distinct from any other bean; they don't pass peak harvest time and get tough as quickly as bush snap beans; and if you keep them picked and fertilized, they just keep bearing.

Over the years I've experimented with all kinds of strings, wires, supports, and trellises for pole beans. Here's my favorite: a tepee made of four poles, each about 6 or 7 feet long and about an inch or two thick.

I lay the poles on the ground and lash the tops of them together with rope or wire. Then I stand the tepee up with the legs 3 or 4 feet apart, pushing each leg 6 or 8 inches into the soil. I put 5 or 6 seeds around each leg, 6 inches from the pole and 1 inch deep. Later I thin them, leaving only three or four of the best-looking plants around each pole. An ounce of seed will be enough for four or five tepees.

In the fall I just pull up the poles (which I get from the woods), yank off the dead vines, and store the poles in the barn.

My favorite pole snap beans are *Kentucky Wonder* (which my dad grew every year) and *Blue Lake* (which I like to grow every year). I don't have a taste for the long, flat, so-called Italian pole beans like *Romano*—but my friends of Italian descent say it's because I'm French.

To side-dress pole beans, give each plant 1 teaspoon of complete fertilizer soon after the first picking and every 3 weeks after that.

Pick beans when they are about the thickness of a pencil. If large seeds start to form inside the pod and the whole bean looks lumpy, they have gone by and are too tough for best eating. Once a bean plant feels it has produced enough mature seed, it will stop producing blossoms and beans. Keep picking and your beans will keep producing.

Beans grow very quickly. After your first picking, you can pick from the same plant in about 3 days.

SHELL BEANS

Lima beans, horticultural beans, and blackeye peas are my favorite shell beans. I pick them when the beans inside have formed but are still soft and tender. They can grow to the dry stage, but if you let them do that, you'll miss out on an early harvest and some very good eating.

Lima beans need 11 or 12 weeks of frost-free weather

To know the real taste of lima beans, you must eat them fresh from a home garden. There's no comparison between fresh and store-bought. Succotash, that terrific blend of fresh corn, milk, butter, and limas, isn't worth a hoot without fresh lima beans.

Jan and I use all the limas we can pick, so I plant them in blocks, wide rows, and in double rows. They yield a lot more than in single rows.

Bush limas are so bushy that I leave at least 3 feet between the rows and 6 or 8 inches between the seeds.

Fresh limas a must for succotash.

Limas are a little slow. Although they need warm soil and 11 or 12 weeks of frost-free weather, they still make sense for gardens in the North. If you have a short season, use seed protectant on your seeds and plant some before the average last frost date.

Pole limas take longer than bush limas, but they can be grown up North, too, especially if you plant the southern favorite *Small Sieva*. It's a good variety which produces early.

Lima beans are ready to be harvested when the beans have formed inside the pods but before they get tough. The pods will look fat and lumpy when the limas are ready. You will find from two to five beans in each pod. If you blanch them for 2 minutes, they'll be easier to shell.

French Horticultural and Vermont Cranberry beans

Besides lima beans, my favorite shelling beans are the *French Horticultural* bean and the *Vermont Cranberry* bean. We use them in succotash which we freeze, or can them. The *Vermont Cranberry* is the better *canning* bean. It keeps its flavor well and has a pleasing pinkish color. Jan puts up about a dozen pints of them each year.

Although the *Vermont Cranberry* has been known for many years as a New England favorite, people can grow it anywhere. Much of the seed for this variety is grown in California.

Southern peas

Southern pea varieties such as *Blackeye* peas are not peas at all—they're beans. I think they're called "peas" because many of the beans are small and round.

When I travel in the South I often hear gardeners talk about them as "crowder" peas. They're referring to southern pea varieties in which the peas are jammed together in the pod.

The name "cream" covers a lot of varieties, too; the cream peas I've seen have a smooth pod and small white peas.

Just because they're called "southern" doesn't mean they can't be grown successfully in the North. All they need is warm soil and a fairly long growing season. If you can grow lima beans, you can grow all sorts of southern peas.

Southern peas are harvested as shell beans but can be allowed to dry. I have friends in Georgia who grow blocks of *Blackeye* peas to improve their soil. But before they till the plants back into the soil, they harvest the peas.

Vermont Cranberry *a fine bean to can.*

DRY BEANS

The *Red Kidney* is my favorite dry bean. I helped my dad and brothers harvest the beans, beginning when I was 5 years old. We gathered them late in the season when the plants were dead and brown and the beans were getting hard. My job was to pull up several plants in a bunch and lay them on the back of the wagon as we traveled across the field. We let the beans dry a little more in the barn before the family pitched in to thresh, winnow, and sort them.

When fully dried, beans are as hard as rocks. In fact, the way to test them is to bite down on a bean—carefully. If you can't make a dent in it, the bean is about as dry as it's ever going to get. Before the beans reach that stage, I pull up whole plants and set them against a fence post or hang them in the garage. You can hang them just about anywhere or even dry them on a floor in a spare room.

Thresh beans in a clean trash can

Threshing, or separating the dry beans from the pods and stalks, is easy and fun—especially with kids helping. One simple way is to whack the plants back and forth on the inside of a clean trash can. Or you can fill a burlap bag with dried bean plants and get the kids to walk or jump on the bag for a few minutes. Then shake the bag vigorously for another minute or so, open it up, and pull out the plants. Inside the bag will be the beans and bits

of broken pods and stems known as chaff.

Separating the beans from the chaff is called winnowing. Wait for a windy day, then pour a basketful of your beans and chaff onto a blanket or canvas you've laid on the ground. Repeat this a

few times and pretty soon all the chaff will have blown away, leaving only the beans. Then sort out any bad beans from the bunch—a job we used to do sitting around the kitchen table. We put the good beans in large glass jars, tightly capped them, and put them in a cool, dry place.

The other dry beans I like besides the *Red Kidney* (a super baking bean, by the way) are: *Soldier, Navy,* and *Yellow Eye* beans.

SOYBEANS

Soybeans need a long season to mature and dry on the vine. Most varieties take 100 days or so to mature. *Fiskeby V* is earlier and probably better suited to northern gardens, but I find the seeds too expensive to be worth the effort. *Frostbeater* is a better buy. Like limas, they are bushier than snap beans, so leave 6 or 7 inches between plants in your rows. If you have a short season, harvest them when the beans inside have formed and are fairly soft.

To shell soybeans, dip the pods in boiling water for a few minutes and they'll give up their beans more easily. With a long season you can let the soybeans dry on the vines, or you can pull out the plants and hang them up to dry. When they are quite hard, thresh and winnow them like other dry beans and store them in airtight containers.

Soybeans are a good green manure crop

Soybeans sprout quickly, grow lush like other beans, and add tremendous organic matter to the soil when you turn them under. I used to plant them in wide blocks for green manure. I tilled them in when they blossomed since I wasn't interested in the harvest. I bought the inexpensive seed of common field varieties at the local grain and seed store.

If you have a long season and want to grow a green manure soybean crop to harvest before tilling it under, get a good table variety.

INSECTS THAT ATTACK BEANS

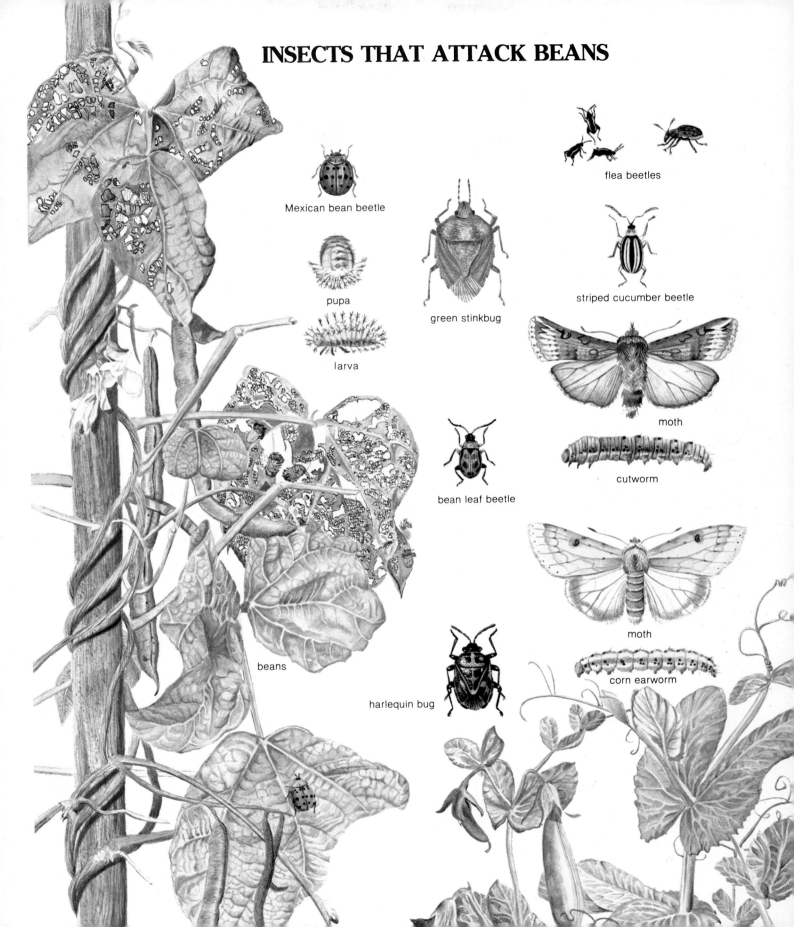

Mexican bean beetle

pupa

larva

green stinkbug

flea beetles

striped cucumber beetle

moth

cutworm

bean leaf beetle

beans

harlequin bug

moth

corn earworm

THE CABBAGE FAMILY

Broccoli

Vegetables in the cabbage family like it cool. I plant them early, at least 3 or 4 weeks before the last spring frost date, and also later in the season so they can mature in the cool weather of fall.

A couple of years ago, Jan and I picked our first heads of broccoli a few days before Memorial Day, and cut the last ones from our fall planting on Thanksgiving Day. If you live south of my homestead, you can easily get a longer season of cabbage family crops—especially in the fall.

The light frosts and cold weather of fall don't hurt the cabbage family vegetables. In fact, a light frost adds tangy sweetness to Chinese cabbage and brussels sprouts maturing in fall.

Brussels sprouts are the hardiest of the whole family. I once picked a basket of them in January. They were frozen right on the stalk but they cooked up beautifully.

My late crop of cabbage tastes great and the heads keep longer because I harvest them at the last possible moment. I put them in my root cellar when it is quite cool down there and will stay that way for months.

Fall crops are nearly pest-free

The best thing about a fall crop is that you'll rarely have a disease or insect problem. Most pests hit hardest in late spring and early summer. By the time the cool weather of fall rolls around, pests are more interested in finding a home for the winter than going on a picnic, so they do little or no damage to your crops. This kind of worry-free gardening is the best.

When you make out your garden plan, aim for two harvests of cabbages, broccoli, brussels sprouts, cauliflower, and kohlrabi—an early one and one late in the season just before you put your garden to bed for the winter.

WHEN TO PLANT A FALL CROP

Vegetable	Weeks before first fall frost date*
Broccoli	10-12
Brussels sprouts	12-16
Cabbage	10-12
Cauliflower	10-12
Chinese cabbage	8-10
Kohlrabi	6-8

*For sowing seed directly in garden. All crops may be started close, perhaps in a short wide row, and (except for kohlrabi) transplanted when 4 to 6 inches tall to another row. (I don't transplant kohlrabi. It grows like a root crop where I seed it.)

The early fall months are prime for harvests of cauliflower (upper left), brussels sprouts (bottom left), and wide rows of tasty red cabbage.

215

Pinch leaves off transplants

When I transplant cabbage family members, I pick off some of the lower leaves on each seedling. I do this both for my early spring crop and for the plants I set in the garden later. These lower leaves yellow and drop off anyway, so why leave them on the plant to sap energy from the roots? Trimming them gives the plant a much better start, especially when they are transplanted late in the summer. The soil then is more apt to heat up and dry out, and whatever you can do to take the strain off the roots will help.

Sometimes I take all the leaves off a small plant, keeping just the center bud of the plant, what I call "a little mouse ear." This mouse ear is the life of the plant. If you snip it accidentally you're out of business.

Crowd your cabbage family

People put their cabbage family crops much *too far apart* in the rows. There's a better way. Put them as close as 10 inches apart. This may seem painfully close to some gardeners, especially when 18 or 24 inches is usually recommended on seed packets. But several *good things* happen when you make close neighbors out of your cabbage family crops:

1. You can fit more plants in each row and have a much bigger harvest from the same space. (My tests on cabbage, for example, show a 50 percent increase in amount of food on a per square foot basis.)

2. Leaves of the plant quickly reach out to their neighbors and shade the ground. This blocks out weeds and keeps the soil moist and cool.

3. You get a *continuous harvest* of cabbage, brussels sprouts, broccoli, and Chinese cabbage. Because these crops are in a wide row, they will mature over a long stretch of time, not just within a few days as often happens with many widely spaced plants in single rows.

In a wide row, some plants get ahead of the rest and grow faster. They take a good share of the nutrients, which keeps their neighbors growing at a slower pace. When the biggest plants are harvested, though, neighboring plants suddenly have more sun, food, and water. They put on a spurt and are soon ready to pick. A long harvest is more enjoyable and easier to manage in the kitchen than a huge harvest in just a few days.

How close is close enough? Here are the guidelines I've found extremely rewarding:

Broccoli	12-16 inches
Cauliflower	12-16 inches
Brussels sprouts	16-18 inches
Cabbage	10-12 inches
Chinese cabbage	10-12 inches

Rotate crops to avoid diseases

The cabbage family crops are susceptible to several diseases—yellows, blackleg, black rot, clubroot, and root knot. Avoid planting members of the cabbage family in the same place two years in a row. Move them to a spot where beans, peas, tomatoes, or other vegetables grew previously.

When you buy transplants, check for disease symptoms such as stunted plants, blemished or yellowing leaves, or wilted foliage. If you discover badly diseased plants in the garden, pull them up, burn them, or toss them in the trash. Don't put them in the compost pile.

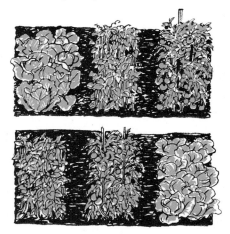

Mustard, collards, and kale

Kale, mustard, and collards are the tasty greens of the cabbage family. But since they grow like other greens and because most people think of them as greens, I've included them as crops in the greens family, pages 236-247.

THE GREAT BACILLUS THURINGIENSIS STORY

No More Worms!

> "When I realized I could grow broccoli without *ever* worrying about worms again, I wanted to get up and dance!"

For a long time I didn't eat much broccoli. I planted a lot of it but each spring when my broccoli was starting to head, a flock of small white butterflies appeared over the rows of broccoli and the other cabbage family crops. I knew they were hunting for places to lay eggs, which would later hatch and produce a horde of small, very hungry cabbage worms. Boy, do those cabbage worms love to eat! They can devour leaves, stems, and broccoli heads, too. The worst feeling in the world is finding them in a dish of cooked broccoli.

As upsetting as it was to discover worms on my plate, I hated to spray my broccoli crop with anything toxic because when you spray broccoli you cover the entire harvest. It's not like cabbage where the spray stays on the outside leaves. With broccoli, bits of spray penetrate all through the tightly packed buds. So I didn't spray.

Some years we were lucky and didn't get many worms; most years we had to soak the harvest in heavily salted water before cooking it. And I kept my fingers crossed during the meal. When a new non-chemical spray to fight cabbage worms was introduced to home gardeners some years ago, I tried it right away on my broccoli. I was amazed at how well it worked. The white butterflies visited the garden as usual, but the worms which hatched died quickly and did no damage. When I realized I could grow broccoli without ever worrying about worms again, I wanted to get up and dance!

The safe, natural non-chemical worm killer

The spray is a naturally occurring bacterium. Its official name is *Bacillus thuringiensis;* it causes a fatal disease in the worms but does not hurt plants, people, or other animals. You can use it on crops right up to the day of harvest. Unlike other sprays, there is no waiting time before harvesting.

The bacteria are sold under several trade names. Dipel, Thuricide, and BT are the most common ones. It's available as a dust as well as a spray. It releases disease-causing spores which the worms ingest. Within a couple of

Here's an easy and economical way to apply Dipel as a dust. Put dust in a bag made of lightly porous cloth . . .

. . . then give the bag a small shake over plants. A light covering is all plants need.

hours the worms stop feeding; they get sick and are unable to digest food; their stomach wall collapses and within a couple of days they die.

I start using it on my garden as soon as I see those white butterflies. I spray all my cabbage family crops and repeat the spray every 7 to 10 days until the harvest is over. This safe regular coverage guarantees that I'll never see a worm in my broccoli, cabbage, cauliflower, kale, mustard, collards, and all other cabbage family crops.

As you can see from the chart below, this non-toxic substance can end your worries about cabbage loopers, the big tomato hornworm, corn earworms, and many other common pests. *I'll put it this way: anyone who grows a garden should have some Dipel, Thuricide, or BT on hand.* Even in a small garden with just a few cabbage family crops, it's worth it. You can mix the spray in an old Windex bottle or plant mister and apply it in just minutes.

Some of the caterpillar pests killed by eating spores of Bacillus thuringiensis:

armyworm	tobacco hornworm
cabbage looper	European corn borer
corn earworm	sod webworm
(tomato fruitworm)	melonworm
(cotton bollworm)	redbanded leafroller
Eastern tent caterpillar	imported cabbage worm
saltmarsh caterpillar	gypsy moth
walnut caterpillar	brown-tail moth
tobacco budworm	grape leaffolder
artichoke plume moth	fall webworm
grapeberry moth	California oakworm
tomato hornworm	

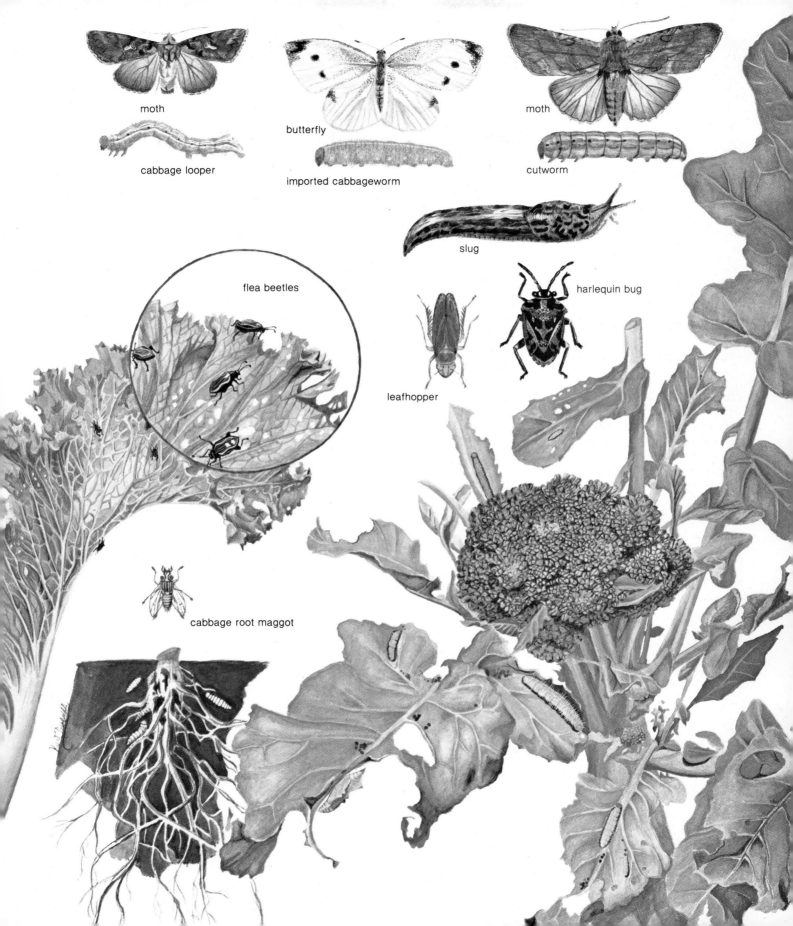

moth

cabbage looper

butterfly

imported cabbageworm

moth

cutworm

slug

flea beetles

leafhopper

harlequin bug

cabbage root maggot

BROCCOLI

Cut broccoli heads just as buds start to spread apart. Then watch bonus sprouts grow.

Non-stop harvest

It's exciting to discover the first thumb-sized broccoli heads in the row and watch them grow. Sometimes they'll get to be 6 or 8 inches wide at the top. Other times the heads will be quite small when it's time to pick them.

The center head must be cut before it blossoms, even if it's on the small side. How do you tell when the head is ready to blossom? A head of broccoli is a cluster of flower buds. When the head is young, its individual buds are packed very tightly. Rub your thumb over them and you will feel that tightness. As long as the buds stay tight, let the head grow. But when the buds loosen up and spread out, they are about to pop up and produce little yellow flowers. Again, pass your thumb across the top of the head—if the buds are loose, you'd better harvest.

The heads may be very small when the buds loosen, but harvest anyway. Because of hot weather, lack of water, or some other stress, the plant is determined to send up flowers and try to make seed. The only way to stop this is by harvesting.

Once you cut out the center head, many smaller heads, or "side shoots," will form on other parts of the stems. These may not be large, but often there are so many of them you can top up your harvest basket in no time. The smaller shoots also will try to send up flower stalks and blossoms. If you let a plant blossom, it will go to seed and stop producing. It's important to keep them picked. In hot weather I go out every other day and snip all the side shoots—even little bite-sized ones—before they can flower. It's almost a non-stop harvest!

There are many dependable early varieties of broccoli, along with purple-headed and late-season types. *Green Comet Hybrid* is a variety you'll often see at nurseries in the spring. It is an early variety, but please note: it produces a large center head with *few,* and sometimes *no, side shoots.* I'd rather plant *Green Comet* as a fall crop because there isn't much time for a long harvest of side shoots anyway.

BRUSSELS SPROUTS

Strip off bottom leaves for bigger harvest

I used to grow brussels sprouts exclusively for a fall harvest because the plants survive so well in very cold weather. Heck, I've picked brussels sprouts as late as Janaury here in Vermont. I had to dig in the snow for them, but they were good.

I don't wait for cold weather anymore. In recent years I've picked tiny sprouts as early as July and continued the harvest from the same plants well into November. People ask me, "Aren't the sprouts bitter when you pick them in the heat of the summer?" "Shouldn't you wait until the sprouts get big and the weather gets cold?" The answer to both questions is, "No." The secret is to start picking when the sprouts are about the size of marbles. As long as they're growing smoothly and you pick them small, they should be tender.

The sprouts form where a leaf grows out of the thick stalk. They'll appear on the bottom of the stalk first. That's the oldest part of the plant.

Stripping leaves directs energy to sprouts

I have a technique that encourages these early sprouts to grow big in a hurry. As soon as I see tiny sprouts begin to form, I break off all the branches, starting from the lowest and continuing up 6 or 8 inches. The sprouts stay in place, but all the branches near them are gone.

Stripping the stalk like this stimulates the plant in two ways: it grows taller so it can add more

Brussels sprouts are 16 to 18 inches apart in my garden. Look how I strip the leaves (right) a week or so before starting my harvest.

leaves and sprouts; and it directs energy to the tiny sprouts at the bottom of the stalk. These grow in a hurry. In 5 or 7 days they are ready for picking. When I harvest them I take a minute and snap off more branches higher up on the stalk. This helps the next harvest grow. I do this through the season, forcing the plant to grow taller, to send out new branches, and to produce more sprouts.

The plants will get pretty tall if you continue to strip the branches. They'll keep growing until winter knocks them out or until some of the sprouts send out seed stalks and blossoms.

When plants get about 3 feet tall, try pinching out the center terminal on a few plants. This will encourage larger sprouts.

CAULIFLOWER

I blanch it with its own leaves

A thriving row of cauliflower is a spectacular sight in the vegetable garden, but few people think they can have great success with it. I think it's as easy to grow as any cabbage family crop. Cauliflower is less tolerant to hot weather than its relatives, though, so it's important to set your plants out very early or plan on a fall crop. If the heads mature in the heat, they're apt to have a bitter taste or go by very quickly.

For your first crop, set out some plants 3 or 4 weeks *before* the average date of the last spring frost. Pinch off a couple of the lower leaves.

As cauliflower heads get to be 4 to 5 inches across, they should be blanched by preventing sunlight from reaching the heads.

Blanching keeps the heads creamy white and sweet tasting. Normal blanching takes 4 to 8 days, but it may take a little longer in the fall. The conventional way to blanch is to pull the larger outer leaves over the top of the head, and tie them together with twine or fasten them with a rubber band. I don't like this method because it traps rain water. The moisture sits on the head and after a while the head may start to rot.

I have an easier method which prevents rot. I cover the heads by taking an outside leaf from

CABBAGE

the plant, breaking it partially at the stem, laying it over the top of the cauliflower, and tucking it in on the other side of the head. I do this on all sides of the plant. This lets air in but keeps the sunlight out. The folded leaves also shed the rain, so you have fewer problems with rot.

When cauliflower heads are about 6 inches across, you can begin to harvest them. Depending on the variety, you can let them get as large as 12 inches across. Be sure to cut the heads before the tight flower buds open. Cauliflower loses its fine texture and taste when the buds start to loosen. Unlike broccoli, cauliflower does not produce side shoots, so once a head is cut, that's it.

Plant for a continual harvest

There are so many nice ways to eat cabbages—raw in salads or cole slaw, as part of our traditional New England boiled dinner, pickled in sauerkraut, or sauteed with Chinese vegetables.

A continual harvest of cabbages is easy. Once the harvest starts there are always some ready-to-pick cabbages somewhere in the garden. I start some seeds indoors early in the season and set the plants out 3 or 4 weeks before the last spring frost date. (They're tough little plants and can take a light freeze.) In the early part of summer I sow more cabbage seeds, some in the

garden and some in flats in partial shade by the barn. In midsummer I set them in the garden and they grow eating-sized heads from late summer right up until the end of the season when the ground freezes.

Most importantly, I put my cabbage plants in wide rows to stretch out the harvest. I use a 20-inch wide row, and set my plants in about 10 inches apart in a 3-2-3 pattern.

As in other wide rows, the leaves of the plants grow to touch each other, shading out weeds and keeping the soil cool. Some plants grow faster and form heads earlier. Cut big heads first to provide extra space and food for the others. Remove all the leaves along with the heads.

How about a six-headed cabbage

Just for fun I like to coax a few of my cabbage plants into producing more than one head. I like to show visitors to my garden that there's really more than one head to a cabbage plant. You can do this in your own garden.

First, harvest a few spring-planted cabbages when the heads are fairly small (about softball size or slightly larger). Leave five or six of the larger outer leaves on the plant. For each leaf, a small head will form. By fall, if you're lucky, you'll get five or six small tasty heads.

Fall cabbage has time to make only one head, so try this trick only with your spring crop.

Cabbage head cracking? Turn off the faucet

Cabbage heads, like all vegetable heads, grow from the inside out. If yours start to crack, this probably means that the cabbages are growing too fast in the center. (This condition is frequently caused by heavy-handed fertilizing.) If you let the cracking continue, the head will split wide open and send up a seed stalk.

If you see a crack, hold the head and twist the whole plant halfway around, like turning a faucet. Don't be shy! Grab the plant and twist it halfway around. This breaks off many of the roots and that slows the inner top growth of the plant. Give the plant another quarter turn in a few days if the cracking continues.

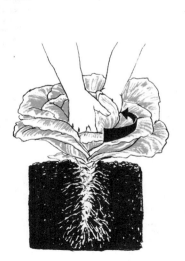

CHINESE CABBAGE

Super for stir-frying

I plant Chinese cabbage in my fall garden every year now. Jan and I really like its crisp, nutlike flavor. When I cook a stir-fry supper in my wok, Chinese cabbage is always one of the ingredients.

Sow Chinese cabbages about 8 to 10 weeks in advance of the expected first fall frost. Use a row about 15 inches wide and gradually thin out the row (or transplant seedlings to *another* row) to leave 5 to 8 inches between plants. Watch out for flea beetle damage when the crop is young. Later the plants may be bothered by cabbage loopers, so use the non-chemical Dipel or Thuricide spray on them.

When plants are 8 to 10 inches tall, blanch them for milder flavor by slipping half-gallon milk cartons (both ends torn open) over them.

Chinese cabbage grown beyond maturity is worthless. Harvest the heads when they are full and tight, much as you would Romaine lettuce. Once harvested, the heads will keep for a couple of weeks in the refrigerator.

Michili is the most popular variety of Chinese cabbage. It matures in about 70 days, grows well in partial shade, and will withstand a few autumn cold snaps. *Bok Choy* produces short, compact heads with a mild flavor and is more tender, sweeter, and crisper than *Michili*. The heads also have wider stalks, which is good for Chinese style cooking.

Blanch several heads for milder taste.

225

KOHLRABI

"Try it, you'll like it"

Nothing bothers kohlrabi. If you want a pest and disease-free plant, kohlrabi is it.

Kohlrabi is what I call an "above ground turnip" because what you eat is a round bulb that forms at the base of the stem. Kohlrabi has a little taste of turnip, along with a hint of cabbage and radish flavor.

Start kohlrabi from seed in wide rows just like turnips or beets. The plants are very hardy and will thrive in almost any kind of soil or temperature.

The best kohlrabies are those that grow quickly. Slowpokes are usually tough and woody. Plant in well-fertilized soil and provide a steady supply of water for the plants.

After thinning, the plants should be 3 to 5 inches apart in the row. If you plant in wide rows, you'll have enough kohlrabi to start harvesting once the first bulbs reach 2 to 3 inches in diameter. I pick kohlrabi all season, slicing the bulbs into bite-sized pieces with my jackknife as I walk through the garden. They're great.

Besides slicing it thin and eating it raw, or with dips or in salads, kohlrabi can be steamed, sauteed, or added to soups or boiled dinners.

CORN

Two ways to have it fresh every week

If you have room in your garden, sweet corn is a must. Nothing tastes as special as corn from your own garden. I like to have the pot of water heating up as I go out to pick some ears for dinner. That's because from the moment the ear is picked the sweet sugars inside begin turning to starch and the precious flavor starts to disappear. You simply cannot find that wonderful taste of freshly-picked corn anywhere else—not in canned corn, not in frozen corn, and not by buying the so-called "stay-sweet" varieties at the supermarket. Once sweet corn is picked, its flavor starts to go downhill.

Here's how to get the earliest sweet corn ever!

I have been able to have my first sweet corn 2 weeks before anyone else, even before the commercial growers. My method is simple, and it will work in your area, too.

This is *not* a method for planting all your corn. It's only for a part of your early crop. *The two most important factors in this method are the section of the garden to plant in, and when to plant.*

Decide the previous fall where to grow this extra-early corn. Choose a dry section of the garden where there is no sod, no manure or other fresh organic matter in the soil, and no green manure crop growing.

Let me tell you why this is so important. Whenever you have a large amount of organic matter in the soil, there's bound to be a lot of activity by soil micro-organisms in the spring. They'll be working to decompose all that organic matter. Normally, this is a good thing, but because your early corn seeds may take 2 weeks to come up, they could become part of the process—the soil life might decompose the seeds along with the organic matter.

If you have an area that slopes slightly to the south or west, great! This is a good spot for extra early corn because the soil will be much warmer there in spring and usually can be worked in advance of other sections of the garden.

No fertilizer at planting time

Do *not* put any plant food in the soil at planting time—no manures, and no fertilizers of any kind. If you've been planting corn for many years, this may seem dumb. But fertilizing early in the year is the worst thing you can do for corn. What happens? The plants usually grow too fast. This makes them tender and a slight nip of frost kills them. The fertilizer may also cause the seed to rot in the ground.

When should you plant? Take a gamble. The first year, try planting at least 3 weeks before the average last spring frost date. If you have good success and most of your plants make it, the next season plant a few days or a week earlier. Keep pushing the date earlier and earlier until you know the absolute earliest time you can plant sweet corn and get a good crop.

I try to have some early corn planted on my birthday—April 13—which is usually about 5 or 6 weeks *before* the last spring frost in Vermont.

Plant your corn a little deeper than normal—1½ to 2 inches deep. (Normal planting depth is about 1 inch.) It may take 2 weeks or more for the plants to emerge, so be patient. The seeds will sprout and start work on their root systems, and then the first leaves will appear.

Suppose the weather turns cold?

Corn seedlings grown this way can survive two or three frosts. I've seen corn lying frozen on the ground and completely brown, only to watch it spring back within a week.

Why is this so? Each corn plant has a terminal growing tip called its "growth point." If the growth point freezes, the plant dies. Fortunately, this growth point doesn't get above the surface until the plant is 6 to 8 inches high. It is in the base of the plant and is underground when the plant is small. That's usually when the coldest weather hits. Although the small leaves above ground may be frozen or set back, the plant can make a comeback if its growth point is insulated in the ground.

Side-dress corn when it's about 6–10 inches tall (top) and also later when tassels appear.

Soil of raised beds warms early, which is good for corn.

You have to plant an early variety if you want the earliest corn. *Spancross* and *Sugar 'N Gold* are two of the varieties that work well. It's important to plant treated seeds. If you have a little extra space, try a mid-summer variety like *Butter 'N Sugar*. With luck, you'll have some of that before anyone else.

One last thing—you'll need some fertilizer to get the best early corn. Side-dress your plants when they're 6 to 10 inches tall and again when the tassels appear.

Corn planting in wet and dry soil

Planting corn on *raised beds* produces earlier corn in wet areas, or in climates which don't get enough sun and heat for great corn. A raised bed is simply a row that is elevated 6 to 8 inches. It dries out and warms up earlier and captures more heat

and sun through the season. When it rains heavily, the raised bed sheds water, keeping the corn roots on the warm, dry side. I have grown all kinds of corn on raised beds with good success— even the tall, long-season *Silver Queen* variety. But if you live in a climate that is cool and cloudy, concentrate on early varieties such as *Sugar 'N Gold* or *Butter 'N Sugar*.

In hot, dry climates plant corn in 3- to 6-inch deep furrows. The furrows will catch irrigation water (or any rain that falls) and channel it to the corn plants. This helps corn germinate quickly, too; there is usually more moisture at the bottom of the furrow.

Once the plants start getting tall it's okay to spill in a little soil to help support them. As long as you keep even a shallow furrow, you'll reap a little extra irrigation water or rain. And because the roots are deeper than corn planted on level ground, furrow-planted corn will need even less watering.

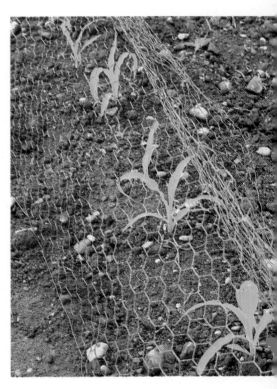

This 12-inch wide mesh wire keeps crows and other birds from digging up corn seedlings. Cover each row immediately after planting. When corn pokes through the top, it's safe to roll up the wire. Use it on later plantings or store if for next year.

229

Tips for a full season of sweet corn:

Corn will provide some summer shade for greens.

● There are two good ways to have fresh corn week after week. 1. Plant early and mid-season varieties the same day. Early varieties will usually produce after 8 or 9 weeks; later ones need 10 to 12 weeks or more. The result is 5 or 6 weeks of steady eating. 2. Stagger planting dates. In my garden I do this with *Butter 'N Sugar* corn, one of my yellow and white favorites. I sow a block of it, and every 10 or 14 days for about a month I plant another section. This way, I get many weeks of tasty corn.

● Corn prefers a full day of sun, so plant it away from trees or buildings. Think about the height of your corn varieties. Will they shade any plants? In hot climates a little shade from your corn can *help* many crops. I put most of my corn rows on the north side of the garden. They don't shade any smaller crops, and provide the added benefit of blocking the strong north and northwesternly winds we get.

● If you're planting popcorn, keep it at least 100 feet away from your other corn. Popcorn tends to "dominate" and if it crosses with your sweet corn, the sweet corn could taste anything but sweet.

● For sturdy corn, plant your seeds in a furrow or trench, then hill the plants as they grow. I plant corn in a furrow about 4 inches deep, with the seeds about 10 inches apart. Firm them in and cover them with 1 inch of soil. As the plants grow, fill the furrow. This supports the plants and also gets rid of weeds.

● Plant late varieties for best flavor. Some gardeners, tempted by the short growing times of the extra-early varieties, plant them all season long. They'll be disappointed. They'll get ears to harvest but they will definitely not be as tasty as late varieties which need 12 or 13 weeks to mature.

● Plant sweet corn in blocks of at least four rows. This assures good pollination.

INCORRECT:	CORRECT:
XXOO	XXXX
XXOO	XXXX
XXOO	XXXX
XXOO	XXXX
	OOOO
	OOOO
	OOOO
	OOOO

x = one variety
o = another variety

INSECTS THAT ATTACK CORN

grasshopper

corn maggot

Japanese beetle

asparagus beetle

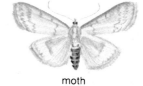

moth

European corn borer worm

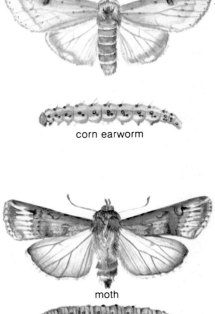

corn earworm

moth

cutworm

root-knot nematodes

stubby-root nematodes

typical nematode (x 100)

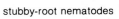

The small spheres form from nematode eggs
laid within the roots of the host plant.

Keep a big patch of corn weed-free with just a wee bit of work

1. The first few weedings are always with the In-Row Weeder. I drag it over the plants as fast as I can walk down the rows. I use it three or four times in every row, starting when the plants are just poking through the soil.

2. I use my roto-tiller to cultivate between the rows and keep any weeds from getting a foothold. By controlling the speed of the machine, I can maneuver quite close to the plants.

3. Hilling corn is very important in fighting weeds the easy way. I use a hilling attachment on my tiller, but you can do the same job easily with a hoe.

I hill the corn first when the plants are about 6 to 8 inches high. The hilling wings spill dirt around the young stalks. This buries and kills many little weeds and also gives a lot of support to the plant as it grows.

I plant my rows of corn 30 inches apart so I can take the tiller down between the rows and hill both sides.

4. I hill a second time when the plants are ¿ foot or more tall. I change the angle of my hilling wings to push soil even higher up on the stalks. The wings scrape away and bury any weeds that are left around the plants.

5. If you hill corn with a hoe, cultivate between the rows first. This will loosen up about 1 inch of soil so you can pull it up easily with your hoe and not have to chop.

In-Row Weeder works until corn is 6 to 8 inches tall.

Hilling soil around plants buries many weeds.

A later hilling gets rid of more weeds and anchors plants.

Pinch instead of peek to be sure corn is ripe

Never open a husk to check if sweet corn is ready to harvest. That's an engraved invitation to insects and birds to ruin your harvest. My method is "touchy-feely" but it works every time and never invites pests.

I locate the top of the ear, knowing that sometimes the ear will not fill out the husk completely. Then I press down on the top of the ear. If it is pointy, it's not ready to pick. (Usually the husks are still quite tight to the ear.) But if the top of the ear is flattish and almost rounded, the ear is ripe. (The husks are also a bit looser at this time.)

Some people have heard this tip in my lectures and have gone home and pinched the *sides* of the ear near the tip. This is incorrect. You have to feel the top, or the peak, of each ear—like feeling the point of a pencil and not its sides.

Pop-pop-pop-pop-corn!

Harvesting popcorn is easier than harvesting sweet corn. You don't have to worry about catching popcorn at the peak of sweetness; leave it in the garden until the stalks and husks are brown and dry.

Popcorn requires an additional 4 to 6 weeks of drying in a warm, well-ventilated place. Pick the ears when the plants have dried, husk them, and place them in mesh bags or spread them out in an area with warm air circulat-

ing around them. We hang mesh bags full of popcorn ears in our carport where they cure for 4 weeks. Then I hang the bags from the ceiling of our root cellar. The corn can keep for years in the cool, dry, dark conditions there.

I strip kernels from a few ears right away and store them in a glass jar in the refrigerator. All popcorn pops better if it spends 24 hours in a refrigerator, and I like to have some ready to pop. When the jar is getting low on popcorn, I go back down in the root cellar and rub two ears head-to-toe against each other to get more kernels.

A little home-grown popcorn goes a long way. One year I got 1½ cups of kernels from every six ears, which were about 5 inches long. Each 1½ cups popped out to 20 cups of popcorn.

Braided ornamental corn makes an attractive gift or wall-hanging.

Thorough drying needed for best popping corn.

233

EGGPLANT

An elegant, drought-resistant vegetable

I grow more eggplant than we need just to have plenty of the gorgeous purple and black eggplant fruits in the garden. I get four or six beautiful eggplants, or "eggs" as my grandson says, from each plant, but you can get lots more if you have a longer, hotter season than mine.

Eggplant is a tender crop. It can't stand frost. I set out a few transplants before our last frost date and surround them with plastic or cover them with hot caps. Most of the plants go in the garden when there's no threat of frost and the ground is warm. I put them in a staggered double row, as I do with peppers and broccoli, and set each one in the soil just slightly deeper than it was in its flat or pot.

Put eggplants in a sunny spot because they thrive on sun and lots of heat. Eggplant is one of the most heat- and drought-tolerant vegetables. A few years ago, gardeners in Texas and Oklahoma had a terribly hot summer with many days of temperatures above 100° F. A friend in Texas wrote to me that the only thing growing in his garden was eggplant. Well, that's because eggplants have a unique response to heat and drought. Instead of continuing to lose moisture through their leaf pores, or "stomates," like most vegetables in hot

Eggplant flowers are striking in color.

When an eggplant's skin is dull, it usually means the plants are past the best harvesting time.

weather, eggplant pores shut down to save the plant's dwindling water supply.

Harvest when glossy

When I set out my eggplants I put lettuce transplants between them. The lettuce plants cover the ground quickly, which saves me some weeding and watering. When the first small eggplant fruits appear, I harvest nice heads of lettuce.

Eggplants don't need a lot of

fertilizer. A tablespoon of 5-10-10 at planting time and another when you see blossoms or the first little eggplants is about all they need.

Eggplant tastes best when young. Start harvesting when the fruits reach one-third their full growth—anytime after their skins appear glossy. The eggplants are past their prime when the outside skin turns dull and you find lots of seeds inside.

Black Beauty is everybody's standard variety, and mine too. But I also plant *Dusky*, which matures earlier and serves northern gardeners well.

THE GREENS FAMILY

Celery   Chard

A full row of tender spinach (far left).
Ruby *leaf lettuce (left, with marigold buds in foreground) is a must in my rows of greens.*

Greens are the greatest. I doubt that any other group of vegetables provides so much good eating for so little effort. From small sections of wide rows, you'll be able to create salads of all kinds, from early spring to late fall. The long harvest is a big reason I like greens so much. They keep my garden going long after frost has nipped my last tomatoes, beans, and corn.

Greens fit in *everywhere*. More and more people are growing them in their flower beds, along walks and driveways, and in all sorts of containers.

Most of the greens grow quickly, which makes them perfect for spot planting. Whenever an area of the garden opens up, sprinkle in some lettuce or chard seeds, cover them with a little soil, and walk away. The only way to grow greens is in wide rows, and if you harvest your greens "crew cut" style, you'll get repeat harvests as tasty as the first without the bother of making another planting.

Beet and turnip tops make excellent greens, too, but I've put them with the other root crops.

Cool weather greens

These crops do best and are tastiest when you plant them early in the spring and then again in late summer for a fall harvest. They don't like hot weather, but they will grow in shady areas during the warm months. . .next to your asparagus bed, near a corn patch, along the side of the shed, or under your pole bean tepees.

Celery	Lettuce
Endive	Mustard
Kale	Spinach

Heat-tolerant greens

A few greens are downright productive during the hot summer months when others have gone to seed or are getting bitter. Where summers are *very* hot it's a good idea to give these crops a little shade.

Chard

Collards

New Zealand spinach

Fertilize after crew cut harvest

Many greens are best harvested by cutting them to an inch above the ground. It's so easy, and you can fill a harvest basket in a minute.

What's even better is that the plants will quickly put on new growth, which means another tasty harvest for you. Sometimes after giving part of the row a crew cut, I sprinkle dehydrated manure or other natural fertilizer around the plants. The next rain will carry the nutrients into the soil to provide some pep for the plants as they come back.

A bread knife for harvesting greens

Here's the first harvest in part of a spinach row. Note how the spinach on the left grows back from a crew cut harvest.

Greens which can be harvested by my crew cut method	Greens to be harvested by picking outside leaves or branches only
Chard	Celery
Endive	Collards
Lettuce	Kale
Mustard	New Zealand spinach
Spinach	

With greens, hardly a disease, only a few pests

The most troublesome insect pests of greens are the small leaf miners which feed on spinach, chard, and mustard (and beets and turnips as well). They are hard to control because they feed inside the leaves, not on them. Tear off the areas of the leaves with miners *before* you harvest; it's easier done in the garden than in the kitchen.

Because they are part of the cabbage family, mustard, collards, and kale can be bothered by the cabbage worm. Routine sprayings with the non-chemical Dipel or Thuricide once you spot the white cabbage moth should prevent any problems.

Aphids can be a problem with greens if they become too numerous. They are small, come in all colors, and hurt crops by sucking plant sap from leaves and stems. In a bad case, the plants will become stunted. Luckily, there are many natural predators of aphids—lady bugs, lacewing larvae, and some wasps. If you notice an unusually large group of aphids feeding on your greens, spray the plants with a soapy mixture, until predators bring the aphid population back to a level you can live with.

Diseases have not bothered any of my greens over the years. The most important step in keeping your greens free of disease is to thin wide rows correctly. The rows must have air circulating through them so plants can dry off after a rain or watering. If they're too thick, the plants will stay wet and that's an open invitation to disease organisms.

CELERY

How I grow this challenging vegetable

Some gardeners are hesitant to try celery and I understand why. It needs a long time to grow—up to 4 months of mostly cool weather. Celery also demands steady water and fertilizer because its root system is near the surface. But if your soil holds water well and has plenty of organic matter in it, you're in good shape, especially if you plant early and harvest early.

Because celery takes such a long time to grow, start the seeds indoors early. Celery seeds are slow to germinate, so you can soak them overnight to speed the process. Plant them indoors 10 to 12 weeks before the average last frost date.

To transplant celery, work the soil, mix in the fertilizer (about 1 cup of 5-10-10 per 10 feet of row), and dig a trench 4 to 5 inches deep. Plant the celery in the bottom of the trench, spacing the plants 8 to 10 inches apart, and set them half an inch deeper than they were in their pots. As the plants grow, fill in the trench a little with sand, soil, mulch or compost. This blanches the lower part of the stalks and keeps the roots cool and closer to water, which celery plants like.

Give the plants a good dose of water regularly. This, plus a side-dressing of 5-10-10, will keep the plants growing smoothly.

When celery runs low on water or slows down its growth for any reason, the stalks will get tough and the flavor will be strong.

I harvest my first stalks when they get big enough to eat; they taste best at this stage. I take the largest outside stalks. The growing center of the plant will produce new ones. I'd rather have smaller stalks that taste good than big ones that are so strong you can only chop them into soups or spaghetti sauce.

Blanch celery by hilling it

I've spent a lot of time blanching celery with milk cartons or boards. Frankly, it doesn't work too well. Blanching is supposed to produce milder tasting celery by shutting out the sunlight, but with standard methods it has never altered the flavor very much. In fact, blanching with milk cartons can cause problems—some stalks may rot because the air flow around them is cut down so much.

I like to hill the plants by bringing loose soil 4 or 5 inches up the stalks. It's easier than fussing with boards and the plants don't mind it. When I pull up the celery I get plenty of good-tasting stalks.

Hilling soil up around celery stalks (top) will lighten their color and produce a milder flavor.

239

CHARD

The day will come when it is more popular than spinach

Chard has a lot going for it. You can plant it as soon as you can work your garden in the spring, and it will provide tasty, nutritious greens for months. Through cold weather or hot, it won't get bitter, tough, or strong as long as you keep it harvested.

With wide rows you can get basket after basket of chard to can or freeze for the winter. To me, it's the perfect green for a wintertime meal. It tastes good, it's nutritious, and it's a lot cheaper than store-bought greens.

In processing chard it doesn't shrink as much as spinach. I'm sure chard will be grown more than spinach someday.

Chard is the easiest wide row crop to grow. It sprouts quickly, and, after an early thinning, it soon shades out any weeds.

It will also stand several freezes both in the spring and in the fall.

Plant chard in wide rows, scattering the seeds 2 to 3 inches apart. After thinning, the plants should be 3 to 4 inches apart.

Keep your chard cut back. Don't pick only the large outside leaves. They are the oldest and toughest on the plant. Cut the whole plant back to an inch above the soil. You'll get tender young leaves mixed in with the older ones. Most importantly, you'll force the plant to grow again. Another harvest will be a

*This is the second harvest of chard here. Right: This is how **Rhubarb** chard looks after cutting it close to the soil. In a few days it will produce new top growth.*

few weeks down the road. If you keep the soil fertilized, you can keep cutting the crop back as long as you want. I know a couple in Eugene, Oregon, who make one planting last 3 years. The weather is mild there and the plants don't freeze, so it's just a matter of fertilizing and cutting the chard when it gets a foot tall.

If you enjoy chard, make two plantings, one in early spring and another in middle or late summer. You can plant it in the fall in the South, and it will grow throughout the winter.

COLLARDS

More northerners should grow them

My southern friends are crazy about collards. These nutritious, flavorful greens can be grown anywhere, even way up North where I live.

Unlike most greens, collards will survive the cool spells of spring and fall weather, as well as the intense heat of summer.

In the South, collards are so widely grown that garden stores and nurseries provide young collard plants for sale in the spring. Setting out these plants is a convenient and reliable way to get an early harvest before hot weather slows them down.

The 4- to 5-inch seedlings resemble cabbage plants, but they'll never head up like cabbage. Some folks refer to collards as "headless cabbages."

I always seed collards directly in the garden in mid-summer for a fall crop. I sow the seeds in a 16- or 20-inch wide row and thin the plants to 8 to 10 inches apart. Fall and winter collards thrive on cool nights and light freezes. They add the zing and succulence to the leaves.

If you live where winters are mild, you'll discover that a fall crop of collards lasts well into winter. It will grow until the temperature dips to 20° F. a few times.

Like other greens, collards can be harvested as soon as there are enough leaves to make a meal. Never cut collards all the way to the ground as you would mustard or chard. Once the central bud is removed, collards won't grow back. Instead, harvest only the bottom leaves of the plant so the central bud will keep putting out branches.

Some gardeners in the South plant a spring crop, harvesting the lower leaves as they need them early in the season. Then they let the plant grow through the summer months and begin heavy harvesting again in the fall. It's much more common, though, to plant collards twice, once in early spring and again in late summer.

Chard comes in different colors. *Swiss Chard* is green with white stems. *Ruby Chard* has bright red stems and reddish green leaves. I prefer the *Ruby Chard* because I like the color it adds to a planting of greens. It also has more of a beety taste, which I prefer. When the stalks get ahead of me and grow large, they are more tender than the large *Swiss Chard* stalks.

However, letting the stalks of *Swiss Chard* grow very large has its advantages, too. I can strip the leaves and cook them like spinach. That leaves the large white stems, which are delicious in Chinese wok cooking.

ENDIVE

Add a touch of class to your salads

Endive is a cool-weather salad green with a distinct clean, sharp taste. A handful of endive leaves mixed into your salad bowl adds a wonderful touch.

Endive doesn't like hot weather, but it can take a few hard frosts. I grow it as a fall crop only, and sow it directly into the garden. You also can start endive indoors like head lettuce. Either way, plants should stand 6 to 7 inches apart.

Some people blanch the endive plants when the heads are getting large to reduce the bitterness, but I don't. I've noticed that the plants nearly blanch themselves. The inside portion of the head stays white, and that's the best tasting part. We cut it up to mix with lettuce or other salad greens.

I like the curly-leaf endive varieties such as *Green Curled*. A green known as *escarole* is actually a less-curly endive with broader leaves.

KALE

The winter wonder crop and nutritionist's delight

Back before lettuce was hauled thousands of miles to market, truck farmers near big cities grew kale in fall, late winter, and early spring. It filled the demand for fresh, nutritious salad greens. Unfortunately, kale has since lost much of its popularity in spite of its high vitamin and mineral content and appealing flavor. I hope we get back to eating more of it.

Kale prefers cool weather, but it can survive quite a bit of heat if you give it some water. I know—I've grown beautiful wide rows of kale in Florida.

In Vermont I plant the seeds in wide rows in midsummer and harvest when the plants are tall enough to have some leaves cut. In some areas of the South you can plant as late as September or October and have fresh kale through the mild winter. A few weeks after planting, thin the kale so the plants are 4 to 6 inches apart. Later on, pull up some plants to give those remaining plenty of room to grow.

Don't pull up or till under kale plants in the fall when you might think it's time to stop gardening. Let them keep growing right into winter. They will survive through cold and snow. The deeper the snow, the greater the thrill of harvesting some crisp blue-green kale.

Because kale is a biennial, another peak harvesting period is

when the snow melts and the plants start growing again. The new leaves are delicious raw, or you can cook them and use them like spinach or as a garnish.

Siberian Kale and *Blue Curled Scotch Kale* are the two varieties you'll most likely see in the seed racks. *Blue Curled Scotch* is better tasting to me and winters over very well. By the way, the *Blue Curled Scotch* makes a nice houseplant in winter. Jan and I dig up a couple each fall, pot them, and place them near a south-facing window. The plants lose some color, but the intricate shapes of the curled leaves are quite pleasing.

We also like to plant flowering or ornamental varieties of kale. Their curly green and maroon leaves are beautiful at the edge of the garden. They also can be potted and brought indoors for the winter.

Kale needs a little elbow room. When a row seems too crowded I pull out a few plants for a harvest.

LETTUCE

Iceberg types—for solid heads, start early

Too many people think head lettuce or *Iceberg* lettuce has to be bought at the market.

I grow wonderful crops of head lettuce and yet every year some new visitor looks at my bright green rows and says, "Hmmmm. I didn't know you could grow that here." Well, you can and it's easy.

All you need is some cool weather in spring or fall. Get started *early;* head lettuce needs as much time as possible developing in *cool weather,* so the earlier you can set out some plants, the better. They will have the best chance to head up be-

fore the scorching days of summer.

Great Lakes, Iceberg, and *Ithaca* varieties have all done well in my garden. I start them indoors in shallow flats or pyramid planters about 6 to 8 weeks before the last expected frost date.

The most important step in early planting is to harden off the plants very well before setting them into the garden. After they are about 4 weeks old, I start giving them some time outdoors. That way they can handle unexpected cold snaps and even a light frost.

I may sound like a broken record by now, but head lettuce belongs in wide rows. When I set transplants out, I first prepare a wide row seedbed 20 inches wide. Then I set the plants 10 inches apart in a 3-2 pattern down the row, two at the edges and one in the middle in the first row. And two in the next row, each 5 inches in from the edges.

Lettuce roots recover quickly from transplant shock. To help them out a bit, I trim some of their outside leaves. Leave the center alone, of course. Don't be afraid to set out even the smallest of transplants. If they have some decent roots, they'll make it.

Lettuce roots recover quickly from transplanting in spring as long as soil stays moist. I've already picked off a couple of outside leaves on this plant to help.

With so many plants in the wide row, you can afford to start harvesting as soon as the leaves are big enough to eat or the first heads are the size of softballs. You'll get plenty of bigger heads later. After all, who needs a whole row of head lettuce at once? Start picking early!

Keep your head lettuce plants supplied with water as they head up.

I use pyramid planters for sure starts

The biggest obstacle to a fall crop of head lettuce is getting the plants off to a good start in late summer when it can be ferociously hot. The answer is to use pyramid planters.

I sow a couple of seeds in each compartment and then pinch out one after the plants are up. I keep the planting trays in a semi-shaded spot so they don't dry out. When it is time to put the plants in the garden (after 3 weeks or so), I give them a good soaking.

Using my jackknife, I slide out a plant without disturbing its root system. This "bump-free" transfer to the garden means that all roots will be intact. The plant will be able to survive hot weather on its own.

I hardly budge roots in transplanting.

Other lettuce favorites

Growing in wide rows helps me get *more* of the very flavorful *Buttercrunch* and *Dark Green Boston* lettuce. These are "soft head" varieties. They form a head, but it's loose.

I sow the seeds directly in the garden early in the spring. (You can start some ahead of time inside if you like.) In a wide row they easily can come up too thickly to form a nice head, so it's important to thin them out as they grow.

Once the row is thinned, you can harvest by cutting the heads an inch above the ground. A lot depends on the weather, but you may get a fine second cutting of leaves later.

The flavor of *Black Seeded Simpson* is probably my favorite among the leaf lettuce varieties. These varieties don't produce heads, but they are ready to eat earlier, and they come back well after a crew cut harvest.

I like *Oak Leaf*, too, because it doesn't get bitter as quickly in warm weather. I always include some *Ruby* leaf lettuce for color and taste in a salad. It looks beautiful in the garden.

Everyone should have a good supply of leaf lettuce seed on hand at all times. Plant short wide rows here and there in the garden through the season starting as early as you can. You'll never be caught without enough salad greens for a small army.

Because *Romaine* doesn't germinate as well as other types, I plant it a lot thicker than the other varieties.

The plants produce heads 10 or more inches high, so they need a little room. Thin your wide rows as the plants reach 3 or 4 inches in height. Pull them as you need them until you have 6 or 8 inches between plants.

In the summer I pick lettuce from the garden minutes before serving. I wash it well and don't chill it because it's so fresh. If you need to store lettuce, wash it first, put it in a bowl, cover it with a damp towel, and put it in the refrigerator. It'll stay crisp and fresh for days. Another way is to put the lettuce in plastic bags without tying up the bags, and store in the fridge.

Ruby lettuce fans out to form a colorful loose head.

MUSTARD

Not the kind you put on hot dogs

Mustard is a cool-weather crop that can be used as a salad ingredient or as a cooked green, which I prefer. The seeds are so fine that you may want to sow them from a salt shaker to insure uniform seeding.

Mustard is great when planted in blocks because you can harvest so much for so little work. Mustard greens shrink a little when you cook them so you need quite a bit anyway.

Harvest mustard as soon as there is enough for a meal. Mustard planted in late summer for fall harvesting is tops. Cold weather and light frosts do much for improving mustard's flavor. If winters are mild in your area, a late summer planting will yield greens all winter long.

Of course, you can plant mustard early each spring, too. In as little as 30 days or so, you can be harvesting young leaves. *Green Wave* and *Tendergreen* varieties give excellent results. *Green Wave* is peppery when raw. *Tendergreen* has a mellow flavor when cooked.

SPINACH

Too many people miss out when spinach plants go to seed. You can gain heftier harvests by planting as early in spring as possible, by mulching and growing in wide rows, and by saving a few seed packets for fall planting.

first day I can work the soil in spring, and again in late summer for a fall harvest. Spinach takes about 10 days to germinate when the soil is still cool.

Start your spinach plantings early. Otherwise, hot weather may send your plants into the seed stage before you harvest it. Don't wait too long to harvest spinach, either. Cut the whole plant back to an inch tall while the leaves are still small and tender. They'll grow back.

I'm not too choosy about spinach varieties, but I always plant some of the *Bloomsdale* varieties. To me, they're tops.

New Zealand spinach

New Zealand spinach is not like spinach at all. I wish it were, though, because it grows right through hot weather without going to seed. The first year I grew it I ate some leaves raw. They tasted lousy. I didn't dare put them in salad. To approach the taste of real spinach, you have to cook *New Zealand spinach*.

Some gardeners advise soaking the very hard seeds for a day before planting to help germination, but you can have good stands of this green without soaking. Just plant early in the season when the soil is quite moist.

The plants grow a foot or two high. Thin them to 8 to 10 inches apart. To harvest, pick off the leaves you need. Don't cut the plants back and don't pick off the tops.

New Zealand spinach can grow tall and become quite bushy.

Harvest bushels, not handfuls with early planting and wide rows

If you've ever grown spinach, you know it doesn't take many leaves to fill a basket. But when you cook them, a lot turns to a little.

To get an abundance of spinach from a small space, I plant in wide rows. If you harvest 6 pounds of spinach from a single row, you can get 20 pounds from a wide row the same length. That's important when it's time to freeze spinach.

Because spinach thrives in cool weather, I often plant it on the

246

OKRA

Harvest pods small and often

Okra likes hot weather, so plant it after the last frost when the ground is warm. I cheat a little in Vermont and plant it early under a grow tunnel to catch extra heat. (I shape my tunnels so they are quite tall and I can leave them on for 2 or 3 weeks.)

To help the seeds sprout, soak them in water for a few hours before planting or put them in the freezer overnight. Either step will help soften or crack the seed coat.

The plants should stand about 12 inches apart so they can spread out. Okra will grow big and bushy in soil rich in nutrients. If you have poor soil, be sure to use a lot of fertilizer.

The okra blossoms are beautiful, but sometimes they fall off without forming pods because of sudden changes in the weather or an up-and-down water supply. If the plants are healthy, they will keep right on blooming and producing pods once the weather improves.

Harvest the pods when they are about 2 inches long. If they get large and woody, they'll lose their flavor. Although some varieties boast that you can let the pods get 7 to 9 inches long and still have a steady harvest, I've found that the more young pods you pick, the more the plant will produce.

Okra grows so quickly in hot weather, that once the harvest begins you might have to pick every 2 or 3 days. Harvesting can be a chore in a big plot. I met a 16-year-old gardener in Georgia who grew 2 acres of okra as a 4-H project. I asked her, "How do you harvest it?" She answered, "With my whole family!"

Gloves and a long-sleeved shirt are practical when harvesting in a big patch. The leaves are covered with little spines you can hardly see. These spines can get

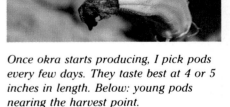

Once okra starts producing, I pick pods every few days. They taste best at 4 or 5 inches in length. Below: young pods nearing the harvest point.

under your skin and make your hands and arms itch.

After the first rush of pods, remove the bottom leaves of the plant to encourage it to bear more.

In the deep South, okra grows very tall. When the plants get too tall to harvest, cut them back to 12 to 18 inches above the ground. This is usually done in midsummer. The plants will sprout again to make a second crop.

THE ONION FAMILY

My garden is always full of onions and their relatives. It's easy to grow a lot of them in wide rows. And their flavors—from the strong yellow keeping onions to the subtle shallots—go with almost everything. How can you cook without them?

Onions, garlic, and shallots will store for many months, and you don't need a root cellar either. Leeks won't hold out like the others but they can be kept in my "perennial patch" in the garden or for a week or two in the refrigerator. The onion family is with us 12 months a year. Jan and I never have to buy any.

There are lots of fun ways to grow these crops in the garden. How about a multiplying shallot patch so you never have to buy expensive shallots again? Or a no-work "Eternal Yield" square of bunching onions to get the earliest scallions every spring? Or a big row of giant sweet onions?

The taller the top, the bigger the onion

There are only a couple of important things to remember about growing plenty of good onions.

Start early in the season, well before the last spring frost date. There are two reasons to get going early: the cold won't hurt onions, and they need as much time as possible to grow big, lush green tops. The more top growth your onions produce, the bigger the bulbs they will form on the bottom. But how do bulbs grow? Where do they get their energy to fatten up? Here's the story:

After onions have been growing a while, they suddenly stop putting energy into their tops when Mother Nature gives them a signal, or "trips" them. This signal is a combination of increasing temperature and the number of hours a day the sun shines. It's complicated, but the point is that suddenly the onions shift gears and the energy from the leaves is transported down to make a bulb. If you have a healthy onion plant with a lot of green tops, you should get a good-sized bulb. If you plant late, the onions may be short on top growth, which means smaller bulbs.

Up to 10 times more onions in wide row

Plant onions according to my wide row method and you'll be harvesting onions sooner, with a steady harvest through the growing season, and have plenty of big ones left to store for the cold months.

In my wide row trials, I found that you can get up to 10 times the harvest of a single row by devoting an equal amount of garden space to a wide row planting. I've often thought I could get rich planting onions in wide rows on just a little bit of land if I could only find some way to sell them all.

I got this big bundle of scallions from thinning a few feet of a wide row, while the smaller harvest was pulled from the same length of a single row.

For a wide row super harvest

I plant most of my onion sets about 2 or 3 inches apart in all directions.

It's important to firmly tamp down the sets.

The In-Row Weeder can be dragged safely over growing onions to keep annual weeds from sprouting.

Let's look at how I grow a wide row of onions to see how such a big harvest is possible. Most of this information also applies to the other onion family members.

Whether you plant seeds, "sets" (little onions which grow up to be big onions), or small onion transplants, the wide row harvest should be far ahead of standard single row plantings.

Close planting. I plant onion sets about 2 or 3 inches from each other in all directions. They're almost shoulder to shoulder! Don't be afraid to crowd them. I've even planted sets as close as 1 inch apart. Hold each set by the point end (this puts the root end in the right direction) and press it firmly in the ground to its full depth. Use a

hoe to tamp them down or the bulbs may pop out of the ground.

In-Row Weeder keeps row clean. Early in the season, pass over the onion row each week with the In-Row Weeder to keep weeds in check without ever bending down. If one or two weeds survive, let them get big enough to pull easily a little later on.

Save some sets in the refrigerator

If you want a continuous harvest of scallions, don't plant all your sets at once. Save a few handfuls and store them in the refrigerator so they won't sprout.

As you finish thinning out your wide rows for scallions, find an open spot in the garden and plant your second-string sets. In a few weeks you'll have another rush of scallions to harvest.

Sets the size of small marbles are best. The bigger ones and some of your onion plants will send up a seedpod early in the game. This must be pinched off or the onion won't grow a good bulb. Snap it off 1 or 2 inches from the base. Check every few days for more seedpods because they grow quickly. Get them while they are small.

Plant once for everlasting bunching onions

Nine years ago I planted one packet of white bunching onion seeds, and I'm still eating from the row. Each year I get the tastiest, earliest scallions you can imagine. I don't do a thing all season except pull a few weeds now and then.

It's important to plant a "bunching" onion variety because these onions will not form a bulb. The bottoms stay thin all year long. Plant them where you won't be tilling, such as next door to a perennial planting. I have mine near my black raspberries.

Plant the seeds thickly in early spring. Thin them a little with a rake when they come up, then let them grow. Harvest some of them when the stems are as big as a pencil, but leave plenty alone. Let them go right into the fall and winter. Don't mulch them—they don't need it.

In the spring they'll come back and you'll be able to harvest some very early scallions. Again,

Close-planted onions ready to be pulled at scallion size.

Pull some early scallions. When onion tops are 6 or 8 inches tall and the stems are as thick as a pencil, pull onions as you need them. This thins the row and helps keep the soil loose near the other onions. In many wide rows I harvest two out of three onions for early eating. The first scallions have not yet formed a bulb, but later, if the plants have small bulbs, Jan uses them for pickling.

be sure to leave plenty of plants in the row. These will go to seed before too long. When they do, don't do anything except admire the beautiful blossoms and watch the bees work them. You want the plants to reseed the row. A whole new group of onions will start to grow. They'll winter over and send up early greentails the next spring. They're about the very *first* thing you can eat from your garden. You can pull some from the bed anytime, but you'll find that the first handfuls in early spring have the best flavor.

Secrets of growing giant sweet onions

Everybody loves those juicy, sweet slicing onions for hamburgers and salads. Let me tell you the secrets of growing the big ones.

I recommend growing or buying transplants. This means that you can get an early start in your garden when the weather is cool and when onions grow so well. The more cool-weather growth your plants can muster, the larger your onions will be at harvest time.

I grow a tasty variety, such as *White Sweet Spanish,* and give them a long hardening-off period before planting. It takes 2 weeks to get them adjusted to outdoor weather. Most folks say that you shouldn't set out your plants until after the last frost, but I disagree. If you harden them off well, they should do fine planted 2 or 3 weeks before the last frost date.

The best transplant is as tall and thick as a pencil, but don't toss out the small guys. Find a place for them in the row, and you'll be surprised at how big

Let some bunching onions go to seed every year.

Big, White Sweet Spanish *onions are easy to grow if you start plants indoors.*

they get by the end of the season.

Transplanting onions is easy. Place the plant on your index finger, and push your finger and the onion into the soil about 2 inches. Lift up just a bit (this gets the roots headed in the right direction) and firm the soil around the plant.

If you buy onion plants from a mail order company, unwrap them as soon as they arrive. Stick their roots in water in a shallow pan and plant them as soon as you can. If you can't plant them immediately, unwrap them, put them in plastic bags, and store them in the refrigerator for a day or two. You can also heel them in the garden and move them later.

To get big onions it's important to side-dress the crop at least three or four times. Use a balanced fertilizer such as 10-10-10; for at least one side-dressing add a little bone meal or superphosphate to give the expanding bulbs extra phosphorus.

Onions need extra fertilizer

No matter what you plant—sets, seeds, or plants—onions should get some extra fertilizer when they are 6 to 8 inches high, and then again 3 or 4 weeks later. A couple of side-dressings will give you a crop to be proud of.

Use dehydrated manure to fertilizer onions. Sprinkle it liberally over the wide rows. If you use 5-10-10, get your hand close to the ground and spread the fertilizer around the bulbs. If the fertilizer contacts the bulbs, it won't hurt them at all, but it can sting the green tops. That's why I don't broadcast it like dehydrated manure.

The drier the onions, the better they store

Pull your storage onions when the plants are dead. The tops will lose their green color, turn brown, and start to wither. That's the time they should be harvested. Don't let them stay in the ground once they are dead.

A warm, sunny day is ideal for pulling onions. Leave them bottom side up in the garden for 2 or 3 days until they are dry. Keep roots away from the ground. The drying kills the roots—they look like little brittle wires. When thoroughly dry, they'll break off easily with a swipe of your hand.

Onions then need a longer drying or "curing" period of up to 2 weeks. Spread them out in a warm, airy place in the shade. I usually put them alongside our gravel driveway. I cover them with a light cotton sheet (do not use plastic). Held in place by stones, the sheet keeps the sun from burning the bulbs, but allows plenty of air circulation. I turn the bulbs a couple of times to promote even drying.

Once the onions are dry (after about 2 weeks), I sort them according to size. Then I put them in mesh onion bags, hang them in the garage, and leave them there for another 3 to 4 weeks.

Finally, I move the onions to my root cellar. I find the drier the onions, the better they store. I hang them from the ceiling so they will get good air circulation around them.

A BUSHEL OF HOME-GROWN ONION SETS
FROM ONE OUNCE OF SEEDS

To grow sets I use seeds of a good keeping onion. An ounce of seed can produce a bushel of sets.

I've never had as much fun and satisfaction growing onions as I have since I began using home-grown sets. I grow about 45 pounds of sets each year in an area 3 feet by 5 feet and it takes only 1 ounce of seeds. The seeds cost about $3, but the sets I get are worth 20 times that!

You probably can't use 45 pounds of sets in your garden, of course, but I bet you have neighbors and friends who would gladly buy some from you in the spring.

Here's how I get such a big, money-saving harvest from a 3- by 5-foot area:

I sow onion seeds in mid-July—about 3 or 4 months before the first hard freezes are due in my area. Timing is important! Onions grown for sets should grow about 4 months before a hard freeze kills the tops. If I planted earlier, the bulbs would get bigger; if later, they wouldn't have enough time to form marble-sized bulbs.

Where you plant is important. I pick a section of the garden where I recently grew a weed-beating green manure crop like peas, beans, or buckwheat.

Onions like to grow fast, so fertilizer is important—especially in midsummer, because by then the rains have carried many nutrients deep into the soil.

I've found that *Ebenezer, Stuttgarter,* and *Buc-*

caneer seeds produce excellent sets. These three are yellow, long-keeping varieties.

I get my onion seeds from a mail order company because I can find all of these varieties, and I can order an ounce or two of seeds at a good price.

To plant them, I rake the soil of the bed one last time to get it as smooth as I can. Then I sprinkle the ounce of seed evenly over the bed. The seeds land about ¼- to ½-inch apart.

I firm them in with a hoe, rake up a ¼- or ½-inch covering of soil from outside the seedbed, smooth it over the seeds, and firm them down again.

Don't be worried about getting the seeds too close together because that's really what you want. A slight crowding will help keep the sets small. You don't want to grow big sets because those go to seed when you plant them next spring.

I weed this bed just like my other wide rows. The first step is crucial—I drag an ordinary garden rake across the bed when the plants are about ½ inch tall. After 5 or 6 days I drag my In-Row Weeder over the plants. I use the In-Row Weeder a few more times at 3- or 5-day intervals.

About frost time, the tops, though small, start to die. They'll grow a little bit beyond a frost, but not much. By the next freeze the tops are usually brown and have fallen down.

I pull them up and spread them out to dry for a week in a warm, airy place such as a porch or carport. Don't wash the onions, and don't worry about the tops. They'll just dry up and fall off.

The last step is very important. Put the best sets in *small* mesh bags. Never load a lot of sets or small onions in a big bag. They'll pack too tightly and the onions in the middle won't get the air circulation they need to keep.

Once I've got them bagged, I put them in the root cellar where it's cool and dry. Any cool, dry place in your house should be okay, too.

Check them once or twice a month, and get rid of sets that sprout or rot.

Pests and diseases

Thrips are tiny insects that feed on onion leaves and cause white, blotchy areas. The plants weaken, and the yield is reduced.

The onion maggot is the off-spring of a small fly that lays her eggs near the base of the plant, or on the bulb itself late in the season. The maggots kill the plant by burrowing into the stem and the bulb. Pull up and destroy any plants with maggots before they mature into flies.

Neck rot is probably the most common onion disease. It often hits just after the harvest or while the bulbs are in storage. All onion varieties can develop neck rot, but the mild-flavored, Bermuda-type onions are especially susceptible. Drying the onions at warm temperatures with good ventilation and then storing them in a cool, airy spot can help prevent this disease.

Hang some braided onions in your kitchen

If you want to braid onion tops, harvest the crop while the drying tops are still flexible. Braid in twine to strengthen the tops, and hang the braids in a warm, well-ventilated, shady spot to cure. Then store them in a cool, dark place and bring out one braid at a time to hang in the kitchen.

GARLIC

Break into cloves to plant

I can't imagine spaghetti sauce without garlic, and I can't imagine my garden without it either. There's nothing better than fresh garlic from the garden—it's a must for our pickles.

Buy a few garlic bulbs from a garden store or supermarket and break each one into individual cloves.

Plant each clove 3 or 4 inches from the next one in a wide row. Push them in to their full depth, pointed end up. Plant them as early as you can, like onion sets, and give them two or three side-dressings during the season. Keep the soil loose around them, and don't let them get dry.

For big garlic bulbs, the plants need to grow mostly in cool weather. That's why some folks plant garlic in the late summer or early fall and mulch the plants over the winter. The plants grow during the cool fall and spring weather before making their bulbs.

When the garlic tops fall over and die, pull up the bulbs, let them dry in the sun for a few days, and cure them in an airy place as you would onions. Store them in mesh bags or braid the tops.

Braid garlic before tops are completely dry. Light reinforcing wire is usually required for a long-lasting braid.

LEEKS

Blanch with soil for beautiful white stems

I start leeks indoors quite early along with my onions, and set them out in the garden as transplants. I grow a short wide row so I can have some good-sized leeks in early fall when the weather is getting cool and Jan and I start thinking about hot soups.

Instead of planting in a wide row, you can set them in the bottom of a narrow furrow 4 to 6 inches deep. Set the plants an inch deeper than they were in their flat. As the plants grow, gradually fill the furrow with soil.

In this way, 4 inches or so of stem beneath the soil will be white—and that's what leeks are all about!

I keep a bed of leeks growing year after year with a bare minimum of effort. Years ago I gave them a good start in a short wide row. Now I let nature do the rest. I harvest leeks each spring and they continue to seed and multiply. The tastiest harvest is in the spring when the plants put on quick, new growth. That's when I harvest many small, mild leeks rather than big ones later. Those can be tough. After the spring harvest I toss a few handfuls of compost around remaining plants. These go to seed in early summer and the bed soon starts adding plants.

Plant leeks in a shallow trench and hill soil around stalks to blanch them.

SHALLOTS

Plant one, get a cluster

If you haven't cooked with shallots, you're missing a mild, distinctive flavor that is great. Paying a high price for them at the store is ridiculous because anybody can grow enough bulbs to use all year and still have some to plant as next year's crop.

Shallots are grown from sets which you may have to buy to get started. That should be your last purchase. Plant the sets, with the pointed end up, to their full depth. Space them 4 to 6 inches apart—they need more room than onion sets.

Side-dress them when they are 6 inches tall and again 3 weeks later.

Shallots are very productive. A pound of sets yields about 5 to 7 pounds of shallots. You'll get a big cluster of shallots for each set you plant. Harvest these bulbs anytime.

I let most of the crop grow until the tops die back. I pull them up, dry them like onions, and stash them in the root cellar. They keep much better than onions—up to 10 or 12 months.

Be sure to save some to plant next year.

PEANUTS

Early Spanish variety grows well in my garden

You can't plant peanuts from the stores if they've been roasted. To find a seed source, look in the mail order catalogs. If you live in the South, a garden store should have them.

Most peanut varieties need 4 or 5 months of warm growing time. If your season is shorter, try *Early Spanish* peanuts. They take less time and bear very well.

A peanut seed consists of a hull filled with nuts. I shell them and plant each nut separately, 1¼ inches deep and 1 foot apart.

Once the blossoms are pollinated, the plants send out long runners or "fruiting pegs." These pegs curve downward, grow into the soil, and produce clusters of peanuts. When the plants get about a foot tall, they should be hilled by pulling a little dirt up around them. This helps the fruiting pegs to bury their tips sooner and form peanuts earlier.

The peanut harvest is near when the leaves turn yellow. This happens because the peanuts underground need the food supply in the leaves for their own growth. Inspect a few pods to see if they are ready.

The best way to harvest peanuts is by slowly prying up the whole plant with a fork. I lift the plant out of the ground, and gently shake off the loose soil. The peanuts will need some drying in a shaded, warm, airy spot. One year chipmunks discovered my drying peanuts and didn't leave me a single one; now I'm careful where I dry them.

Dry peanuts for 2 to 3 weeks to allow the moisture content of the peanuts to drop. When the plant leaves become dry and crumbly, pull the nuts off the plants. They should be ready for roasting and storing.

Tasty boiled peanuts

An Extension Service friend in Florida showed me how to use peanuts in the "green stage," that is, after they are well-formed but still not mature. The hulls are thin and soft at this stage.

Dig them with a fork and pull the peanuts right away. Boil them, hulls and all, in salt water for 5 to 10 minutes. Take them out, salt them again, and roast them for 10 to 15 minutes. Eat them, shells and all. They're delicious!

A young peanut plant (far left) and blossoming (center). Peanuts form just under the soil and can be easily dug or pulled.

257

PEAS

My plant 'n pick pea patch produces even in hot climates

Peas are the ultimate crop for the lazy gardener. Using my wide row method, you can plant them in minutes and come back weeks later to harvest them. There's no weeding, side-dressing, staking, or hilling. . .there's just no work at all to growing tasty fresh peas anywhere in any climate.

People in the South often complain to me, "Dick, it's just too hot down here to grow English peas. They start growing okay when the weather is cool but then it gets hot and the peas don't produce." My wide row method solves this problem.

I once brought 2 bushels of fresh-picked peas from my Florida test garden to a class I was giving nearby. I set the peas down in the middle of the crowd and said, "Taste for yourself." These Florida gardeners sampled the peas and said, "They're great!"

This wide row of peas (top left) won't have to be staked at all. About 2 weeks after peas blossom (below, left) there will be plenty of pods to pick. The work goes easier if you've got a stool to sit on.

The secret to "no-work" peas and a good harvest in warm climates is to plant them in wide rows. Choose a dwarf variety such as *Little Marvel, Progress No. 9,* or *Wando* (which fills its pods well in warm weather). Try *Snow Peas* in wide rows if you do Chinese cooking. You'll have plenty. Then, as early in the season as you can, work your soil a couple of times.

Because peas are legumes, they don't need much fertilizer—especially nitrogen. A day or two before planting, I broadcast 1 or 2 pounds of 5-10-10 commercial fertilizer over each 100 square feet of garden space. I work it into the top 2 to 3 inches of soil.

Don't worry about cold weather—peas will stand many freezes. Treat the seeds with a protectant and sow them in rows at least 16 inches wide. (I often grow peas in 3- or 4-foot-wide rows.) Tamp them down and cover with soil from alongside the row, or simply roto-till them in a few inches.

No weeding

When the peas come up, they'll quickly screen out the sun from hitting weeds which are trying to grow up through the peas. You never have to weed a good wide row of peas. Most important for southern gardeners, the shade keeps the soil cool and moist. This practically assures steady growth of vines, pods, and peas. In a single row of peas, you don't get this cooling, moisture-saving effect. In the South, single rows

of peas dry out, the roots and plants become parched, and the harvest, if there's any, is puny and not too tasty. But with wide rows, as I learned in Florida, the peas are prolific and sweet even in a very hot season.

As they grow these peas will block more and more sunshine from striking the soil.

With a dwarf variety like *Little Marvel* you'll find that the plants in a wide row won't need staking. The only pods in the wide rows that sometimes hit the ground are those on the outside of each row. Most of the peas will be in the air, dry, and easy to get to when you're picking.

Use two hands to pick peas, so that you won't damage the brittle vines or uproot the plants. Hold onto the pea vine with one hand, and pick off the pods with the other.

English peas are very sweet because of their high sugar content. However, after picking, the sugar starts turning to starch. That's why it's important to rush the peas into the kitchen, so you can shell and cook them.

Climbing peas growing up a trellis of brush cut from my woods.

PEPPERS

Climbing pea trellises

Many people like to grow climbing peas because they're easy to pick and bear very well. The *Alderman* pea and the new *Sugar Snap* pea (which has edible pods) are good examples. They grow so high they need a support, like a chicken wire fence, trellising, or brush.

A lot of people rave about *Sugar Snaps* but I can't share the enthusiasm. To me, they just don't measure up as a real pea, so I grow *Alderman*.

My dad liked to grow peas on brush. One of my winter chores as a kid was to gather all the brush he used to support the plants.

I plant double or triple rows and then set brush in the middle of the rows, about 2 or 3 inches from the plants. If you use a chicken wire trellis, set it up first and then plant a row of peas on each side. You may have to help the plants up the trellis a little.

Pests and diseases

Peas aren't usually seriously troubled by disease or insect problems. Nevertheless, it's a good idea to know what enemies you might encounter in the pea patch. Northerners will find that aphids and pea weevils are the most common insects, while southerners most often have to contend with the cowpea curculio. Blight, fusarium wilt, mosaic, and root rot are the most common diseases of peas. The preventive measures I prescribed for beans will work for peas.

260

The biggest mistake is over feeding plants

Peppers are the prettiest plants in the garden, especially when they're loaded with dozens of red, green, orange, and yellow peppers.

Peppers are easy to grow, but people have trouble with peppers because they push them too hard. Giving them too much fertilizer is the number one mistake. I have a big stack of letters from people who say, "My plants are tall and dark green, but I don't have any peppers yet!" This is a sure sign of too much fertilizer.

Peppers don't need much fertilizer, and what they get should come in small doses. Give them a teaspoon of a complete fertilizer like 5-10-10 at planting time and no more than a teaspoon or two at blossom time.

Each year I grow pepper plants that at first glance seem awfully small, yet when you look closely you discover 15 or 20 peppers on each plant.

Bad weather can plague peppers, too. Sometimes blossoms will fall off in a cold spell. Nothing can be done about this. You have to wait for more blossoms to appear.

If you start peppers indoors, put your flats in a warm place. Peppers need more heat than other crops to get going. They are one of the best crops for rais-

I love peppers—all kinds of them. I've listed some of my favorites on page 263.

ing under fluorescent lights inside, because they never get leggy, which can be a problem with other crops.

There's a saying that for good production, the leaves of pepper plants should touch when they're full grown. I agree. I put my peppers 12 to 14 inches apart in a staggered double row. With this close spacing I can pack the row with plants and get a big harvest.

I laugh when I see red bell peppers in the store priced higher than the green ones. There's no special trick to growing red peppers. Leave the pepper on the plant and it will turn red. A few varieties will turn yellow or orange when they mature, but most peppers, including the popular *California Wonder* bell pepper, will turn red.

Green peppers mature to red if left on the plant.

If you're having trouble getting the pepper crop you dream of, I have two tips for you.

1. At planting time put some matches in the soil underneath your plants.

Matches contain a little sulfur, an element which lowers soil pH. Since peppers like to grow in slightly acid soil, matches can

help give them the soil condition they prefer.

Rip out half the matches in an ordinary pack and sprinkle them around the bottom of the hole where you're going to set in a plant. Cover them with 2 inches of soil. It's important that the roots of your transplants do *not* come in contact with the matches right away. If they do, they may be severely shocked.

There may be another benefit to using matches. I have a hunch that the matches make fertilizer in the soil less available to the plant, and peppers don't want big helpings of fertilizer.

2. Spray your plants with Epsom salts when they start to blossom.

Epsom salts are a wonderful source of magnesium, a plant food peppers need to set fruit. I mix a teaspoonful of Epsom salts

in a Windex spray bottle filled with lukewarm water. I shake it well and spray the mixture on the leaves and blossoms when the plants first blossom, and again 10 days later. The leaves quickly turn dark green, and soon after, I have an abundance of peppers.

I'll hang this string of dried hot peppers in the kitchen. One pepper is usually enough to flavor a pot of spaghetti sauce.

Decorating with hot peppers

Jan and I string up some of our dried hot peppers with a needle and strong thread. We hang these strands in the kitchen for convenience and color. They keep well there. Here's a tip if you string hot peppers: your needle will pick up a lot of hot juice piercing the peppers, so wear rubber gloves and don't out of habit wet the needle with your lips.

I grew a pepper orchard!

1	2	3	4	5	6	7	8
Large Red Hot Cherry	**Cubanelle**	**Gedeon Sweet**	**Italian Sweet**	**Hungarian Wax**	**Golden Bell**	**Cayenne Hot**	**Sante Fe Grande**

9	10	11	12	13	14	15	16
Anaheim Hot	**Tabasco Hot**	**Gypsy Hybrid Sweet**	**Big Jim**	**Sweet Banana**	**Jalapeno**	**Chile Tatong**	**Pepper Oritani**

I love peppers! One year I started a big variety of peppers indoors and set them out in what a friend called a "pepper orchard." I enjoyed showing friends and neighbors what a crazy assortment of peppers they could grow. The orchard was easy to care for and produced basket after basket of sweet peppers, hot peppers, and some extra-hot types that were almost volcanic! The variety *Tabasco*, for example, is called by some "the hottest pepper in the world." No one around our place dared to nibble them raw, so we saved them to use sparingly in spaghetti sauce.

My orchard was a treat for the curious pepper lovers who visited the garden—and for my wife, Jan, who had a great time creating new spices for her favorite relishes.

Seeds for all the varieties listed here are available by mail. The ones you can't find in your favorite seed catalogs are usually available from Horticultural Enterprises, P.O. Box 340082, Dallas, TX 75234, a firm that specializes in pepper seeds.

POTATOES

Start with certified seed potatoes—they're disease-free

A good potato crop starts with good seed potatoes. Get the best ones you can because you don't have many chances at planting time. A garden store will have certified seed potatoes that are free of disease. These are the best. Don't rely on old potatoes from your root cellar because they could be carrying disease organisms without showing it.

When you buy seed potatoes, you'll get some small ones. Plant these whole. Cut the bigger ones into two or three blocky pieces, being sure to cut them so that each piece has two or three buds, or "eyes." I cut up seed potatoes a day or two before planting and leave them in a warm place. This gives the cut surfaces time to heal over and dry out a little.

I also douse seed potatoes with sulfur immediately after cutting them up. Sulfur powder is a cheap, natural protectant available at most drug stores. Two ounces will protect 10 pounds of seed potatoes. Put the cut and whole potatoes in a paper bag. Add 1 or 2 tablespoons of sulfur and shake the bag. The powder

sticks to the potatoes and helps keep out rot organisms. This sulfur also will lower the soil pH around the potatoes a bit. That's good because potatoes like an acid soil.

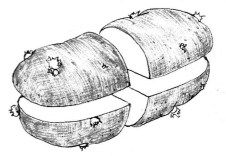

I plant my earliest potatoes 5 to 6 weeks before the last expected frost and use *Red Norland* potatoes because they will produce early. A frost before the plants come up is no problem. The soil will insulate them. But if the young leaves have popped through the soil and there's a frost warning, I push the soil from the walkways up over each plant. In a few day the leaves grow back up through the soil as if nothing had happened.

*When the plants blossom (left), potatoes are starting to form underground. From top, two of my favorite varieties, **Red Norland** and **Kennebec**, along with the novelty potato **All Blue**. Blue spuds look strange but they taste like ordinary potatoes.*

Can't find certified potatoes? Try this.

Nothing beats a good baking potato, and the Idaho varieties, called "Russets," are some of the best ones to grow. Trouble is, certified *Russet* seed potatoes aren't available where I live. That's because Russets don't do their best in New England's wet and humid summers. The certified potatoes are all grown and used out West.

Still, I like to grow a row or two of them. Here's how I get my seed potatoes:

About a month before planting I go to the supermarket and get a few pounds of some good-looking Idaho potatoes. Back home I spread out a layer of them in a shallow box and put the box in a warm room near a sunny window. Over the next few weeks the potatoes will wear down the anti-sprout chemicals they were treated with. They'll slowly begin to send out shoots. Because they are in the light, these shoots won't grow fast—they'll stay small. (Not like potatoes kept in the dark.) A few potatoes may not sprout at all. I don't plant those.

At planting time I gather up the sprouted potatoes, cut the large ones up like other seed potatoes, and plant them.

Whether the potatoes are diseased and what our summer weather is like determine how this crop performs. I usually get a pile of potatoes as big and flavorful as the "bakers" straight from Idaho.

A second crop for winter keeping

After the average last frost day in our area, I plant a larger crop of potatoes, including plenty of the *Kennebec* variety—a super potato that stores well.

I want the potatoes from this second planting to go into the root cellar just before the first frost of early fall. My root cellar is cool at that time of year, perfect for keeping potatoes.

As with other vegetables, I stick with my tried and true varieties, *Red Norland* and *Kennebec*. But it's always fun to plant some others, such as *Katahdin, Green Mountain*, the novelty variety *Lady Finger* for early boiled potatoes, or a short row of *Idaho* baking potatoes.

Plan ahead for a potato patch

To get the best potatoes, I look ahead at least two or three seasons. Since potatoes like soil pH from 4.8 to 5.5 I hold off on liming future potato areas. The soil pH in these areas will gradually drop into the potato range.

One benefit of this plan is that my potatoes rarely have scab on them. Common scab is a fungus disease which can be very active if the soil pH is 6.0 or higher. Scab doesn't ruin potates but it disfigures their skins. You must peel them before using.

If you use manure in your garden, treat it like lime because it also promotes scab. Do not use it on your potato patch a year before planting.

Plant deeply to grow fuller hills

Potatoes need to be planted in a deep trench, and for good reason. You see, a potato plant will form its potatoes *above* the seed piece that you put in the ground. To get a good crop, you must provide the plant with room to form and develop those potatoes. The trick is to start low in a trench.

I plow a deep trench, at least 6 or 8 inches down, with my tiller and furrowing attachment. Then I put a balanced fertilizer (such as 5-10-10) in a thin band along the bottom of the trench. I add a small handful of superphosphate (0-20-0) at 10- or 12-inch intervals right over the other fertilizer. This will furnish the plants with vital phosphorus as they develop their roots. I put this fertilizer at 10- or 12-inch intervals because I plant a seed piece directly above the superphosphate and I want 10 to 12 inches between my potato plants. Please note: there should be a buffer of 2 or 3 inches of soil between the seed piece and the first band of fertilizer. If the seed piece touches the nitrogen in the 5-10-10, it may burn and rot.

The easy way to do this is to push soil from the side of the trench over the fertilizer and firm the seed piece—cut side down—into the soil, all in one motion. It's a quick way to plant a lot of potatoes.

The final step is to cover the row of seed potatoes with 4 inches of soil and tamp it down.

Later hillings add more soil around plants. I plant potatoes in rows 36 inches apart to have lots of soil available for hilling.

I start mounding soil around plants, or "hilling," when they are quite small.

I give potatoes a *second* hilling

Potato plants have to be hilled. They need lots of soil around them above ground to create a place for the plants to grow their potatoes, or "tubers."

I hill most potato rows *twice*—the first time when the green tops of the plants are 3 to 5 inches tall. I use my tiller with a hilling attachment because I have a large potato patch. I put the rows 36 inches apart so my tiller can do the job with a single pass between each row. I get it done in minutes. Many of the plants are almost covered with loose soil. That's fine. They'll keep growing and show themselves in a day or two.

It's easy to hill by hand, too. Use the broadest hoe you have so that you can bring up a lot of soil with one pull. Loosen the soil between your rows with a quick cultivation to make the job a lot easier.

You'll notice that hilling eliminates many small weeds. They are smothered by the soil and won't come back.

I do a *second* hilling when the plant tops have grown 8 or 10 inches tall, about 3 or 4 weeks after the first hilling.

Think twice before you plant potatoes under mulch

You've probably seen articles about planting potatoes under a deep layer of mulch without digging trenches or hilling up rows. This no-work method *is* easy and fun, but it *won't* give you as big a crop as planting in rows. In fact, with all that mulch (usually hay) lying around, you're apt to get invaded by mice who first nibble on seeds in the mulch and then turn their attention to your potatoes. Mice have another bad habit—they attract snakes. I tell gardeners, "If you reach through the mulch to grab a potato and it *shakes,* let go!"

Despite these risks, I grow some potatoes under mulch—but more for fun than for a reliable crop.

To plant them, till up an area of soil, say 10 or 15 feet square, and mix fertilizer into the soil. Put the small seed potatoes or cut pieces about a foot apart in all directions. Push them into the soil cut-side-down. Cover the potatoes with 1½ to 2 feet of mulch, such as straw or hay that has as little seed as possible in it.

Forget about them for a while. The tops will grow up through the mulch and new potatoes will form on top of the ground where it's roomy and shut off from sunlight. As the season goes on, reach under the mulch from time to time. If you feel a potato big enough to eat, grab it. In the fall, rake back the mulch and pick the potatoes.

Potato plants growing in mulch sometimes are hardly bothered by hungry potato beetles. No one really knows why, but a Department of Agriculture researcher once offered me a theory. He said potato beetles often seem hesitant to travel over thin, unsteady materials and so may not be eager to walk across a deep loose mulch to get from plant to plant.

Protecting your crop

Consider using a standard potato dust or spray regularly. It is a mixture of chemical insecticide and fungicide which prevents troublesome diseases such as early and late blight. It thwarts some pests, too, such as the Colorado potato beetle. To be effective, most standard dusts must be applied to the potato foliage every 7 to 10 days, beginning when the plants emerge.

You may have a disease problem in the potato patch one year and none the next. The weather plays a big part. Moisture and temperature conditions trigger certain diseases which will spread rapidly through the potato rows.

Sneak a few potatoes early

The first new potatoes of the season are a tasty treasure. Some that I pick are only the size of golf balls, but nothing tastes better. They are ready 7 or 8 weeks after planting, if the plants grow without trouble. Some varieties will send out a few blossoms at this time. That's a signal to reach into a hill with your hand and search for some small boiling-size potatoes. Robbing the plants won't harm them. They'll continue to develop more potatoes and fatten the ones you leave.

When the soil is moist, you can dig up a whole plant with a fork, take the potatoes you want for supper, and put the plant back in its hole. If the soil stays moist, the plant will bounce back and deliver more potatoes. One year I dug up the same plant three times to steal potatoes.

After digging them, leave the potatoes in the row for an hour to dry. Most of the soil stuck on them should drop off. Do not brush or wash them because it could encourage rot in storage.

When the potatoes are dry, I put them in bushel baskets and take them to the root cellar. Potatoes must be stored in total darkness. Don't put them in burlap bags, because light will shine through the burlap and turn the outside potatoes green.

I put them in slatted bins which are raised off the floor a few inches. This allows air to reach all the potatoes and carry off excess moisture. This is important for long storage. The bins are near the floor because that's the coolest spot in my root cellar and potatoes like it cool. I never pile potatoes more than 12 inches high in the bins, either.

To dig potatoes, use a 5- or 6-pronged manure fork and start at the edge of each hill. Dig down and then under potatoes to avoid skewering any.

Give your spuds the storage test

My storage crop is ready to harvest in early fall when the days are getting cool and frost is not far off. That's when the tops of the plants are dying and sending the last of the vine energy down into the potatoes.

To be sure the crop is ready to store, I dig up a hill or reach in for a few potatoes. I rub my thumb hard on the potatoes. If the skin rubs off easily, I know they are too young to store. They need a little more time to mature. Potatoes with a thicker, tougher skin that won't rub off will last the longest in the root cellar.

Easy digging and safe storage

Many people dig potatoes with a spading fork or a shovel, but when it's time to dig up the potatoes, I grab what I think is the best tool of all—a 5- or 6-pronged manure fork. I stick the fork in at the outside of the hill, carefully move it down in, and lift. The dirt falls between the prongs and I'm left with a forkful of potatoes. With this kind of fork, I don't have to do much bending.

After you dig a few hills, you'll realize that all the potatoes are pretty much at the same level in the hill. With this knowledge, you'll injure fewer potatoes as you dig.

I always spike a few potatoes—usually the biggest ones. I set these aside because they won't store well. Jan and I use them within a few days.

Store potatoes in slatted bins raised off the floor.

SWEET POTATOES

Plant slips on raised beds for big potatoes

To grow sweet potatoes, start with "slips," which are tiny plants sprouted from sweet potatoes. Here's how I grow the slips I need each spring.

About 7 to 8 weeks before the average last frost date I get some sweet potatoes from the market. I cut them in half lengthwise and lay the pieces cut-side-down in aluminum cake plates filled with moist peat moss. I put a shallow covering of moist peat moss over the potato pieces and wrap the works in a plastic bag.

As soon as the slips appear, I take off the plastic and put the plants in a sunny window. After our last frost date, I pull each slip and plant it separately. It will grow to a full-sized sweet potato plant.

You can also get slips by sprouting a section of sweet potato in a jar of water. Like sprouting an avocado pit, most of each piece should be submerged in water on the kitchen window-sill.

In warm climates, start slips from sweet potatoes planted in cold frames or in soil at the edge of the garden. In case of a very cold night, make sure they're covered up.

You can also send away for sweet potato slips. Specify the date you want to receive them—when your soil has warmed up and the danger of frost is about past. (Northern gardeners: try the *Centennial* variety first. It does best in cooler summers.)

I plant the slips in raised beds, about 6 to 8 inches high. Raising the soil in beds, or "ridges," is especially important with clay soil. Heavy soils compact and restrict the growth of the roots underground, resulting in rough and odd-shaped potatoes. These soils also tend to drain poorly. Don't prepare your beds more than a day before planting, or weeds will start growing before your sweet potatoes.

Put sweet potato pieces in a shallow cake plate of moist peat moss. Wrap with plastic until first sprouts appear.

How to fertilize

Fertilizing is a delicate matter with sweet potatoes, as too much plant food, especially nitrogen, will produce skinny potatoes and lush vines. Yet too little fertilizer cuts down on the harvest.

When using commercial fertilizer, the basic guideline is about 4 or 5 pounds of 5-10-10 for each 100 feet of row. The simplest way to apply the fertilizer is to broadcast over the lanes where you'll be making your ridges.

Set the slips 12 to 15 inches

Nice sweet potatoes from my Vermont garden.

apart in the row, and about 5 to 6 inches deep. Make a little hole for them. Set them in and gently water after firming the soil around them. If you have some short slips, put them into the soil with one leaf showing above ground; they'll do fine.

Watering is very important in the next few days. Keep the soil around the slips wet, so the roots can expand quickly. Once the roots have anchored the plants, sweet potatoes can be considered drought-hardy.

After the plants take hold but before their vines really start to run along the ground, you should give them more fertilizer as a side-dressing. Try a tablespoon of

5-10-10 for each plant. Bone meal, high in phosphorus, is also good side-dressing fertilizer. Apply 1 cup for each 10 feet of row.

Harvest before frost

Sweet potato plants will grow as long as the weather stays warm. Their vines don't die and signal the harvest as white potatoes do. Most gardeners wait until their sweet potatoes are pretty large, then harvest all of them. For super eating earlier in the season, harvest sweet potatoes when they're not much bigger than your finger. Reach in the

hill and steal them from the plant.

A fall frost can hurt sweet potatoes even though they're underground, so harvest them before cold weather. When frost kills and blackens the vines above the ground, decay to the roots.

Dig the sweet potatoes on a dry day. Dig gently around the hills, starting from a few feet away; you don't want to slash any wandering potatoes with your shovel or fork.

Dry the potatoes on the ground for an hour. If you dig late in the day, don't leave them out overnight. Never wash the potatoes after the harvest, either.

Select any badly cut or bruised potatoes to eat first; they won't keep well. Sort the rest according to size in boxes or baskets to cure before storage.

Curing, which is important for sweet potatoes, takes 10 to 14 days. Keep them in a warm, dark place with some ventilation. The temperature should be around 70° to 80° F. with high humidity.

Sweet potatoes bruise easily and suffer in storage when handled roughly. The less you handle the crop, the better.

Sweet potatoes will spoil in a short time in cool storage. Jan and I cook our sweet potatoes right at harvest time—in 1½-inch chunks with no seasonings—and pop them in the freezer.

THE ROOT CROP FAMILY

One of the joys of growing root crops is that you can store most of them for free in a root cellar. I can keep them there through the winter with no trouble. Jan pickles some beets and carrots as a special treat, but it's nice to have crisp, tasty root crops straight from the root cellar in the off-season.

When spring rolls around, root crops mark the start of the outdoor garden. As soon as the ground thaws and I can prepare some seedbeds with my tiller, I start planting. Root crops love cool weather. Frosts usually don't bother them, so it pays to plant early. With radishes ready to eat in 3 weeks, why wait? Fall frosts are no problem either. In fact, parsnips and carrots get sweeter after a couple of frosts. (The carbohydrates in their roots change to natural sugars in cold weather.)

272

I sow root crops in wide rows. This is the only way to plant them. They don't need extra fertilizer, are easier to weed than people think, and yield a tremendous harvest through weeks and weeks of picking. Once I start pulling carrots from a wide row, I don't stop. I can pull some every day and still have a big crop to store in the fall.

Harvest as soon as there's something in the row big enough to eat—finger-sized carrots, beet greens with only marble-size bottoms, tiny radishes, or turnips. It's an early bonus for the kitchen, but it's also important for the other plants in the wide row. By picking and thinning out the eating-size crops first, you leave room for the other plants in the row to grow quickly and reach harvesting size.

For prize-winning root crops, use a raised bed

Building your rows up to form raised beds can help you grow better root crops. Sometimes in heavy clay or shallow soils it's a hassle getting long, straight carrots or parsnips, or large, well-shaped beets. The answer is to create a raised bed and heap extra topsoil onto the row from the walkways. It sounds like a lot of work but it's not.

No matter what kind of soil you plant root crops in, get the seedbed smooth and as free of clods and rocks as possible. In rocky, clumpy ground, all the seeds won't poke through the soil at the same time. This is a problem when you rake-thin and weed the first time.

When you plant carrots (left) on raised beds, you can expect a straighter, better-shaped harvest.

Coaxing carrots with 0-20-0

To coax the best root crops possible from your soil, add a little phosphorus fertilizer to the seedbeds before planting. Broadcast a common commercial fertilizer such as 5-10-10. Use about 1 quart for each 100 square feet and mix it in the top 2 or 3 inches of soil.

Stake out the wide rows, then sprinkle a handful of bone meal or superphosphate (marked "0-20-0" on the bag) over each 6 to 8 square feet of seedbed. It won't burn the seeds because it does not contain nitrogen.

Phosphorus is important for fast, steady root growth, so this extra boost in the row helps deliver a fine harvest of root crops. There's no need to side-dress root crops later in the season if the soil is stocked with nutrients early.

Again, don't be afraid to thin with a rake

To make sure I get a full stand of plants with no gaps, I sow my seeds thickly. Root crops, especially parsnips and carrots, are slow to come up. Rather than waiting for each plant to poke up through the soil, I sprinkle in some insurance seeds.

Extra seeds don't cost much. and they bring peace of mind. Even if all the seeds come up together, I can thin them quickly with my garden rake.

No matter how you plant them, root crops need a good thinning early. In my wide rows it's essential. If you don't thin root crops in a wide row, you don't get any. And timing is important, too.

If you're not sure of the technique, experiment. Grow and thin your main crop of carrots and beets as you normally would, but plant some extra seed in a few wide rows and thin them out with a rake. Then it won't matter if you "ruin" your rows. But I'll bet you won't! In fact, I'll bet you'll have plenty of root crops without much work.

The code of thinning

1. Thin early, when the root crops are barely poking out of the soil.
2. Drag your garden rake across the row with the teeth going only ¼ inch deep. Do this in clay soil when the soil is loose. A good time is when the top of the seedbed has just about dried out after a rain, but before it bakes down. If you don't get much rain,

274

you can water the row gently in the morning and thin in the afternoon.

3. Usually one pass with the rake across the row is all it takes. If you see that a section of row is very thick, make another gentle pass over the area.

People first think that rake-thinning will ruin a row. It doesn't. It may be a horrible experience the first time to drag plants out of a row with a rake. But you'll get used to it after you see how your crops benefit.

White Icicle radishes good companions

White Icicle radishes help me grow better root crops. I plant them in with my carrots, parsnips, beets, and other root crops. The *White Icicles* help me thin the row, keep the soil of the row loose, and trap extra water.

After I've sprinkled the seeds of the main crop over the wide-row seedbed, I drop a pinch of *White Icicle* seeds throughout the row. They probably number 5 percent of the other seeds. I tamp all the seeds down, cover the row with soil, smooth it out, and tamp it down again. It's like planting any wide row.

The *White Icicles* sprout quickly. Their tops do not spread out like other radishes, so they do not block other seedlings trying to come up. They put a lot of energy into growing a deep straight root as quickly as they can. I let them grow.

MY FOOT-WIDE HOME-MADE SEED TAPES

There's a guaranteed way to get hard-to-germinate parsnips and carrots to come up in a few days!

Parsnips, carrots, and other slow-germinating seeds take so long to come up—often 2 weeks or more—that weeds often overtake the row.

If you'd like to get these slowpoke crops to come up in just a few days (or if you want to speed up other crops such as onions, lettuce, beets, etc.), my wide-row seed tape planting idea is for you.

1. Roll out one layer of reinforced paper towel. Get the toughest towels you can. The cheap brands fall apart during the sprouting stage.

2. Moisten the paper towel, using a spray bottle.

3. Sprinkle the seeds evenly over the entire towel surface. A salt shaker is a good tool for this job. The seeds should land about ½ inch apart. Plant them just as you would in a wide row in the garden.

4. Cover the seeds with another layer of strong paper towel and moisten it with the spray bottle.

5. Roll the towels up together loosely; don't wrap them too tightly. The sprouts will need room to grow.

6. Put the roll in a plastic bag, seal it, and place the bag where the temperature is warm and constant.

7. In 3 or 4 days the carrots will sprout; parsnip seed may take 5 to 8 days. When the time is up, unroll the towels and take a peek. If you can see tiny roots growing out of the seeds, get ready to plant. If they haven't germinated, roll them back up.

8. In the garden, work the soil, add fertilizer, and smooth out the wide row seedbed with a rake.

9. Unroll the paper towels together and set them on the seedbed. Toss in a few radish seeds.

10. Cover the towels with about ¼ or ½ inch of soil, using a rake to pull some up and over.

11. Smooth the soil over the towels, then lightly firm the soil with a hoe.

12. Stand back and watch 'em grow. The sprouts will be poking through the soil in a few days. You'll be able to thin and weed earlier than ever.

Just for the fun of it, I tried planting a whole series of crops on the same roll of paper towels: radishes, lettuce, carrots, beets, onions, and chard. This is an unusual but sure way to get a whole row of crops off to an earlier start.

When the main crop, say of carrots, has some big enough to eat, I start to harvest. At the same time I pull some of the icicle radishes. They are much bigger than the carrots at this stage.

When I pull them, they leave a tremendous hole in the soil. This traps water and helps the soil to breathe better. The big advantage, though, is that it creates extra growing space for early carrots. And in a heavy clay soil, the *White Icicle* keeps the soil loose. It plunges into the soil, allowing air and water to get through the heavy soil to nourish other plant roots.

White Icicles are good to eat, too, especially when I pull them out late in the season from my rows of fall root crops. The cool weather gives them a nice taste. If you happen to grow one all by itself, look out. It could get big. At a gardening talk once in Atlanta, a woman presented me with one that weighed 7½ pounds! I've tried other white radish varieties, but none works as well for me as the great *White Icicle*.

Down-to-earth storage

It's easy to keep root crops from the fall garden for months in your root cellar. Keep these points in mind:

Your late crop should be as late as possible. The later you can harvest and store them, the longer they'll keep.

Pull or dig your storage crop after 2 or 3 days of dry weather. Leave the crop out in the sun for an hour. The vegetables will dry quickly and the soil on them will fall off easily.

Don't wash or brush the vegetables. As soon as you dig them, "top" them right in the garden, but don't cut the tail roots of your carrots or beets. Leave about an inch of stem on beets so they don't bleed. Cut the tops close on other root crops. Wash the roots when you're going to use them, not before.

If you bruise or break any root crops, use them first in the kitchen.

I put root crops in big plastic trash bags, punch a few holes in them, tie up the tops, and store the bags in a cold area of the root cellar.

A cardboard root cellar

If you have no root cellar, you can store some root crops in a cardboard box—even if you live in an apartment. I pack some carrots in a box each year and store it in my root cellar, but any cool room will work.

You need some damp peat moss or sawdust and a large, sturdy cardboard or wooden box.

Dig the carrots (or other root crops) you want to store. Don't wash them. Clip the tops close and let them dry for an hour in the sun. Line the bottom of the box with a 4-inch layer of peat or sawdust. (My father used sand, but the carrots often tasted a little sandy.) Put in a layer of carrots. The carrots can touch, but keep them 3 or 4 inches from the sides of the box. Cover the carrots with ½ inch of peat moss. Alternate carrots and peat moss to within 5 inches of the top. The idea is to insulate the roots so they'll stay at an even temperature. Top the box off with a layer of peat moss.

Keep the box in a fairly cold area. A garage, basement, back porch, even an unheated room is fine.

Tops of root crops should be cut off before putting vegetables in the root cellar. Be sure to leave ½ inch of beet tops to prevent bleeding.

Peat moss is a good substitute for sawdust when storing carrots.

Overwinter root crops right in the garden

If I lived in the South, I'd store root crops in the ground through the winter. It's an easy way to extend the harvest. But it's a lot easier to get to them there during the winter than up here in Vermont, where 2 feet of snow may cover the garden. It's easy for me then to talk myself out of using outdoor vegetables to cook up a stew.

If your soil freezes, insulate the ground around your roots so they won't go through a freezing and thawing cycle. Put at least 12 to 18 inches of mulch over the row. Use whatever you have—hay, straw, or leaves. Extend the mulch out from both sides of the row at least 12 or 18 inches. In the winter move the mulch aside and dig up some fresh vegetables.

Vegetables stored in the ground don't have much keeping power once you dig them, so be sure to eat them in a day or two.

Side step root maggots

Small white maggots are the toughest pests of root crops. It's frustrating because often you don't know they are digging into your crops until you harvest them. They bother radishes, rutabagas, turnips, and parsnips more than beets or carrots.

Root maggots (technically known as "cabbage maggots") appear when the weather warms up in late spring. (I like to plant *early* so I'll harvest radishes and turnips before any damage is done.) Small flies emerge from the soil and lay eggs around the base of plant stems and in the soil of the row. The maggots hatch from these eggs and work their way into the soil where they start eating the roots and stems. If your root crops have tiny tunnels in them, you have a root maggot problem.

I've had good luck with very early crops. The radishes I grow under plastic tunnels have been free of root maggots—perhaps because the flies can't land near plants under a tunnel.

Stagger your plantings. Put in one row very early in the season and then follow with extra sowings through the season. Although there are several generations of maggots in one season, your crops may reach eating size when there aren't many maggots in the feeding stage. The most effective control is using a soil insecticide such as diazinon before planting.

INSECTS THAT ATTACK ROOT CROPS

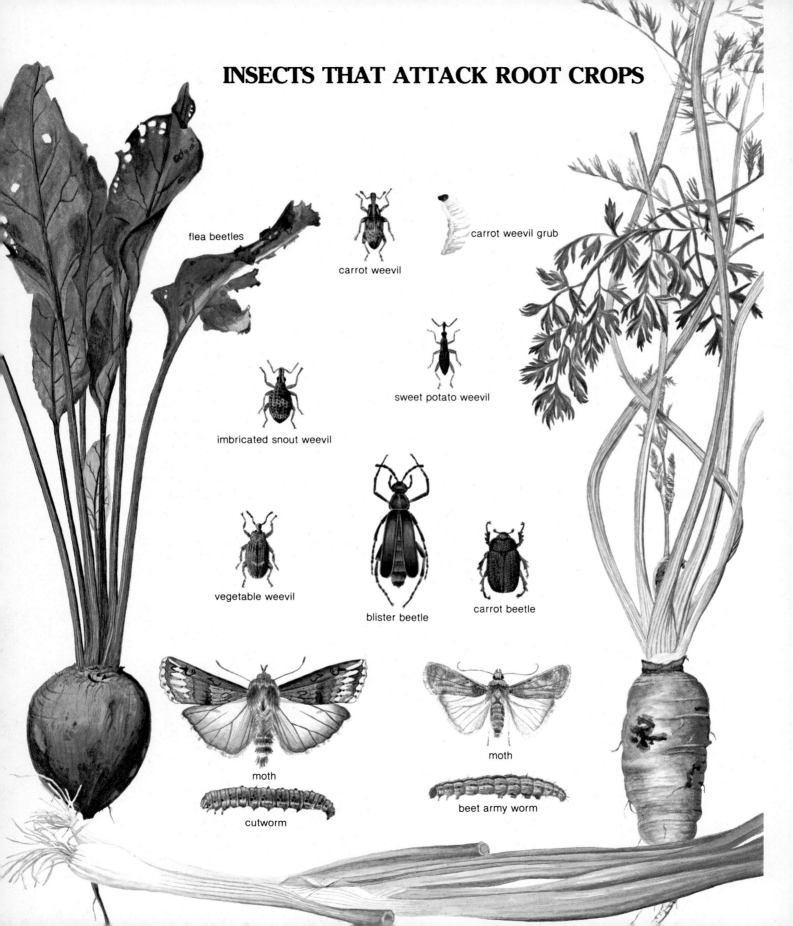

flea beetles

carrot weevil

carrot weevil grub

imbricated snout weevil

sweet potato weevil

vegetable weevil

blister beetle

carrot beetle

moth

cutworm

moth

beet army worm

BEETS

Eat the whole thing, from top to bottom

A neighbor of mine once called the beet "a poor man's steak." He said, "They're juicy, tender, red, and good for you." I still like a good cut of meat, but I agree that beets make fine eating.

I plant plenty of beets so we can enjoy an early feast of beet greens, summer dishes of Harvard beets and cold beet salads, beets for pickling, and a big bunch to store in the root cellar. The early harvests are especially rewarding, because we use the whole beet plant, the green tops and the tasty bottoms.

Beet seeds are unusual. They look like pieces of cork and are larger than other root crop seeds. Each one is a cluster of seeds from which several seedlings will sprout. Rake-thinning will separate these seedlings. If you try to pull the clustered seedlings apart by hand, you'll damage the remaining ones.

Beets sprout easily in early spring when the ground is moist, but sometimes germination is poor in warm weather. It can be especially tricky in sandy soil. If the heat is on, I cover my summer rows of beets with a thin layer of mulch—only about ¼ inch thick. This is thick enough to shade the soil, but not too thick to keep plants from coming up. A light watering from time to time until the plants come up also helps.

Detroit Dark Red is the best producer I've grown. Like all beets, it can be grown for both greens and roots. *Golden Beets* are a novelty. The beets are carrot-colored but they taste like red beets and don't bleed. Try some if your kids don't like the red beets.

Lutz beets get very large and are surprisingly good at all stages, though they're best when small. If you want to do some bragging, grow a row of *Lutz* beets.

CARROTS

A vitamin-rich snack

My grandson Brian is a real carrot fan. When he sees the feathery carrot tops in the garden he can hardly wait to start pulling up his orange snacks. Kids like discovering buried treasure and I've taught Brian how to find the biggest carrots in the row—by looking for the darkest green tops. (Works almost every time.) To get the most of your carrots' vitamin A and other minerals, don't peel them. A good scrubbing with a vegetable brush is all they need.

I try a lot of carrot varieties each year, all lengths and shapes. My friend Ed told me about the *Danvers* variety which I grow every year. He said it was developed a long time ago in the area around Danvers, Massachusetts. When he was a kid he weeded carrot fields there by hand for a summer job and received $4 a week!

Any variety of carrot can be eaten when it's as big around as your finger. These fingerlings are

great fresh and they are about the only size you can freeze. They stay sweet, but older carrots lose their quality when frozen.

Small carrots are the only ones we freeze.

Carrot seeds aren't the best starters in early spring, so I plant them about 2 weeks *after* my first sowing of beets and turnips.

You can give carrot seeds a head start with my paper towel seed tapes or by soaking the seed in warm water for a few hours before planting them. Use extra seed because some stick together and are hard to thin.

You also can start them in sprouting jars as you would alfalfa seeds or mung beans, soaking them first, then rinsing them once a day. When the seeds sprout, prepare your seedbed, sprinkle the seeds over the row, and cover normally.

PARSNIPS

Slow to grow but worth the wait

It's hard to understand why more gardeners don't grow parsnips. It's true, they take a long time to germinate and need a long season to grow, but their delicious flavor makes them well worth the wait. Once you've grown and cooked parsnips, you can't give them up.

A few years ago an 85-year-old neighbor of mine moved to a nearby city to live with his relatives. Unfortunately he didn't have room to garden there. Before he left, he brought some parsnip seeds to my house and said, "Dick, will you grow some parsnips for me? I'll have my son drive me out to help you dig them up. I just love 'em!"

My wife, Jan, is the real parsnip fan in our house. Her chicken soup is not really chicken soup unless it has fresh

parsnips cut into it. And have you noticed in the supermarkets that the packages of cut vegetables labeled "Soup Greens" have lots of parsnips in them? Somebody knows what makes soups taste good.

I start parsnips when I start carrots. Once they're up, which can take 2 weeks or more, I thin them, then let them grow all summer. After a few frosts in the fall I dig up some of the row to use right away. I mulch another part of the row so I'll be able to dig some during the winter, and I leave the rest of the row alone.

As soon as the ground thaws in the spring, I dig in this last part of the row. The parsnip flavor is best when they are dug and eaten within a day or two. Once the plants start growing, a few weeks later, they start using the energy they've stored to send up new growth. As a result the roots get soft and unappetizing.

Jan never cooks chicken soup without parsnips.

RADISHES

In my garden *Cherry Belles* pop up everywhere

I rarely grow radishes by themselves. They function so well as a companion crop that I keep a pouch of seeds handy and sprinkle a few in with almost every vegetable, especially other root crops. That's explained in more detail on page 131.

You might think "a radish is a radish" but there are many varieties to choose from. The *Cherry Belle* is my favorite red radish. It's crisp and flavorful and ready to pick in a few weeks. Root maggots bother it less than other varieties. The white radishes and black radishes grow deep like carrots but they take more time than red ones.

For the tastiest radishes, keep your crop growing quickly. Fertil-ize the seedbed before planting, and give the plants a steady supply of water.

My most flavorful, crunchiest radishes grow under plastic tunnels early in the spring. The tunnel traps moisture rising from the ground, so the plants never hurt for water. They grow quickly and don't get woody.

When you plant radishes, plant a lot, but be sure to thin. You'll have so many radishes growing, you won't have to wait for big ones before you start eating.

Make a few plantings late in the season with the last one about the time you figure it's *got to be too late*. More often than not you'll get a bonus crop when it's time to put the garden to bed.

RUTABAGAS AND TURNIPS

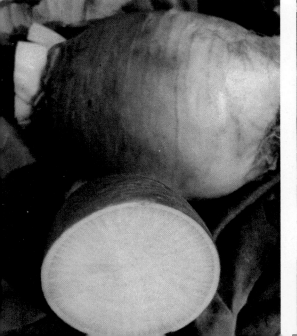

Delightful all-season eating

I think of rutabagas and turnips as twins. They look alike, are grown the same way, and to some folks even taste the same. I think, though, that rutabagas have a slightly milder flavor than turnips, and they keep much better.

I take plenty of big rutabagas to my mountain camp each fall. We get plenty of visitors there—often 12 or more staying for supper—and rutabagas are a staple. I like to boil a lot of them with just a couple of potatoes, mash them, and serve them with salt, pepper, and butter mixed in. The potatoes seem to reduce any bitterness there might be in the rutabagas. This rutabaga dish goes great with spaghetti and tossed salad. (Sometimes my guests don't realize they're eating rutabagas, but they love 'em!)

I don't grow rutabagas for greens because their stem is thick and tough. Turnip greens taste much better. I plant turnips almost as soon as I can till the soil. I pull most of them for greens. Later I plant more turnips and rutabagas for some good-sized roots to store for the winter.

I pack rutabagas and turnips in large plastic bags, poke a few holes in each bag, and store them in a cold spot in the root cellar. Because rutabagas keep longer than turnips, we eat the turnips first and save the rutabagas for meals in late winter.

SUNFLOWERS

Seeds for you and the birds

Everybody loves giant sunflowers! Grown just to look at, or for seeds for you or the neighborhood birds, sunflowers are easy to grow, even for the beginning gardener.

I plant sunflowers directly in the garden a couple of weeks before the last frost. Because young sunflower seedlings transplant so well, they can also be started indoors very early in the spring and set out in the garden around the time of your last frost.

If you had a crop in the garden last year, look around for some early "volunteers"—those plants sprouting from dropped seeds. Scoop them up with a trowel, set them where you want them, and water them.

Sunflowers should be grown where they won't shade shorter crops in need of full sunlight. The north side of the garden is an excellent place for them. Plant them in your corn rows or in back of them.

Late in the summer, when the seed heads begin to mature and bend toward the ground, you'll have to protect them from birds.

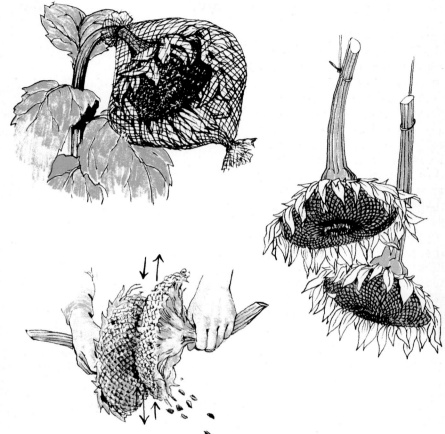

The best material to wrap around the heads is the plastic mesh that onion bags are made of. Don't cover them too early. Wait until you see the first bird poking at them. Birds are reluctant to stick their beaks through the mesh. Of course, if you're growing sunflowers for the birds, just relax and watch them. It always amuses me to see how birds will perch on top of the head and peck at the seeds while they are almost upside down. They just dig in, hold on for dear life, and eat away.

When harvesting sunflowers for your own use, cut the seed heads with about a foot of stem still at-tached, and hang them in an airy place where birds and mice can't get to them. Once the heads are dry (in 2 to 3 weeks) you can re-move the seeds by rubbing them off with a stiff brush, or by rub-bing two heads together. There's no need to remove the seeds until you need them.

Jan and I save some whole heads for winter birdfeed. We hang a head from a tree limb. Trouble is, it lasts only a day and a half. The bluejays will eat the head clean unless we woo them away with some whole corn. That gives the cardinals a chance to en-joy the sunflowers for a while.

Wrap light mesh material around heads to protect against birds. After cutting mature heads, hang them to dry for 2 or 3 weeks. One easy way to pry out sunflower seeds is to rub two of the heads together.

TOMATOES

Without a doubt, the most popular garden crop in America is tomatoes. Approximately 35 million families grow them. They're growing varieties that bear tomatoes from the size of marbles to the size of grapefruits; pink ones, red ones, and even yellow ones. There are tomatoes which grow in the coolest, cloudiest, and shortest growing areas and there are those developed to withstand the heat of hot southern summers. No matter where you are, there's a tomato variety for you.

What I've learned about planting tomatoes

Almost everybody grows tomatoes by setting out transplants. How you treat these young plants and transplant them has a lot to do with your harvest. For *more* and *better* tomatoes, here are my best planting tips:

Shop for the best plants

I'm amazed each spring when I stop at the greenhouses and nurseries and see people selecting tomato plants that are too tall and leggy! Perhaps they think that bigger means better; but with tomato transplants that's not the case.

The best transplants are fairly young and small. Good ones are 6 to 7 weeks old, and about 8 inches tall. They should have plenty of dark green leaves and most importantly, a solid, thick stem. If you get some tall plants, don't worry. My planting method takes advantage of the length of the stem and helps you get the most from every plant.

Inspect all plants closely. If you see signs of disease or insects (particularly the small whitefly), put them back.

Try several varieties

It's good insurance to get two or three varieties. In the case of disease or drought, you may find that one variety fights off trouble better than another.

If you get early, mid-season, and late varieties, you should have a steady harvest. A good trio for many areas is the *Pixie* (which sets fruit in cool weather), *Supersonic* (a fine mid-season tomato), and *Beefmaster* (a hefty late variety which needs about 3 months of growing after you set it in the garden).

For many people, an ample harvest of red-ripe tomatoes is the highest achievement in gardening.

These tomato plants were hardened off for 10 days. Setting them in the garden now won't shock them much.

Harden off plants

Whether you buy plants or grow them at home, they need to be hardened off for a week or so. Start by setting them on the back porch. Then gradually shift them out to a sunny open spot where they can take the weather all day long and all night, too, if there's no chance of a surprise frost.

Transplant on a cloudy day

I like to set out tomatoes in the late afternoon or evening. If it's cloudy and mild, all the better. Plants don't appreciate hot sun or a whipping wind for their first few days in the garden. The shock of transplanting is bad enough; they prefer to take on the elements a little at a time. Have your tools on hand before you take a single plant out of its flat. Water the plants to hold roots and soil together. When you lift out a dry plant, the dirt goes everywhere and the roots get shocked.

Two ways to put fertilizer under my plants

I plant tomatoes *two ways* and I have *two ways* of adding fertilizer. If I set the tomatoes in *individual holes,* I first dig a hole 5 or 6 inches deep. I add a handful or two of good compost or a tablespoon of 5-10-10, mix this with soil at the bottom of the hole, then cover it with an inch or two of soil.

I sometimes make a 6-inch-deep *trench,* the entire length of my row. I spread a thin band of 5-10-10 along the bottom of the trench. The fertilizer should be covered, so I drag a hoe along one side to spill 2 or 3 inches of dirt into the trench.

Don't forget the cutworm collar

It's a shame to lose a transplant to pesky cutworms. Even if I'm not really expecting a problem with them, I wrap a newspaper collar around the stem of each plant. The collar should be at least 2 inches wide, 1 inch below ground and 1 above.

Set the plants in a shallow trench

With this technique, most of the root system is only 2 or 3 inches away from the surface. This helps the plant gather plenty of heat and produce extra roots.

To transplant, I carefully take a plant from its flat or container and cup my hand securely around the roots. I don't want soil to fall away from the roots.

I pinch off most of the lower leaves, leaving just the top cluster. The cutworm collar goes on, and then I lay the plant in the ground and cover the root ball and exposed stem with 2 or 3 inches of soil.

Most of the stem is buried. All along it, new roots will form. Like the main root system, these new roots will reach down for food and water as the plant grows. In a dry spell, these extra roots can be a lifesaver.

I plant most tomatoes horizontally after pinching off all but the top leaves . . .

I position the plants so that each top cluster of leaves is 18 inches away from the next. They can be a little closer if you plan to stake your plants.

Planting tomatoes this way helps me grow an *earlier* crop. After all, the bulk of the root system is quite shallow at first, so it heats up early every day. Tomatoes love this, especially in springtime. If I planted them deep in a hole, the roots would sit and shiver for weeks.

Now's the time to stake plants

After the soil is firmed around the plants, drive your stakes. Doing it later could damage some roots, especially if you set your plants in horizontally.

Keep wind direction in mind when you stake. I put my stakes on the east side of each plant because where I live the winds are mainly out of the west. When the wind is strong, the plant will be held up against the stake. If I did

A plastic shield around young tomatoes traps plenty of heat. Cutting off the wind helps them recover quickly from transplant shock.

it the other way, a stiff wind could push the plant against my tie-ups and perhaps break the stem.

. . . You can see the mass of roots which grows from the bare stem.

Don't skimp on water

Tomato plants need lots of water for 3 or 4 days after transplanting. Soak them after planting and keep the ground moist for a few days after. Don't skimp—pour it on. I've never seen anyone overwater a tomato plant.

Trap heat and block out the wind

Whatever you can do to gather extra heat for your plants or to shut out winds will help. Use old tires, plastic wrap-around cages, cardboard, or whatever else you have.

In one experiment, researchers used 1 foot-high strips of black roofing paper to circle their just-planted tomatoes. The paper blocked winds and brought in extra heat. Result? A 50 percent increase in yield.

How to Have the First Ripe Tomatoes in Your Neighborhood

I've always tried to have the very first tomatoes in the area. When Jan and I had our market garden it was very important. If we could get folks to come to our stand for their early tomatoes, they'd probably be regular customers for the rest of the season.

Now I've worked out a system that puts vine-ripened tomatoes on our table in the middle of June. That's only 4 weeks past our average last frost date! Most folks in my part of the country pick their first tomatoes at the end of July! This method will work for you no matter where you live.

Get the seeds of an early tomato variety. I've found *Pixie* to be tops. It will grow quickly and set fruit in cool conditions. The name might lead you to think that this is a small cherry-type tomato, but it isn't. The *Pixies* I grow get about the size of a tennis ball.

Plant the seeds indoors in a shallow flat about *10 to 12* weeks before the average last frost date. This may seem way too early— and it is for your main crop—but it's a must for the "first on the block" harvest. Starting this early means you may have blossoms or even little green tomatoes formed on the plant when it's time to set them out.

When the seedlings are 4 to 5 inches tall, repot them into much deeper containers. Pick off the lower leaves, and set the plant in the new pot up to the top cluster of leaves.

Transplant the plants again when they are 8 inches tall. Again, pinch off the lower leaves, leaving the top cluster, and set each plant up to its neck in a half-gallon milk carton. This will encourage an extensive root system.

About a month before the average last frost date, start giving the plants a little time outdoors. Because it can be so harsh and cool at this time of the year, take 10 days or so to harden off the plants.

Set the plants in the garden about 3 weeks before the last frost date. This is very early for tomato plants, but if you've hardened off your *Pixie* plants well, they should be fine.

There's no need to pick off any leaves or to lay the plant down horizontally. The plants are too big for that. Soak the milk carton well, then plant the *Pixies* an inch or so deeper than they were in the milk cartons.

Use heat-gathering techniques right away—hot caps, old tires, or circling the plant with plastic. The more heat you draw to the plant, the sooner the harvest. In case of frost danger, cover the plants with hot caps, paper bags, or bushel baskets.

To insure good fruiting, spray the flower clusters twice a week with "Blossom Set," a hormone spray which helps to make sure the blooms turn into tomatoes. This is not necessary, but it's good insurance, especially if you are growing an early variety other than *Pixie*.

Growing in cages

The simple way I get juicy, even-ripening picture perfect tomatoes

Everybody has a favorite way of growing their prized tomatoes. My way is to support them with cages. After many years of experimenting, I've settled on caging as the easiest and best way to care for tomatoes. Tomato plants support themselves easily inside a cage. Because they receive very little pruning, they grow enough leaves to shade the tomatoes. This protects them from sunscald and helps them ripen evenly.

Garden stores sell cages, but you can make better ones at home.

Tomatoes grow freely, but upright, in cages.

A wooden stake helps anchor this cage.

Cages should be strong, at least 5 feet tall (to handle the big varieties) with holes big enough so that you can harvest big tomatoes.

Concrete reinforcing mesh is often regarded as the ideal cage material, but I don't think it is. It's hard for many people to find, it's somewhat expensive, and it rusts quickly. I prefer a sturdy galvanized wire mesh that you can use for years. The cages can be from 12 to 30 inches in diameter. You need about 3 feet of material for every 1 foot of diameter. I like a cage diameter of 24 or 30 inches, especially for my main crop tomatoes like *Better Boy* and *Big Boy,* so I make them from mesh 6 to 7½ feet in length.

I tie down the cages on two sides to short stakes I drive into the ground. Then I know the cages won't *ever* topple.

Here's an easy way to give your caged tomato transplants a boost early in the season. When you put the tomato plants in the ground, set the cages over them immediately, push the bottom wires firmly into the ground, and secure with small stakes.

Then make a tight circle of foot-high black felt roofing paper (or dark plastic) around the outside of the cage at ground level. Staple together the overlapping ends of the paper. The black paper will gather heat for the tomato plants and will protect them from bruising winds.

289

Other systems have good points, too

Staking Tomatoes

ADVANTAGES

■ Staking saves space. You can grow more tomato plants in a row, staking them as close as 18 inches from each other.

■ Keeps vines and tomatoes off the ground so the harvest is cleaner and there's less rotting. No slugs either, and that's a big plus for many gardeners.

■ Earlier harvest. The pruning that staked tomatoes need forces more of the plant's energy into ripening the fruit. Tomatoes tend to be larger when a plant is staked. Again, this is the result of pruning: more energy goes into fewer tomatoes.

■ Easier to pick tomatoes and to work around the plants.

DISADVANTAGES

■ It takes time and effort to set the stakes, train the plants up the stakes, and prune them.

■ Tomatoes are more prone to cracking, blossom end rot, and other problems because they are standing up and are much more exposed.

■ Decreases yield.

■ Plants usually need plenty of mulching.

■ Staked plants need *more* water than unstaked ones.

It's time to loosely tie the main stems of these plants to their stakes. Keep only one or two main stems for best results.

Trellising Tomatoes

ADVANTAGES

■ Like staking, trellising holds tomatoes off the ground for cleaner, easier-to-pick harvest.

■ Usually doesn't require as much pruning as staked tomatoes. Most common trellising methods let you grow two or three main stems.

Here's one example of a trellis support system. There is work in setting it up, but tomatoes are kept off the ground and are easy to tend and harvest.

DISADVANTAGES

■ Trellising can be hard work, especially for a big planting. Poles, wires, and braces usually needed.

■ Requires weekly maintenance to keep plants running up the trellis. Often the plants need to be tied to trellis wires.

■ Takes time at end of the season to disassemble the trellis and store parts.

Letting Tomatoes Run

ADVANTAGES

■ Very little time spent caring for crop. Little or no pruning, no staking and training, no supports to build or buy.

■ Total yield seems to be higher than staked or caged plants.

If you let tomatoes run free and sprawl, many fruits will lie on the ground. Rot or animals will often claim a share of the harvest.

DISADVANTAGES

■ In wet weather many gardeners will have rot or bug problems with tomatoes on the ground. Slugs can be bad news around free-growing tomatoes.

■ Requires more room in the garden. Sprawling plants will bush out quite a bit.

■ Sometimes it is hard to pick tomatoes close to ground or even hidden by thick growth.

Let's relax about pruning tomatoes

It's not necessary to prune tomatoes. However, in my garden all the tomato plants get a little pruning. Staked and trellised plants need the most because you want them to grow only one or two main stems which will make the plants easier to tie up.

Pruning means pinching off the shoots, or "suckers," that grow out from stems right above leaf branches. By restricting the vine growth somewhat, you'll get bigger tomatoes. If you let these suckers grow, each becomes another big stem with its own branches, blossoms, and fruits—even its own suckers. I prune my plants in cages and those growing freely early in the season,

Prune suckers like these.

and then I let them grow. You should go on sucker patrol at least twice a week during the heavy growing season to keep your staked plants from getting hard to control.

In a very hot, sunny area, you can let some of the suckers put on a couple of leaves and then pinch out the top to stop its growth. The extra foliage will help the plant manufacture food and will help shade tomatoes.

Don't mulch too early

A thick mulch around tomato plants, especially staked ones, will help them get a steady supply of water, but it could hurt if you mulch too early.

Wait at least 4 to 6 weeks after

Mulch tomatoes only after your soil thoroughly warms up—that's usually 4 to 6 weeks after planting.

you set out your plants before mulching them. By that time the soil will be warm. If you mulch too early in the season, you insulate the ground and keep it from warming up. This can delay the harvest 2 or 3 weeks.

Slugs and mice visit the garden when you use hay or other natural mulches. That's why I mulch tomatoes only if I stake them.

The problem with black plastic

Some folks use a black-plastic mulch early in the year to capture *heat* as well as block out weeds and hold water in. I've tried black plastic a few times and, frankly, I don't like it. Once, when it was wet, I slipped on the plastic and fell right on my rear. But that's not the only thing contributing to my poor opinion of it. It's not cheap or easy to use. It's a bother to lay down in the spring and take up in the fall. I also hate to use a mulch that earthworms and soil life can't dine on someday. In my view, black plastic detracts from the natural beauty of a garden.

A piece of advice from a Tennessee old-timer

I visited an older market gardener in Tennessee some years ago. His early tomatoes were just hitting the stand. Business was brisk around the baskets of tomatoes. I complimented him on the fine-looking tomatoes, and told him I had a question.

"Go ahead and ask it," he said, smiling.

"Well," I said, "the other growers around here don't have many tomatoes to sell yet, and here you are tucked behind a ridge where it must be cool sometimes . . . just how are you getting tomatoes so early?"

He laughed. "Come on out back and I'll show you."

Going past the barn he picked up a round-pointed shovel and carried it along. We stopped in front of a tomato plant loaded with clusters of large green tomatoes.

"Watch," he said. He dug deep into the soil 6 inches from the plant. He spaded a few more times to make a half-circle cut around the plant. "They'll be ripe inside of a week," he said flatly.

He said he "root-pruned" some plants with his shovel three times. "The plants don't know what's happening," he said. "They just figure it's high time to ripen those green tomatoes. They do it quickly, too."

Each year I try this trick in my own garden on a few plants—especially the early ones. My soil is sandy and I can use a long bread knife to cut a semicircle around the plant in a jiffy. If you try it, be sure the green tomatoes are about as large as they're going to get. Root-pruning at that point will bring the quickest results. The plants recover from this root shock and continue to yield throughout the season.

I use a bread knife to root-prune some early tomatoes. I cut a semi-circle around the plant, 6 inches from the stem and about 8 inches deep. I'm careful, with trench-planted tomatoes, not to cut stem.

Only one tomato to a windowsill!

I've given up thinking I can convince people that tomatoes ripen better in the dark, and *not* on a sunny windowsill. I've tried for years and I'm getting nowhere.

It's true, though. The fruits ripen gradually from the inside out; keeping them in the sun can burn and redden them (not *ripen* them) before they ripen naturally from the inside. A warm, dark place is best for even, sweet ripening.

Would gardeners be interested in a compromise? How about keeping just one or two big tomatoes on the kitchen windowsill? The room will still have that nice garden aroma and gardeners can display these prize tomatoes—while stashing the rest of the harvest in a dark area for best ripening.

Some tomato troubles

How to prevent blossom end rot

Blossom end rot can be a killer. Your tomatoes may be growing just fine and starting to ripen, when suddenly there's a hot, dry spell. After a few days you notice large brown or black spots showing up on the bottom side of all your tomatoes. This is blossom end rot. The rot spreads and the prospects for a great harvest suddenly go out the window.

There is no cure for blossom end rot once it hits your tomatoes. The best thing to do is pick the tomatoes that have been hit and toss them on the compost pile. No use wasting any of the plant's energy on damaged goods.

You can avoid blossom end rot only by expecting it. A steady moisture supply is crucial, because the rot starts when there isn't enough moisture in the ground to travel all the way through the plant out to the ends of the tomatoes. Mulch staked plants or watch them regularly in dry times because end rot hits them first. And make sure *all* your tomatoes get the water they need during a dry spell.

Scientists say a good supply of calcium in the soil is important, too. To provide this, add lime. It has a lot of calcium in it.

Top: Prevent blossom end rot by giving tomatoes a steady supply of water. Middle: Abnormal development of tomato blossoms will result in odd-shaped fruits. Bottom: The pale streak on this tomato indicates the start of sunscald.

Other lesser ailments

Catfacing. This is a type of scarring. Tomatoes develop unusual swellings and streaks. It is not a disease; it's caused by abnormal development of the tomato flower. Cool weather is believed to cause the problem.

Blossom drop. Some years early blossoms will fall off. This is caused by temperatures below 55° F. at night. Some varieties, such as *Pixie,* will keep their blossoms and set fruit in cool weather, but most varieties won't. Some blossom drop will also occur when night temperatures get above 75° or 80° F. in the summer.

Curling of leaves. Curling, or "leaf roll," is very common, but don't worry, it does not harm production. Heavy prunings may promote curling.

Sunscald. This occurs when green or ripening tomatoes get too much sun. At first, a yellowish-white patch appears on the side of the tomato facing the sun. The area gets larger as the fruit ripens and becomes grayish-white. If this is a problem for you, grow varieties that develop heavy foliage. To guard against sunscald, don't over-prune plants. Or grow them in cages where they'll develop lots of protective foliage.

The Colorado potato beetle lays its orange eggs on undersides of leaves. Collect adults and rub out egg masses to avoid problems.

Tomato diseases and pests

Early blight is one of the most common and most harmful diseases. It is caused by a fungus and appears first as a brown spot, surrounded by yellow, that spreads outward on the leaves. The lower leaves wither. Higher leaves are hit, too, and the crop can be badly damaged. To control early blight, mulch to reduce splashing and use an all-purpose tomato dust.

Late blight is a serious disease in areas east of the Mississippi and is more pronounced in cool, moist weather. Leaves develop large, brown spots and wither. Spots on tomatoes turn brown and harden.

Leaf spot is a fungus disease that can hurt production. It's often a problem in the Southeast and some northern areas that have warm, moist weather. The leaves have small spots with light centers. They may turn yellow and drop off. The fungus that causes the disease lives on old tomato vines, in the soil, and on perennial weeds. Rotating crops is important to keep the disease in check.

Flea beetles are small, tiny black or brown insects which eat small holes in the leaves, most often early in the season. Spray or dust with Sevin or rotenone.

Blister beetles and **Colorado potato beetles** feed on tomato foliage, and may also be controlled with rotenone, Sevin, or an all-purpose dust or spray for tomatoes.

Aphids can bother tomato plants all season long. They suck the sap from the plants and weaken them, and spread disease.

Hornworms are huge, green, caterpillars with thornlike horns at their back end. They eat both leaves and tomatoes. They work quickly, too. Hand-picking these creatures is the best bet in the home garden because you usually discover them at harvest time when it's unwise to spray. The non-toxic spray Bacillus thuringensis (available as Dipel or Thuricide) is effective.

A season-long pest which eats tomatoes big and small is the *tomato fruitworm* or *corn earworm*. Control worms with Dipel as soon as you notice them.

Stink bugs are mostly a southern problem. Like aphids, they suck sap from the plant. To control, keep weeds in check in the garden and spray with Sevin or malathion.

Keeping tomatoes healthy

Rotate the crop each year to avoid diseases that live in the soil. I like to wait 3 years, if possible, before planting tomatoes where I've had them before. I never plant tomatoes where I grew potatoes or eggplant the previous season, since some diseases attack all these vegetables and live in the soil from year to year.

Plant resistant varieties. Many varieties are resistant to verticillium wilt and fusarium wilt—two troublesome diseases for which there is no cure. Some seed companies list resistance to these diseases by putting "F" (fusarium) or "V" (verticillium) after the variety name. "N" stands for resistance to nematodes, the tiny worms that plague many southern gardens and cause stunting of the plants and poor crops.

Don't let anyone smoke near tomato plants since they can infect tomato plants with tobacco mosaic virus, a serious disease which cuts down on the harvest.

Consider a spray program. To insure a long life for your tomato crop, dusting or spraying with a standard tomato formula is very effective. Start a week after setting out the plants and repeat the application every 7 to 10 days.

Green tomato roundup

Tomatoes succumb to the lightest frost, but don't panic at the first frost if your tomato vines are still loaded with green fruit. You can protect the plants by covering them with sheets, burlap bags, or big boxes. It's worth the effort because the next frost is often 2 or 3 weeks after the first.

If a heavy freeze is on its way, pick all the tomatoes. Green tomatoes about three-fourths their full size will ripen eventually.

Some people pull the whole tomato plant, hang it upside down in a dark basement room, and let the tomatoes ripen gradually. Check them regularly so you can catch the ripe tomatoes before they fall on the floor—splaat!

We put green tomatoes on a shelf in the root cellar and cover them with newspaper. Some people wrap each tomato individually, but that's too much work, especially when you check for ripe tomatoes. You have to open each one. Instead, we lift the newspaper cover, select the ripe tomatoes, and remove any that are starting to rot.

Your own fresh tomatoes for Christmas

I've got a great way to have fresh home-grown tomatoes for the Thanksgiving and Christmas holidays. I start at the end of summer. From my *Pixie* tomato plants I pinch off suckers that are 6 inches long. I pinch off the bottom leaves and put them in water for an hour or two to get them to start rooting. Then I plant them deep in large pots filled with garden soil or Pro Mix.

Two plants will fit in a 10-inch pot. For smaller pots, one plant is plenty.

I keep the soil moist for a week or so to ensure that the suckers root. I put the pots outdoors in the sun. When the frosts come, I bring them inside and set them on a table near our two south-facing picture windows. Once they bloom, I spray the flowers with Blossom Set. When the holidays roll around we usually pick the first of many small but juicy and flavorful vine-ripened *Pixies*!

INSECTS THAT ATTACK TOMATOES

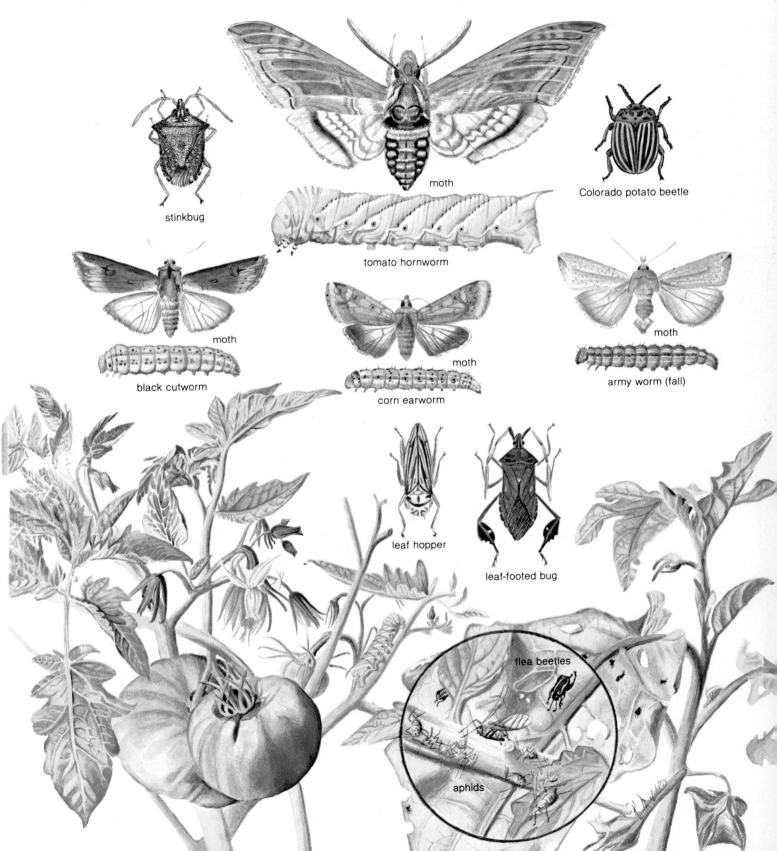

stinkbug

moth

Colorado potato beetle

tomato hornworm

moth

black cutworm

moth

corn earworm

moth

army worm (fall)

leaf hopper

leaf-footed bug

flea beetles

aphids

THE VINE CROPS FAMILY

There's no greater variety of flavors, shapes, and colors than in the vine family of vegetables. Picture a dill pickle next to a *Big Max* pumpkin and you begin to see what I mean. Vine crops are more popular than you might think. Most of us eat from the vine crop family two or three times a week, even if it's only a pickle.

More people are growing vine crops because many varieties now do *not* grow long vines. Bush or "compact" strains of cucumbers, melons, and squash now have a place in small gardens. I know I'd grow *Gold Nugget* winter squash no matter how small a garden I had.

Even if you are short on ground space, you can grow vine crops on trellises. I used to talk people out of using them, since they seemed like a lot of work, but not anymore. I nearly drove off the road once when I spotted a garden with big pumpkins growing on a trellis. I stopped immediately and saw for myself how even heavy vine crops can produce as they swarm over a sturdy trellis.

Many vine crops are planted and grown the same way, but the harvest is wonderfully varied. Far left: Jan picks cucumbers for pickle-making. Above left: watermelon rests on overturned can to sweeten. Bottom: small pumpkins for pies and big ones for jack-o'-lanterns.

Planting in hills is an invitation to trouble

If you examine seed packets of the vine crops you'll probably always find a recommendation to sow the seeds in small circles, or hills. This is an invitation to disaster. Let me tell you why.

In a hill only four or five seeds are planted. If they all come up, folks usually thin out one or two. The hills may be 6, 8, or 10 feet apart, depending on the crop. If insects attack the hill, it's easy to lose every plant. And many times it's too late to replant. You're left with a huge gap of bare soil in the garden because the vines from other hills will take many weeks to reach the empty hill, if they do at all. Having spots of bare soil runs counter to my whole gardening method of covering as much soil as possible with thriving green plants.

I plant my vine crops in rows. If insects become a problem, I may lose four or five plants from the row, but there are many other plants nearby to fill in. And they do it in a hurry.

Without replanting I can maintain the important covering of living plants over the soil. It's also a lot easier to cultivate near the plants early in the season.

In short-season areas, start some cucumbers in individual peat pots. These are at a good size for transplanting.

Pre-sprout some seeds for a worry-free start

The vine crop family can't take a frost, so if you have a short growing season, start your cukes or melons indoors. Plant them in individual peat pots or pyramid planters. Sow the seeds 3 or 4 weeks before you want to set them out. They mustn't be too big at transplanting time. Be careful when you transplant vine crops—their roots are slow to recover from any transplant shock.

I also sprout some of my cantaloupe and watermelon seeds indoors—using my paper towel method—to gain time on the season.

If gambling on early planting, sprout cantaloupe and other vine crop seeds indoors. Watch for first sprouts and then plant seeds carefully outside.

300

Warm your soil, avoid killer frosts with tunnels and hot caps

Ordinarily, vine crops are planted after the last frost date because they are so tender and need warm soil. But I like to give some of my melons, cucumbers, and summer squash a 3-week start by planting them under hot caps or plastic tunnels which trap a lot of heat. I use more tunnels than hot caps because I can place them over a long row and be-cause they circulate hot air better. With hot caps, the plants sometimes get *too much heat,* which sets them back. My tunnels have openings at both ends so hot air can escape easily. Both materials protect the plants well in case of frost.

To plant early, I work the soil once or twice a few days before planting and then one last time right before sowing the seeds. I plant either treated seeds or pre-sprouted seeds which will come up quickly. I always sprinkle a few radish seeds for bug control. I usually don't fertilize at this time. I prefer to wait a few weeks until the plants are up and growing. Anytime you put fertilizer under early-planted seeds, you risk burning them.

After planting the seeds, covering and tamping them down, I put the tunnels or hot caps over them.

Once the plants sprout and start to get big, I check the hot caps regularly. On sunny days it's wise to take them off for part of the day.

When the weather warms up for good and the danger of frost has passed, I lift off the hot caps and tunnels, and my vine crops will be well on their way.

Cucumbers can be planted 3 or 4 weeks earlier under plastic tunnels. Close the ends of the tunnels on cold nights.

Planting in review

If you have a big garden and a tiller, use this method to plant vine crops and you'll save a *lot* of time.

1.

I till the planting area about 6 to 8 inches down. Then I slip my furrowing attachment onto my tiller and plow a 4- or 6-inch furrow where the row will be. The straighter the better.

2.

I sprinkle in compost or other natural fertilizers, or place a thin band of 5-10-10 fertilizer at the bottom of the furrow. Vine crops like fertilizer; put it where the roots will find it.

3.

I cover the fertilizer with soil from the sides of the furrow and level it out. (Whenever I plant seeds, I get the soil as smooth and level as possible.)

DISTANCE BETWEEN VINE CROP ROWS

Cucumber	4-6 feet
Pumpkins	6-10 feet
Winter squash	6-10 feet
Cantaloupe	4-5 feet
Watermelon	6-10 feet
Summer squash and zucchini	3-4 feet
Luffa sponge and gourds	4-8 feet

4.

I place the seeds at appropriate intervals down the furrow. The planting surface will be an inch or two below ground level. That's fine. Don't always "go by the book" when you plant vine crop seeds. The plants may do best 10 to 12 inches or more apart, but that doesn't mean you should space the seeds that way. If a few don't come up, you will have unproductive gaps in the row. Instead, plant them a little thicker and thin them after they come up.

5.

Tamp the seeds down with the back of the hoe and cover them with ¾ to 1 inch of soil. Sprinkle in a few radish seeds and firm the row down one last time.

I like to plant this way because it's fast. I do each job completely before moving on to the next. With hill planting, however, it's just the opposite. You're continually moving from your hoe to fertilizer bag, to seed packet, to hoe, and back to fertilizer bag.

Try a two-story garden

Here's a sturdy trellis where even pumpkins do well with a little extra support.

It's possible to grow many of the vine crop family on trellises. Cucumbers grow well on a trellis and so do gourds, some varieties of winter squash and even pumpkins (with a little bit of extra support).

The most sensible trellis is one that lasts. I make mine out of sturdy posts and tough 3- or 4-foot chicken wire. Install your trellis on or before planting day. (If you pound stakes into the ground later, you may injure the roots.)

I place mine on a slight slant so that the prevailing winds will push the plants onto, and not away from, the trellis. Slanting the trellis also makes it easier for the plants to climb.

Trellises are not maintenance-free. You have to guide the plants up the trellis and sometimes tie vines to it. Heavy gourds, small pie pumpkins, or some acorn squash may need additional tie-ups to hold the vegetables against the trellis.

There's always open soil on the back side of my trellis early in the season. It's a good spot for a crop of lettuce, onion sets, or a quick crop of greens like turnips or chard. It's a way to have a "two-story" garden—a vine crop climbing above and another crop huddling near the trellis at ground level.

If you grow vine crops on a trellis, watch their water supply. Trellised plants, because they are more exposed to wind and sun, can lose moisture quickly.

Keep vine crop stems tied loosely to trellis and support heavy squash with cloth sling. Cucumbers need least attention.

303

Let me explain cross-pollination once and for all

Too many gardeners worry about cross-pollination of vine crops, but there's nothing to worry about unless you plan to save seeds to plant next year.

Sure, vine crops can cross-pollinate, but this does not affect the crop you're growing. You may notice an unusual looking squash or melon in the patch, but this is only the result of a cross-pollination that occurred the previous season.

Feel free to plant your vine crops wherever you want them. If you decided to save seeds from a crop, isolate it 100 feet or more away from other vine crops.

Cucumber beetles spread disease

The worst pests of vine crops are the striped cucumber beetle and the spotted cucumber beetle. They can wreck a whole crop of cucumbers, melons, pumpkins, or squash because they attack the plants as they come out of the ground. The plants aren't tough enough to ward them off. What's worse, the striped cucumber beetle infects the plants with a bacterial disease which can cause the plants to go limp and die in mid-season. Watch carefully for the beetles' first appearance, then spray with malathion or Sevin. Treat the base of the plant since the beetles attack there.

The beetles hatch three or four broods of eggs, so you may have to repeat the spraying every week or so. However, if you get rid of the beetles early, you avoid repeated sprayings.

Two other insects to watch for are the squash bug and the squash vine borer. Squash bugs can be controlled by trapping adults under boards placed near the plants or by spraying with Sevin. The borer is tough to control. You can avoid a serious problem by staggering your plantings over several weeks or a month.

Another way to prevent disease, besides stopping the cucumber beetle, is to select disease-resistant varieties. Normal gardening practices, too, go a long way toward preventing problems. If you notice a diseased plant, pull it to keep the disease from spreading to healthy plants. Diseases move quickly among vine crops, especially cucumbers, and speed up in wet weather.

Side-dress—stand back and watch 'em grow!

Side-dress your vine crops if you want the best harvest. I give my plants a fertilizer boost when they blossom. The energy they get then will help produce good-sized fruits and new vine growth. They really take off after a feeding.

To side-dress I place about a tablespoon of 5-10-10 or similar fertilizer in a band 3 to 4 inches from the stems of the plants. It's important to cover the 5-10-10 with soil so that the leaves don't flop down on it and get burned.

To side-dress vine crops put fertilizer in shallow trench . . .

. . . and hoe some soil over the fertilizer to keep rain from splashing it on plant leaves.

INSECTS THAT ATTACK VINE CROPS

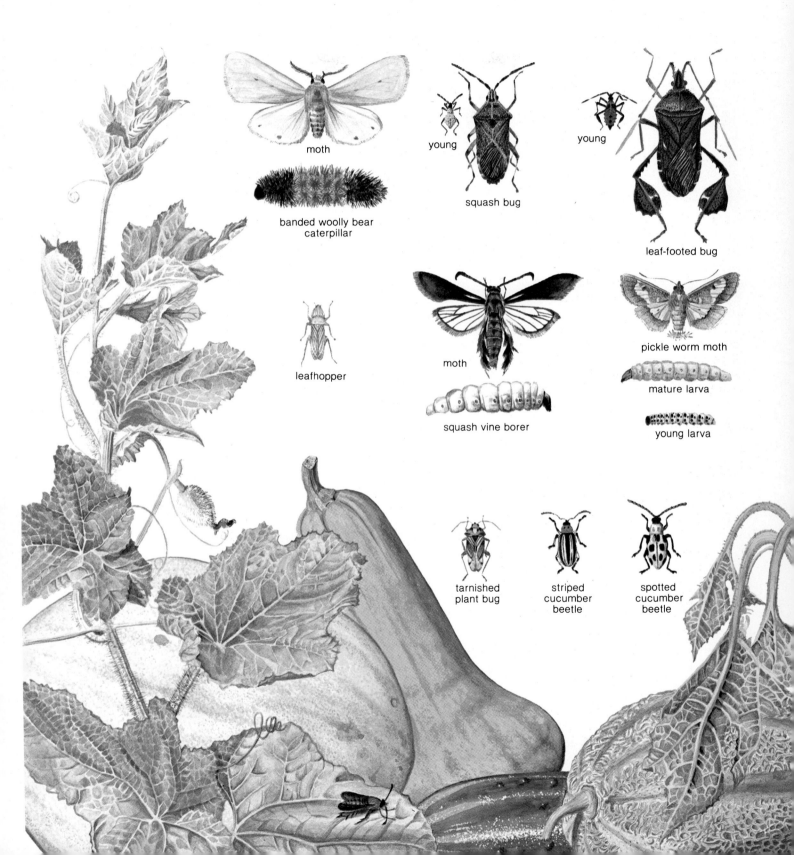

moth

banded woolly bear
caterpillar

young

squash bug

young

leaf-footed bug

leafhopper

moth

squash vine borer

pickle worm moth

mature larva

young larva

tarnished
plant bug

striped
cucumber
beetle

spotted
cucumber
beetle

CUCUMBERS

Three plantings for an avalanche of cukes

I'm the most impatient man in the world when the first cucumber harvest is getting close. I just can't wait. As soon as I find a cucumber 2 or 3 inches long I pick it, brush it off, and eat it.

Because I like cukes so much and because Jan is always trying out new pickle recipes, we grow a lot. I make three plantings: 3 or 4 weeks *before* the average last spring frost date, using grow tunnels or hot caps; about the time of the last expected frost; and 3 or 4 weeks later. This way we get a long harvest of cukes lasting into the fall.

I like the smaller "pickler" varieties for our pickles (though you can preserve any small cucumber). *Wisconsin SMR 18* is my favorite because it is disease resistant and prolific. For bigger slicing cucumbers, my mainstay is *Marketmore 76*. If I miss harvesting some, they stay at table quality a long time.

Most people are afraid to pick a lot of early cucumbers, but it's hard to over harvest them. Keep picking the pickle-sized cucumbers, and the plant won't get the chance to produce mature seeds. It will continue to produce female blossoms. Harvest all the small cucumbers you want.

Plant some dill as soon as you can work the soil in the spring for your dill pickles and other recipes. Here's a tip for making good, crisp pickles. Harvest cucumbers early in the morning while they're crisp and before the sun has a chance to heat them up.

Grow a big pickle in a small bottle

Two cucumber sizes for pickling—small ones are used to make gherkins; slightly larger ones make good dill pickles.

Pick cucumbers when small to encourage plants to stay productive. It's hard to over-harvest cucumber plants.

Why a bitter cucumber?

People ask me why their cucumbers are sometimes bitter. It's strictly a weather problem. If the weather gets too hot or the plants get low on water, some cukes will develop a bitter taste, especially in their skins. Scientists are still trying to find out how and why it happens. Peel the cucumbers a little deeply and hope for the best. Later pickings from the same row may be okay.

Growing a "cuke in a bottle" is a fun project for young gardeners—and old ones, too. Find a small cucumber and stick it into a small necked bottle without damaging the stem or vine. Keep the bottle shaded with a cloth or leaves while the cucumber grows. Without shade it will get too hot. When the cuke reaches the bottom of the bottle, harvest it. Pour some brine in the bottle to pickle it. Top with a cork. The "cuke in a bottle" makes a great gift. But instead of a "thank you," you'll get a "how the heck . . .?"

GOURDS

seeds overnight to speed germination.

Healthy gourds can spread quite a distance. If space is a problem, train them up a trellis or fence where they will receive full sun. Plant at 1-foot intervals. Keep the gourds off the ground to prevent misshapen ones and to increase your yield. If a gourd vine is threatening to take over your backyard, halt its progress by pinching off the fuzzy growth tips.

Harvest only when your gourds are fully mature, or they won't last long. Wait until the stem shrivels. If frost is expected before your gourds are ready, protect them with a sheet or newspapers.

Leave a few inches of stem when harvesting them, and handle them carefully to avoid nicks and bruises. Let them cure for 1 or 2 weeks. Then dip them in alcohol or diluted bleach to ensure good keeping.

Decorations, centerpieces, dippers, and birdhouses

Gourds can become a bowl or brightly colored objects polished to perfection; a fall centerpiece; a child's pride in his or her first gardening effort; or a garden conversation piece that lasts for months and months.

Gourds, such as the *Bottle, Dipper* and *Birdhouse*, need 140 to 150 days to reach maturity. They need to be started indoors if your season is short. I gain a few extra days by soaking gourd

LUFFA

Home-grown sponges, hard or soft

Luffa plants grow quickly and produce club-shaped gourds from 10 to 20 inches long. The spongy interiors can be cleaned out, dried, and used as bath sponges, scrubbers for light scouring or carwash wipers. I've found them very handy.

Luffas grow much the same as cucumbers, although they are more sensitive to cold and need more room.

They also need a long season, so you might have to plant them before the last frost and use hot caps for protection.

If you need a soft sponge, pick the luffa while it is green. Want a tougher quality? In time, the outer skin will yellow and dry out some. That's the time to pick it for a coarse sponge useful for scrubbing.

After picking, "unzip" the luffa by peeling off the skin—it's like peeling an orange—then rinse it under running water to wash away the oily covering surrounding the spongy skeleton. Dry them in the sun and shake away the seeds. Whiten the sponge if you like in a weak bleach or peroxide solution, or soften it further by boiling briefly in water. Your home-grown sponge is ready to use or sell. I've seen them at market stands for $1.50 each.

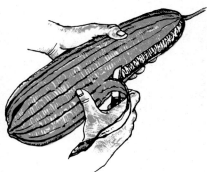

Peel mature luffas as you would peel an orange.

Squeeze and wash fibrous, spongy interior under fast flow of water. Then set luffas in a sunny spot to dry. When dry, shake out any remaining seeds.

CANTALOUPES &

Pushing melons for the earliest and sweetest

Gardeners everywhere want melons to ripen earlier and to taste sweeter. This is understandable in the North where the season can sometimes be too short for many melon varieties.

It's also true in the South,

Here's what makes a good melon

A good watermelon or cantaloupe needs a smooth start in warm, well-drained soil, a steady water supply especially when the melons get big, and plenty of heat at ripening time.

Anything northern gardeners can do to trap extra heat for their plants will help them grow bigger, better melons. In the warm states, a steady supply of water is most important.

Melons like well-drained soil and lots of water. It's not a contradiction. They like to "keep their feet dry" but still get regular drinks of water. Go out to the farmstand with the biggest and sweetest melons and you'll probably discover the melons are growing in well-drained sandy soil. If your soil is heavy clay and does not drain too well, you'll get better melons on raised beds.

WATERMELONS

where the season is long and hot and where you'd think there would be no difficulty in growing superior melons. But it's important to give melons an early start in the south so you can harvest them before the very hot, dry spells of summer. Drought is very harmful, because good melons must have water as they get big and start to ripen. It pays to push your crop so the melons will mature when the chances of getting a few good rains are good.

If you're interested in trying to get those cantaloupes, watermelons, and honeydew melons to ripen earlier, try these tips:

■ Sprout your seeds a few days before you plant, or start seedlings indoors 3 or 4 weeks before planting time.

■ Plant outside 2 or 3 weeks earlier than usual. Use hotcaps or plastic grow tunnels (along with a few radish seeds for insect control) in case the weather turns cool.

■ When there are plenty of melons on the vines, pick off the fuzzy ends to concentrate the plants' energy into producing flowers and fruit, not more vines.

Smell those cantaloupes. . .

My favorite way to tell when a cantaloupe is ripe is to smell it. When it gives off a strong "musky" or perfume-like scent around the stem end, it's ripe. This technique works in the supermarket, too. Don't squeeze, tap, rap, or punch the cantaloupes. . .smell 'em.

Some varieties will indicate ripeness when the skin changes from green to yellow or tan and the netting becomes very pronounced.

Also, when a melon is ripe its stem will usually separate or slip from the melon with very little pressure.

Thump those watermelons. . .

Judging when a watermelon is ripe is a guessing game.

One way is to "thump" the melons. I wasn't sure about this technique when I first tried it a few years ago, but it works.

A watermelon that still has a way to go will make a sharp thump when you rap it, like rapping on your forehead.

A melon that is ripe will sound a little muffled. This is like rapping on your chest.

An overripe melon will be heavier and more muffled than a ripe one, like the sound from rapping your stomach.

If you think you have a good ear for sound, and are willing to give yourself a few hard knocks, this ripeness test might be fun.

Another sign of ripeness is the color of the spot where the watermelon rests on the ground or tin can. As the melon ripens, that ground spot turns from white to a deep, creamy yellow, then towards orange, when it's ripe. The shiny surface of some varieties will dull somewhat when ripe.

Watch the watermelon stem to judge ripeness, too. There is a small tendril next to the point where the stem of the melon comes out of the vine. When this tendril turns brown and dries up like a pig's curly tail, the melon is ripe.

I've noticed that animals, birds, and bees like cantaloupes and watermelons. If you spot a pencil-thick hole in a cantaloupe, be careful. . .might be a few yellow jackets inside.

My advice on varieties

Watermelons—If you have a short growing season, look for fast-maturing varieties. Try some of the smaller icebox watermelons such as *Sugar Baby* which ripen in 75 to 85 days. We chill them, cut them in half, hollow out the centers a bit, and put in ice cream—now that's a nice dessert.

Dixie Queen and *Charleston Gray* are two of the most popular standard watermelons. They do well in warmer climates, but I've grown them successfully here in Vermont, too. Just ask my grandsons how they tasted!

Cantaloupes—I like the hybrid varieties of cantaloupes. I have a short growing season and want the best chance of success. My favorite hybrids are *Gold Star, Burpee Hybrid,* and *Harper Hybrid.*

Lift your melons for extra heat

■ Save large cans such as coffee cans. When the melons are the size of baseballs, place the tin cans near them. The open ends should be facing downward, and the cans should be buried deep enough so they won't tip over.

■ Gently lift each melon onto a can. Melons like heat and as the first sunlight of the day hits those cans, the melons will get warm earlier than usual. It's like making the day longer. In northern gardens, this helps melons ripen faster.

In warm climates, this step is *not* necessary. There is usually enough heat to ripen melons. The water supply is more critical. When the weather is hot, they need 1 or 2 inches of water a week.

■ Near the end of the season, pick off little green melons which won't ripen before a frost. This keeps the energy on the plant headed where it can best be used.

PUMPKINS

For my grandchildren, fall means pumpkins

If you fertilize pumpkins they'll get very big and take up a lot of garden space—but they're worth every inch I give them.

We grow a lot of pumpkins for our grandchildren—they like them big—plus plenty for making pumpkin pies. The smaller varieties have better flavor than the big ones, so we use them for pies.

The bigger jack-o'-lantern types, such as *Big Max,* can be used for pies but I don't think they're as good.

There's no secret to growing a super-sized pumpkin that might win a ribbon at the fair. Here are the steps:
• Dig a big hole and put in about a bushel of aged manure or compost, or a pound of commercial fertilizer, or some combination of the two. Cover the fertilizer with 3 inches of soil.
• Select seeds like *Big Max,* a favorite large pumpkin.
• Plant three or four seeds in a hill. Once they sprout and grow two or three leaves, save the healthiest plant and remove the others.

• After the plant blossoms and sets three small pumpkins, pick off any additional blossoms that appear. Also pick off the fuzzy tips of the vines to focus all the plant's energy into those three little pumpkins.

• When the pumpkins are soft-ball-size, save the best-shaped one, and pick the other two. All plant food will head into that one pumpkin.

• If you want a pumpkin with a perfect shape, roll it gently every now and then to keep it from flattening out on one side or the bottom. Be careful when you do this.

•Side-dress the plant three or four times as it's growing and give it plenty of water.

•Pumpkins should be harvested when they are full-sized and mature. They should not be left out when a frost hits because they will be injured and won't keep long. Don't remove the stem when you pick them. If it breaks off, the pumpkin will be a poor keeper.

Your children will love their own autographed pumpkins

A treat for our grandchildren is a crop of autographed pumpkins.

When some of our pie pumpkins are about softball-size or slightly larger, I write their names on separate pumpkins. I use a ballpoint pen and lightly break through the skin when I write. As the pumpkins expand, so do the names.

The kids don't see these until it's time to pick a few pumpkins for Halloween. By then their names have grown 10 times. It's a joy for Jan and me to watch them discover a pumpkin with their own name on it—and it's the greatest thrill in the world for them.

WINTER SQUASH

Delicious out-of-season eating without canning, freezing, or even a root cellar.

Our Thanksgiving meal is not complete without a serving of home-grown winter squash. We store *Blue Hubbard, Gold Nuggets, Butternut, Acorn,* and *Buttercup* in the root cellar. For Thanksgiving, we choose our favorite, *Blue Hubbard.* I have yet to taste as flavorful a squash.

Winter squash is getting more popular with gardeners. Perhaps it's because they require very little work, yield well, and keep for months in a cool place. You don't even need a root cellar.

If you have a small garden, try the *Gold Nugget.* This winter squash takes up as much space as a zucchini plant and yields a bundle of small, delicious squash. We cut them in half and bake them—they're wonderful.

The *Spaghetti* squash keeps very well. It has tender, stringy flesh when baked, with a texture surprisingly like spaghetti. Some people like it so much that they serve it with their favorite spaghetti sauce.

I plant winter squash in rows about 10 feet apart after the frost danger is past. Between the rows, I plant a swath of inexpensive dry beans 4 or 5 feet wide. I weed around the squash once or twice and never work the beans at all. They sprout up and start shading out weeds right away.

The nice thing about this system is that I cover the soil quickly with plants, and both crops are ready to harvest at the same time.

Let squash grow as long as you can. The longer they grow and mature, the less water they will contain. That's important for long keeping. Winter squash which *haven't* matured will be a little watery when you cook them up—but still good.

Curing squash for longest keeping

I wait until the vines die or just before the first fall frost to harvest winter squash. They should not be exposed to frost because it will soften their skins and they won't keep as well. Fully mature squash are the ones with the tough skins. Check by sticking your thumbnail into them. If you break the skin easily, it hasn't matured and will keep only for a short time.

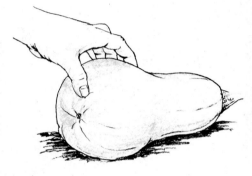

Harvest your crop on a sunny day, after a few days of dry weather. Cut them off the vines, leaving 2 or 3 inches of stem. If the stem breaks off, set the squash aside. It won't keep well and should be used first.

Roll the squash over and leave them outside overnight if there's no danger of frost. Pick them up the next afternoon—the dirt clinging to them should be dry and drop off easily.

Be careful not to bruise the squash you want to store—they won't keep well.

Never carry them by the stems. (That goes for pumpkins, too.) And never wash them until you are ready to cook them.

Winter squash should be cured in order to dry and harden their shells before being stored.

Ideally, they should be aired in a warm, well-ventilated place for 1 to 2 weeks. It's usually too cool to achieve the perfect temperature outdoors, but you can group them near your furnace, wood stove, or on a sunny back porch.

I cure my winter squash in the root cellar, running a small, portable fan on them around the clock for a week or so. Even though my root cellar is cool, the circulating air from the fan does the curing.

Then I pile the vegetables two or three deep on shelves located halfway between the floor and ceiling of my root cellar. It's warmer there than near the floor where I keep my potatoes, and the squash like higher temperatures.

My root cellar is fairly dry, but most cellars are too damp for storing vine crops. They keep best in a cool place (50° to 55° F.) with *low* humidity.

In the past, folks stashed their winter squash and pumpkins under their beds, but beds were high off the floor and bedrooms unheated in those days. Any cool, dry, dark spot is fine—a spare room, closet floor, attic floor, or even a large cool kitchen cupboard.

Check them regularly. Remove any that are getting soft or look as if they're starting to rot. Some will keep better than others.

If some squash have started to soften, cook them without butter or seasonings, and freeze them in containers.

SUMMER SQUASH AND ZUCCHINI

Don't let them get more than 6 inches long

Summer squash and zucchini varieties are space-efficient, fast-maturing, and one of the easiest crops to grow. In fact, they're too easy. First-timers find out in a hurry that you don't have to plant much summer squash to get a big yield.

I've heard the suggestion that gardeners should practice "ZPC"—zucchini population control. I'll bet that if only one out of three gardeners planted zucchini, there would still be plenty for everyone, and with much less waste.

I used to think that *everyone* had a problem with too *much* summer squash and zucchini. But I discovered "that ain't so" when I visited the Pacific Northwest region. There, gardeners complain about *too little zucchini*—because they don't get enough heat and sun for zucchini to thrive. A good strategy there is to grow them on raised beds for extra heat.

Summer squash are tenderest and most delicious when young, 5 to 6 inches in length. Don't let them get longer. Picking them small will keep the vines producing. If you plant the *Crooked Neck* summer squash, pick it very young. To me it gets too large too fast. I much prefer the *Straight Neck* variety.

Too few people know about harvesting squash buds and blossoms. They are a real delicacy. Pick the buds just before they open into blossoms. Wash them and saute them in butter. Or dip them in batter and deep-fry. They're also delicious in soups, with meats, and in stews. Squash plants will continue to produce buds as long as you keep them harvested, so don't worry that taking some buds will limit your squash harvest.

Squash and zucchini produce best when they grow unchecked; don't allow the soil to dry out, and make certain you've given the plants plenty of food.

GARDEN PERENNIALS

Asparagus   Horseradish   Jerusalem artichokes   Rhubarb   Strawberries

Perennial vegetables will last for years with proper care. My asparagus bed is almost 10 years old and is getting better each season. Maybe I'll still be harvesting when it's 30 years old, an age any asparagus bed can reach with some care.

Rhubarb will keep going for a long time with my easy prescription for handling it. Horseradish and Jerusalem artichokes seem to grow forever. The biggest job with them is how to keep them under control. They're the "space invaders" of a garden.

To grow one or more of these crops, put the bed where it won't be in the way of tilling and planting your annual vegetables and flowers. Your perennials will have to live in one spot for a long time, so it pays to work a lot of organic matter and compost into the soil before planting.

One of the biggest problems in growing perennials is not pests or diseases (those are rare) but moving before you've harvested much of a crop. It's most serious with asparagus which needs about 3 years in the garden before you get a decent harvest. I have an old friend who just moved back to my neck of the woods after some years away. He said, "Dick, you're not going to believe this, but I planted asparagus three times in 6 years. Trouble is, I moved so much I never got to harvest one spear!"

Weeding is the main difficulty for the folks who do stay put. You can avoid a lot of weeding by planting in a part of the garden which is relatively weed-free. This might be where you have grown several thick green manure crops in succession.

319

RHUBARB

Four plants go a long way

Rhubarb grows from root divisions which you can buy in a garden store or from a seed catalog. Often the best way is to get some roots from a neighbor. Three or four root crowns will produce all you can eat.

In the spring, dig planting holes several inches deep and 18 inches apart. Put some compost or fertilizer in each hole. Place a single piece of root in each hole, covering it with about an inch of soil. Do not harvest from these plants the first year. Give them a few side-dressings through the season so they'll grow lots of tops and in turn nourish the developing root system.

The next season you can harvest some stalks. When they get 8 to 10 inches tall, gently pull out and up on the ones you want to tear away from the plant. Harvest the largest stalks first. Don't eat the leaves. They are toxic.

During the second year, the rhubarb plant may put out tall seedpods. Remove these so the roots will produce tasty stalks all season. The more stalks you harvest, the more the plant will produce.

Divide your plants to keep them thriving

To keep your rhubarb plants thriving for many years, they must be divided. I like to do it every 4 or 5 years in the fall, though it can be done in the spring before growth starts.

I drive a shovel down into the middle of the plant and dig up half the root. I fill in the hole with compost. This forces the plant to produce younger, better crowns the following year. With young crowns you'll have tender, flavorful rhubarb. The half of the plant I dig up can be saved in the root cellar, planted right away, or given to a friend. In another 4 or 5 years, I repeat the process and remove the older part of the plant.

I store some of these rhubarb plants in my root cellar and "force" a few. They are amazing!

After I dig the roots in the fall, I put some in a box filled with peat moss or sawdust and keep it in a dark place in the cellar. In January, I soak the peat moss or sawdust with water, and keep the box cool and in the dark.

In a few days, the rhubarb sends out little stalks. These look just like the rhubarb shoots that come out of the ground in the spring, except they have no leaves. They look a little like asparagus shoots, and they taste great. We thaw some frozen strawberries, mix in the tender rhubarb shoots, and make a tangy strawberry-rhubarb pie.

A final note—the roots used for indoor forcing will not produce well if planted outdoors in the spring.

One good plant will provide the rhubarb for 6 or 8 strawberry-rhubarb pies.

320

JERUSALEM ARTICHOKES

Deliciously low in starch and calories

Jerusalem artichokes are grown for their underground tubers which are delicious, practically starch-free, and low in calories. They will grow almost anywhere in the United States and can be planted either in the fall or as early as the ground can be worked in the spring.

One of the nicest things about Jerusalem artichokes, besides their taste, is that they are almost completely free of diseases and pests. They are so prolific that if you do not watch them closely, they will take over the whole garden, your lawn, your woods, and any nearby roadside ditches. Any tuber left in the soil will sprout the next year and send out roots.

I grow mine in a circular bed near the back fence in my garden. I left a lot of room around the bed so I can roto-till a deep swath around the plants to prevent them from spreading.

Start Jerusalem artichokes by planting tubers which you can buy, or dig from a friend's garden. You will need six pieces, cut in quarters, for a 25-foot long row. Cut the tubers into pieces with an eye in each and plant them about 4 inches deep, spacing them a foot apart. Leave 3 to 4 feet between the rows so you can till next to them. When Jeru-

salem artichoke plants are mature, they will be 6 or more feet tall, so plant them where they will not shade other plants.

Jerusalem artichokes need a very long growing season—about 125 days. Start harvesting in late fall or after the frost has killed the tops. They also can be harvested in the spring before they sprout again.

There are many good ways to eat Jerusalem artichokes. Cook them or eat them raw in salads. They don't need to be peeled, just give them a good scrubbing. Thinly sliced, they substitute for water chestnuts in stir frying.

ASPARAGUS

The best way to grow an asparagus bed is to plant 2-year-old roots which you can order from a seed catalog or pick up at a garden store. One-year-old roots may be cheaper, but the savings are not worth waiting an extra year for your first harvest. I think the 2-year-old roots are more reliable in transplanting.

If you live in the North, set out asparagus roots in the early spring. In the South, set them out in the fall because it can be so dry and hot in the summer that the plants may not make it through.

Asparagus will grow in most types of soil, but since it must have dry feet, it does best in soil that drains well. Place the plants about 2 feet apart with 5 feet between rows. Twenty-five to 30 crowns will produce enough asparagus for a family of four once the bed is established, which takes three seasons.

Dig a trench 12 to 18 inches deep, the length of your row, and add 6 or 7 inches of aged manure, or compost, or a little peat moss. Sprinkle on a dusting of 10-10-10, add a couple of inches of soil from beside the trench, and mix everything together.

With this mixture, build up mounds at the bottom of the trench about a foot apart. Set each crown on top of a mound and drape the roots down just the way you'd put a wig on a head. This enables the roots to get moisture and food throughout a depth of 4 or 5 inches of soil. If you place the roots flat on the ground they can feed only at one level and it will be a while before

Roots are draped over soil and compost at planting time.

they grow down and get water and food from a deeper level.

Place the top of the crowns at least 4 inches below the soil surface. Fill up the trench to cover them with a couple of inches of soil. This puts the soil level of the row a little below the rest of the garden. When the shoots grow up, fill in the trench with a little more soil to give the stalks excellent support.

Don't harvest any asparagus the first year. The plants need to grow as much top, or "ferns," as they can. As the tops die down in the fall, the energy they've captured from the sun will be transferred to the roots below. After three seasons the roots will have enough energy to send up plenty of thick asparagus spears that you can harvest. You must allow some to develop into lush ferns. They will continue the yearly job of gathering energy for the roots.

While you're waiting for the first harvest season to come around, you still have to take care of the crop.

First year

You may want to put a thick mulch around the small spears *after* they come up to keep the weeds down and hold in moisture. Let the new plants grow through the summer and fall without cutting the shoots or ferns. Let the tops die down in late fall. Don't do a thing to them.

Second year

Every spring, starting with the second year, you'll have to do a little maintenance on your asparagus bed *before* it starts to grow again. I cut the old ferns that

died over the fall and winter and clear them out. I also remove any mulch that's left. Then I fertilize the plants. I use a cupful of 5-10-10 or similar fertilizer for each 3 feet of row. I also cultivate a couple of times with my tiller between the rows each spring. Till at a shallow depth to avoid cutting any spreading roots.

As the weather warms, the asparagus will poke through the soil. Don't harvest the second year. When the spears are tall enough to mulch, I weed and then mulch around them.

Third year

Early in the third spring, again cut away old ferns, pull the mulch back, and fertilize. You'll probably be able to harvest some spears. They are at their prime when 6 to 8 inches tall. If they are as thick as your finger, pick some. If they are skinny, let them grow into ferns.

Harvest with a knife and cut the spears a hair below the soil surface. Cut with care. Another spear may be about to come up right next to the one you're harvesting.

Following years

As your asparagus plants get stronger and stronger over the next few years, you can harvest for 5 to 8 weeks each spring before letting the plants concentrate on growing ferns.

Here's a harvest tip: don't toss out the tough bottom ends of the spears. Cook them separately, puree them, then freeze them in ice cube trays. Use the asparagus "cubes" in soups. They're great.

Weeds are the biggest hassle

After the last harvest of my bed, I pull all the weeds. I fertilize the bed again, and mulch heavily around the spears. This halts all weed growth.

Here's another method I use to block weeds. After the last harvest I weed the bed. Then I sprinkle in some *annual ryegrass* seed and scratch it into the soil. The ryegrass will grow very thickly. It becomes a living mulch for the bed, choking out weeds that try to come up. Because it's an annual, it will die over the winter and insulate the soil and roots. In the spring it is partially decomposed and easy to pull away from the bed.

Once your bed is established, there's a simple way to stretch out the harvest period. Early in the spring, pull the mulch away from only part of your patch. The asparagus will come up faster when the soil is exposed to the warmth of sunlight. The mulched soil in the rest of the bed will stay cool longer, delaying the growth of the remaining asparagus. Wait a couple of weeks and then pull the mulch off the rest of the row. If you see spears poking through the mulch before the two weeks are up, pull the mulch back. Otherwise, some of the asparagus spears may curl over when they come up.

My instant asparagus bed

Some years ago, before Jan and I moved to our present home, I planted an entire asparagus bed with roadside plants to get a harvest the first year. The best time to dig and transplant asparagus is in early spring, before the plants start growing. You have to know exactly where the buried roadside crowns are. So, just before the asparagus tops died down in the fall, I stuck yellow stakes near the plants I wanted to dig.

Early the next spring I went back with my shovel and some bushel baskets. You wouldn't believe how big and wide some of those asparagus root systems were. I had to cut them in pieces to get them out of the soil, and even then each piece filled a bushel basket. I trucked them to my house and planted them in big holes with manure and compost at the bottom. It was a long, tough job. I didn't enjoy it at all . . . but when I think about the excellent harvest we got that very first year, it doesn't seem so bad.

HORSERADISH

I have a new technique for coaxing my horseradish bed to produce the straightest roots I've ever seen. Straight roots are the easiest to clean and process.

First, let me explain that I harvest most of my horseradish roots quite early in the spring. The taste is real hot in spring and I like hot horseradish.

I fertilize after the harvest and let the plants get about 6 inches tall. Then I till half the bed as deeply as I can. This chops up the roots and mixes the pieces into the soil. Many of the pieces are near the surface where they will quickly sprout and grow again. The important thing is that my roto-tiller leaves the soil so soft and fluffy that the roots have an easy, unobstructed path down into it.

The next year the tilled part of the bed will be full of super-straight, delicious horseradish roots, easy to clean and process. After the harvest, I till the other half of the bed to get thick, straight roots growing there. I plan to keep up this tilling rotation over the years.

Start with roots from a friend

To start a bed, get some roots from a friend who has one. A horseradish grower won't mind because the plants expand quickly; unless you till around it several times a year they will try to invade neighboring crops. I once mentioned on the local radio that I had some horseradish roots to give away to folks who wanted to start a bed. People came for 3 days, and from as far as 40 miles away. Luckily, my bed was so big I could give a few roots to everybody.

You'll need only six root pieces. Plant them as early in the spring as you can.

Till or spade the area to a depth of 6 to 8 inches. Dig a hole or furrow 4 to 6 inches deep and put a handful of fertilizer or compost at the bottom. Cover this with 2 inches of soil.

Push each root piece in the soil at a 45° angle rather than straight up and down. This way, the roots that form along the length of each cutting can grow straight down without getting tangled up. The top of the root cutting should be 2 inches below the soil surface.

(Note: if you buy roots at a store, one end will be cut on a slant. That slanted end should be planted downward. If you dig roots in a friend's garden, cut them the same way so you'll get the right end planted downward.)

Horseradish roots can be dug, ground up, and eaten anytime, but I think spring is the best. A kitchen blender or a food processor is great for making horseradish sauce. Mix together 2 cups peeled horseradish chunks, 1 cup distilled white vinegar, and 1 teaspoon salt. Grind the mixture to the texture you prefer. I like a fine mince. Horseradish sauce keeps very well refrigerated.

STRAWBERRIES

Here's my recipe for growing great strawberries

Plant your berries in a sunny location for the sweetest berries and the healthiest plants. Try for an open spot on a slight south-facing slope. Low spots on your property could be trouble since cold air flows like water down a slope and will collect in pockets. Frosts will hit these low spots first.

Strawberry plants are usually set out in the early spring (March or April) in the North, but southern gardeners often have the best luck with fall planting.

Soil

Fertile, well-drained soil is a must. If you have heavy clay, make raised beds. These keep plants from sitting around with "wet feet" which lowers production. Raised beds also prevent plants from being heaved out of the ground by frost during the winter. Add plenty of organic matter to help loosen up clay soil.

In sandy soil, organic matter boosts water- and nutrient-holding capacity. I put a lot of compost, leaves, and other plant residues into new strawberry soil. I never use manure, however; it is usually full of weed seeds.

Test your soil. Strawberries like a slightly acid soil, with pH readings from 5.8 to 6.5. If your pH is below 5.8, add lime during the

For best berries, choose two or three varieties proven successful in your area.

fall preceding planting. If it's above 6.5 (often the case in some western states), add sulfur.

Start with certified, virus-free plants

Good plants will produce more berries over a longer time. The plants should look healthy and be free of insect or disease injury. Robust young stock with good-sized root systems grow big plants with lots of berries.

Selecting varieties that do well in your area is as important as choosing quality plants. There are varieties adapted to every part of the country. Ask your Extension agent or good local strawberry growers which ones do best in your neck of the woods. Plant two or three recommended varieties to extend your harvest and to provide insurance for that season when one variety doesn't do very well.

Strawberry plants usually are sold in bunches of 25, and one or two bunches are enough if you're starting a bed.

326

My planting pointers

Mound soil and compost in a trench . . .

. . . spread roots over the mound like a wig.

Plant as early as you can and use only dormant plants. If the plants have already started growing, they will experience more of a setback when planted. Set out on a cloudy day or late in the afternoon to avoid exposing young plants to stressful sunshine and heat.

Soak the roots with water while you make a furrow in the row where the strawberries will be planted. I plant in rows 4 feet apart. Add a bushel of organic matter and 4 cups of 5-10-10 fertilizer for every 25 feet and mix well into the soil. Then build up a small dome of soil every 12 to 16 inches.

Trim roots so they are 4 to 5 inches long. This encourages healthy, new root development. Some plants will arrive with the beginnings of green top growth. I pick off these leaves, leaving only one leaf in the center of the plant. This gives the roots a break, since they won't have any top growth to support right away.

Place the trimmed roots over the dome of soil, like putting on a wig, with the crown right at the peak.

Add soil and make certain the base of the crown is just at the soil surface. Then firm the soil around the plant and water well.

You're bound to hear about "June-bearing" and "everbearing" varieties. *June-bearing* strawberries produce one large harvest in June in many of the northern states. Many varieties of June-bearers are available, and they produce a large number of daughter plants.

Everbearing strawberries produce berries throughout the season, but bear most at two periods—in June and again in the fall. Everbearers don't produce many runners, which makes them ideal for space-conscious growers. Fewer varieties are available, but they are worth trying to see if they perform for you.

Keep strawberry blossoms picked off during the first season of growth.

After planting, strawberries need tender-loving care

Keep your berries weed-free. Mulching is the best way to beat weeds in a strawberry patch. Build up a 4- to 6-inch layer of a weed-free mulch such as wheat straw, chopped cornstalks, or a late cut of hay.

Place a little mulch around the young plants early in the season and add more as it packs down. A 2-inch layer of composted mulch should do the job of keeping the weeds down and still allow daughter plants to root.

In early summer, shallow cultivation between rows will get rid of small weeds. If you spot large weeds next to the plants, pull them carefully so that the berry roots are not disturbed.

Side-dress about one month after planting. Young plants require a steady supply of nutri-ents. If your plants are healthy and vigorous by fall, they'll set plenty of blossoms for you next summer. Healthy plants also produce a large number of daughters to extend the life of the bed. Side-dress with about a bushel of compost or one pound of 5-10-10 for each 100 square feet.

Pinch off all the blossoms. Kids are good helpers at this job. By keeping the flowers picked off the first year, the plants put their energy into developing runners. This is the key to a long-lasting productive bed.

Space daughter plants. I let the daughter plants root themselves away from the mother plants, but sometimes I help them to an open spot. I don't want them too crowded.

Control insects and diseases. Study the most common strawberry diseases and insect pests. If you see trouble signs early, you'll be able to take control measures while the problems are still minor.

Get ready for winter. Strawberry plants need winter protection—the fruit buds of the plant must be shielded. They are dormant in the crown and should not go through freezing and thawing cycles.

The best protection is a 6-inch layer of straw or weed-free mulch placed directly over the plants once they've been hardened by several hard freezes. The plants are sufficiently hardened when the leaves lay flat on the ground instead of being upright the way they are all summer.

A heavy snowfall after mulching helps—it adds to the insulation.

A job for next spring. A couple of weeks before the expected last frost, carefully take the mulch off the plant and check for new growth. You can leave some mulch in the rows and between the plants to keep weeds down. Do not fertilize now. That encourages too much leaf growth and a small, soft crop of berries.

Protect the plants from a late frost. Knowing the advance signals of a coming frost helps every grower. For example, low daytime temperatures followed by a windless, cloudless night could mean a frost. If the temperature sinks below 32°F., any tender blossoms are in danger. Put mulch over the plants, or cover them with sheets of newspapers. If you have a small patch, a sprinkler can rescue the plants. Turn it on late at night and leave it on until sunrise.

How I keep my strawberry bed productive year after year

Setting my plants out in rows 4 feet apart allows me to weed out old plants easily and to have a new crop of plants to set fruit.

After harvesting the second year, I till down the middle of my original rows, turning under the mother plants. This leaves a tilled area about 2 feet wide. After several days, I till again, this time adding dehydrated manure, compost, or fertilizer.

Now the daughter plants, which are going strong on either side of this newly tilled pathway, will become mother plants themselves, sending out runners and establishing new plants where the original ones had been. Sometimes these runners will have to be encouraged to grow toward the newly opened ground, but this is easily done with a rake or by hand. Each year I till under the older rows and let them fill in again from the runners of the remaining plants. Shifting the rows back and forth this way keeps my bed healthy and productive for years.

During the first season of growth, "daughter" plants will root from the runners. The second year, after the harvest, I will turn under just the mother plants. This will encourage the daughter plants to send out their own runners into the tilled area.

GARDEN PESTS

A secure fence is the best line of defense

I encourage gardeners with animal problems to put a fence around the garden. Nothing beats a secure fence for keeping out rabbits, woodchucks, raccoons, dogs, and cats. It even helps to control the traffic of neighborhood kids scooting through the yard.

Get your fence up early, *before* animal pests make their first forays. Once they get a taste of what's in your garden they are determined to get back in for extra helpings.

I use fences made of 3-foot-high chicken wire (1- or 1½-inch mesh), topped by a single strand of electric wire 1 inch above the top. An electric fence is the best way to keep raccoons out of the corn patch. The jolt a raccoon gets when he grabs the electric wire convinces him to try a garden somewhere else. The only time I hitch up the battery and energize the wire is before and during the corn harvest. I run it from late afternoon until early morning.

I like gates that are at least 5 feet wide. It's easy to get my big work cart through one. And if I ever want to get a vehicle of some kind into the garden, I have an entrance that's wide enough.

A fence is expensive, but it's a wise investment. Just think of how much food money you save from a productive garden. It's easy to grow $500 or more worth of food from a 30 by 40-foot garden. Isn't the value of a garden worth protecting? If you use good materials and build your fence solidly, it should easily last 10 or 20 years with only a little upkeep each season.

Early spring is a good time for fence-mending. Check around the base of the fence for open spaces where animals can sneak under. Sometimes the freezing and thawing of the ground will raise a few fence posts and open gaps. Drive the posts back into the ground. As the season passes, cut the grass and weeds around the fence. If you let some get tall they can short out the wire strand on top and allow animals a free pass into your garden.

Fencing a 30-by-40-foot garden my way

(Fence will be 40 feet by 50 feet to allow 5 feet from fence to garden on all sides)

Materials Needed

180 feet 3-foot-high chicken wire 1-inch by 1-inch mesh

1 box porcelain or plastic insulators

180 feet 12-gauge electric wire

1 "fencer" to boost up battery voltage

1 6-volt "hot shot" battery

20 posts

1 gate handle

set of gate hinges

What I've learned about animal pests and how to stop them

WOOD

RABBITS

Black pepper or bloodmeal may chase them out

If you have rabbits in your neighborhood, you have *lots* of rabbits. They mate several times a year and each litter can have six or seven young ones. You don't need a calculator to figure that the possibilities are tremendous.

Rabbits like to feed at twilight, but they have no rules. I've watched them feeding at dawn and in the middle of the day. They'll seek out a garden in the spring when their normal food supplies aren't as plentiful. Rabbit damage can be rough in spring. Just a few bites into your broccoli, lettuce, cabbage, or cauliflower transplants can set them

back. And if they nibble the center bud, the plants won't ever produce. They can do a number on young beans, too.

There are only a few defenses if you don't have a fence. In a small garden, sprinkle black pepper on your transplants in the evening. Rabbits sniff everything and after a sneezing fit they'll move on. If you can find their path to the garden, you can scatter some *moth crystals* along it. Don't use mothballs; they are dangerous and kids think they are candy. Some folks say if you sprinkle bloodmeal at the edge of the garden and on some plants, rabbits will avoid your garden. I guess if they smell blood they think someone means business. If you tie a dog near the garden, you can usually keep rabbits at bay.

If you can get them to relocate, they'll leave you alone

A woodchuck will eat anything green it can gets its teeth into. Woodchucks, often called "groundhogs," come out of their underground burrows at dawn for their first meal. They're lazy and like to make their home near a convenient food source—like a nice vegetable garden. (I have a woodchuck that tries each fall to nest in my garden!) You can tell if a woodchuck is eating your crops because it moves efficiently down one row at a time, eating everything in its path. You couldn't do a neater job with a lawnmower.

After their morning eating binge, woodchucks go back underground to sleep it off. You might spot them later in the day coming out for another meal. What a life!

CHUCKS

They prefer not to travel very far from home to get food. If you can get them to relocate their burrows away from your garden, they may not bother you again.

Find all the woodchuck holes around your garden. They like dry spots for a burrow and they dig two entrances. Pour some moth crystals down each entrance or pour in a little liquid creosote, which is available at paint stores. Don't get any creosote on your hands as it will burn. That's what it does to the woodchuck's belly. He'll be smart enough to look for new quarters. Pouring some used motor oil down both entrances will often discourage them. They like to keep their fur clean and dry.

Woodchucks are easy to catch in "Havahart" traps. Be sure to release them at least a mile or so from your garden.

RACCOONS

They hate the taste of moth crystals on their paws

There are many old-time tricks to keep raccoons out of the corn patch, but only one rule: put your defense in action *before* the raccoons set foot in your garden. Don't wait until their first attack. Once raccoons get a taste of your sweet corn, it will be almost impossible to keep them out.

If you are growing extra-early sweet corn, get ready to protect it. The local raccoons will sniff it out because it will be sweet and delicious well before any of your neighbors' corn. I find that once the farmers near me have corn in their fields that's ready to eat, the raccoons don't bother my crops as much.

One trick I had good luck with—before building my electric fence—was spreading moth crystals between corn rows at each edge of the garden. Raccoons hate the taste of moth crystals on their paws. I put out the crystals at dusk because raccoons will hunt for food as soon as it gets a little dark. I never had to use them down the entire row—working the edges did the job. If it rains, you'll have to put down more crystals.

If you are a careful observer, you may find paths through tall grass that raccoons take to the garden. If so, sprinkle a little creosote along the path. Raccoons don't like getting this on them either, and it may discourage them.

SQUIRRELS & CHIPMUNKS

Tough nuts to crack!

Squirrels and chipmunks are fun to watch, but they are the hardest to keep away from your corn and sunflowers. A fence won't keep them out, not even an electric one. They jump so well and scurry into the garden so fast that an electric shock doesn't stop them. They're in the garden while they're still feeling the zap.

In the sweet corn or popcorn rows, squirrels climb right up the stalks and eat the ears. They're smart. Often they only work the inside rows so you won't notice them. A few times I have seen squirrels trying to haul away whole ears of corn. In a row of sunflowers they can jump from one stalk to the next as if they were in a tree.

In a small garden you may be able to use old stockings or cheesecloth on the sunflower heads and corn ears to foil the squirrels at harvest time. In a big garden, an active cat or an eager dog may be your only hope.

SKUNKS

Let them eat in peace!

A skunk is not a serious garden pest. In my garden, they have dug up some seeds early in the spring. Later in the season I spotted one reaching up for some sweet corn. I thought, "Well, if he wants it, he can have it." Other than that, they have caused very little damage.

Skunks do have some redeeming qualities. They eat insects, grubs, rats, and mice, and thus help control pests in and around the garden.

If you have a surplus of skunks, almost any fence will keep them out of the garden. They won't climb, though sometimes they will try to dig under a fence.

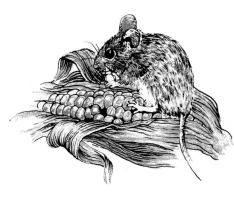

MICE

Let an active cat earn his keep

Field mice can be destructive. When the season is still young, they sometimes dig up big seeds before they have a chance to germinate. Unsuspecting gardeners often think that they've planted wrong or had a bad batch of seeds.

Mice are troublesome at harvest time, too. They love the wide rows of beets in my garden. They can hide under the lush foliage and nibble away to their heart's content. In bad years, they'll take bites out of almost every beet in some rows. Carrots, potatoes, and strawberries are favorite targets, too.

To control mice, keep a cat. With a cat lurking around the garden, most of the rodents will stay away. Also, avoid using heavy mulches until well into the gardening season. Mice will take shelter and breed in a thick mat of hay or straw when the weather is still cool. If you can, use mulches that contain few seeds. Mice just love hay seeds. This is especially important if you plant potatoes under mulch, because after eating a lot of seeds they'll chew the potatoes.

MOLES

Three-inch-long blackberry canes can chase them away

If there are moles in your garden, you'll know it. Their zig-zagging tunnels are easy to recognize. Moles burrow close to the surface searching for earthworms, grubs, snails, and slugs, and this burrowing can really damage a garden. Moles can lift seeds and transplants out of the ground, and those west of the Rockies (slightly bigger than the "eastern" moles) may eat root crops, flower bulbs, or even sprouting pea and corn seeds.

There are several good techniques for repelling moles. I used one when I discovered a number of mole tunnels around our new house the day after we graded and seeded the lawn. I cut up some thorny blackberry canes into 3- or 4-inch sections. I used a piece of wire to make small holes into the mole tunnels at different spots. Then I pushed a short thorny cane down through each hole into the tunnels. Moles have tender skins and they were so annoyed that they left.

You also can squirt a little creosote on the runs every 6 or 8 feet and the moles will probably leave. Another good idea is to drop moth balls into the first run you see to discourage moles from tunneling further in the area.

BIRDS

Birds are usually nice to have near a garden because they eat many kinds of insect pests, but they can be a problem, too.

Crows and blackbirds are notorious for digging up corn seeds and small plants. I've tried the commercial coatings you put on the seeds before planting, but they don't work very well. By the time the birds discover they're getting a stomach ache, they've dug up two-thirds of the row.

I put some 12-inch-wide wire mesh over my corn rows, shaping it like a tent, until the plants get too big for the birds to pull.

This works well.

Birds can be destructive at harvest time. As berry growers know, robins, bluejays, and other birds love to gorge themselves on all kinds of berries and grapes just as you're getting ready to pick them. Netting is the top deterrent here. Birds love sweet corn and sunflower seeds, too. People often tear open an ear of sweet corn to see if it's ready. Don't do this; it's just gives birds a helping hand. Put mesh bags over the sunflower heads when you see the first bird trying to peck some seed.

Fight insect pests with home remedies first

We home gardeners are lucky. We don't depend on the garden for our livelihood. Gardening is not a business for us. We don't have to worry about keeping our crops totally free of blemishes and damage so they will bring top prices at the market. We can afford to share a part of the harvests with insects and not get upset by it. We can use and enjoy slightly damaged crops.

The charts on the following pages will help you identify insects which might be feeding on and damaging your vegetables. Check your garden at least every 2 or 3 days so you can spot bugs before they do much damage. When you see some unusual insect activity, take a good look at it. Be sure the bugs actually pose a serious problem before you take steps to control them.

Fight insects with "home remedies" first. A home remedy is often the easiest and simplest control measure you can take, especially if you are close to harvesting the crop. There's no point in delaying the harvest with a chemical spray or dust when a home remedy can do the job.

The only exception is the bacterial insecticide spray, sold under such names as Dipel and Thuricide, which kills worms that bother cabbage family crops, tomatoes, and corn. Dipel is not a chemical spray; it contains bacteria which paralyze the worms' digestive systems. You can use it even on the day of the harvest. It is very safe for people, pets, and plants. I heartily recommend it.

Use organic pesticides such as rotenone or pyrethrum spray or dust, and choose chemical pesticides such as Sevin or malathion only as a last resort. Follow all label instructions carefully.

A home-made duster saves money

Dusters cost money, but you can make one for free that will do a perfect job. I make a pouch out of a porous cloth material, such as a cut-out section of burlap bag. I put the dust in, and tie the pouch at the top. To apply it, I hold the pouch over a plant and shake it downward with a quick snap so that a mist of dust drifts from the bottom onto the plants. This cloth bag stores easily, too.

Army cutworm

If you choose chemical sprays or dusts, use the correct one for the job

If insect pests get out of hand and you decide to use a commercial chemical insecticide, use the *least* toxic and *most* effective one. It helps to know how the problem insect is feeding. Flies and aphids suck their food—their jaws have been fused together into a sort of tube to withdraw liquid from the plants. Diseases can enter a plant through the puncture holes made by sucking insects. A contact poison, such as malathion or methoxychlor, is needed to kill them. Beetles chew leaves and stems, and can be killed with a stomach poison such as Sevin.

Some pests, such as the root maggot that attacks cabbage, do most of their damage underground by feeding on plant roots. These soil-dwelling pests can be killed with the chemical Diazinon.

The chart on pages 338–342 lists sprays which have been approved for garden pests as of this publication. You should keep abreast of any changes by contacting the nearest Extension Service office each spring and asking for the latest information on home garden sprays.

Japanese beetles

Tomato and potato dusts must be used early

I'm always extra-watchful when it comes to potatoes and tomatoes, because for many years we depended on big crops of each to store and preserve for winter. Several crippling diseases can hit these crops. Our growing season is often wet and humid, which creates perfect conditions for these diseases to spread—especially early and late blight.

I use a commonly available "tomato-potato dust" which contains a fungicide, a chemical that will kill tiny disease spores before they spread. The important thing is to start early, when the plants are 6 to 8 inches tall, because you can only stop these diseases before they happen. I use a tomato-potato dust every 7 to 10 days up to the harvest period to keep my plants protected. One or two dustings won't do it. Regular applications are the only way.

337

Insect Pest Chart

APHID

Description: The aphid is a 1/10 to 1/5 inch long, soft-bodied teardrop-shaped insect with a hollow, piercing mouth tube used to suck out plant juices. It has two wax-secreting tubes on the posterior end of the body which secrete a sticky, sugary substance called honeydew.

Damage: There are many kinds of aphids and most produce many generations. They emerge early in the growing season and cluster on the tips of young leaves or stems. They suck out plant juices and inject toxins, causing plants to yellow and lose vigor. Aphids transmit viruses and other serious plant diseases. Aphids are found throughout the United States.

Plants affected: Many plants are affected, especially beans, eggplant, okra, peas, pepper, potato, and tomato.

Home remedies: Rub aphids off the leaves or spray with a mild solution of soapy water. Aphids have natural enemies in the garden: the ladybug beetle and the trichogramma wasp.

Commercial remedies: Spray with rotenone, pyrethrum, or malathion.

ASPARAGUS BEETLE

Description: Larvae are plump, up to 1/3 inch long, olive green to grayish, with dark head and legs. The adult is ¼ inch long, bluish-black with four white spots and an orange margin on the wing covers.

Damage: Beetles as well as larvae feed on the foliage and young shoots.

Plants affected: Asparagus.

Home remedies: If plant debris is removed at the end of the season there will be less shelter for beetles to overwinter.

Commercial remedies: Spray plants with rotenone, Sevin, or malathion.

BEAN LEAF BEETLE

Description: Larvae are small white grubs, with dark heads and tails. The adult is reddish orange with two pairs of black spots down the middle of the wing covers and black band aroung the exterior. It is usually about ¼ inch long.

Damage: Adults feed on the undersides of leaves, pods, and stems. They typically eat out round holes. Larvae feed on roots and stems. This beetle is especially troublesome in southeastern states.

Plants affected: Beans and peas.

Home remedies: It is important to control weeds around the garden; handpick adult beetles. Till under debris as soon as harvest is over.

Commercial remedies: Spray with rotenone, Sevin, or malathion. Be certain to spray under the surface of the leaves.

BEAN WEEVIL

Description: Small beetle, 1/8 inch long, brown with reddish legs, with snout.

Damage: Adult beetles chew holes in bean pods and lay eggs. Small white grubs hatch and eat their way into seeds. Dry beans in storage may be attacked, with several generations growing and feeding. Occurs throughout the United States.

Plants affected: Beans in garden as well as dry beans in storage.

Home remedies: Heat dried beans to 135⁰ F. for 3 to 4 hours; this kills all stages of the beetle.

Commercial remedies: If a bad problem is noticed early enough in the garden, malathion can limit damage.

BLISTER BEETLE

Description: The adult is a slender beetle which ranges in size from ½ to 1 inch. It is gray-to-black in color and is sometimes striped or spotted.

Damage: The adult blister beetles feed on plant leaves and may cause significant damage when present in large numbers.

Plants affected: Chard, beets, spinach, tomato.

Home remedies: Pick the beetles off plants by hand. Wear gloves for protection. These beetles have an oil on their bodies that causes blisters.

Commercial remedies: Spray plants with Sevin, rotenone, or methoxychlor. (Long waiting period with methoxychlor.)

CABBAGE ROOT MAGGOT

Description: The larva is a small, white, legless maggot. Adults are dark flies similar in appearance to horse flies, only half as large. The cabbage maggot overwinters as a pupa. The flies emerge in the early spring and begin to lay eggs.

Damage: Larvae bore into roots leaving tunnels in vegetables with fleshy roots. Small roots may be completely eaten causing rot. The above-ground portion of the plant will be yellow and look unhealthy. Cabbage root maggots are especially troublesome in northern regions.

Plants affected: Cabbage family, some members of root crop family, and others.

Home remedies: Rotate crops and don't plant in areas where maggots have been a problem before. To prevent the fly from laying eggs in the soil, cover plant area with cheesecloth, fine netting or a tunnel.

Commercial remedies: Treat the soil with diazinon.

CABBAGE LOOPER

Description: Larvae are green with light stripes on each side of their bodies. The adult is a brownish moth with a silvery spot on each forewing. This moth is nocturnal. The cabbage looper overwinters as a pupa. Moths emerge in the early spring and lay eggs.

Damage: The looper eats large holes in the leaves of plants and also bores into cabbage heads.

Plants affected: Cabbage family crops and several others.

Home remedies: Cover the young plants with netting to prevent the moth from laying eggs. Pick the worms by hand or sprinkle the plants with salt, flour, or wood ashes.

Commercial remedies: Spray every 5 to 7 days with *Bacillus thuringiensis,* sold as Dipel or Thuricide.

COLORADO POTATO BEETLE

Description: The larva is red with two rows of black dots running down each side and has a humped appearance. The eggs are yellow orange and stuck to the lower surface of the leaves. Adults have yellow wing covers with black stripes.

Damage: Larvae and adults feed voraciously on the leaves and stems and may completely defoliate plants. There is usually one generation in the North and two or three generations in warmer climates.

Plants affected: Eggplant, pepper, potato, tomato.

Home remedies: Handpick beetles and larvae and crush all egg masses underneath the leaves. Growing under mulch seems to help. Rotate crops and till late in the fall to expose hibernating adults.

Commercial remedies: Dust crops with all-purpose potato dust, rotenone or Sevin.

CORN EARWORM

Description: Larvae vary in color from green to brown or pink with light or dark stripes running down their bodies. They reach 1½ inches at maturity.

Damage: Earworms usually enter at the tip of the ear, feed on the silk, then eat the kernels right down to the cob.

Plants affected: Beans, corn, okra, tomato (known here as the tomato fruitworm).

Home remedies: Squirt mineral oil with a medicine dropper into the tip of each ear after the silk begins to wilt. Tilling in the fall disturbs pupa in the southern regions where earworms overwinter. Early corn has less damage.

Commercial remedies: Spray with Sevin or *Bacillus thuringiensis,* sold as Dipel, Thruricide, BT, etc.

CUTWORM

Description: The worms are smooth, fat, 1½ to 2 inches long, brown, gray or blackish. They are nocturnal feeders, hiding in the soil by day.

Damage: These pests cut off the plants above or below the ground. Plants fall over, stems are gnawed. this insect is most troublesome east of the Rocky Mountains. There will usually be one generation a year in the North with more in the South.

Plants affected: Corn, eggplant, pepper, tomato

Home remedies: Mix wood ashes into the soil and till in late fall and early spring. This disturbs the overwintering pupa. Use a cutworm collar barrier on all transplants set out in the garden.

Commercial remedies: Ring a solution of diazinon around each plant.

EUROPEAN CORN BORER

Description: The larva is flesh-colored with a dark brown head and spots running down the back. It may grow up to 1 inch. European corn borers overwinter as larvae in the leftover corn stalks. By early spring they are pupae and change to moths which appear throughout the summer.

Damage: Larvae bore into ears and into stalks causing the plants to weaken and fall over. Bending or broken tassels are early signs of borer activity. Borers appear throughout the eastern states, south to Georgia and west to Idaho.

Plants affected: Corn.

Home remedies: Till in or pull out old corn stalks after harvest to prevent borers from overwintering. When borers appear, make a small slit in the stalk and remove the insect. Rotation of crops is helpful.

Commercial remedies: Spray with Sevin.

FLEA BEETLE

Description: Larvae are tiny, whitish-tan grubs with dark heads. They live in the soil and feed on roots and tubers. The adult is a tiny (1/16 to 1/8 inch) black jumping beetle with chewing mouth parts that greatly damage young plants.

Damage: Adults chew many tiny holes in leaves. They weaken the plants and allow entrance of plant diseases. There is a "buckshot" appearance and young plants are especially harmed. These beetles emerge in early spring and usually produce one to two generations a year.

Plants affected: Eggplant, pepper, potato, tomato, young plants.

Home remedies: Dust with wood ashes or spray with a garlic or hot pepper solution. Rotate your crops. Till in or pull up crop debris and put on the compost pile.

Commercial remedies: Spray with rotenone, Sevin, or malathion.

HARLEQUIN BUG

Description: The adult is red and black, spotted, flat, shield-shaped, 1/3 inch long. Nymphs resemble the adults but are more teardrop shaped. The eggs are barrel-shaped, white and black striped masses found on the undersides of leaves.

Damage: The nymphs and adults suck the sap out of plants. This often causes them to wilt, brown out, and die. These bugs are especially troublesome in the southern states.

Plants affected: Cabbage family and other crops.

Home remedies: Handpick the bugs and crush any egg masses. Keep nearby weeds to a minimum and destroy or till under all crop residues at the end of the season.

Commercial remedies: Spray during the nymph stage with rotenone or pytethrum.

IMPORTED CABBAGE WORM

Description: The larva is green velvety worm with a fine light stripe down its back. Size ranges up to 1½ inches. The adult moth has black dots on its wings.

Damage: Larva may bore into the vegetables, particularly cabbage heads, eating large holes through the leaves.

Plants affected: Cabbage family, mustard, kale, collards.

Home remedies: Cover the young plants with netting to prevent the moth from laying eggs. Pick the worms by hand. Sprinkle plants with salt, flour, or wood ashes.

Commercial remedies: Spray every 5 to 7 days with *Bacillus thuringiensis*, sold as Dipel or Thuricide.

JAPANESE BEETLE

Description: Larvae are white grubs that live in the soil. The adult is metallic green with copper-colored wing covers. Its size reaches ½ inch long. Japanese beetles emerge in mid-summer.

Damage: Adult beetles feed on corn silks and tips of the ears, bean leaves, etc. They are especially troublesome east of the Mississippi River.

Plants affected: Corn, many other vegetables.

Home remedies: Till in the early spring, allow the birds to eat the grubs and don't plant in recently sodded areas. Beetles may be picked by hand from the plants. Beetle traps are available at many garden stores.

Commercial remedies: Spray with rotenone, Sevin, malathion, or methoxychlor. Use milky spore bacteria in sod areas to control the grubs.

LEAFHOPPER

Description: The adult is a tiny 1/8 to 1/5 inch, wedge-shaped, hopping insect. It is usually pale green and may have white spots. These insects have sucking mouth parts. Nymphs look similar to the adults, except they are smaller and have no wings.

Damage: The tips and edges of potato leaves brown out, curl inward, and die. This is thought to be caused by toxin injected into the plant by the hopper's feeding. Leafhoppers transmit viruses and cause plant yields to be reduced.

Plants affected: Beets, eggplant, lettuce, potato, tomato.

Home remedies: It is helpful to cover plants with cheesecloth or fine netting and to keep weeds out of the garden.

Commercial remedies: Spray plants with Sevin, malathion, or methoxychlor.

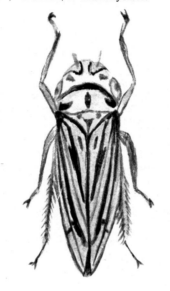

LEAF MINER

Description: Larvae are tiny, yellowish-white grubs. The adult is a small, grayish-black fly that is about 1/8 inch long. Leaf miners overwinter as pupae in the soil. The adult flies emerge in the early spring and lay eggs on the undersurface of the leaves.

Damage: Larvae tunnel within the leaves causing long, winding trails or whole blotches.

Plants affected: Beets, chard, spinach.

Home remedies: Tear off affected parts before harvesting, and burn them to destroy the maggots. Cover plants with cheesecloth or fine netting to prevent the flies from laying eggs. Keep weeds down in the garden.

Commercial remedies: Spray with malathion or diazinon.

MEXICAN BEAN BEETLE

Description: The larva is yellow and has a fuzzy appearance because of numerous black-tipped spines on its back. It is about 1/3 inch long. The adult is ¼ inch long, oval, and copper-colored with 16 black dots on its back.

Damage: Larvae and adults feed on the leaves, stem, and pods. They feed on the undersurface of leaves. These beetles are found throughout the United States, except in the westernmost states.

Plants affected: Beans, (especially lima and snap beans).

Home remedies: Till under crop residues at the end of harvest and be careful to crush egg masses under the leaves. Plant beans early so the crop matures before most beetles arrive. Use beetle traps.

Commercial remedies: Spray with rotenone, Sevin, or malathion as soon as the earliest beetles appear.

MITES

Description: There are many different kinds of mites. Most are very small with colors of yellow, green, red or brown.

Damage: Most feed on leaves, often clustering on underside. Fruit trees near garden will often see more damage.

Plants affected: Onion, melons, beans, potato, peppers.

Home remedy: Soapy sprays, dusting with sulphur or lime.

Commercial remedies: Not usually necessary in vegetable garden. In western areas where mites are more common, miticides may be available.

NEMATODES

Description: The adult is a microscopic eelworm that attacks the plant roots.

Damage: Damaged roots will have knots, galls, root rot, and be excessively branched. Tubers may be deformed and the plants will be stunted, with yellowed, wilted leaves. Nematodes are most prevalent in southern states. There may be many generations in one year.

Plants affected: All (especially okra, sweet potato and tomato).

Home remedies: It is helpful to plant resistant varieties, to use crop rotation, and to plant healthy, nematode-free sweet potato slips.

Commercial remedies: For severe problems, soil fumigation may be necessary. Contact the local Extension Service agent for advice.

ONION MAGGOT

Description: Maggots are white, legless, about ⅓ inch long. They overwinter as pupae. Flies emerge in the early spring and lay eggs at the base of plants.

Damage: The maggots bore into bulbs, killing young plants outright and allowing rot organisms to destroy older bulbs. This insect is troublesome in the North, particularly in wet seasons.

Plants affected: Onions.

Home remedies: Pull and burn infested bulbs. Following the harvest, all residue should be tilled into soil.

Commercial remedies: Spray with malathion or diazinon.

PEPPER WEEVIL

Description: Larvae are white with brown head. Adults are small, 1/8 inch long, black, long-snouted beetles.

Damage: The larvae burrow within the fruit, causing it to drop or to be misshapen. Adult weevils feed on pepper leaves.

Plants affected: Pepper.

Home remedies: Pick off and burn the infested fruit.

Commercial remedies: Spray or dust with rotenone or Sevin.

SEED CORN MAGGOT

Description: The larva is a yellowish-white maggot. It is legless, pointed at the head, and about ¼ inch long. Adults are grayish-brown flies about ¼ inch long.

Damage: The larvae tunnel into newly-planted seeds, preventing germination, and causing those that do develop to be weak and sickly.

Plants affected: Corn, beans.

Home remedies: Plant in warm season to speed germination. If the soil is too wet, plant on a raised bed. Tilling in early spring or fall helps disturb maggots or pupa. Rotating crops also helps.

Commercial remedies: Plant seeds treated with diazinon or lindane. Also use diazinon in the soil before planting.

SLUGS

Description: Slugs resemble snails without shells. They range in size from ¼ inch to 8 inches long, and thrive in moist, cool climates.

Damage: Slugs are very active at night or on rainy days. They feed by crawling on leaves and chewing large, ragged holes in them.

Plants affected: Many crops, especially lettuce and greens.

Home remedies: Lay board in walkways. Check each morning and kill slugs hiding underneath. Slugs dislike crawling through or over scratchy materials such as lime, sharp sand, wood ashes, etc.

Commercial remedies: Many types of slug baits are available.

SOUTHERN GREEN STINK BUG

Description: The nymph is small with reddish markings. The adult is a flat, shield-shaped, green bug about ½ inch long.

Damage: The stink bug sucks sap and then injects toxin into the plants, causing pods or fruit to drop or to be deformed. This insect is common in the southeastern U.S.

Plants affected: Okra, tomato, beans and others.

Home remedies: Destroy and remove all plant debris to prevent stink bugs from overwintering.

Commercial remedies: Spray with Sevin.

SQUASH BUG

Description: Adults are flat, grayish-black bugs about 5/8 inch long. Nymphs resemble adults, only they are grayish-white, smaller, and wingless. The eggs are brownish-red and are found on the undersurface of the leaves. The squash bug overwinters as an adult living on dead vegetation. The bugs reappear in the spring to mate and lay eggs.

Damage: Squash bugs suck juices out of plants causing runners or whole plants to darken and die. They breed one generation a year.

Plants affected: Vine crop family (especially pumpkin and winter squash).

Home remedies: Clean up all crop residue. Dust plants with lime and wood ashes mixed together. Hand pick insects from plants, and crush all eggs. Put a slightly raised board in the garden at night to attract the bugs. The next morning kill those that have congregated.

Commercial remedies: Spray with rotenone, Sevin, malathion, or methoxychlor.

SQUASH VINE BORER

Description: The larva is about 1 inch long, flat, and white with a dark head. The adult is a colorful red and brown moth. Squash vine borers overwinter as pupae or larvae in the soil. In the spring, moths emerge and begin to lay eggs. The larvae hatch and bore into stems and vines.

Damage: Sudden wilting of vines caused by tunneling larvae. Greenish-yellow excrement is pushed out of holes in the stems. When vines are cut open, they are hollow with borers inside. Found east of the Rocky Mountains.

Plants affected: Cucumber, pumpkin, squash.

Home remedies: Clear away and burn any infested vines. Till deeply in the fall and again in the spring to kill overwintering insects. Make a small slit in the stem, remove borer, and mound soil over injured stem.

Commercial remedies: Spray or dust early with rotenone or malathion. Once the borer is within the stem it is difficult to kill with insecticides.

SPOTTED CUCUMBER BEETLE

Description: Larvae are yellowish-white with wrinkled brown heads. Adults are ¼ inch long, yellowish-green, with 12 black spots on back.

Damage: Adults eat pods and leaves of many garden plants. Larvae tunnel into roots and stems of beans and corn. Adults infect vine crop family with bacterial wilt.

Plants affected: Beans, vine crop family, corn and others.

Home remedies: Cover plants with fine netting when they are young. Beetles hibernate at base of weeds, so keep garden and nearby areas clean.

Commercial remedies: Spray plants, especially near base with Sevin, malathion or methoxychlor.

STRIPED CUCUMBER BEETLE

Description: Larvae are ⅓ inch long, slender and white with brown coloring at both ends. They feed on underground portions of the plant. The adult beetles are about ¼ inch long and are yellow with three black stripes on their wings.

Damage: Beetles emerge in spring and begin to chew holes in leaves and stems of vine crops. They inject a bacterial wilt disease into the plant while they are feeding.

Plants affected: Cucumber, melon, squash.

Home remedies: Cover plant area with cheesecloth or fine netting.

Commercial remedies: Spray base of plant with rotenone, Sevin, methoxychlor, or malathion.

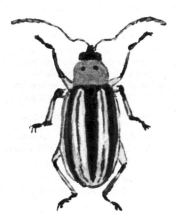

SWEET POTATO WEEVIL

Description: The larva is fat, white, and legless with a dark head. The size is usually less than ¼ inch. The adult is a slender, ¼-inch long, snout-nosed beetle. It has a bluish black head and wing covers, with red thorax and legs.

Damage: Sweet potato tubers are riddled by larvae tunneling. This weevil is very troublesome in the Gulf states.

Plant affected: Sweet potato.

Home remedies: Plant only healthy, non-infected slips. All infested tubers should be destroyed and all crop debris tilled under immediately following harvest. Rotate crop.

Commercial remedies: Contact your local Extension agent for information on handling a bad infestation.

THRIP

Description: The nymph and the adult are both very small, only about 1/25 inch long.

Damage: The thrip sucks the juice out of onion stems and leaves. White blotches may develop and whole onion tops may brown and fall over if infestation is severe. Bulbs will be small and malformed. Damage is more severe in dry seasons.

Plant affected: Onion.

Home remedies: Keep weeds down in the garden area, rake up and burn onion tops after harvest, and till in the fall to eliminate debris where thrips may overwinter. Some sweet Spanish varieties are resistant to thrips.

Commercial remedies: Spray with malathion or diazinon.

TOMATO HORNWORM

Description: The tomato hornworm is the larvae of the hawk moth. It has a black appendage that resembles a horn. It is 3 to 4 inches long and is green with light white stripes running at an angle along each side of the body.

Damage: The larvae feed heavily on foliage and fruit. They are camouflaged by the leaves due to their green color. They breed one or two generations a year.

Plants affected: Eggplant, pepper, potato, tomato.

Home remedies: There are two controls found in nature: Trichogramma wasps and Braconid wasps. Another method is to handpick them.

Commercial remedies: Spray or dust with non-toxic *Bacillus thuringiensis*, sold as Dipel, BT, Thurnicide, etc.

WIREWORM

Description: The larva is a hard-skinned, tannish-brown, shiny worm that feels stiff like a wire. It doesn't curl up.

Damage: Larvae tunnel into tubers, roots, and stems, leaving the plants open to the entry of disease organisms. There is only one generation per year. They emerge when the soil has warmed.

Plants affected: Beets, carrots, onion, potato.

Home remedies: Rotate crops. Don't plant potatoes or root crops in areas recently in sod.

Commercial remedies: Spray or dust diazinon into the soil.

Disease Chart

ANTHRACNOSE

Description: Fungus disease that may over-winter on infected seed, plant debris, or in the soil.

Damage: Appears as dark brown circular sunken spots on pods or fruit. The centers of the spots may ooze pink spores. On the leaves, anthracnose shows up as reddish discoloration of the veins. Disease favors areas of high humidity, plentiful rain and warm temperatures.

Plants affected: Beans, cantaloupe, cucumber, melon, pepper and tomato.

Home remedies: If you have trouble with anthracnose, don't save your own seed for planting. Use western-grown seed because anthracnose is not a problem there. Be sure to rotate your crops. Avoid working in the garden when it is wet as this encourages disease spread.

Commercial: Treating seeds with a fungicide. Fungicide sprays or dusts containing zineb or maneb help prevent this disease. Start spraying vine crops when runners are 6 to 8 inches long.

BACTERIAL BLIGHT

Description: This disease is usually spread by infected seeds.

Damage: Brown and water-soaked spots appear on the leaves and pods. Infected areas often turn yellow, then brown, and finally die. Spots on the pods enlarge and often exhibit reddish markings.

Plants affected: Beans, peas.

Home remedies: Rotate crops and clean up old debris. Don't work among wet plants, as this may help the disease spread. If you have a problem, do not save any seed.

Commercial: None.

BACTERIAL WILT

Description: Wilt organisms live within cucumber beetles and are transmitted to the vine crop through their feces. The bacteria clog the water and nutrient "transport" system of the plant.

Damage: First appears as wilting of a few leaves or a small portion of the vine. The rest of the vine wilts within a week or so. When the vine is cut, a white substance oozes from the stem. This disease is most severe east of the Mississippi River.

Plants affected: All vine crops.

Home remedies: Pull out and destroy infected plants before the disease spreads. Keep cucumber beetles away. (See spotted and striped cucumber beetles on pest chart.)

Commercial: Spray with Sevin or malathion to control cucumber beetles.

BLACKLEG

Description: Blackleg is caused by a fungus that is carried on seed and lives in the soil.

Damage: Lower stem blackens and is completely girdled. Young plants yellow, wilt and die.

Plants affected: Broccoli, Brussels sprouts, cabbage, cauliflower.

Home remedies: Practice crop rotation. Clean up plant debris at the end of the season.

Commercial: None effective.

CLUBROOT

Description: A fungal slime mold causes this disease which lives in the soil and enters the plant through the roots.

Damage: Roots become enlarged and swollen (clubbed), often cracking or rotting. Young plants are killed, while older, larger plants have reduced yields. The above ground portion of the plant will yellow and wilt during the day, but recover at night.

Plants affected: Cabbage family crops.

Home remedies: Use a 4-year crop rotation plan as spores can survive in the soil a long time.

Commercial: The disease thrives in acid soil so it is helpful to keep soil pH above 6.0.

DOWNY MILDEW

Description: This fungus disease overwinters in crop residues and spreads through infected seeds.

Damage: Lettuce and spinach have pale spots on the leaves with furry whitish growth on the underside. Lima beans have white, felt-like growths on the pods, with a possible reddish discoloration around the white areas. Mostly eastern United States because high humidity and cool to warm temperatures help it spread.

Plants affected: Lima beans, lettuce, onions, spinach, all vine crops.

Home remedies: Pull up and destroy infected plants and all crop residues. Plant resistant varieties. Be certain to rotate crops yearly.

Commercial: Spray or dust with zineb or maneb.

343

EARLY BLIGHT

Description: Early blight is a fungus disease.

Damage: Leaves develop spots that are dark brown with a series of concentric rings within each one giving it a target-like appearance. These spots usually appear on the older leaves first. Under favorable conditions, especially in warm, wet weather, the disease will spread rapidly over the entire plant. Serious infections will cause reduced yields and defoliation of the plant.

Plants affected: Potato, tomato.

Home remedies: Rotate crops, remove plant debris to prevent the disease from overwintering, and be certain to use healthy seed potatoes and tomato seedlings.

Commercial: Spray with all purpose tomato/potato dust or a fungicide such as maneb or captan every 7 to 10 days. Begin early in the season.

Early blight.

FUSARIUM WILT (VERTICILLIUM WILT)

Description: Fusarium wilt is a fungal infection of vascular tissues. The fungus lives in the soil and infects plants through the roots. Very similar to Verticillium wilt.

Damage: Leaves and stems turn yellowish. Plants wilt and have a brown discoloration inside the stems. Plant growth is stunted and yields are reduced. Fungus develops during hot dry weather.

Plants affected: Potato, tomato, eggplant, pepper, okra.

Home remedies: Crop rotation is important as well as the planting of resistant varieties where available. Practice a 4-year rotation plan for okra.

Commercial: None effective.

LATE BLIGHT

Description: Late blight is a fungus disease that first appears as wet-soaked or light spots on the leaves. As it progresses, these spots turn black and a white fungal growth may be seen on the underside of the leaf.

Damage: The disease spreads rapidly under cool, wet conditions causing all the above-ground parts of the plant to become soft and blighted. At this stage there will be a strong odor characteristic of this disease.

Plants affected: Tomato, potato.

Home remedies: Use resistant varieties, rotate your crops. Don't follow either tomatoes or potatoes by each other. Clean up all crop debris at the end of the season. Use clean seed potatoes.

Commercial: Spray or dust with an all purpose potato/tomato dust every 7 to 10 days starting early in the season.

LEAF SPOT

Description: Fungus disease that overwinters on seeds or infected crop debris.

Damage: The plant leaves are dotted with small, tannish spots. These spots have purplish borders. The disease may cause leaves to drop later in the season and is most troublesome east of the Rocky Mountains.

Plants affected: Beets, chard.

Home remedies: Practice crop rotation. Till in all crop residues at the end of the season.

Commercial: Spray or dust with a fungicide like zineb.

MOSAIC

Description: This virus disease overwinters in perennial weeds. In the spring it is transmitted by aphids to vine crops and other host plants.

Damage: Shows up as a yellow and green mottling of the leaves. Plants are stunted and yields are greatly reduced. Infected fruit is mottled, bumpy and misshapen.

Plants affected: Beans, cucumber, melon, pepper, squash, tomato.

Home remedies: Plant healthy seeds. Plant mosaic resistant varieties. Control aphids. Pull and destroy plants that become infected. Keep weeds down around the garden.

Commercial: Apply a spray containing malathion to control aphids when they appear.

NECK ROT

Description: Neck rot is a fungus disease. It usually attacks onions in storage and overwinters in infected bulbs.

Damage: Onions have brownish, dry rot areas around the neck. If the disease has progressed the entire bulb may be rotten. Neck rot usually appears in storage.

Plants affected: Onions.

Home remedies: Allow onions to mature completely in the field before harvesting. Cure and store them properly. Don't try to store bulbs that have been bruised or damaged. Sweet varieties tend to be more susceptible to neck rot.

Commercial: None.

ROOT ROT

Description: Root rot is caused by fungi that live in the soil.

Damage: Root rot causes yellowish, unhealthy looking plants, often with withering of the lower stem.

Plants affected: Peas.

Home remedies: Rotate your crops yearly. Plant in well-drained soil. Raise your beds if the soil is too wet.

Commercial: None.

RUST

Description: This fungus overwinters on infected plant residue.

Damage: Numerous tiny, rust-colored spots appear on the leaves, turning darker in color as they mature. Leaves turn yellow and then die. High humidity or wet weather causes more rapid growth of the disease.

Plants affected: Asparagus, beans, sunflowers.

Home remedies: Plant rust-resistant varieties, cut and burn infected ferns as well as removing all crop debris at the end of the season.

Commercial: Spray with sulphur or dust with undiluted sulphur.

SCAB

Description: Fungus disease that over-winters on seed, infected crop debris, and also in the soil.

Damage: Scab appears as dark, sunken spots on fruit. In severe cases, these will be like small craters over the entire fruit. There may be ooze or a fungus growth from infected areas. Cool, wet weather is favorable to disease development.

Plants affected: Cucumber, melon, squash.

Home remedies: Plant resistant varieties. Practice crop rotation. Clean up all plant debris.

Commercial: None.

SMUT (CORN)

Description: Fungus disease that over-winters on crop debris and in the soil.

Damage: First appears as whitish-gray galls on the ear or other part of the plant. As galls mature they turn black and finally burst, releasing thousands of spores. This disease occurs throughout the United States and favors warm, dry seasons.

Plants affected: Corn.

Home remedies: Remove and destroy smut galls before they break open and spread spores. Be sure to clean up all crop debris. Rotate your crops. Use varieties of corn which are somewhat resistant. Don't use diseased plants in compost.

Commercial: None.

YELLOWS (ASTER)

Description: Aster yellows is caused by mycoplasmas that overwinter in weeds and other perennial plants.

Damage: Plants will be yellowed and stunted. Yields are reduced; infected plants usually don't head. This disease is spread by leafhoppers.

Plants affected: Celery, lettuce, spinach.

Home remedies: Control leafhoppers. Keep weeds down around the garden. Plant lettuce in sheltered areas as leafhoppers prefer open spaces.

Commercial: Spray or dust with malathion or Sevin to control leafhoppers. Start when plants are small and repeat treatment once a week.

VEGETABLE PLANTING GUIDE

Here are 57 vegetables and recommendations on how to plant them so you have plenty for the whole family.

This chart offers suggestions on how much of each vegetable to plant per person. Of course, how much you plant depends on how much you and your family like to eat each vegetable and whether you want to store some as well. These recommendations should result in a generous supply of each vegetable with plenty to eat and some to store. Use this as a guideline to be adjusted to your personal preferences.

This chart also includes recommendations on the length of wide rows per person, assuming a wide row to be 16 inches wide. Recommendations for single-row vegetables are offered in a separate column.

This chart provides basic information that should be useful as you lay out your garden and order seed. Use it as a starting point for a super garden!

Vegetable	Amount to plant per person	Length of wide row per person	Length of single row per person
Asparagus	10 crowns		20 ft.
Beans, dry	¼ lb.	10–15 ft.	---------------
Beans, lima	½ lb.	10–15 ft.	---------------
Beans, snap	¼ lb.	10–15 ft.	---------------
Beets	Up to a pkt.	2–3 ft.	---------------
Broccoli	5–7 plants	4–6 ft.	---------------
Brussels sprouts	5–7 plants	4–6 ft.	---------------
Cabbage	5–7 plants	2–3 ft.	---------------
Carrots	Up to a pkt.	2–3 ft.	---------------
Cauliflower	5–7 plants	2–3 ft.	---------------
Celery	6 plants	---------------	3–5 ft.
Chicory	Up to ½ pkt.	1–2 ft.	---------------
Chinese cabbage	5–7 plants	2 ft.	---------------
Collards	3–5 plants	2–3 ft.	---------------
Corn	1 oz.	---------------	25–50 ft.
Cucumber	Up to ½ pkt.	---------------	8 ft.
Eggplant	2–3 plants	1 ft.	---------------

Distance between plants in row	Depth to plant seed	Hardiness	Days to harvest	Helpful hints
24 in.	6–8 in.	Hardy	2 years	Start from 2-year-old crowns. Don't cut ferns in fall or winter. Harvest sparingly second year after planting.
4–8 in.	1 in.	Tender	65–110	Let bean pods dry on vine before harvesting. Put in burlap bag, beat bag to separate bean from chaff.
4–8 in.	1 in.	Very tender	65–80	Can be grown as bush or pole bean. Likes warm soil. Pole limas will keep producing if picked continually.
3–6 in.	1 in.	Tender	50–60	Bush bean excellent wide row crop. Keep beans picked for continual harvest.
2–4 in.	½ in.	Hardy	50–65	Thin early with rake and again when beets are young and tender. Greens are nutritious and tasty.
14–16 in.	¼ in.	Hardy	50–80 (from transplant)	Plant in a 2-1-2 pattern. Will produce sideshoots if main head is cut before it blossoms.
14–16 in.	¼ in.	Hardy	65–75 (from transplant)	Break off bottom leaves to keep plant producing. Can take many freezes. Excellent fall crop.
10–12 in.	¼ in.	Hardy	60–90 (from transplant)	Grow in 3-2-3 pattern in wide row. Harvest when softball-size to allow growing room for remaining plants.
2–3 in.	¼ in.	Hardy	55–80	Thin when finger-size for tender young carrots. Excellent in wide rows.
10–12 in.	¼ in.	Hardy	65–80 (from transplant)	Plant in 3-2-3 pattern. Fold outer leaves over head when head is 2–3 in. wide. Head will be ready in 4–10 days.
8–10 in.	¼ in.	Semi-hardy	80–150	Start plants 8–12 weeks indoors. Hill soil around celery as it grows.
6–8 in.	¼ in.	Hardy	45 (greens) 120–140 (roots)	Can be eaten as green or roots roasted as coffee-like drink.
8–10 in.	½ in.	Hardy	70–90	Prefers cool weather. Blanch for milder flavor by putting milk carton (ends cut out) over top of plant.
12–15 in.	¼ in.	Hardy	60–70 (from transplant)	Good fall crop. Flavor improves with frost. Can stand cold or hot weather.
8–12 in.	1 in.	Tender	60–95	Sow 4–6 inches apart and thin to 8–12 inches. Plant early and late varieties.
8–12 in.	½–1 in.	Tender	50–70	Plant in row, thinning plants to 8–12 in. apart. Pick when small for continual harvest.
12–14 in.	½ in.	Very tender	80–90	Plant in 2-1-2 staggered pattern. Start early indoors. Harvest when fruit is still glossy.

Vegetable	Amount to plant per person	Length of wide row per person	Length of single row per person
Endive	up to ½ pkt.	1–2 ft.	--------------
Garlic	12 single cloves	8 in.	--------------
Gourds	--------------	--------------	--------------
Horseradish	3–5 roots	--------------	3–5 ft.
Jerusalem artichoke	5–10 roots	--------------	6–12 ft.
Kale	Up to a pkt.	2–3 ft.	--------------
Kohlrabi	Up to a pkt.	1–2 ft.	--------------
Leeks	5–10 plants	1–2 ft.	2 ft.
Lettuce, head	8–10 plants	2–3 ft.	--------------
Lettuce, leaf	Up to a pkt.	2–3 ft.	--------------
Muskmelon	Up to a pkt.	--------------	10–15 ft.
Mustard	Up to a pkt.	2–3 ft.	--------------
Okra	3–5 plants	--------------	3–5 ft.
Onion sets	1 lb. sets	3 ft.	--------------
Onion seeds	½ pkt. seed	3–4 ft.	--------------
Parsley	Up to ½ pkt.	2 ft.	--------------
Parsnips	Up to a pkt.	2–3 ft.	--------------
Peanuts	30–40 nuts (shelled)	--------------	15–20 ft.

Distance between plants in row	Depth to plant seed	Hardiness	Days to harvest	Helpful hints
6–10 in.	¼ in.	Semi-hardy	80–90	Prevent bitterness by tying leaves overhead a week before harvest. Harvest entire head, like head lettuce.
3–4 in.	2 in. (for planting clove)	Hardy	60–100	When tops fall over in fall, pull and dry in sun a few days. Store in mesh bag.
4–6 in.	½–1 in.	Very tender	130–150	Can be grown on fence or trellis to save space. Hollow dipper gourds grow well in South.
12–16 in.	2 in. (for planting root)	Hardy	45–55	Harvest roots in spring for strongest flavor. Keep away from rest of garden—plants spread.
18 in.	3 in. (for root)	Hardy	180	Can be left in ground all winter and harvested as needed.
6–8 in.	¼ in.	Hardy	50–65	Excellent fall crop. Taste improves after frost. Can also be planted as edible cover crop.
3–5 in.	¼ in.	Hardy	50–70	Harvest when bulb is 2–3 inches in diameter. Has mild taste and can be eaten raw with dip.
3–4 in.	½ in.	Hardy	80–130	Plant indoors and set out transplants in wide row or single-row. Furrow hill or fill in furrow to blanch.
8–10 in.	¼ in.	Semi-hardy	45–50 from transplant	Plant in 3-2-3 pattern in wide rows. Begin harvesting when heads are small. Doesn't like hot weather.
2–3 in.	¼ in.	Semi-hardy	35–50	Excellent in wide rows. Harvest by cutting entire plant 1 inch above soil. More will grow back.
8–10 in.	½–1 in.	Very tender	75–100	Likes warm soil. When melons are small, set them on tin cans to quicken ripening.
2–3 in.	¼ in.	Hardy	35–45	Fast-growing green can be harvested at any stage and eaten cooked like spinach or as salad green.
10–12 in.	½ in.	Very tender	50–55	Likes hot weather. Harvest when pods are 4 inches or less for continual harvest.
2–3 in. 2–3 in.	Width of set ¼ in.	Hardy Hardy	30–45 75	Plant sets and seeds close together in wide row and thin for scallions.
3–5 in.	¼ in.	Semi-hardy	120–150	Seeds slow to germinate. Harvest at any stage.
3–4 in.	¼ in.	Hardy	120–150	Flavor improved by freeze. Store in ground over winter and harvest in spring.
12 in.	1½ in.	Very tender	110–120	Needs long, hot season. For short growing season, use quick-maturing variety. Hang to dry after harvest.

Vegetable	Amount to plant per person	Length of wide row per person	Length of single row per person
Peas, English	½ lb.	10–12 ft.	--------------
Peas, Southern	¼ lb.	10–15 ft.	--------------
Peppers	6–8 plants	3–4 ft.	--------------
Potatoes	5 lbs.	--------------	25 ft.
Pumpkins	Up to ½ pkt.	--------------	12 ft.
Radishes	Up to a pkt.	2–3 ft.	--------------
Rhubarb	1–2 roots	--------------	3–6 ft.
Rutabaga	Up to a pkt.	2–3 ft.	--------------
Salsify	Up to a pkt.	2–3 ft.	--------------
Shallots	½ lb.	2–3 ft.	--------------
Soybeans	¼ lb.	10–15 ft.	--------------
Spinach	Up to a pkt.	3–5 ft.	--------------
Spinach, New Zealand	Up to ½ pkt.	5 ft.	--------------
Squash, summer	Up to ½ pkt.	--------------	5 ft.
Squash, winter	Up to ½ pkt.	--------------	12 ft.
Strawberries	15–25 plants	--------------	15–25 ft.

Distance between plants in row	Depth to plant seed	Hardiness	Days to harvest	Helpful hints
2–3 in.	1 in.	Hardy	50–80	Plant as soon as ground can be worked. Plants in wide rows support themselves without need for trellis.
3–5 in.	1 in.	Very tender	55–80	Likes hot weather. Harvest green or after pod has dried. Can be planted in block.
10–12 in.	¼ in.	Very tender	60–100	Plant in 3-2-3 pattern in wide row. Avoid heavy side-dressing; peppers like fertilizer in small doses.
10–12 in.	4 in.	Hardy	80–120	Hill up plant to give tubers growing room. Ready to harvest when foliage dies.
8–12 in.	1 in.	Very tender	100–120	Give plants plenty of room or grow on trellis. When thumbnail won't penetrate skin, it's mature.
1 in.	¼ in.	Hardy	25–35	Sprinkle radish seeds in wide rows with other crops. Also plant with vine crops as decoy for insects.
30–36 in.	2 in. (root)	Hardy	1 year	The more you harvest the more it will produce. Don't harvest first year. Keep seed pods cut.
4–6 in.	½ in.	Hardy	80–90	Good fall crop. Takes longer to mature than turnip but is better keeper. Harvest early for greens.
3–4 in.	½ in.	Hardy	120–150	Harvest after frost. Can be stored in ground through winter. Grows like a carrot; has oyster taste.
3–4 in.	Depth of bulb	Hardy	30–40 for green tops	Can be picked for green tops or for bulbs. Bulbs store well; harvest 2 weeks after tops die.
3–4 in.	1 in.	Very tender	85–100	For freezing, harvest when young and green. Cut off blossom ends. Blanch in shell, cool, squeeze out bean.
3–4 in.	¼ in.	Hardy	40–50	Cut entire plant to one inch above ground for additional harvest. Will bolt in hot weather.
8–10 in.	½ in.	Semi-hardy	75–80	Will hold up in hot weather. Pick outer leaves; don't cut back to ground.
8–12 in.	½–1 in.	Tender	50–70	Pick when fruit are small for continual harvest.
8–10 in.	1 in.	Very tender	85–120	Needs lots of space for large vines. Harvest late for winter storage. Some bush varieties available.
12 in.	-------------	Semi-hardy	1 year	Pick off blossoms the first year to strengthen plant. Allow runners to take root. Harvest second year.

Vegetable	Amount to plant per person	Length of wide row per person	Length of single row per person
Sunflowers	--------------	--------------	--------------
Sweet potatoes	10–12 plants	--------------	10–15 ft.
Swiss chard	Up to a pkt.	3–5 ft.	--------------
Tomatoes	3–5 plants	--------------	6–12 ft.
Turnips	Up to a pkt.	3–5 ft.	--------------
Watermelon	Up to ½ pkt.	--------------	8 ft.
Zucchini	Up to ½ pkt.	--------------	6 ft.

Distance between plants in row	Depth to plant seed	Hardiness	Days to harvest	Helpful hints
10–12 in.	1 in.	Semi-hardy	68–80	Protect seeds from birds with mesh or cheesecloth. Harvest before first frost, allow to dry.
12–15 in.	—————	Very tender	90–120	Sprout seed pieces indoors, and set out when plant is 4–6 inches high.
3–4 in.	½ in.	Semi-hardy	45–55	Will take hot as well as cold weather. Cut entire plant to 1 inch above ground for 3 or 4 harvests.
24–36 in.	¼–½ in. (seed)	Tender	55–90	Sow seeds early indoors. Plant different varieties for early and late harvests.
4–6 in.	¼ in.	Hardy	40–60	Harvest when root is 2–3 inches wide. Also harvest tender young greens.
8–10 in.	1 in.	Very tender	75–100	Toward end of season, pick off the smallest melons to help larger melons ripen more quickly.
8–10 in.	½–1 in.	Tender	50–70	Pick when fruit are small and keep picking for continual harvest.

FIRST EXPECTED FROST DATE IN THE FALL

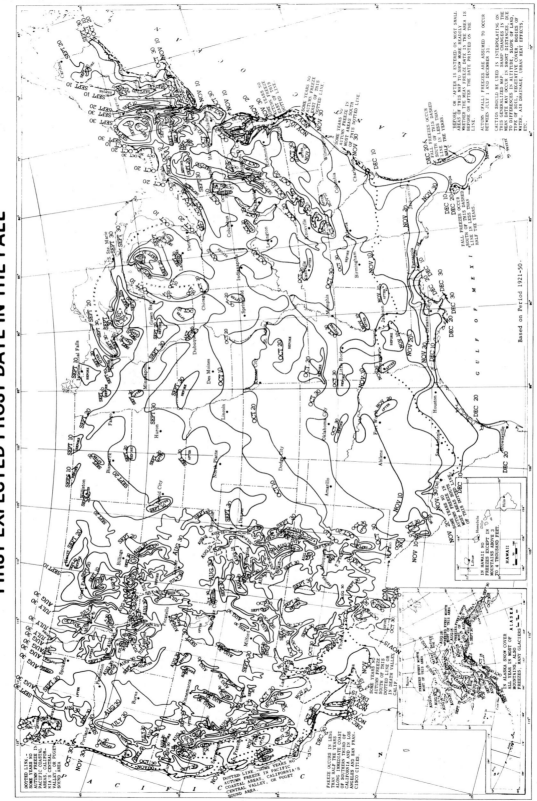

Based on Period 1921-50.

LAST EXPECTED FROST DATE IN THE SPRING

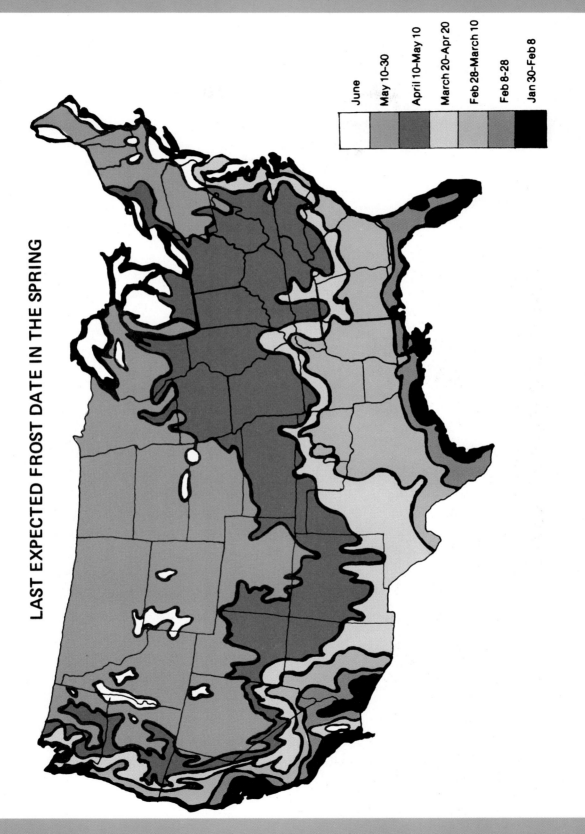

June
May 10-30
April 10-May 10
March 20-Apr 20
Feb 28-March 10
Feb 8-28
Jan 30-Feb 8

WET RESISTANT

The following varieties perform well under wet conditions:

Brussels sprouts: Prince Marvel
Carrots: Spartan Fancy
Corn: Jubilee
Lettuce: Ithaca MTO, Minetto
Muskmelon: Supreme Delight

COLD TOLERANT

The following have demonstrated the best tolerance to cold weather:

Beans: Sungold, Greencrop
    LIMA: Henderson
    SHELL: Dwarf Horticultural
Broccoli: Waltham 29
Brussels sprouts: Long Island
Corn: Blitz, Quicksilver, Early Sunglow, Spancross Hybrid, White Sunglow
Cucumbers: Marketmore 76
Lettuce: Prizehead, Deep Red, Butter-crunch, Green Lakes
Muskmelon: Minnesota Midget
Peas: Wando
Pepper: New Ace, Merrimack Wonder, Staddon's Select
Tomato: Earlirouge, Coldset, Early Girl, Springset
Watermelon: Sugar Baby, Summer Festival

HEAT RESISTANT

Heat can be as much of a problem in some parts of the country as cold is in others. Excessive hot weather can cause some vegetables like lettuce, cabbage and broccoli to mature too quickly. Some types of vegetables burn, others, like tomatoes and cucumbers, may refuse to set fruit if the temperature rises too high.

The following varieties have proven the most successful under hot conditions:

Broccoli: Green Comet
Cabbage: Red Head, Savoy King Hybrid, Stonehead
Cauliflower: Snow King, Panda
Cucumbers: Marketmore 76, Poinsette 76, Green Star
Eggplant: Classic
Lettuce: Buttercrunch, Parris Island Cos, Salad Bowl, Green Ice
Peas: Wando, Sugar Snap
Peppers: Staddon's Select
Tomato: Globemaster, Floramerica, Better Boy
Watermelon: Charleston Gray

DROUGHT TOLERANT

The water content of some vegetables is as high as 90 percent. Obviously vegetables will not mature to their full potential unless they receive a regular supply of water. One inch of water per week is recommended for most vegetables. But the following varieties have proven to be tolerant of dry conditions to some degree:

Beans: DelRay, Greencrop Fordhook, Henderson
Corn: Harmony, Iochief
Cucumbers: Slicemaster, Burpless #25
Eggplant: Classic, Burpee Hybrid
Lettuce: Ithaca MTO
Peppers: Staddon's Select
Squash, Winter: Table Queen Acorn
Tomato: Globemaster, Floramerica

NUTRIENTS IN ONE POUND
OF FRESH VEGETABLES

(Based on figures in USDA Handbook No. 8)

	Calories	Protein (grams)	Fat (grams)	Carbo-hydrate (grams)	Vitamin A (Int'l unit)	Ascorbic Acid (ml. grams)
Asparagus	66	6.4		12.7	2,290	84
Beans, Snap	128	7.6	.8	28.3	2,400	76
Beets	78	2.9	.2	18.0	40	18
Beet Greens	61	5.6	.8	11.7	15,490	76
Broccoli	89	10.0	.8	16.3	6,920	313
Brussels Sprouts	188	20.4	1.7	34.6	2,300	426
Cabbage	86	4.7	.7	19.3	470	169
Carrots	112	2.9	.5	26.0	29,440	21
Chard	104	10.0	1.3	19.2	27,120	132
Corn, Sweet	240	8.7	2.5	55.1	1,000	31
Cucumber	65	3.9	.4	14.7	1,080	48
Kale	128	14.1	2.7	20.1	29,880	420
Kohlrabi	96	6.6	.3	21.9	70	219
Lettuce, Iceberg	56	3.9	.4	12.5	1,420	28
Lettuce, Looseleaf	52	3.8	.9	10.2	5,520	54
Mustard Greens	98	9.5	1.6	17.8	22,220	308
Onions, Bulbing	157	6.2	.4	35.9	160	42
Onions, Bunching	157	6.5	.9	35.7	8,710	139
Parsley	200	16.3	2.7	38.6	38,560	780
Parsnips	293	6.6	1.9	67.5	120	62
Peas	145	10.9	.7	24.8	1,100	47
Peppers, Bell	82	4.5	.7	17.9	1,540	476
Potatoes	279	7.7	.4	62.8	Trace	73
Radishes	69	4.1	.4	14.7	70	106
Rhubarb	33	1.2	.2	7.6	200	18
Rutabagas	177	4.2	.4	42.4	2,240	166
Spinach	85	10.5	1.0	14.0	26,450	167
Squash, Summer	84	4.8	.4	18.5	1,800	95
Squash, Winter	161	4.5	1.0	39.9	11,920	43
Tomatoes	100	5.0	.9	21.3	4,080	118
Turnips	117	3.9	.8	25.7	Trace	140
Turnip Greens	127	13.6	1.4	22.7	34,470	628

From *16 Steps to Gardening in Alaska*, 1977, Cooperative Extension Service of Alaska.

Varieties for canning, freezing, or drying

COLD STORAGE

Beets: Lutz Green Leaf

Cabbage: Bonanza, Amager Green Storage LD

Carrot: Nantes Forto, Scarlet Keeper

Onions: Early Yellow Globe, Yellow Sweet Spanish Buccaneer, Nutmeg

Rutabaga: Burpee's Purple-Top Yellow

Squash, Winter: Buttercup, Ebony Acorn, Waltham Butternut

Tomato: Long Keeper (Burpee)

PICKLING

Beets: Early Wonder, Gladiator

Cabbage: Penn State Ballhead, Red Danish Ballhead

Cucumbers: Saladin, Carolina

Onions: Crystal Wax

JUICE

Beets: Detroit Dark Red

Carrots: Gold Pak

Tomatoes: Roma, Heinz 1350, Campbell

CANNING OR FREEZING

Beans: Greensleeves, Tendercrop, Goldcrop Wax, Royal Burgundy
LIMA: Kingston

Carrot: Royal Cross, Red Cored Chatenay

Cauliflower: Snowball, Royal Purple

Corn: Jubilee, Early Sunglow, Iochief

Peas: Burpeeana Early, Oregon Sugar Pod, Sparkle, Little Marvel, Victory Freezer

Rutabaga: American Purple-Top

Spinach: Early Smooth #424 (Park), America

Squash, Winter: Blue Hubbard, Buttercup

Tomato: Roma, Heinz 1350, Campbell

DRYING

Beans: Dwarf Horticultural, Soldier (white kidney, Black Turtle Soup, Red Kidney, Pinto, White Marrowfat

Peas: Extra Early Alaska

Corn (for meal): Garland Flint, Mandan Bride, Rhode Island White Cap Hickory King (for grits, hominy & corn nuts)

Popcorn: White Cloud, Popwhite

JAN'S VARIETIES FOR CANNING OR FREEZING

What makes a vegetable variety a good candidate for canning or freezing? Taste, of course. It should be flavorful, high in sugars and nutritional value. The variety also should have a texture that is fleshy but firm enough to withstand the heat of blanching. And it should have a stable color which will not fade, bleed or brown during the process. Many of these qualities have been bred into the following varieties, making them good bets for home preservation.

Beans: Top Crop

Beets: Detroit Perfected

Broccoli: Italian Green

Brussels Sprouts: Long Island Improved

Corn: Golden Cross Bantam

Peas: Little Marvel

Squash: Crookneck

METRIC CONVERSION CHART

DIMENSION	WEIGHT	VOLUME
1 INCH equals 25.4 MILLIMETERS *therefore:* ____ INCHES × 25.4 = ____ MILLIMETERS ____ MILLIMETERS × .04 = ____ INCHES	**1 POUND equals 454 GRAMS** *therefore:* ____ POUNDS × 454 = ____ GRAMS ____ GRAMS × .002 = ____ POUNDS	**1 QUART (dry) equals 1.1 LITERS** *therefore:* ____ QUARTS (dry) × 1.1 = ____ LITERS ____ LITERS × .91 = ____ QUARTS (dry)
1 INCH equals 2.54 CENTIMETERS *therefore:* ____ INCHES × 2.54 = ____ CENTIMETERS ____ CENTIMETERS × .394 = ____ INCHES	**1 POUND equals .454 KILOGRAMS** *therefore:* ____ POUNDS × .454 = ____ KILOGRAMS ____ KILOGRAMS × 2.2 = ____ POUNDS	**1 QUART (liq.) equals .95 LITERS** *therefore:* ____ QUARTS (liq.) × .95 = ____ LITERS ____ LITERS × 1.06 = ____ QUARTS (liq.)
1 FOOT equals .305 METERS *therefore:* ____ FEET × .305 = ____ METERS ____ METERS × 3.28 = ____ FEET	**1 PINT (dry) equals .55 LITERS** *therefore:* ____ PINTS (dry) × .55 = ____ LITERS ____ LITERS × 1.82 = ____ PINTS (dry)	**1 PECK equals 8.81 LITERS** *therefore:* ____ PECKS × 8.81 = ____ LITERS ____ LITERS × .114 = ____ PECKS
1 OUNCE equals 28.4 GRAMS *therefore:* ____ OUNCES × 28.4 = ____ GRAMS ____ GRAMS × .04 = ____ OUNCES	**1 PINT (liq.) equals .47 LITERS** *therefore:* ____ PINTS (liq.) × .47 = ____ LITERS ____ LITERS × 2.11 = ____ PINTS (liq.)	**1 BUSHEL equals 35.24 LITERS** *therefore:* ____ BUSHELS × 35.24 = ____ LITERS ____ LITERS × .028 = ____ BUSHELS

Material	Thickness Used To Control Weeds	Advantages	Disadvantages	Comments
Aluminum foil or foil-backed paper	one layer	Good for shady gardens as it increases the light around the plants; aphids and other insects avoid foil mulched plants; can be used more than once.	Foil can tear if handled roughly; can be expensive; is artificial-looking.	Keeps ground very cool, so better for mid-summer than spring.
Compost	1–2 inches	Also serves as fertilizer; partially decomposed compost will continue decomposition quickly into humus.	Must have had sufficient heating period to kill any weed seeds and bacteria or diseases.	Plan and start ahead so compost will be ready when you need it.
Cottonseed Hulls	2–4 inches	Readily available in areas of the South; have a fertilizer value similar to cottonseed meal.	Very light so wind can scatter.	For weed control sift between plants; can be covered with a very thin layer of other mulch to prevent scattering by wind.
Grass Clippings	2–3 inches	Improves soil by adding organic matter—available almost everywhere.	May carry weed seeds or herbicide residues.	May be mixed with other materials to prevent packing down; bottom layer may decompose rapidly so additional layers needed. Should be dried for a few days after cutting to prevent rotting.
Hay	6–8 inches	Often available in large quantities; legume hays, such as alfalfa, add large amounts of nitrogen to soil.	First cut hay usually full of weed seeds; not best for weed control.	Second or third cut hay more likely to be free of weed seeds; chopped hay may be more attractive. May not have to add more during season—just fluff up what is there.
Leaves	2–3 inches	Readily available to most people; contain many trace minerals; best food for earthworms.	May become soggy and pack down, becoming hard for water to penetrate to soil. Also may blow away.	Chopping will prevent packing down or matting. Mixing with other mulch materials will also prevent this.

MULCHING GUIDE

Material	Thickness Used To Control Weeds	Advantages	Disadvantages	Comments
Peat Moss	1–2 inches	Clean and free of weed seeds.	Extremely absorbent so water will not readily penetrate to soil; can be expensive. Adds little or no nutrients to soil.	Very good as soil conditioner to loosen up heavy soil and improve water retention on sandy soil. Is acidic; long decomposition time.
Pine Needles	3–4 inches	Light; usually free of weed seeds; absorbs little or no moisture. Can be used more than once; does not pack down.	Decompose very slowly; sometimes earthworm activity beneath them.	Add extra nitrogen fertilizer if faster decomposition is wanted; slightly acidic in nature.
Polyethelene (black)	one layer	Can use more than once; free of weed seeds; absorbs no moisture. Very effective weed control, even with perennial weeds.	Difficult to apply properly. Is not penetrable so rain cannot get through; may make soil too warm; not always attractive.	Warms soil in spring; effective with warmth-loving crops. Ground must be moist before applying. Does not add any nutrient or organic matter to soil.
Salt marsh hay	4–6 inches	Usually weed free; free and easy to gather in marshy areas or along marshy coast. Long lasting and can be used a 2nd season.	Not available to everyone; expensive if purchased.	Can be tilled under at end of season, chopping may make more attractive and easier to handle; does not decompose rapidly.
Seaweed	3–4 inches	Can be used more than once; available at little cost or free to those along coast; water penetrates to soil easily.	Not readily available inland unless sold (packaged) at store; may have excess salt content; not necessarily attractive.	Salt can be washed out if left outside in a number of rains, or washed often with hose or soaked in tubs of water with water changed often. Decomposes slowly.
Straw	6–8 inches	Readily available in some areas.	One of the best mulching materials. Sometimes difficult to obtain; can be difficult to handle; can be a fire hazard.	Chopping may make more attractive and easier to handle.

Index

Acidity/alkalinity of soil (pH), 82
Acorn squash, *see* Squash, winter
Alfalfa meal, 89–90
  and compost, 90, 161
Animals, as pests, 330–35 and *illus.*
  birds, 335
  chipmunks, 334
  mice, 335
  moles, 335
  rabbits, 332
  raccoons, 333
  skunks, 334
  squirrels, 334
  woodchucks, 332–33
Ashes, added to soil, 82, 86
Asparagus, 322–24 and *illus.*
  mulching, 323, 324
  transplanting roots, 322–23 and *illus.*
    from roadside plants, 324
  weed control, 324 and *illus.*

Bacillus thuringiensis, 217–18
Bean(s), 206–13 and *illus.*
  insects and diseases, 208, *table*, 213
  planting, 208
Bean(s), bush (green and yellow), 28, 207, 209
  as green manure crop, *illus.*, 186, 187
  tunnel-grown late crop, 127, 174
  varieties, 209
  see also Bean(s), lima
Bean(s), dry, 35, 207, 211
  threshing and winnowing, 211
  varieties, 211
Bean(s), lima, 210
Bean(s), pole (green and yellow), 29 and *illus.*, 207, 209
  side-dressing, 159, 209
  tepee for, how to make, 209
  varieties, 209
  see also Bean(s), lima
Bean(s), shell, 210
Bean(s), snap, *see* Bean(s), bush; Bean(s), pole
Beet(s), 279 and *illus.*
  harvesting, 59
  storage, in root cellar, 202
  see also Root crops
Beet green(s), 279
  in salad garden, 21
  in summer garden, 28
Birds, as pests, 335
Blackeye pea(s), 210
Block planting, 66–71 and *illus.*
  advantages of, 67
  method, 68 and *illus.*
  for peas, 6 and *illus.*
Braiding garlic or onions, 254 and *illus.*
Broadcasting seeds, 3, 7, 46–47 and *illus.*
Broccoli, 28, 220 and *illus.*
  in fall garden, 175 and *illus.*
  side-dressing, 158
  varieties, 220
  see also Cabbage family of vegetables
Brussels sprout(s), 221–22 and *illus.*
  side-dressing, 158
  see also Cabbage family of vegetables

Buckwheat:
  as green manure crop, 180, *illus.*, 188, 189
  as smother crop, 144 and *illus.*, 145
Bunching onions, 251
Bush bean(s), (green and yellow), 28, 207, 209
  as green manure crop, *illus.*, 186, 187
  tunnel-grown late crop, 127, 174
  varieties, 209
  see also Bean(s), lima
Buttercup squash, *see* Squash, winter
Butternut squash, *see* Squash, winter

Cabbage, 223–24 and *illus.*
  cracking (problem), 224
  harvesting, 53
  planting, and distance apart, 52 and *illus.*
  side-dressing, 158
  storage, in root cellar, 202
  in wide rows, 4 and *illus.*, 29, 223
Cabbage, Chinese, 225 and *illus.*
  see also Cabbage family of vegetables
Cabbage family of vegetables, 214–25 and *illus.*
  fall crop timetable, 215
  insects and diseases, 215, 216, 217–18, *table*, 219
  planting distances, 216
  transplanting, 216
  see also Broccoli; Brussels sprout(s); Cabbage; Cauliflower; Chinese cabbage; Kohlrabi
Canning vegetables, 167–68
Cantaloupe(s), 310–12
  ripeness, 311
  varieties, 312
  see also Melon(s)
Carrot(s), 279–80 and *illus.*
  "fingerlings," 279–80 and *illus.*
  harvesting, 59, 166
  in salad garden, 20
  sprouting, 280
  storage:
    freezing, 280
    in root cellar, 202
  in wide rows *vs.* single rows, 2 and *illus.*
  see also Root crops
Cauliflower, 222–23
  blanching, 222–23 and *illus.*
  harvesting, early, 53 and *illus.*
  side-dressing, 158
  in wide rows, 4, 29 and *illus.*
  see also Cabbage family of vegetables
Celery, 239 and *illus.*
  blanching, 239 and *illus.*
Chard, 240–41 and *illus.*
  harvesting, 9 and *illus.*, 58 and *illus.*, 59
  in salad garden, 21
  side-dressing, 158
  varieties, 241
  in wide rows *vs.* single rows, 3 and *illus.*
  see also Greens
Chinese cabbage, 225 and *illus.*
  see also Cabbage family of vegetables
Chipmunks, as pests, 334 and *illus.*

Clay soil, 81
  breaking up crust on, 51
  and green manure, 179
  and raised beds, 94
  tilling, 78
Cold frame, *illus.*, 118, 119 and *illus.*
Cold weather, protection from, 120, 124 and *illus.*, 125
  see also Hardening off; Hot cap(s); Tunnel growing
Collards, 241 and *illus.*
  see also Greens
Compost, 160–65 and *illus.*
  how to make pile, 162–63 and *illus.*
  how to use, 164
  sheet method (tilled into garden), 165 and *illus.*
  trench method, 165
Container-grown vegetables, 23 and *illus.*
  tomatoes, 296 and *illus.*
Corn (sweet), 227–33 and *illus.*
  continuous harvest, tips for, 230 and *illus.*
  early, 227–28
  hilling, 140–41 and *illus.*, 232 and *illus.*
  in raised beds, 229 and *illus.*
  ripeness, checking for, 233
  side-dressing, 158, *illus.*, 228, 229
  varieties, 34, 229
  weeding, 232 and *illus.*
Crops (selection of), *see* Vegetables (selection of)
Crowder pea(s), 34, 210
Cucumber(s), 306–07 and *illus.*
  bitterness, 307
  harvest, continuous, 167, 306
  pickling variety, 35, 306
    grown in bottle, 307 and *illus.*
  side-dressing, 159, 304 and *illus.*
  started indoors, 107
  on trellis, 21 and *illus.*
  see also Vine crops
Cultivation, *see* Weeds and weeding
Cutworm(s), 122, 286

Damping-off, 40
Dill, 28, 306
Diseases, *see* insects and diseases *under specific vegetables*
Double row, 70
"Driveway garden," 23 and *illus.*

Earthworm(s), 81
Eat'n Store Garden, 30–35 and *illus.*
  plan for, 32–33
  vegetable selection for, 34–35
Eggplant, *illus.*, 234, 235 and *illus.*
  side-dressing, 159
Endive, 242 and *illus.*
  see also Greens
Equipment and tools:
  hoes, 138–39 and *illus.*
  for soil preparation, 74
  for starting seedlings, 109
  for watering, 153
  see also In-Row Weeder; Roto-tiller and roto-tilling

"Eternal Yield" garden, 194–97 and *illus.*

Fall garden, 173–75 and *illus.*
  planting dates, *table*, 173
Fence, 331 and *illus.*
Fertilizer, 85–90
  natural, sources of, 90
  numbers on labels of, 87
  and planting, 44–45 and *illus.*, 130 and *illus.*
  and seedlings, 110, 117
  side-dressing, 156–59 and *illus.*
    compost as, 164
    and succession crops, 170
Freezing vegetables, 167–68
Frost, protection from, 120, 124–25 and *illus.*
  see also Hot cap(s); Tunnel growing

Garden, new:
  setting up, steps, 75
  testing soil in, 82–84
Garden plans, 14–33 and *illus.*
  for Eat'n Store Garden, 32–33
  for Salad Garden, 19
  for Summer Garden, 26–27
Garlic, 64, 254 and *illus.*
  storage, 254
    braided, *illus.*, 254
    in root cellar, 202
Germination of seeds:
  and seedbed, smooth, 46–47 and *illus.*
  testing for, 41 and *illus.*
  see also Seedlings, started indoors
Gourd(s), 308 and *illus.*
  luffas, 309 and *illus.*
  see also Vine crops
Grass:
  as weed, 142–43 and *illus.*
  see also Ryegrass, annual
Green bean(s), 28, 207, 209
  as green manure crop, *illus.*, 186, 187
  tunnel-grown late crop, 127, 174
  varieties, 209
Green manure, 79, 176–93 and *illus.*
  planting, 192–93 and *illus.*
  see also "Eternal Yield" garden
Greens, 236–47 and *illus.*
  fertilizing, 237
  harvesting, 9 and *illus.*, 59, 167, 238, *illus.*, 239
  and hot and cold weather, 237
  insects and diseases, 238
  see also Beet green(s); Celery; Chard;
    Collards; Endive; Kale; Lettuce; Mustard
    (greens); New Zealand spinach; Spinach

Hardening off, 117
  see also Cold Frame
Harvesting, 166–68 and *illus.*
  early and continuous, 53 and *illus.*
  multicrop, 64
  picking vegetables when small, 166–67
  wide rows, 8–9 and *illus.*, 58–59 and *illus.*
Hay, as mulch, 151 and *illus.*
Hill(s) and hilling:
  for celery, 239 and *illus.*
  for corn, 140–41 and *illus.*, 232 and *illus.*
  for potatoes, 140–41 and *illus.*, 267 and
    illus.
  for vine crops, 128, 299
Hoe(s), 138–39 and *illus.*

Horseradish, 325 and *illus.*
Horticultural bean(s), 210
Hotbed, 119 and *illus.*
Hot cap(s), 124 and *illus.*
  for vine crops, 301
Hot-climate garden:
  corn in, 229
  peas in, 259
  succession crops in, 169
  watering, 153
  wide rows in, 11
Hubbard squash, *see* Squash, winter

In-Row Weeder, 57, *illus.*, 136, 137–38
  to break crust on seedbed, 51
  for corn, 232 and *illus.*
  for multicrop, 63
  for onions, 250 and *illus.*, 253
Insecticides, 336–42
  Bacillus thuringiensis, 217–18
Insects, 336–37
  list, 338–42
  and radishes, 131
  see also insects and diseases *under specific*
    vegetables

Jerusalem artichoke(s), 321 and *illus.*

Kale, 242 and *illus.*, 243
  in fall garden, 175 and *illus.*
  thinning, 29
  varieties, 243
  in wide rows, 6 and *illus.*
  see also Greens
Kidney bean(s), *see* Bean(s), dry
Kohlrabi, 226 and *illus.*
  see also Cabbage family of vegetables

Lawn garden, 102, 103 and *illus.*
Leek(s), 255 and *illus.*
  blanching, 255 and *illus.*
  side-dressing, 159
Lettuce, 243–45 and *illus.*
  harvesting, 28, 53 and *illus.*
  head type, 243–44
  started indoors, 107
  tunnel-grown late crop, 127
  varieties, 244
  in wide row, 5 and *illus.*, 243–44
  see also Greens
Light(s), fluorescent, 108–09
Lima bean(s), 210
Lime, 82
Luffa sponge, 309 and *illus.*
  see also Vine crops

Manure (animal), added to soil, 88–89, 178
  see also Green manure
Melon(s), 35, 310–13 and *illus.*
  early ripening, tips for, 311
  side-dressing, 159
  started indoors, 107
  varieties, 312
  see also Vine crops
Mice, as pests, 335
Moles, as pests, 335
Mulch, 150–51 and *illus.*
  for asparagus, 323, 324
  black plastic, 292–93
  for moisture retention, 51

Mulch, *continued*
  for potatoes, 268 and *illus.*
  for strawberries, 329
  for tomatoes, 292 and *illus.*
Multicropping, 16 and *illus.*, 60–65 and *illus.*
  harvesting, 64
  how to plant, 62–63 and *illus.*
Mustard (greens), 245 and *illus.*
  see also Greens

New Zealand spinach, 246 and *illus.*
  see also Greens
Nitrogen in soil, 85, 88

Okra, 246 and *illus.*
  side-dressing, 159
Onion(s), 248–54 and *illus.*
  bunching type, 251
  container-grown, 23
  fertilizing, 252
    side-dressing, 159
  grown from seed, 105, 253
  harvesting, 252
  insects and diseases, 254
  planting, 7 and *illus.*, 250 and *illus.*
  in salad garden, 20
  storage, 252
    braided, 254
    in root cellar, 202, 252
  in summer garden, 29
  sweet type, 251–52
  transplanting, 252
  wide rows, 2, 249, 250 and *illus.*
Organic matter, added to soil, 73–74, 79, 80,
  81–82, 177
  and water preservation, 155
  see also Green manure; Mulch
Overwintering:
  kale, 242–43
  root crops, 277 and *illus.*
  parsnips, 280

Parsnip(s), 280 and *illus.*
  storage:
    overwintering, 280
    in root cellar, 202
  see also Root crops
Pea(s), *illus.*, 258, 259–60 and *illus.*
  block planting, 6 and *illus.*
  climbing variety, 260
  as green manure, *illus.*, 184, 185
  insects and diseases, 260
  in wide rows, 11, 28, 259
Peanut(s), *illus.*, 256, 257 and *illus.*
  harvested "green," 257
Pepper(s), 261–63 and *illus.*
  as decoration, 262
  fertilizing, 261
    side-dressing, 159
  "orchard," 263 and *illus.*
Perennials, 318–29 and *illus.*
  see also Asparagus; Horseradish; Jerusalem
    artichoke(s); Rhubarb; Strawberry/ies
Pests:
  animal, 330–35 and *illus.*
  insect, 336–37
    list, 338–42
  see also insects and diseases *under*
    specific vegetables
pH (acidity/alkalinity) of soil, 82

363

Phosphorus in soil, 86, 88
Picking vegetables, *see* Harvesting
Pickle grown in bottle, 307 and *illus.*
Planning chart, 37
Plans for gardens, 14–33 and *illus.*
  eat 'n store garden, 32–33
  salad garden, 19
  summer garden, 26–27
Planting seeds:
  in blocks, 66–71 and *illus.*
    advantages of, 67
    method, 68 and *illus.*
    for peas, 68 and *illus.*
  by broadcasting, 3, 7, 46–47 and *illus.*
  and fertilizer, 44–45 and *illus.*, 130 and
    illus.
  for multicropping, 62–63 and *illus.*
  with rototiller, 67
  in single rows, 129
  small seeds, using jars, 47 and *illus.*
  in wide rows, 42–51 and *illus.*
Pole bean(s), (green and yellow), 29, 207, 209
  side-dressing, 159, 209
  tepee for, how to make, 209
  varieties, 209
  see also Lima bean(s)
Popcorn, 231 and *illus.*, 233
  storage, 233
Pot(s) for starting seeds, 110–11 and *illus.*
Potassium in soil, 86, 88
Potato(es), 264–70 and *illus.*
  early, 28, 269
  harvesting, 269–70 and *illus.*
  hilling, 140–41 and *illus.*, 267 and *illus.*
  insects and diseases, 268
    scab, 266–67
  mulching, 268 and *illus.*
  seed, 265, 266 and *illus.*
  side-dressing, 159
  for storage, 34
    varieties, 266
  storage of:
    readiness for, 269 and *illus.*
    in root cellar, 202, *illus.*, 270
Pumpkin(s), 34, 313–14 and *illus.*
  autographed, 314 and *illus.*
  storage, in root cellar, 202
  see also Vine crops
Pyramid planter, 111 and *illus.*
  for lettuce, 244 and *illus.*

Rabbits, as pests, 332 and *illus.*
Raccoons, as pests, 333 and *illus.*
Radish(es), as companion crop, 131, 275–76,
  281 and *illus.*
Raised bed(s), 81, 92–99
  benefits of, 94–95
  for corn, 229 and *illus.*
  how to make, 96–97 and *illus.*
  with tiller, 98
  maintenance of, 99
  for root crops, 95, 274 and *illus.*
  for zucchini, 319
Rake-thinning, 54–55 and *illus.*, 135
  root crops, 274
Rhubarb, 320 and *illus.*
Rocks in garden, 79
Root cellar, 198–203 and *illus.*
  building plans, 201
  cardboard box as, 276

Root crops, 272–82 and *illus.*
  fertilizing, 274
  harvesting, 59, 273
  insects, *table*, 278
    root maggot, 277
  in raised beds, 95, 274 and *illus.*
  seed tapes, homemade, 275
  storage, 272, 276
    see also Root cellar
  thinning, 274–75
  in wide rows, 273 and *illus.*
  see also Beet(s); Carrot(s); Parsnip(s);
    Radish(es); Rutabaga(s); Turnip(s)
Rotation of crops, 194–97 and *illus.*
Roto-tiller and roto-tilling, 76–77 and *illus.*
  for hilling, 140 and *illus.*, 141, 232
  for planting:
    green manure crop, 192–93 and *illus.*
    seeds, 67
  for raised beds, 98
  for sheet composting, 165 and *illus.*
  for soil preparation, 42–43 and *illus.*, 73,
    74, 78
  for turning crops back into soil, 169–70
  for weed control, 78, 99, 135
Rutabaga(s), *illus.*, 272, 281 and *illus.*, 282
  storage, in root cellar, 202, 282
  see also Root crops
Ryegrass, annual, 102, 145
  in asparagus bed, 324
  as green manure crop, *illus.*, 190, 191

Salad Garden, 15 and *illus.*, 17, *illus.*, 18
  location of, 22–23 and *illus.*
  plan, 19
  vegetable selections, 20–21 and *illus.*
Sandy soil, 80
  and green manure, 178
Scallion(s):
  continuous harvest, 250, 251
  in Salad Garden, 20
  in Summer Garden, 29
  in wide rows *vs.* single rows, 2
Seed(s):
  amount needed, 36 and *table*
  date on packet, 40
  disease–resistant, 39
  germination of:
    and seedbed, smooth, 46–47 and *illus.*
    testing for, 41 and *illus.*
    see also Seedlings, started indoors
  hybrid, 39
  planting, *see* Planting seeds
  treating (methods), 40 and *illus.*
  varieties:
    new, 39
    "old reliables," 38
Seedbed:
  keeping moist, 51 and *illus.*
  preparation, 42–45 and *illus.*
  smooth, 46, *illus.*, 47
    advantages of, 47 and *illus.*
Seedlings, started indoors, 105–17 and *illus.*
  dates for starting, 106
  and fluorescent lights, 108–09
  hardening off, 117
  tending, 116–17
  transplanting, 120–23 and *illus.*
  in trays, 112–15 and *illus.*
Seed rot, 40

Seed tape, homemade, 275
Shallot(s), 256 and *illus.*
Sheet composting, 165 and *illus.*
Shell bean(s), 210
Side-dressing, 156–59 and *illus.*
  compost as, 164
Single rows:
  planting, 128–29 and *illus.*
  vs. wide rows, 2–3 and *illus.*
Skunks, as pests, 334 and *illus.*
Smother crops, 144 and *illus.*, 145
Snap bean(s), *see* Bean(s), bush; Bean(s), pole
Sod pot(s), homemade, 108
Soil:
  acidity/alkalinity (pH) of, 82
  clay, 81
    breaking up crust on, 51
    and green manure, 179
    and raised beds, 94
    tilling, 78
  crusty, 51
  nutrients, 85–87
    see also Fertilizer; Organic matter added
      to soil
  sandy, 80
    and green manure, 178
  sterilizing, 110
  and succession crops, 170
  testing, 82–84
  tilling, *see* Roto-tiller and roto-tilling
  wet, 74
    and raised beds, 94
Soil-less mix, 107
Soybean(s), 207, 212 and *illus.*
  as green manure crop, 187, 212 and *illus.*
  shelling, 212
  varieties, 212
Spaghetti squash, 315
Spinach, 247 and *illus.*
  early, 29, 247
  see also Greens
Squash, summer, 317 and *illus.*
  blossoms and buds, 317
  side-dressing, 159
  see also Vine crops; Zucchini
Squash, winter, 29, 315–16 and *illus.*
  curing, 316
  side-dressing, 159
  storage, 35
    in root cellar, 202, 316 and *illus.*
  see also Vine crops

Squirrels, as pests, 334 and *illus.*
Sterilizing soil, 110
Storage of vegetables:
  canning, 167–68
  freezing, 167–68
  root cellar, 196–201 and *illus.*
  see also Overwintering; *and under specific
    vegetables*
Strawberry/ies, 326–29 and *illus.*
  buying plants, 326
  care of plants, 328–29 and *illus.*
  planting, 327 and *illus.*
Succession crops, 28–29, 168–71 and *illus.*
Sulfur in soil, 82, 88
Summer garden, 24–29 and *illus.*
  plan, 26–27
  vegetable selections for, 28–29 and *illus.*
Sunflower(s), 282–83 and *illus.*

Sweet potato(es), 270–71 and *illus.*
Swiss chard, 240–41 and *illus.*
  harvesting, 9 and *illus.*, 58 and *illus.*, 59
  in salad garden, 21
  side-dressing, 158
  varieties, 241
  in wide rows *vs.* single rows, 3 and *illus.*
  see also Greens

Terrace, 101 and *illus.*
Thinning wide rows:
  multicrop, 63
  with rake, 54–55 and *illus.*, 135
    root crops, 274–75
    vegetables appropriate for (list), 56
Tiller and tilling, *see* Roto-tiller and roto-
  tilling
Tomato(es), 284–97 and *illus.*
  buying plants, 285
  in cages, 289 and *illus.*
  container-grown, 23 and *illus.*, 296 and
    illus.
  early, 288, 293 and *illus.*
  in fall garden, 174
  fertilizing, 286
    side-dressing, 159
  green, storage in root cellar, 202
  harvesting green, 296
  insects and diseases, 294–96 and *illus.*
  mulching, 292 and *illus.*
  Pixie variety, 174, 296 and *illus.*
  pruning, 292 and *illus.*
  ripening in dark, 293, 296
  in Salad Garden, 21
  sprawling, 291 and *illus.*
  staking, 287, 290 and *illus.*
  started indoors, 106
  in Summer Garden, 29
  transplanting, 123 and *illus.*, 286–87 and
    illus.
  trellising, 291 and *illus.*
Tools and equipment:
  hoes, 138–39 and *illus.*
  for soil preparation, 74
  for starting seedlings, 109
  for watering, 153

Tools and equipment, *continued*
  see also In-Row Weeder; Roto-tiller and
    roto-tilling
Trace minerals in soil, 87
Transplanting, 120–23 and *illus.*
  "3–2 staggered row" system, 52 and *illus.*
Tray(s), for starting seeds, 110
  method of using, 112–15 and *illus.*
Trellis:
  for peas, 260
  for tomatoes, 291 and *illus.*
  for vine crops, 303 and *illus.*
    for cucumbers, 21 and *illus.*
Troy-Bilt Roto-Tiller, 76–77 and *illus.*
Tunnel growing, 126–27 and *illus.*, 174
Turnip(s), 281 and *illus.*, 282
  greens, 282
  storage, in root cellar, 202, 282
  see also Root crops

Vegetables (selection of):
  for block planting (list), 69
  for early harvesting (list), 59
  for Eat'n Store Garden, 34–35 and *illus.*
  by families (list), 205
  planning chart, 37
  for root-cellar storage (list), 200
  for Salad Garden, 20–21 and *illus.*
  for side-dressing (list), 156–57
  started indoors (list), 106–107
  started outdoors (list), 107
  for Summer Garden, 28–29 and *illus.*
  for wide-row method (list), 13
Vermont Cranberry bean(s), 210
Vine crops, 298–317 and *illus.*
  cross-pollination, 304
  hilling, 299
  insects and diseases, 304, *illus.* 305
  planting, 129 and *illus.*, 302
    distances, *table*, 302
  side-dressing, 159, 304 and *illus.*
  sprouting indoors, 300 and *illus.*
  on trellises, 303 and *illus.*
  tunnels (plastic) for, 126–27 and *illus.*, 301
    and *illus.*
  see also Cucumber(s); Gourd(s); Melon(s);

Vine crops, *continued*
    Pumpkin(s); Squash, summer; Squash,
    winter; Zucchini

Watering, 152–55
  after planting, 51
  raised beds, 95, 99
  seedlings, 116
  tools for, 153
  wide rows, 10
Watermelon(s), 310–12
  ripeness, 312
  varieties, 312
  see also Melon(s)
Wax (yellow) bean(s), 28, 207, 209
  as green manure crop, *illus.*, 186, 187
  tunnel-grown late crop, 127, 174
  varieties, 209
Weeds and weeding, *illus.*, 132, 133–35, *illus.*,
  134, 142–47 and *illus.*
  and hilling, 140–41 and *illus.*
  in raised beds, 99
  and roto-tilling, 78, 99, 135
  and smother crops, 144 and *illus.*, 145
  and wide rows, 10
  see also In-Row Weeder
Wide-row method, 1–13 and *illus.*
  basic steps (list), 71
  compared to single rows, 2–3 and *illus.*,
    12 and *illus.*
  development of, 11
  garden plans for, 14–33 and *illus.*
  harvesting, 8–9 and *illus.*, 58–59 and *illus.*
  planning chart, 37
  planting, 42–51 and *illus.*
  thinning, 54–56 and *illus.*
  vegetables appropriate for (list), 13
Wintering-over:
  kale, 242–43
  root crops, 277 and *illus.*
  parsnips, 280
Woodchucks, as pests, *illus.*, 330, 332–33

Zucchini, 29, 317 and *illus.*
  harvesting small fruits, 167
  side-dressing, 159
  see also Squash, summer; Vine crops

Other Garden Way Books by Dick Raymond

DOWN-TO-EARTH VEGETABLE GARDENING KNOW-HOW

A bible for beginners, *Down-to-Earth Vegetable Gardening Know-How* is chock-full of practical advice and step-by-step instruction. From planning and planting, to picking a healthy harvest, Dick walks you through all the basics of successful gardening. Introduces Dick's wide row gardening technique to double, even triple your garden's yield. $7.95.

HOME GARDENING WISDOM

Dick Raymond teams up with his wife, Jan, to take 55 favorite vegetables from seed to table. Dick shows just how to plant, fertilize and care for each vegetable so you'll have the biggest and best harvest to carry into the kitchen. Then Jan steps in with a lifetime of home-tested recipes and preservation know-how to help you make the best use of that bountiful crop! Combines the best of Dick and Jan's gardening and cooking wisdom. $9.95.

WIDE ROW PLANTING (Garden Way bulletin A-2)

Wide row planting increases yields, saves time and space, and makes harvesting easier than ever before! Dick Raymond tells why wide rows work, how to plan and plant wide rows, what crops do well in wide rows. All in a complete, concise, 32-page bulletin. $1.95

These Garden Way Books are available wherever good books are sold, or may be ordered directly from Garden Way Publishing, Dept. F511, Charlotte, Vermont 05445. If your order is less than $10.00, please add $1.00 postage and handling.